A LITERARY
HISTORY OF GREECE

ROBERT FLACELIÈRE

A LITERARY HISTORY OF

GREECE

Translated by
DOUGLAS GARMAN

ALDINE PUBLISHING COMPANY
CHICAGO

Originally published in 1962 under the title
HISTOIRE LITTÉRAIRE DE LA GRÈCE
by Librairie Arthème Fayard, Paris

Copyright © 1962 by Librairie Arthème Fayard

English translation copyright © 1964 by
Elek Books Limited

First published 1964
ALDINE PUBLISHING COMPANY
64 East Van Buren Street
Chicago, Illinois 60605

Library of Congress Catalog Card Number 64-11944

Printed in Great Britain

CONTENTS

v

LIST OF PLATES

The Publishers gratefully acknowledge the sources of the illustrations appearing in this volume:

Antikensammlungen, Munich, 11, 13
British Museum, 3
De Foscherare, 10
Laboratoire photographique de la faculté d'architecture d'Athènes, 7, 14
Mansell-Alinari, 4, 9, 15
Mansell, 1, 2, 5, 6, 8, 12
Radio Times Hulton Picture Library, 16

FOREWORD

There are several good histories of Greek literature of various shapes and sizes, but my purpose here is not simply to consider the literature of ancient Greece as an isolated subject, treating each of the literary modes—epic, lyric, drama, history, philosophy, rhetoric—in terms of its own evolution. What I have attempted to do is to provide a Greek history that deals with all the important works of Hellenic literature that are still of interest to contemporary readers; and to do this in chronological order with an accurate account of their historical background. Naturally, since it is a literary history, attention is mainly focussed on the writers and their works, but by displaying these in their political, social, artistic and scientific setting, I hope to contribute to a better understanding of the production and significance of these wonderful achievements of the human spirit.

For the classical centuries, so rich in talent and genius, I have tried to follow the successive generations step by step and to distinguish the special features of each, what it owes to the preceding generation and how it paves the way for the next.

A number of Hellenized Jewish writers, such as Philo of Alexandria and Flavius Josephus, as well as the New Testament and the works of the apologists and Fathers of the Greek Church doubtless belong to the literary history of Greece. But they are not dealt with here. To have attempted to do so would have meant exceeding not only the physical limits laid down for this book, but also the bounds of my own competence. Moreover, if I stop short at Plotinus, it is because he, through the history of neo-Platonism that extends far beyond him, seems to me, rightly or wrongly, to be the last representative of pure and authentic Hellenism.

Not long ago, in a book describing everyday life in Greece, I felt myself to be primarily concerned with the external and commonplace aspect of things, precisely because this is their most 'everyday' aspect. I wrote about the narrow, malodorous streets of down-town Athens, not the monuments of the Acropolis; about the humblest crafts, not the masterpieces of painting and sculpture; about the functioning of the popular assembly and the law courts, not the eloquence of Demosthenes; about the organization of theatrical performances, not the plays of the great tragic poets; about the education of children and sport, not the progress of history and the achievements of philosophy and science. What I have hoped to do here is to provide the counterpart to this; to show the other, more brilliant panel of the diptych by presenting a picture of Greek civilization seen above all through the work of its best writers.

If to be in love with one's subject were sufficient to make one write well and to draw others to share one's love, I should feel confident of success.

I wish to thank my friend Pierre Demargne, Professor of Classical Archaeology at the Sorbonne, who has been good enough to read the short accounts at the beginning of each chapter dealing with the history and principal works of art referred to, for the many corrections and additions that he has suggested to me.

TRANSLATOR'S NOTE

The translations of the many passages quoted from the *Iliad* and the *Odyssey* are taken from the admirable versions made by Dr E. V. Rieu for the Penguin Classics, and I take this opportunity of thanking him and his Publisher for permission to use them. In the case of other Greek writers, I myself am responsible for the English versions of the passages quoted.

If I have occasionally modified Dr Rieu's spelling of proper names, e.g., substituting Ajax for Aias and Hecuba for Hecabe, it has been to bring it into line with the practice adopted elsewhere in this translation. In the absence of any generally accepted method of transliterating Greek names into English, I have preferred to retain spellings sanctioned by long usage, while keeping as close as possible to the Greek in the case of less well-known names. Having thus committed myself to inconsistency, I can only hope to have been consistent in it.

D.M.G.

THE TROJAN WAR: HOMER

> No one in Troy had a harder burden to bear . . . ill-starred
> couple that we are, tormented by heaven to figure in the songs
> of people yet unborn.
>
> (HELEN: *Iliad* VI, 357–8)

HISTORICAL BACKGROUND

Even if Helen's beauty was not its only cause, and though Homer's
account of it may not be completely reliable, the Trojan war did
nevertheless take place. It is an historical fact, which was later magnified
and enriched by legend.

The names 'Greece' and 'Greeks' are comparatively late and were
only used from Roman times onwards. In the classical age the Greeks
referred to themselves as Hellenes, the people of Hellas. But at the
time of Homer's *Iliad* and *Odyssey* the Hellenes were as yet no more
than a tribe in southern Thessaly, subjects of Achilles, also known
as the Myrmidons. When Homer wants to refer to all the various
peoples who took part in the expedition against Troy under the
leadership of the Atreidae, he uses three names: Achaeans, Argives or
Danaans. Here we shall use the first as being the most comprehensive.

In the widest sense, it is true, Homer's Achaeans were already
Greeks. They spoke an archaic Greek dialect of which we now possess
specimens in a syllabic, not yet alphabetic, script, that is inscribed on
tablets of clay found by archaeologists at Cnossos in Crete, at Mycenae
in Argolis and at Pylos in Messenia; that is to say, in the capitals of
Idomeneus, Agamemnon and Nestor. The fact that we are able to
read these tablets today is due to the brilliant discovery of an English-
man, Michael Ventris, who in 1953 succeeded in deciphering this
writing, which consists of some eighty signs.

If an historical epoch is defined as that for which we have written and
comprehensible documents, Ventris may be said to have 'promoted'
the Achaeans as Champollion did the ancient Egyptians: he transformed

them from a prehistoric to an historic people. Unfortunately the texts inscribed on these clay tablets are little more than inventories and accounts, enough only to whet our appetite. Nevertheless it is possible to derive some information from them, particularly about the system of land ownership and the social organization of the Achaeans. But it is for the history of the Greek language that these tablets are of capital importance: before they had been deciphered, the history of Greek began with the *Iliad*, composed perhaps about 800 B.C., and the language spoken by the Achaeans in 1200 B.C. was completely unknown to us. Now we have scientific confirmation that the heroes of Homer spoke an archaic form of Greek which we can study and compare in detail with that of the *Iliad* and the *Odyssey*.

I cannot resist adding my own tribute to the Greek language: clear, supple and musical, it took shape for literary purposes in the service of poetry, yet was able to adapt itself effortlessly to the eloquence of Demosthenes or the philosophical thought of Plato; a tongue fluid as a spring, melodious as a song, yet thanks to its particles as strictly organized as a temple built of highly polished and precisely laid blocks of stone.

Linguistically it belongs to the Indo-European group like Sanskrit, Latin, the Germanic languages and most of those spoken in Europe today. The words for 'father' and 'mother', for example, are to be found in almost identical form in all these languages. There can be no doubt that all the peoples speaking one or other of the dialects belonging to this group originated in the far distant past, perhaps the fourth millennium B.C., from the same stock and probably inhabited the region which today corresponds to southern Russia and central Europe.

The Achaeans were not the first inhabitants of Greece. They succeeded a people called by the Greeks of the classical period Pelasgi, of whom little is known and who were certainly not Indo-Europeans. Indeed the Achaeans adopted certain Pelasgian words such as *labyrinthos* and *thalassa* and others with similar endings which can be shown by the methods of comparative linguistics not to be of Indo-European origin.

Since *thalassa* means 'sea', it would seem probable that before their arrival in Greece the Achaeans had spent so long in some inland country remote from the sea that through lack of use they had forgotten the word for it in their own language and therefore borrowed the Pelasgian word *thalassa*. As for the word *labyrinthos*, it suggests a

2

connection with the labyrinth of Daedalus at Cnossos from which the hero Theseus escaped alive and victorious, thanks to the ball of thread given to him by his mistress Ariadne—and therefore with Crete. This large island played an important part in human history, especially from about 2500 to 1400 B.C. Admirably situated for receiving influences from Europe, Asia and Africa and re-transmitting them, it was also the seat of a great indigenous civilization, known either as Minoan after Minos the legendary king of Crete, or as Aegean because thanks to his powerful fleet Minos succeeded in extending his sway over most of the islands of the Aegean Sea.

Then, at some date still in dispute, though almost certainly in the second half of the fifteenth century, the Achaeans, who had also built themselves a navy, landed in Crete and captured Cnossos. Yet in defeat Crete triumphed over her savage conquerors, in the same way that later Greece, after defeat by the Romans, was to mould and educate the victorious 'barbarians'. The uncouth Achaeans finding the Cretan civilization, something of which was already known to them from earlier raids, superior to their own adopted it and were assimilated by it. Thus was born the civilization that we call either Achaean or Mycenaean from Mycenae, the royal town of Agamemnon, where the finest relics of the heroic age were later to be found. In the *Iliad* the Cretan Idomeneus is a vassal of Agamemnon, whereas in the legend of Theseus it is Minos who imposes a tribute on the Athenians: this is explained by the fact that in the interval the Achaean conquest of Crete had led to a reversal of roles.

Eventually the Achaean expansion turned eastwards, especially towards Cyprus and Asia Minor where it was brought to a halt by the town of Troy, also known as Ilium, whose inhabitants were possibly related by blood to the Achaeans. The geographical position of Troy made her the queen of the Hellespont or Dardanelles, the only entrance to the sea of Marmora, the Bosphorus and the rich and fertile shores of the Black Sea. The strategic and commercial importance of this wealthy city, whose treasures held promise of valuable loot, was enough to make it the chosen target of the Achaeans. Since the *casus belli* proclaimed by the aggressor is seldom the true underlying reason for war, whether the rape of an Achaean princess, sister-in-law of the king of Mycenae, by one of Priam's young sons was a fact, used by Agamemnon as a diplomatic pretext, or whether it was purely legendary, will never be known, though the second hypothesis seems the more likely.

3

The Trojan War—a long and monotonous siege, a 'phoney war' with occasional skirmishes—lasted for ten years and was only brought to an end by the crude strategy of the wooden horse. According to the traditional chronology of the great Alexandrian scholar Eratosthenes, the town was taken in 1183, though certain modern historians date it a century earlier in 1280. The archaeologists who excavated the ruins of Troy on the mound of Hissarlik discovered there the superimposed remains of several successive towns, one of which was the city of Priam.

The expedition against Troy was the last major undertaking of the Achaeans, whose victory was swiftly followed by decline. On his return to Mycenae, Agamemnon found that he had been supplanted, and he died beneath the axe.

The Minoan civilization of the Cretans and the Mycenaean civilization of the Achaeans both belong to the Bronze Age: though the use of iron was not completely unknown, it was then a rarer and more precious metal than copper. The decline of the Achaeans was completed, in Greece, by new invaders from the North, the Dorians, who were also Hellenes. According to legend, this was the 'return of the Heracleidae', for the leaders of the Dorians were the sons of the great hero Heracles who like Theseus belonged to the generation before the Trojan war. These invaders brought with them iron as the metal in everyday use.

Under pressure from the Dorians, many of the Achaeans embarked once more and reached the shores of Asia Minor; no longer in search of new conquests, but hoping to find a place there alongside the earlier emigrants. There in Ionia and Aeolis the memory of the great Achaean heroes was preserved for centuries; their exploits were recounted, embroidered with all the magic of reminiscence, and the minstrels, the *aoidoi*, put these stories of war and glory into verse. Thus was born the Greek epic.

One of these minstrels who may have been born at Smyrna and lived at Chios at some undetermined date, which I personally would place between 850 and 750, more than three centuries after the fall of Troy, was a poet of genius. It was he who had the idea of isolating from the huge cycle of epics relating to Ilium and treating separately two episodes that seemed to offer subjects of outstanding significance, the wrath of Achilles and the return of Odysseus. According to ancient tradition, this poet was Homer.

MINOAN ART

In order to appreciate fully the character of the civilization described in the *Iliad* and the *Odyssey*, we are today fortunate enough to be able to visit the ruins of Cretan palaces and Achaean citadels as well as the museums at Cnossos and Athens. Certainly such a visit is the best introduction to the reading of the Homeric poems.

The palace of Cnossos, excavated—and very considerably reconstructed—by Sir Arthur Evans, astounds us by its huge dimensions and the splendour of its ornamentation. Its bold and complex plan, which freely replaces walls by large bays framed by supporting columns, furnishes a succession of dark passages and rooms suddenly lit up by 'wells of light'. This architecture, very different from that of classical Greece, may well have aroused in the minds of the Hellenes the idea of the 'labyrinth'. Columns of painted wood, tapering downwards, with plinths and capitals, support richly carved porticos. The so-called 'Queen's bathroom' bears witness to the comfort enjoyed by the inhabitants of the palace (since the word Homer uses for 'bath', *asaminthos*, has the same ending as *labyrinthos* it is of pre-Hellenic origin). The throne room is decorated with painted frescoes representing, against a field of flowers, griffins crouched in heraldic attitudes. Other well-known frescoes represent the 'Prince with the Fleur-de-Lys', the 'Vase-Bearer' and the 'Parisienne', so called because of her arch and expressive features. The Minoan women, as may be seen from the terra-cotta figurines of priestesses that have been preserved, wore flounced, bell-shaped skirts, leaving the breast freely exposed: a type of dress radically different from that of the Greeks of the classical period.

Many other palaces have been discovered in Crete, at Mallia, Phaestos and Hagia Triada. A magnificent sarcophagos from Hagia Triada, painted on all four sides, depicts scenes from the funeral rites: the making ready of a sacrifice on a tomb, the ghost of the dead man. The work of the Cretan jewellers and goldsmiths is even more superb than that of the painters; necklaces, pendants and jewels of all kinds, chased and ornamented ceremonial swords, and drinking vessels. The golden goblets found at Vapheio in Laconia were made by Cretan craftsmen and their repoussé decoration showing men capturing wild bulls is quite amazing.

The memory of these Minoan splendours is preserved in the *Iliad*. In the 'Catalogue of Ships' there are references to Crete and 'its

5

hundred cities', and elsewhere to Minos, the son of Zeus, who after
his death was considered worthy of becoming one of the judges in
Hades. In Book xvIII, the poet describes the marvellous shield that
the lame Hephaestus made for Achilles:

Next the god depicted a dancing-floor like the one that Daedalus designed
in the spacious town of Cnossos for Ariadne of the lovely locks. Youths
and marriageable maidens were dancing on it with their hands on one
another's wrists ... (xvIII, 590–4).

According to tradition, Daedalus of Athens had been the architect
of the labyrinth, that is to say of the palace, of Minos. Though it had
been destroyed six centuries earlier, one might almost imagine that
Homer had actually visited it, so closely do the palaces of Circe and
of Odysseus in Ithaca resemble those that have been revealed by
excavations in Crete. But it is above all in Books vII and vIII of the
Odyssey where he describes those peaceful seafarers and prosperous
traders, the Phaeacians, that the poet seems to have been inspired by
memories of the Minoan civilization. When Odysseus beholds the
splendour of the palace of Alcinous he is overwhelmed:

His heart was filled with misgivings and he hesitated before setting foot on
the bronze threshold. For a kind of radiance like that of the sun or moon
lit up the high-roofed halls of the great king. Walls of bronze, topped with
blue enamel tiles, ran round to left and right from the threshold to the back
of the court. The interior of the well-built mansion was guarded by golden
doors hung on posts of silver which sprang from the bronze threshold
(vII, 82–7).

The life of continual feasting, to the accompaniment of music and
dancing, led by the Phaeacian king and queen amongst their nobles,
evokes the kind of luxury that must have existed at the Minoan court.
And it is also to the fashions of the Cretans that the poet looks when
he wants to describe the elegance of the Olympian goddesses. In
Book xIV of the *Iliad*, when Hera is getting herself ready to seduce
her husband Zeus in order to distract his attention from the Trojan
battlefield, she pays particular attention to her toilet:

With this [oil] she rubbed her lovely skin: and then she combed her hair,
and with her own hands plaited her shining locks and let them fall in their
divine beauty from her immortal head. Next she put on a fragrant robe

of delicate material, that Athena with her skilful hands had made for her and lavishly embroidered. She fastened it over her breast with golden clasps and, at her waist, with a girdle from which a hundred tassles hung. In the pierced lobes of her ears she fixed two ear-rings, each a thing of lambent beauty with its cluster of three drops (XIV, 175–83).

These locks and golden clasps and heavy ear-rings were part of the armoury of feminine coquetry in the time of Minos—and also, it is true, in Achaean times.

MYCENAEAN ART

Long before 1900, when Evans began to investigate the ruins of Cnossos, Heinrich Schliemann, a wealthy German business man who had conceived a passion for Homer, had attacked the site at Troy; later in Argolis, he turned his attention to the acropolis of Mycenae, Agamemnon's capital (1876) and the acropolis of Tiryns (1884). Schliemann was the great pioneer of archaeological excavation.

In contrast to the Cretan palaces, the dwellings of the Achaean chieftains were real fortresses, smaller in size and comparable to the castles of our own Middle Ages. Moreover, the social organization of this period was of an essentially feudal type: Achilles was one of the great vassals under the suzerainty of Agamemnon.

The citadel of Tiryns was surrounded by an outer wall, built of great blocks of stone with little or no bonding. Impressed by the vast size of these ramparts, the Greeks of the classical period described them as 'cyclopean', as though they could only have been constructed by creatures with the superhuman stature and strength of the Cyclops. The system of defence was completed by galleries, casemates and posterns. Entering by a deep portico and courtyard, one reached the vestibule, beyond which was the great hall, or *megaron*, almost square, with a central hearth between four columns that supported the roof, in which was a kind of louvre to let out the smoke. The rude Achaean masters of this fortified manor employed artists who, if not actually from Crete, must have been trained in the Minoan school, for at Tiryns some splendid frescoes were discovered, representing a boar hunt, two women in a chariot, and a woman carrying a chest and dressed in Cretan style.

At Mycenae, the principal entrance is set between two walls of regularly bonded ashlar, disposed in such a way that assailants would find themselves exposed to attack from three sides at once. A huge

7

lintel, weighing approximately twenty tons, displays a triangular relief of two lions, erect and confronting one another on either side of a column, with their fore feet resting on its base. Their heads, which were originally turned to face the attackers and were intended to terrify them, have since disappeared.

Within the citadel is a large circular area, surrounded by dressed stones, beneath which Schliemann discovered the tombs of the lords of Mycenae still intact. They had been buried with their ceremonial arms, their jewels and elaborate funeral furnishings, including many objects made of gold, notably their death masks. Thus Homer was justified in calling Mycenae the town 'rich in gold'. All this gold could only have been obtained by raids carried out by the Achaeans on countries as far away as Asia. In 1951, Papadimitriou discovered more tombs, also full of gold and other art works, outside and below the citadel, enclosed in a grave-circle similar in size to that of the acropolis.

When Schliemann made his sensational discovery at Mycenae he thought he had found the bodies and death masks of Agamemnon and Clytemnestra. In reality these tombs date from long before the Trojan war, probably from the sixteenth century B.C. Two hundred years later, in the fourteenth century, the 'beehive graves' were built at some distance from the citadel on the slope of the hill, the most famous of which is known as the 'Treasury of Atreus', Agamemnon's father. A passage open to the sky leads between two walls to the majestic façade. The doorway, narrower at the top than at the base, used to be flanked by two half columns of green marble and supported, above an enormous lintel weighing a hundred tons, a triangular roof vault. The inside is shaped like a hive, the curved surface of this false dome being formed by a remarkable disposition of cantilevered stones, subsequently re-cut. Such tombs, though not on the colossal scale of the Egyptian pyramids, are nevertheless a testimony to the power of the rulers of Mycenae and the skill of their architects.

Many of the objects found at Mycenae, at Tiryns and in other Achaean citadels (at Pylos, Nestor's capital; on the Acropolis in Athens, in the palace of Erechtheus; and in Boeotia at Gla, Orchomenos and Thebes) might well serve as illustrations to the *Iliad*. For example there is a dagger whose inlaid blade represents a lion hunt, a scene often referred to in Homeric similes. There is a funeral stele at Mycenae showing a war chariot, and the Tiryns fresco with its bi-lobed shields in the form of a figure eight, or the so-called 'Warriors' Vase' at Mycenae, on which may be seen helmeted soldiers wearing greaves and carrying lances and short, square shields, rounded at the corners. Or again there is a goblet at Mycenae that vividly reminds one of these lines from Book XI of the *Iliad*:

On the table [Hecamede] put a bronze dish . . . and a magnificent beaker adorned with golden studs, which the old man had brought from home. It had four handles. Each was supported by two legs; and on top of each, facing one another, a pair of golden doves were feeding (XI, 632–5).

The golden goblet at Mycenae has only two handles and two doves, but it enables us to understand the poet's description, for the two birds are stooped over the edge as though drinking and the two handles are connected at the bottom by bars of metal forming the feet.

THE HOMERIC QUESTION

So far, we have been speaking of Homer as though he had really existed and had composed the two poems that have come down to us under his name more or less in the form in which we read them today. But as with Shakespeare, though in very different terms, a serious problem arises with regard to Homer; and the 'Homeric question' cannot be evaded.

Can we, today, fully share the optimism of Fénelon in whose opinion the unity of composition displayed in the *Iliad* was so obvious that he saw it as an argument proving the existence of God? 'Who could believe that a poem as perfect as Homer's *Iliad* was not the result of the powerful genius of a great poet? . . . Let people argue and split hairs as much as they like; no sensible person will be persuaded that mere accident was the author of the *Iliad*. Why, then, should any sensible person believe about the universe, which is certainly still more marvellous than the *Iliad*, what his good sense will not allow him to believe about this poem?' (*On the Existence of God*).

Undeniably, as the Ancients were already aware, additions have been made to the text of both poems. For example, Plutarch refers to the tradition according to which Solon, supporting the claim of his own country, Athens, to the island of Salamis, the possession of which was disputed by Megara, inserted in the 'Catalogue of Ships' in Book II of the *Iliad* two lines that are still to be found there: 'From Salamis, Ajax brought twelve ships, Beaching them alongside the Athenian forces'.

The purpose of this close association of Ajax's contingent from

Salamis with the Athenian army was to provide an 'historical' argument in support of Attica's claim to the island, a falsification from which Solon's patriotism would certainly not have shrunk.

Other interpolations were much longer. The great Alexandrian critics, Aristophanes of Byzantium and Aristarchos, both of whom prepared editions of Homer, considered the last authentic line of the *Odyssey* to be the one that describes Odysseus and Penelope at last surrendering themselves to their happiness 'and returning to their bed and its earlier rights' (XXIII, 293). And it is, indeed, probable that the end of Book XXIII and the whole of Book XXIV were added later to provide a connecting link with the *Telegonia* written by Eugammon of Cyrene in the sixth century with a view to continuing the story of the events that constitute 'the Epic Cycle'. Telegonos was a son that had been born to Odysseus, in the course of his wanderings between Troy and Ithaca, either by Circe or Calypso.

Furthermore a number of epics certainly existed before Homer. The poet of the *Iliad* makes many allusions to a Theban Cycle telling of the battles between the Seven Chieftains, a subject which Aeschylus was later to take for one of his tragedies. In Book IX of the *Iliad*, where Achilles is described resting in his tent, withdrawn from the battle and accompanying himself on the lyre as he 'sings of the deeds of heroes', it is clear that these were taken from an epic earlier than Homer's. Similarly in Book VIII of the *Odyssey* the minstrel Demodocus sings before the court of the king of the Phaeacians a number of rhapsodes, notably the bawdy tale of the 'Loves of Ares and Aphrodite' and the episode of the 'Wooden Horse', an account of the taking of Ilium that does not occur in the *Iliad*.

In addition to this, philologists have noticed that there are linguistic differences between various parts of the two poems. Thus an ancient letter of the Greek alphabet, the *digamma*, that was tending to disappear from most Greek dialects in the time of Homer,[1] affects the versification in some places, but not in others.

But above all there are inconsistencies and contradictions to be found in the *Iliad* and the *Odyssey*, which long ago caused the Latin poet Horace to say that 'sometimes great Homer nods'. In the *Iliad*, Zeus' intention that the Trojans shall win as long as Achilles remains absent from the battlefield only begins to take full effect in Book XI. True, from Book II to Book X, Achilles never takes part in the fighting,

[1] Thus the Greek word *ergon* meaning 'work' is spelt in ancient inscriptions *wergon*, which corresponds to the English *work*.

but several episodes in the intervening Books, such as the 'Catalogue of Ships' in Book II, 'Helen on the Walls of Troy' and the 'Duel between Paris and Menelaus' in Book III, would seem to be more appropriate to an epic recounting all the events of the ten-year siege than to the *Iliad* whose subject is restricted to a few weeks in the tenth year of the war. For instance, is it likely that Priam would have waited so long before getting Helen to name the principal leaders of the Achaean army?

In the *Odyssey* the 'Assembly of the Gods' with which Book I opens reaches no conclusion and it is only at the second 'Assembly' in Book V that the decision is taken to free Odysseus from Calypso's spell. One cannot escape the conclusion that the whole of the account of the 'Voyage of Telemachus', interpolated between the two 'Assemblies', must have been added to the poem, and in such a clumsy manner that the 'cobbling' is only too obvious.

Yet again, both the *Iliad* and the *Odyssey* still seem to be oral literature like the primitive type of epic. True, in a certain sense it may be said that the whole of Greek literature, even in the classical and Hellenistic periods, is essentially oral, in that it was written above all to be recited and listened to: the Ancients, even when they were alone with a text, were in the habit of reading it aloud, which is why one of Plutarch's treatises devoted to the reading of the poets is called *The Proper Manner of Listening to Poetry*. But it cannot be denied that there is one feature of the Homeric poems which in this respect gives them a quite special character: the 'formulary' style which facilitated their composition for the poet and reduced the effort of memory required by the minstrel. Thus Athena is the 'goddess of the greenish-blue eyes', Hera the 'white-armed' or 'ox-eyed' goddess, and Zeus 'the gatherer of the clouds'. Achilles is always the 'light-footed' hero, even when he remains peacefully sitting in his tent: and the ships are always described as 'swift', although they have remained drawn up on the beach for almost ten years.

This formulary style appears also in the almost mechanical conjunction of a number of words forming a hemistich which in order to complete a line can be tacked on to a number of other hemistiches, almost equally 'prefabricated'. This may be seen especially, though not only, in the lines that serve to introduce a speech. The phrases 'the cunning Odysseus', 'light-footed Achilles', 'Nestor, master of the chariots', can all be followed either by 'spoke these winged words' or by 'answered him thus'.

It has therefore been assumed that, long before they were written down, the Homeric poems had been composed by various minstrels at the request of audiences who liked to listen to some particular episode, and that the rhapsodes simply remembered them by heart. However, the fact that, thanks to the ingenuity of Ventris (see pp. 1–2), we can now read pre-Homeric Greek rather suggests that Homer and his successors may have been able to transcribe their poems, even if their audiences could not read. In the same way today musicians can easily read their scores, although the majority of those listening to a concert would have great difficulty in doing so. But the hypothesis cannot altogether be excluded that, between the decline of the syllabic script of the Mycenaean tablets and the introduction of an alphabet borrowed from the Phoenicians, writing had fallen out of use.

The Homeric question has given rise to long and impassioned debates ever since the time of François Hédelin, Abbé d'Aubignac, whose *Academic Conjectures* and *Dissertation on the Iliad* were written in 1666, though not published until after the author's death in 1715. According to him the *Iliad* and the *Odyssey* were made up 'of a number of separately composed poems that were afterwards compiled and put together'. But it was the more tentative *Prolegomena ad Homerum*, written by the German scholar F. A. Wolf in 1795, that started the real controversy.

For the Romantics, with their enthusiasm for Ossian, the *Iliad* and *Odyssey* represented a primitive kind of poetry, the spontaneous creation of folk genius. They regarded the two poems as being the result of running together a number of separately composed epic 'lays' in which the soul of the Greek people had been expressed by their bards.

Then came the 'homerizing' Hellenists who erected innumerable theories, stuffed with erudition but destined to collapse like card castles. The ruins of these elaborate constructions that today litter the field of scholarship remind one of a simile in Book xv of the *Iliad*:

Then, with equal ease, the god knocked down the Achaean wall, like a boy at the seaside playing childish games with the sand, building a castle to amuse himself and then with his hands and feet destroying the whole work for fun. That is how you, Lord Apollo, spoilt the Argives' work and started a panic in the men who had toiled at it so painfully (xv, 361–6).

In fact many of these 'carvers-up' of Homer did not leave it to other Hellenists to destroy their tottering edifices: they subsequently defected to the ranks of those who believed in single authorship.

Some, like Kirchoff and Victor Bérard, considered that comparatively short poems, 'rhapsodes', were grouped together in single entities of unequal value and that the linking up of these entities constituted the two poems. According to this view, the *Odyssey* consists of three main parts of which only the central one, the 'Tales of Alcinous', from the beginning of Book v to the middle of Book XIII, can be regarded as worthy of the poet of genius we call Homer; while the two others, the 'Voyage of Telemachus' (Books I–IV) and the 'Vengeance of Odysseus' (Book XIII, l. 185 to Book XXIII) were the work of 'epigonei' of lesser stature. These three parts would then have been cobbled together to the best of his ability by someone else, though certain scholars are of the opinion that Homer himself was responsible for this final arrangement, thus relegating him to the end of this long poetic process instead of the beginning. One can understand why Bernard Shaw wittily remarked: 'The *Iliad* and the *Odyssey* are not the work of Homer, but of another poet who happened to have the same name.'

Other scholars, like Niese and Maurice Croiset, have supposed that the *Iliad* and the *Odyssey* are the result of accretions around a primitive 'kernel', (the *Ur-Ilias* and *Ur-Odyssee* of the Germans), a small number of lays subsequently drawn together by the addition of 'developing' and 'connecting' lays. According to Croiset, the primitive kernel of the *Iliad* consisted of the 'Quarrel' from Book I, the 'Exploits of Agamemnon' from Book XI, the 'Patrocleia' from Book XVI and the 'Death of Hector' from Book XXII—all the rest being adventitious.

The great Hellenist, Paul Mazon, was less radical. He thought that the primitive *Iliad*, the actual work of Homer, consisted of Book I, together with Books XI to XVIII and XX to XXIV, that is to say fourteen, or more than half, of the total number. This already represents a considerable advance on the views of the earlier separatists. But in his *Introduction to the Iliad* he also wrote: 'What constitutes perhaps the most difficult aspect of the problem is that, in the two groups (Books II–VII and VIII–X) that were added to the original plan of the *Iliad*, are to be found some of the most beautiful passages in the whole poem: Book III is the wittiest; v contains the most vigorous battle scenes; the scene at the end of VI, the conversation between Hector and Andromache, is one of the most sensitive and touching in the whole of Homer; IX is psychologically the richest and, as literature, the most eloquent passage in Greek epic; and none of these Books differs basically from Books I and XI–XXIV. Thus it is not absolutely impossible that they are by the same author.'

For my part, it is precisely the converse that strikes me as impossible: I cannot see how any poet other than Homer, even one brought up in his school, could have been capable of inserting into the carefully devised structure of the *Iliad*, passages which, in the main, are in such admirable harmony with the work of the original creator of the poem and which, both in inspiration and style, so closely resemble him. Similarly, as regards the *Odyssey*, surely it is hard to conceive that the splendid account of the 'Vengeance of Odysseus', for example, was not written by the same poet as the 'Tales of Alcinous?'

Comparing the flowering of the epic with that of tragedy, Mazon considered it possible that there had been several successive generations of epic poets of genius, as was later to be the case with Aeschylus, Sophocles and Euripides This may well have been so, and if the *Iliad* and the *Odyssey* were to be attributed to two different poets, an idea that had already occurred to some of the Alexandrian critics, I should see no serious objection. But what Mazon asks us to accept is that each of the poems was the result of collaboration by a succession of poets, as though a tragedy begun by Aeschylus were to be continued by Sophocles and completed by Euripides. Had this been so, however, any experienced Hellenist would soon have been able to show which parts were the work of which poet and it would not have taken the critics long to reach agreement.

'Let us not forget', Mazon concludes, 'that collective works are not necessarily lacking in inspiration and unity: there is scarcely one of our cathedrals where the plans of the first architects have not been modified in the course of construction; nor, though they are the result of changing and successive endeavour, can the Louvre or Versailles be dismissed as mediocre achievements'. Analogy is not proof, however, and the only parallels Mazon puts forward are from architecture. Of all the great literary works known to us that form a single great entity, the *Iliad* and the *Odyssey* would be the only ones to have been produced by a joint creative effort persisting over a century, perhaps longer. In the analysis of the two poems that we make later, their essential unity will be clearly brought out.

On the hypothesis that the two poems were collective works, this unity cannot be explained by reference to any literary parallel. By contrast, on the hypothesis of a single author, there is no dearth of parallels to explain their weaknesses, disparities and contradictions. Lamartine's *Jocelyn*, for example, which is beyond doubt the work of a single poet (true, a little absent-minded sometimes, but then so was Homer), bristles with instances of carelessness and incoherence, compared with which even the 'resurrection' of Pylaemenes, killed in Book v but capable in Book xiii of following his son's funeral, appears a very pardonable slip. Anyone responsible for merely arranging the poem would have been at the greatest pains to avoid such incongruities and would easily have done so; a great poet is more careless about details. Genius can afford to be absent-minded.

Faced with the collapse of so many separatist theories, in which Homer is subjected to *post-mortem* examination, the most sensible thing is to return to the unitary conception of the Ancients. True, there have been interpolations in the original text, but in most cases it is impossible either to prove them or to determine their extent. The greater part of the *Iliad* is the work of Homer and the *Odyssey* can also be attributed to him, if we admit that the *Iliad* was the work of his maturity and the *Odyssey* of his old age.

THE STRUCTURE OF THE *Iliad*

The wrath of Achilles is my theme, that fatal wrath which, in fulfilment of the will of Zeus, brought the Achaeans so much suffering and sent the gallant souls of many noblemen to Hades, leaving their bodies as carrion for the dogs and passing birds. Let us begin, goddess of song, with the angry parting that took place between Agamemnon King of Men and the great Achilles, son of Peleus (*Iliad* i, 1–7).

This invocation to the Muse, with which the poem opens, indicates precisely the subject of the *Iliad*: the anger of Achilles and its disastrous consequences. By virtue of his promise to Thetis, the 'will of Zeus' was to favour the Trojans at the expense of the Achaeans, until such time as Agamemnon's outrage against Achilles after their quarrel should be expiated.

In these few lines Homer, a lucid poet always conscious of his art, underlined the originality of his work. Aristotle, who was able to compare the *Iliad* and the *Odyssey* with other poems of the Epic Cycle, most of which are no more than names for us, says in the *Poetics*: 'For a poem to have unity, it is not enough for it to recount the deeds and achievements of a single hero, as do the *Heracleid* and the *Theseid*

15

and other epics of this kind. Homer, superior in every respect, seems to have taken the correct view on this point also, thanks to his knowledge of art and to his genius . . . both his *Iliad* and his *Odyssey* are constructed around a single action' (*Poetics* VIII 1–3).

The subject of the *Iliad* can be resumed in a few lines. A warrior prince, Achilles, picks a quarrel with his overlord Agamemnon. Outraged by the seizure of his prisoner Briseis, he ceases to take part in the battle. So serious is the effect of his absence on the Achaean army that it comes near to being defeated by the enemy and, since Hector is on the point of burning its ships, to being prevented from returning to Greece. At this point Achilles, despite his anger, decides to lend his own armour to his friend Patroclus and to send him into battle. Patroclus is killed by Hector. From that moment, Achilles' resentment is overcome by grief and the desire for revenge. He returns to the fight and kills Hector.

Thus, like a classical tragedy, the *Iliad* consists of a beginning, the quarrel; followed by a peripeteia, the 'Patrocleia'; and an end, the death of Hector. The unity of action is psychological, since all the important events are determined by the feelings of Achilles, so that the treatment of the subject always brings us back to the portrayal of his character. The unity of place is relative: for, while everything takes place in the restricted area between the ships of the Achaeans, drawn up on the shore, and the nearby citadel of Troy, the actual scene frequently shifts from the Achaean camp to the plain, where the battles are fought, and to the city of Ilium. The unity of time is even less strictly observed: nevertheless, though the siege of Troy lasted ten years, all the events that take place between the quarrel in Book I and Hector's funeral in Book XXIV occupy less than two months. Yet despite this concentration, which is the sign manual of his work, the poet certainly intended to provide a survey of the whole war, which accounts for his frequent allusions to events that had happened before the quarrel or after Hector's funeral.

In the preface to his first Book, known as the 'Archaeology', reflecting on the *Iliad* as a historian, Thucydides says: 'From shortage of supplies, the Achaeans had only brought a small number of troops, limited to what they hoped to be able to maintain during the course of the fighting. But having arrived and proved their superiority—as was certainly the case, otherwise they would not have built the wall to protect their camp—one can see that, even then, they did not make use of all their forces: dispersing their efforts, they cultivated the

Thracian Chersonese and engaged in piracy in order to obtain supplies. It was this dispersal of their opponents that enabled the Trojans to maintain the struggle for ten years: it meant that, at any given time, the strength of their own forces was roughly equivalent to that of the enemy' (I, 11). And, indeed, Homer does mention numerous raids carried out by the Achaeans against the islands and cities in Asia Minor that were allied to the Trojans. Achilles surprises Aeneas and his cattle on mount Ida, puts him to flight, pursues him to Lyrnessos where he seeks refuge and, having captured the town, loots it, taking for himself as the 'share of honour', Briseis (II, 689–93; XX, 187–94). He also seizes Pedasos, another town in Troas (XX, 92), captures Priam's son, Lycaon, and sells him into slavery at Lemnos (XXI, 76–9). Later, he leads an expedition into Cilicia and destroys Thebes-under-Placos, the city of Andromache's father, Eëtion (VI, 414–28). The daughter of Chryses, the priest of Apollo, called after her father Chryseis (as the daughter of Brises was called Briseis), happened to be staying in Thebes with Eëtion's sister; she is captured by the Achaeans and when the booty is shared out given to Agamemnon (I, 366–9). It was Chryses' visit to the Achaean camp to try to buy back his daughter, and Agamemnon's brutal refusal, that led Apollo to avenge his priest by visiting the Greeks with the plague—the plague that was the origin of the quarrel between Achilles and Agamemnon at the assembly of the warriors described in Book I.

Paul Mazon has clearly shown that each of the twenty-four books of the *Iliad* forms a whole and that almost all of them are remarkably well constructed. This is especially the case with Book I. The story proceeds at a lively pace. The plague lasts for nine days, then twelve more elapse between Thetis' promise to Achilles and its carrying out; this second interval is skilfully taken up with an account of the journey undertaken by Odysseus in order to restore Chryses' daughter to him and thus appease the wrath of Apollo. Everything is logically connected, from the arrival of Chryses in the Achaean camp to the scene in Olympus, for the assembly of the gods has already been intimated by Zeus to Thetis (518–9), when he warns her of the conflict with Hera.

Thus Book I covers a period of about three weeks, the only other Book that embraces so long a period being the last. Everything takes place as though Homer intended to equate the short crisis described in the *Iliad* with the whole duration of the war.

Admittedly, the opening of Book II is at first sight disconcerting.

In order to achieve his aims, Zeus sends a false dream to Agamemnon but the latter suddenly decides to put his troops to the test and advises them to re-embark: they obey him all too readily and Odysseus has the greatest difficulty in preventing a general stampede. Here it should be understood that Agamemnon despairs of being able to lead his army into action while they are in the state of demoralization resulting from nine years of 'phoney war'. In lines 235–42, Thersites is certainly expressing the feelings of the exhausted and discouraged soldiers. In this state of confusion, Agamemnon therefore decides to test the army so as to avoid the risk of being disobeyed when he gives the order to attack to men who have already decided to run away. It is true, however, that Homer, who was accepted as a master of the art of war as of all others, was here offering an example to military strategists that it would be very dangerous to follow.

At the solemn moment when the two armies are preparing for battle, the poet addresses a new invocation to the Muses, and then proceeds to the so-called 'Catalogue of the Ships', a list of the principal Achaean and Trojan chiefs, with the strength of the contingents under their command. This enumeration provides a survey, which appears to be historically correct, of Mycenaean Greece: the towns noted by Homer are precisely those where excavation has brought to light the richest remains of the Achaean epoch. Moreover, this catalogue is not, as has sometimes been asserted, out of place here, for, as the poet several times reminds us, this is the first time that the two armies have confronted one another in set battle: up to this point the Trojans, from fear of Achilles, have not ventured beyond the walls of their city.

In Book III, the two armies face one another, but large-scale action is delayed by the single combat between Menelaus and Paris which provides the occasion for a truce, guaranteed by an understanding that the duel between the two principals shall bring the war to an end. Profiting from this pause, the poet now takes us to the walls of Troy, where Helen, prompted by curiosity, is chatting with Priam and the other Elders of Troy. What grounds are there for denying Homer's authorship of this admirably composed Book, one of the most attractive in the whole poem? The scene moves with ease from the army to the walls of Troy, then from Troy to the army and back again, before finally ending with the army in the concluding lines, where Agamemnon sums up the results of the duel. This rich diversity has been obtained without the poet having once had to describe actions that are taking place simultaneously.

In the scene on Olympus, with which Book IV opens, Zeus speaks as though he had forgotten his promise to Thetis, but it must be remembered that his intentions are secret and that, as he himself has already said (I, 549), he had decided upon them 'without consulting the other gods'. To have spoken openly of them beforehand to the assembled gods would have been to give himself away and confirm Hera's suspicions. Besides, Zeus is clearly asserting his own sympathy with the Trojans. Then he orders Athena to bring about a rupture of the pact, agreed upon by Agamemnon and Priam before the single combat: a rupture that is necessary if he is to fulfil his promise to Thetis. When the arrow of Pandarus the Lycian scratches Menelaus' thigh, full-scale battle becomes inevitable.

Agamemnon reviews his troops, thus completing the 'Catalogue' in Book II and in turn exhorts Idomeneus, the two Ajaxes, Nestor, Odysseus and Diomedes; announcing, by the attention he pays to the latter, the leading part he is to play in Books V and VI. At the end of Book IV the battle begins and continues till Book VII; the first of the four great battles described in the *Iliad*.

Book VIII opens, like Book IV, with an Olympian prelude, but this time Zeus is determined to impose his will from the start, and he forbids any of the gods to intervene in the battle. This is one of the Books that has been regarded as a mere link, full of inconsistencies and written by some 'arranger' to serve as preparation for the 'Embassy' in Book IX. Undoubtedly it contains one or two peculiar features, like the four-horsed chariot driven by Hector (185), whereas usually the chariots in the *Iliad* have only two horses; or the purple standard borne by Agamemnon (221). But it also has a number of lovely passages: for instance, the episode of Nestor's wounded horse (80–90); the exploits of the archer Teucer, shooting his arrows from the shelter of his brother Ajax's huge shield; or the comparison of the dying soldier, his head bowed down by the weight of his helmet, with a poppy drooping on its stalk (306–8), a simile imitated by Virgil in Book IX of the *Aeneid*.

The story of the second day of battle takes up the whole of Book VIII, but the battle is broken off and starts again next day, in Book XI. Meanwhile, two episodes occur during the night: the embassy to Achilles (Book IX), and the expedition of Odysseus and Diomedes who surprise and kill the Trojan spy Dolon (Book X).

Book XI, to which the orators of old turned for examples of eloquence, has always been one of the most admired in the whole poem, and Homer's authorship has never been doubted. Its structure is masterly: the three successive replies that Achilles gives to Odysseus, Phoenix and Ajax, though identical in their immediate refusal, are nevertheless subtly modified in such a way as to express a progressive withdrawal from his first decision to quit Troas the following day (427–9): to Phoenix he declares that he will make up his mind on the morrow whether to stay or go (617–19), but then he tells Ajax that, if Hector attacks his camp and his ships, he will start fighting again (650–5), which implies that he means to stay. This last resolve he will effectively recall later when he sends Patroclus into battle (xvi, 61–3). Sometimes it would appear that there are three ambassadors, Phoenix, Odysseus and Ajax, sometimes only two, Odysseus and Ajax. But this presents only a minor difficulty, for Phoenix, an intimate friend of Achilles who has been appointed ambassador by Nestor, sets out first and the two others, who regard him as a companion rather than a colleague, only join him later.

More serious is the fact that on two later occasions in Book xi and Book xvi, Achilles speaks as if he had never received an embassy from Agamemnon. The reason for this is that his enemy has not really humbled himself before him; though Agamemnon offers him presents, he still insists upon his authority. Moreover, for Achilles, whose wrath remains undiminished, these gifts are without meaning: since his mind is still filled with resentment, he either forgets about them at once, or, if he remembers them, prefers not to speak about them because 'he holds them in horror'. On the other hand, Books xviii and xix contain several formal allusions to the embassy.

Book x, with the episode of Dolon, is the only one about which one of the ancient scholiasts expresses doubt, not of its authenticity (he accepts Homer's authorship), but as not belonging to the original plan of the *Iliad*: 'It is said that this book was composed separately by Homer and to begin with was not part of the *Iliad*; but that it was Peisistratus who first introduced it into the poem'. However, to me it appears that Homer intended it to take the place it now occupies, for he makes a number of precise allusions that connect it with Books viii and ix.

With Book xi begins the third battle of the *Iliad*, which will only be brought to an end in Book xviii—or rather, it is here that the second battle, started in Book viii, begins again on the following day. The Olympians, in obedience to the command of Zeus at the beginning of Book viii, do not intervene—apart from Zeus himself. Eris, the personification of discord, is present at the battle and does her best to stir it up. Five Achaean heroes in succession are wounded, three of them by Paris' arrows. Three of them, Agamemnon, Diomedes and Odysseus, are protagonists; the other two, Machaon and Eurypylos, only minor characters. The wounds of the two last are vividly described by the poet in preparation for the third part of this Book where we are taken behind the Achaean lines. The reason for this is that it is now time to introduce the peripeteia: the sending of Patroclus into battle. In this respect, line 604 is of great significance, for here, at the moment when Patroclus leaves his tent at the appeal of his friend, the poet anticipating the future says: 'And this, for him, was the beginning of misfortune'. As he leaves Nestor, to whom he has been sent by Achilles, Patroclus looks after the wounded Eurypylos whom he meets on the way.

Book XII relates the story of the attack on the Achaean wall and its capture, the poet having previously announced its destruction. The battle for the wall is naturally followed by the battle for the ships, the account of which starts in Book XIII. The intervention of Poseidon, who disobeys the orders of Zeus, delays Hector's victory.

At the end of Book XI, Nestor was left in his tent, talking to the wounded Machaon, while Patroclus, having taken Eurypylos home, was looking after his wounds. In Books XIV and XV respectively we once more encounter Nestor and Patroclus exactly as we left them several Books earlier. For them time seems to have stood still. Unable to describe everything at once, Homer is obliged to turn back, but he manages the connection between these various events with masterly assurance.

The 'Patrocleia' in Book XVI, already foreseen by Zeus (VIII, 476), is scrupulously led up to by the group of Books XI–XV, and fits in with them perfectly. Book XVII, which in the manuscripts is called the 'Exploits of Menelaus', might be more accurately entitled the 'Struggle for the Body of Patroclus'. It is cleverly and carefully constructed and centres around the account of the horses of Achilles lamenting over the body of Patroclus (425–542). At the same time, it seems to me that some of the criticisms that have been made of this Book are justified. For example, the poet unnecessarily multiplies the interventions by the gods which are sometimes irksome and contradictory; and the Book, longer than it need be, in places gives an impression of 'padding'.

By contrast, Book XVIII is extremely rich, brilliant and varied.

Though by its subject it is essentially transitional, a 'link' in the language of the separatists, the talent of the poet is displayed in each of its parts and the description of the shield of Achilles with which it ends is one of the jewels of Greek epic poetry.

Desire to avenge the death of Patroclus suffices to bring Achilles back into the fight, which is why Book XIX, telling of the solemn reconciliation of Achilles and Agamemnon, has struck many critics as being superfluous. But to argue thus is to miss the point: if Achilles returns to the struggle only in order to avenge Patroclus, logically he will once again become inactive after Hector's death. Now this would be contrary to the legend, according to which, as his horse Xanthos here warns him (404–17), Achilles will be killed in battle. The solemn reconciliation is therefore necessary to the plan of an *Iliad* that is seen as part of the whole Trojan cycle. And, as we have already several times pointed out, having once strictly delimited his subject, Homer did everything possible to relate his partial account to the legendary cycle as a whole.

Book XX opens with another assembly of the gods, but now that Zeus has fulfilled his aim and kept his promise to Thetis he is no longer concerned, as in Book VIII, to forbid any intervention by the other gods. If they seem to be helping the Trojans, it is in order to prevent Achilles taking Troy immediately and thus forestalling fate. This is the purpose of Apollo and Poseidon in leaving the Achaean camp for that of the Trojans during this fourth day of battle, which will be brought to an end in Book XXII with the death of Hector. Twice in Book XX Achilles finds himself in the presence of Hector, but without any definite result.

There is a certain casualness in the way in which the poet, having ranged the gods against one another, suddenly, at the instance of Poseidon, puts an end to the heavenly strife before it has really begun. It is true that this passage introduces an episode that will be important for the following Book. Yet one cannot escape the feeling that the poet is rather wasting his time and drawing things out, as in Book XVII.

In Book XXI, the episode of Xanthos, however strange it may appear, is not lacking in grandeur. All the same it has to be admitted that, for the modern reader, the war of the gods is a sad disappointment. After the urgent preparations for it at the beginning of Book XX, one expects something better. These encounters between the Olympians strike us as being devoid of seriousness; and they lead to nothing beyond provoking Zeus to a 'gentle smile' (508). However, on ancient

1. The North Gate of the palace of Cnossos (p. 5)

2a. 'La Parisienne', one of the frescoes from the palace of Cnossos (p. 5). *Heraklion Museum*

2b. One of the golden goblets found at Vapheio in Laconia. They were made by Cretan craftsmen and depict the capture of wild bulls (p. 5). *National Museum, Athens*

audiences they may not have made the same impression of exaggerated caricature.

If Books XVII, XX and XXI seem to us to have a number of weaknesses as well as passages of unmistakable beauty, the last three Books of the poem are completely admirable. The death of Hector in Book XXII ends the fourth and final day of the battle, since the only Trojan still outside the walls has perished. It might even be said that this event exhausts the theme of the poem: the anger of Achilles, first against Agamemnon, then against Hector, the slayer of Patroclus. But the *Iliad* is not yet finished: we have still to learn what happened to the bodies of Patroclus and of Hector, and the two last Books are amongst the finest that Homer wrote.

Book XXIII extends over three days: the evening of the last day of the battle when the Myrmidons in their chariots hold a wake over the body of Patroclus; then, after a night during which the shade of Patroclus appears to Achilles, the day of the funeral ceremonies; and finally, after Achilles has watched beside the pyre of his friend, the day of the games. This Book, then, covers a longer period than the preceding ones but not as long as the final one.

These funeral games in honour of Patroclus are, so to speak, the prototype of those to be held later in such pan-Hellenic sanctuaries as Olympia and Delphi, and it is certain that these great trials of strength and skill were in the first place instituted as an accompaniment to the burial of heroes and kings. The account is extremely picturesque, varied and realistic: it was to be imitated by Virgil in Book V of the *Aeneid* and was enthusiastically praised by Goethe and Schiller.

In Book XXIV, the gods deliberate the fate of Hector's corpse which day after day Achilles is continuing to drag through the dust, tied to the back of his chariot. Zeus orders Thetis to persuade Achilles to restore the body in return for a ransom and dispatches Iris to Priam to get him to visit his son's killer. Priam consents and Achilles receives him courteously, though at times he cannot prevent his anger bursting out against the old man: 'So do not exasperate me now, sir, when I have enough already on my mind. . . .'

In his *Introduction to the Iliad*, Paul Mazon says: 'What is so beautiful in this Book is the way in which, though dedicated to peace, the memory of wrath still persists, ready at any moment to break out and ruin everything. In the soul of Achilles it struggles with a profound lassitude, an immense melancholy at the thought of the wretched lot in store for all human beings, reducing them, whatever their age or rank, to equality. For the closing chapter of a poem so charged with humanity as the *Iliad*, it is hard to imagine scenes that could be more impressive. There had always been but one possible conclusion to the *Iliad*: not the death of Achilles, but the death of the anger in the depths of his soul. And the portrayal of this death, which does not come about without agonized and convulsive struggle, is a worthy pendant to the scenes in Book 1, where we witnessed the birth of this anger in all its fresh and stinging bitterness.'

With Priam's return to Troy comes the first appearance of Cassandra, who is to play such a major part in the continuation of the epic cycle at the time of the wooden horse and the taking of the city. Then, finally, Andromache, Hecuba and Helen, each in her own manner, give expression to the grief they have endured.

This last Book lasts for more than three weeks, since Achilles, having dragged the body of Hector round the walls for twelve days, then grants Priam a truce of eleven days for the preparation and observance of Hector's funeral. The only other book that covers so long a period is the first. In this way the poet harmoniously relates his subject to the long drawn out siege. Just as he recalls events from the past, so he announces others that will happen in the future: the approaching death of Achilles, the capture of Troy, the slaying of Priam and Astyanax, the captivity of the Trojans, the return of the Achaeans to their homeland, the complete destruction of the wall built to protect the ships, the reign of Aeneas and his descendants in Troy, and the ultimate fall of the great Achaean cities.

This relationship of the critical period described in the *Iliad* with the legend as a whole is achieved with the same consummate artistry as the internal connection between the various parts of the poem itself. But Homer does not insist, he never exaggerates this dual relationship; he is content to bring it out by brief allusions, by the merest suggestion of similarities. The subtlety of his writing, so subtle as to have misled a number of critics, reminds one of the saying of the philosopher, Heracleitus of Ephesus: 'Harmony when it is concealed is worth more than when it is apparent' (*Fragment* 54).

However, though I am personally convinced that, apart from one or two interpolations, all the books of the *Iliad* are by Homer, I do not go so far as to assert that they were composed in the same order as that in which they appear in the complete poem. It is possible that Homer, having at the start established the overall plan that he intended to follow, may have written Books ix and x, for example, after the group XI–XVII. Such a hypothesis would suffice to remove the greater part of the difficulties that the separatists make so much of in their efforts to deny Homer's authorship of this or that section of the *Iliad*.

THE STRUCTURE OF THE *Odyssey*

The hero of the tale which I beg the Muse to help me tell is that resourceful man who roamed the wide world after he had sacked the holy citadel of Troy. He saw the cities of many people and he learnt their ways. He suffered many hardships on the high seas in his struggles to preserve his life and bring his comrades home. But he failed to save those comrades, in spite of all his efforts. It was their own sin that brought them to their doom, for in their folly they devoured the oxen of Hyperion the Sun, and the god saw to it that they should never return. This is the tale I pray the divine Muse to unfold for us (*Odyssey* I, 1–10).

This is the invocation with which the *Odyssey* opens. Like that at the beginning of the *Iliad*, it defines precisely the subject of the poem: the return of Odysseus. True, the poet does not expressly mention either the 'Voyage of Telemachus' or the 'Vengeance of Odysseus', but this is quite natural: his purpose is to indicate the central theme of the poem, not to provide a table of contents of all its ingredients.

Aristotle, in the passage from the *Poetics* I have quoted above (p. 15–13), observes that the action of the *Odyssey*, like that of the *Iliad*, is one, since Homer 'does not recount all the events in the life of Odysseus', but only his return to Ithaca from Troy. Yet though there is unity of action, 'it rests on a two-fold order of facts, so that its structure is more complex than that of the *Iliad*. The theme of the *Odyssey* is easily told. A man wanders far from his country for many years, ceaselessly watched over by Poseidon, and alone. Moreover, such things are done in his household that his fortune is squandered by his wife's suitors and his son is caught up in their snares. He arrives home in a state of distress and, having made himself known to a few people, he attacks and survives, while his enemies perish. This is what properly belongs to the subject: the rest is episodic' (*Poetics* XVII, 10).

At first sight, the *Odyssey* seems to have no unity of place: Odysseus stays in or passes through a number of places, more or less far away from his homeland where Penelope awaits him; while Telemachus in an attempt to obtain news of his father travels in the Peloponnese, to Pylos and Sparta. But, from Book XIII onwards, after Odysseus has returned to Ithaca, unity of place is strictly observed; throughout the second half of the poem, the whole action takes place between the fields and the town, between the hut of Eumaeus and the palace of Odysseus.

If the account of the wrath of Achilles primarily suggests a tragedy, the wanderings of Odysseus would at first sight seem to be an adventure story. There are a whole series of 'recognitions' such as we shall find later in the Greek novels of Hellenistic and Roman times: Odysseus is recognized successively by Eurycleia, Eumaeus and Telemachus, then by the suitors, and finally by Penelope and his father. Before this, the miraculous and often disastrous landfalls of the hero —in the land of the Cyclopes, on the island of Circe, at the entrance to hell and finally at the palace of Calypso—have occurred far from the real, everyday world, in a fairyland setting.

Another marked difference between the two poems is that the *Iliad* ends sadly with the funerals of Patroclus and Hector, whereas the *dénouement* of the *Odyssey* is happy: the wicked suitors and their abettors are punished, Odysseus and Penelope are re-united after twenty years of separation and enjoy the happiness they thought they had lost for ever. Is it so surprising that a poet who had written a poem of underlying pessimism in his maturity should in old age have written another more optimistic one? Does this really provide justification for following the Alexandrian 'separatists' who attributed the two poems to different authors? Surely this diversity of tone[1] may be less a matter of the poet's personality than of the nature of his themes: deadly battles are a more sombre subject than the return of the demobilized soldier to his own hearth, even when his way home is beset by redoubtable difficulties.

So far I have said nothing about the unity of time. At first sight the events described in the *Odyssey* cover more than ten years, from his departure from Troy to the punishment of the suitors: Odysseus spends a year with Circe and seven with Calypso, and to these must be added the time spent afloat and the many other shorter landings. This is as long a period as the whole Trojan war, only one brief moment of which is dealt with in the *Iliad*. In reality, however, the poet succeeded in compressing time in the *Odyssey* as dramatically as in the *Iliad*, but in a different way. In the latter he chose a crisis, the wrath of Achilles, and only referred to the rest of the war by allusion. In the former he plunges the reader *in medias res*, then leads him

---

1 Bentley went so far as to maintain that the *Iliad* seems to have been written for men and the *Odyssey* for women.

back into the past by making the hero describe it. This device, this 'summoning up remembrance of things past', which was to play so important a part in the later literature of Greece and of many other countries, was here perhaps being used for the first time.

In fact, the *Odyssey* begins at the moment when Odysseus is about to leave Calypso for the country of the Phaeacians where he will make a very short stay before returning direct to Ithaca. Everything that happened prior to this moment of departure will be recounted by Odysseus to the Phaeacians so that between the 'Assembly of the Gods' at the beginning of Book I and Penelope's recognition of Odysseus in Book XXII a period of only forty days elapses, less than that covered by the *Iliad*.

Surely Aristotle was right in pointing to these two different ways of achieving the same result, dramatic concentration, as being the sign manual of the great poet almost unanimously known in antiquity as Homer? In a remarkable treatise, possibly by Plutarch, *On the Life and Poetry of Homer*, we read: 'Form is the primary aspect of art. Homer never lost sight of this, as may be seen especially from the way he begins his two poems. In the *Iliad* he does not start by going back to remote events; he seizes upon the moment when the action is most striking; while he is content to recall less notable happenings briefly by means of allusion. He does the same thing in the *Odyssey*, beginning his story at the last stage of Odysseus' wanderings, at the moment when he decides to introduce Telemachus and the insolence of Penelope's suitors. What had happened before is then recounted by Odysseus, and Homer makes the account of these adventures all the more moving and probable by putting it into the mouth of the man to whom they had happened'.

Nine years after the fall of Troy, 'all the survivors of the war had returned to their homes, and so put the perils of battle and of the sea behind them'—all save Odysseus, held in thrall by Calypso. After wandering for eight years in Egypt and elsewhere, Menelaus is back in Lacedaemon. As for Agamemnon who returned to Mycenae much earlier, the fate that was awaiting him is already known. In the 'Assembly of the Gods' at the beginning of the *Odyssey*, Zeus speaks of the murder of Aegisthus by Orestes, Agamemnon's son, as having occurred recently: thus some nine years must have elapsed between the death of Agamemnon and Orestes' act of vengeance, time enough for the latter to have grown up.

The goddess Athena, still, as in the *Iliad*, devoted to the interests of Odysseus, profiting from the absence of Poseidon his enemy, intercedes with Zeus on behalf of her protégé, who has been kicking his heels for the last seven years under Calypso's spell. Zeus agrees and Athena suggests to him that he should send Hermes to her with orders to let Odysseus go. The goddess adds that she herself will go to Ithaca to advise Telemachus to undertake a journey in the hope of obtaining some news of his father.

It is this 'Voyage of Telemachus', which takes up the first four books of the poem, that raises the major problem of the composition of the *Odyssey*. Was it, as the 'separatists' have supposed, an addition to the work of Homer?

Two decisions have been taken by the gods, one concerning Odysseus, the other concerning Telemachus. But it is impossible for the poet to describe everything at once and he therefore does here what he has already done several times in the *Iliad*: first of all he narrates the story of Telemachus' voyage, then, taking up Athena's suggestion, to which Zeus has already assented, he turns to Hermes' embassy to Calypso. Furthermore, Book I is not solely concerned with the preparations for Telemachus' journey. It also gives us a picture of Ithaca in the weeks preceding the return of Odysseus: we take part in the feasting of the suitors, as they listen to the minstrel Phemios singing of the return of the Achaean heroes; we watch Penelope coming down from the women's quarters (as she will do again in Book xx) to be sharply rebuked by Telemachus her son who, now aged twenty, assumes the authority of master of the house, though when Odysseus set out for Troy he had still been only a baby—the baby referred to in the *Iliad*, when Odysseus says to Thersites: 'Let Telemachus be called no son of mine, if I don't lay hands on you. . . .' (II, 260–1).

To me, this first Book would seem to be the aptest possible prelude to a poem which, eventually, is going to show Odysseus and Telemachus jointly exacting vengeance from the suitors. The fugitive appearance of Penelope is also a happy stroke, for it introduces to the audience the woman for whom throughout his wanderings Odysseus maintains the deepest tenderness and longing. Essentially, indeed, the *Odyssey* is devoted to the exaltation of married love—a rare example in the classical literature of Greece which so often celebrates love of quite a different kind.

To maintain that the 'Voyage of Telemachus' is a later addition to Homer is therefore, I am convinced, to mistake the nature of the poet's art and his feeling for form. True, this journey produces no definite results: neither at Pylos nor at Sparta does he find any certain news of his father's fate. But Homer, not without a sense of humour, is the first to recognize this apparent futility. When in Book XIII Odysseus learns from Athena of Telemachus' voyage in quest of news, he replies very sensibly: 'But why, in your omniscience, did you not tell him the truth? Do you want him to scour the barren seas in misery while strangers eat him out of hearth and home?' To which Athena, who cannot give the true reason because it is a purely literary one, replies rather lamely: 'I myself arranged the journey for him feeling that the adventure would redound to his credit'. Homer is concerned on the one hand to relate the return of Odysseus to the legend as a whole by taking us to the homes of Nestor and Menelaus, both already back from Troy; and, on the other and more especially, to give us a glimpse of Ithaca, with Telemachus, Penelope and the suitors, before the arrival of the hero.

Book II concludes the account of the situation in Ithaca with an animated description of an assembly of the people and of Telemachus' preparations for departure, helped and advised by Athena who has assumed the shape of Mentor.

Book III tells of Telemachus' visit to Nestor at Pylos, and the greater part of Book IV is taken up with his reception at the court of Sparta by Menelaus and Helen, whom we are surprised and delighted to find there once more playing the part of a devoted wife and accomplished mistress of the house. Then, suddenly the scene changes (620), and the poet takes us back to Ithaca where the suitors, having got to hear of Telemachus' departure, are preparing an ambush for him when he returns, intending to kill him. Once again we see Penelope who has been warned of their intentions by the herald Medon and is filled with apprehension for her son. She is only soothed by a dream that is sent to her at night by Athena. And this Book, which concludes the first, brilliantly many-sided part of the poem, is brought to a close on a note of suspense: will Telemachus fall victim to his enemies or not? Here Homer seems to me to be the ancestor of our novelists, at least of those who for purposes of serialization end their chapters with some agonizing situation, leaving their readers desperately anxious to know what happens next. The way in which he here breaks off the action might well serve as a model to many dramatists and script-writers.

We shall not encounter Telemachus again until Book XV and then it will be at Sparta where we have just left him. This technique of story-telling reminds us of that used in the *Iliad*, where Patroclus and Eurypylos disappear from the story for a time (from Book XI to Book XV); though there, it must be admitted, the reader is not left in the same state of suspense as here. In this case, we are only reassured about the fate of Telemachus after a long interval of eleven Books.

True, this suspense is achieved at the expense of a certain verisimilitude, though this is only apparent to someone concerned to establish the detailed chronology of the *Odyssey*; and there would scarcely be many such amongst a minstrel's audience. From the time it would have taken Odysseus to get from the island of Calypso to Ithaca, by way of the country of the Phaeacians, Telemachus must have spent a whole month at Sparta—a long sojourn, even if one assumes that he was detained by the ripening charms of Helen. The poet must have been aware of this difficulty, for in Book IV he makes Menelaus say to Telemachus: 'And now, my friend, I invite you to stay on in my palace. Stay for twelve days or so, and then I'll send you off in style' (587–8). But the young man who has left his ship at Pylos with its crew wisely declines this invitation, though doubtless prepared, later, to submit to the power of Helen's charms.

The truth is, we here have an example of what Edouard Delebecque has well called 'dead time', a device required by the technique of epic story telling, so much closer to that of the drama than of the novel: 'The law of succession in time, making the simultaneous account of events impossible, obliged the poet to immobilize one character in a period of "dead time", so that he might bring a second into play, and then to put the second into cold storage while the first is once more shown in action. As an epic poet, without any of the novelist's resources for reversing the flow of time, Homer was bound by this law. The demands of epic forced him to accept the rules of dramatic action which, being based on his characters, made it necessary for him to show them in action chronologically. As soon as the action begins to take place on two levels, such a law inevitably produces complications. All the faults that we discover in the structure of the *Odyssey* today, simply arise from our inability to hear it as the Ancients would have done; our minds have become warped by reading too many novels.' The hypothesis that the 'Voyage of Telemachus' must have existed prior to and independently of the *Odyssey* seems to me to be absurd: unless these four Books are an integral part of a poem which, as a whole, is concerned with the return of Odysseus, they lack significance and lead nowhere. But there is another possible hypothesis: that the poet himself, having first written the tales told to King Alcinous, may have realized, when it came to following these tales with the story of Odysseus' vengeance, that it would be a good idea to interest his public in the fate of Telemachus, and to introduce Penelope and the suitors from the start. This would provide a better explanation of the fact that the 'Assembly of the Gods' with which Book v begins seems to be in part a repetition of the 'Assembly' in Book I. In the same way, we have already admitted with regard to the *Iliad* that perhaps Homer did not write all twenty-four books in the order in which they appear in the completed poem.

This second 'Assembly', however, is not an exact repetition of the first, since Athena now draws the attention of Zeus to Telemachus' perilous position, threatened by the suitors with death. And what is important for the continuation of the action is that, at last, Zeus orders his messenger, Hermes, to go and insist that Calypso shall set Odysseus free, as Athena already suggested in Book I. From this point, the story follows a straight line and there is general agreement that Books v to VIII are amongst the finest in the *Odyssey*: the building of the raft, his first glimpse of the country of the Phaeacians, the storm unloosed by Poseidon and Odysseus' struggle as he swims to shore (v), the charming interlude with Nausicaa (VII), his arrival at the palace of Alcinous (VII), his welcome and the games in which Odysseus takes part and the three lays sung by the minstrel Demodocus (VIII).

In the Books that follow, IX to XII, Odysseus describes his adventures to the Phaeacians, with only a short break in Book XI to palliate the improbability of such a lengthy monologue by recalling the presence of Alcinous and his courtiers. The hero tells them his name and briefly describes his departure from Troas, passing over in silence those events that Nestor has already recounted to Telemachus (IV): the quarrel between Agamemnon and Menelaus and the great sacrifice offered at Tenedos before the leaders dispersed. Clearly, the poet is anxious to avoid repetition and therefore begins Odysseus' account at his first landing, when he finds himself alone with his own ships (twelve of them, according to the 'Catalogue 'in Book II of the *Iliad*) —the landing in Thrace, the country of the Cicones.

Just as Odysseus' ships are getting ready to double Cape Malea, before heading north-west for Ithaca, they are blown off their course for ten days by a storm. From this moment until his arrival home in Book XIII, all Odysseus' landfalls will be in mythical countries, not to be found on any map. These are the countries Plutarch refers to in the opening passages of his *Life of Theseus*: 'The geographers relegate the regions of which they know nothing to the edges of their maps, inscribing beneath them: "Beyond is nothing but arid desert, infested with wild beasts", or "Gloomy Marshes", or "Frozen Scythia", or "Ice-bound Sea" ' (I, p. I).

Some bold spirits have attempted to identify these unknown lands and seas, an intellectual pastime not without charm. According to Victor Bérard, Homer, though living in Ionia, must have had access to Phoenician harbour lists and detailed information about the western end of the Mediterranean. His thesis now finds few supporters but the game continues. On the whole, Bérard's suggested identifications are less improbable than others that have been proposed and if one really insists upon having a map of these imaginary countries, his hypothesis is as acceptable as any other. A more recent suggestion is that Scheria, the island of the Phaeacians, ought to be transferred from Corfu to the coast of Libya: in which case Nausicaa would have been an African, perhaps a Negress. But we shall be better advised to stick to the opinion of Eratosthenes, the great geographer of the third century B.C., who had far more critical spirit and common sense than many modern 'Homer specialists'. According to Strabo, who disapproved of his temerity, he said: 'If we really want to know the route followed by Odysseus, the first thing we must do is to find the currier who made Aeolus' leather bag'

After the Cicones, Odysseus visits the Lotus Eaters, then the Cyclopes and, still in Book IX, there is the celebrated account of his stay in Polyphemus' cave. In Book X he is admitted to the floating island of Aeolus, the ruler of the winds, who as a friendly gesture presents him with the magic leather bag in which he keeps the hurricanes and tempests; and the hero begins to think his adventures are nearing their end. Unfortunately he falls asleep and his sailors overcome by curiosity, open the leather bag and let loose a terrifying storm. This time Aeolus drives him away without pity and he lands in the country of the Laestrygonians, man-eating giants like the Cyclopes except that they have two eyes instead of one. Here Odysseus' fleet encounters its worst disaster: all the ships perish except that of the hero himself, who manages to get away with a crew of some fifty men. Then follows the famous episode on the island of the enchantress Circe where Odysseus and his surviving companions spend a whole year. She sends him to consult the prophet Teiresias in the Halls of

Hades (xi), which provides an admirable opportunity for the poet to describe his moving meetings with the shade of his mother Anticleia and those of his ancient companions in arms, Agamemnon, Achilles and Ajax. This Book comprises two fairly long interpolations.

Book xii brings us back to Circe, and then recounts the passage of Odysseus' ship past the isles of the Sirens, then between Scylla and Charybdis, and his stay on the island of the Sun, where his companions, despite the warning of Teiresias, eat the sacred flocks and call down upon themselves the anger of Zeus. In the shipwreck that follows Odysseus loses the last of his crew and one realizes that this final disaster had already been announced at the beginning of Book i, in the invocation to the Muse quoted above; for it is now that Odysseus is deprived of all human society, and he reaches the island of Calypso entirely alone, clinging to a piece of wreckage.

In Book xiii, a Phaeacian ship takes him back to Ithaca where his goddess, Athena, who up to then has effaced herself because of Poseidon's anger, welcomes him and becomes his guide and counsellor. Here the story of his vengeance begins and the structure of the poem offers no further serious problem. First of all, Odysseus meets Eumaeus whose rustic hospitality is described with such charm (Book xiv) and at whose house Telemachus, back from Sparta and, thanks to Athena, having escaped the suitors' ambush, discovers and recognizes him (xv–xvi). Henceforward unity of place and action are maintained until the end.

Book xvii describes Odysseus' arrival at his palace and the touching scene with his dog, Argus. The pace of the story slows down in Books xviii–xx in the same way that we noted in Books xvii–xxi of the *Iliad*: it would almost seem that the poet, sure of his effect, has decided to make his audience wait for the dénouement so as to increase their interest and, ultimately, their pleasure. Moreover, these Books contain some admirable passages, like the recognition of the hero by his old nurse Eurycleia (xix).

In Book xxi comes the contest with Odysseus' bow, then, at the beginning of Book xxii, the great dramatic moment which everyone has been waiting for, but which is nevertheless so extraordinarily effective: Odysseus throws off his beggar's rags and begins the slaughter of the suitors. The savage grandeur of the account recalls the brutality of the scenes of carnage in the *Iliad*.

Finally in Book xxiii we reach the longed-for conclusion, Penelope's recognition of Odysseus, with its final surprise: to make quite certain, Penelope puts the wily hero to a last test but ultimately submits in the face of the evidence. 'Her surrender melted Odysseus' heart, and he wept as he held his dear wife in his arms, so loyal and true.' And soon the servant Eurynome leads them to their room, 'and glad indeed they were to lie once more together in the bed that had known them long ago' (296).

With this line the *Odyssey* is completed. The end of Book XXIII and the whole of Book XXIV are, as I have said, unmistakably additions to Homer's work.

HOMER'S PORTRAYAL OF CHARACTER

The *Iliad* has more than fifteen thousand lines, some three thousand more than the *Odyssey*. The Alexandrian editors of Homer noticed that the *Iliad* quite naturally divided into twenty-four Books, each of which they designated by one of the twenty-four letters of the Ionian alphabet. For the sake of symmetry, they also chose to divide the *Odyssey* in the same way, but here for several reasons the division appears to be artificial and open to dispute.

Many of the Ancients held the *Iliad* in higher esteem than the *Odyssey*. In the *Hippias Minor* Plato says: 'I have heard Apemantos say that the *Iliad* is Homer's masterpiece, as superior to the *Odyssey* as Achilles is to Odysseus.' And in his *Treatise on the Sublime* Pseudo Longinus declares: 'Homer wrote his *Iliad* at a time when his mind was at the height of its vigour . . . whereas the *Odyssey* may be compared to the sun when it is setting, as mighty as ever, but no longer having the same heat and strength.'

All Homer's characters, in the *Odyssey* as well as in the *Iliad*, are amazingly true and alive. He spends but little time describing their physical appearance, though we know that Ajax was taller than all the other Achaeans and had broader shoulders. When Odysseus had bathed and dressed himself, he appeared to Nausicaa 'radiant with comeliness and grace'. Indeed, all Homer's heroes are more or less good looking, as all his heroines are beautiful: this 'embellishment' is one of the laws of epic poetry, like the 'magnification' of warlike deeds into superhuman exploits. The ordinary soldier Thersites serves as a foil to the physical beauty of the high-born lords and ladies, though in describing him Homer resorts to caricature: 'He was the ugliest man that had come to Ilium. He had a game foot and was bandy-legged. His rounded shoulders almost met across his chest;

and above them rose an egg-shaped head, which sprouted a few hairs, (*Iliad* II, 216–19).

Homer is above all a great creator of character. True, the psychology of his heroes is relatively simple and reduced to a few, though constant and strongly marked, features; but in the most completely natural way, and with an ease that is at once naïve and masterly, he makes them speak and act according to the feelings he has endowed them with.

Achilles is all impetuous valour, frank, wrathful and cruel; but in love and friendship he is also capable of tenderness and, in the end, he expresses the melancholy of a young man who feels himself ineluctably doomed to an early death. At the time of the quarrel, just as he is about to unsheathe his sword to kill Agamemnon, Athena stops him and says: 'Come now, give up this strife. . . . Sting him with words instead.' And Achilles is not slow to respond, displaying a redoubtable vocabulary:

You drunken sot, with the eye of a dog and the courage of a doe! You never have the pluck to arm yourself and go into battle with the men, or to join the other captains in an ambush—you would sooner die. It pays you better to stay in camp . . . flourishing at your people's cost because they are too feeble to resist (*Iliad* I, 211 and 225 ff.).

When at last he receives the ambassadors, he does so with courtesy, but before long he is irritated by the words of Odysseus because they remind him of the outrage he is continually brooding over and he brutally exclaims that he is not the kind of man to hide his thoughts:

I had better tell you point-blank how I feel and what I am going to do. I loathe like Hell's Gates the man who thinks one thing and says another (*Iliad* IX, 308–13)

Achilles displays all the signs of a thoroughly irascible nature; his feelings are the basis of the whole action of the poem and all its events derive from them. The public humiliation he has undergone and the sadness he feels at the loss of Briseis whom he loves have reduced him to a state of morose and sulky inaction: 'I sit here by my ships, an idle burden on the earth' (XVIII, 104). Only his terrible grief at the death of his closest friend Patroclus can make him forget everything else. And in the end when he has avenged Patroclus by killing Hector, it is only with the greatest difficulty that he can force himself

35

to restore the body to Priam, and his discussion with the old king is filled with bitter melancholy. As he had said to the young Trojan Lycaon before killing him in battle:

Yes, my friend, you too must die. Why make such a song about it? Even Patroclus died, who was a better man than you by far. And look at me. Am I not big and beautiful, the son of a great man, with a goddess for my mother? Yet Death and sovran Destiny are waiting for me too (XXI, 106–10).

Again, the bitterness tearing at his heart is impressively brought out in the vow he made to Patroclus:

Ah, Father Zeus, Athena and Apollo, how happy I should be if not a Trojan got away alive, not one, and not an Argive either, and if we two survived the massacre to pull down Troy's holy diadem of towers single-handed! (XVI, 97–100).

He will burn twelve young Trojans alive on Patroclus' funeral pyre, but the cruelty of his heart, filled with anger and the thirst for vengeance, is displayed even more clearly in his reply to Hector, who asks him to agree that the victor in their duel shall restore the body of his victim to his friends:

You must be mad to talk to me about a pact. Lions do not come to terms with men, nor does the wolf see eye to eye with the lamb—they are enemies to the end. It is the same with you and me. Friendship between us is impossible, and there will be no truce of any kind till one of us has fallen and glutted the stubborn god of battles with his blood (XXII, 261–77).

Lycaon, who had done nothing against him personally, he could call 'friend', but not Hector who had killed Patroclus.

Between the period of the *Iliad* and that of the *Odyssey*, Achilles has perished before the Schaean Gate, as his horse Xanthos had foretold at the time of Hector's death. In the *Odyssey* Odysseus congratulates the shade of Achilles for continuing to reign amongst the dead as he had in his lifetime over the Achaeans:

'For you, Achilles, Death should have lost his sting.' To which he replied, 'My good lord Odysseus, spare me your praise of death. Put me on earth again, and I would rather be the serf of some landless man, with little enough to live on, than king of all these dead men that have done with life' (xi, 486–91).

Thus the after-life, as conceived of by Homer, is not happy and the irremediable misfortune for man is the loss of life on earth. Achilles says to the ambassadors in the *Iliad*: 'But you cannot steal or buy back a man's life, when once the breath has left his lips' (ix, 408–9). Yet Achilles, though he could choose between many years without glory and a short life and immortal fame, preferred to die young, not in order to enjoy a state of dubious blessedness in the beyond, but to ensure his lasting renown amongst men. He is wretched and knows that he will always be; his only consolation is his conviction that he will be 'celebrated by the poets of the future', as in those exploits of the heroes of old with which he delights his leisure hours.

Can it be said that the action of the *Odyssey* is based entirely on the character of Odysseus? It is not the same here as in the *Iliad*, where the decisions that modify the course of events, such as the sending of Patroclus into battle, depended on Achilles; for the will of Odysseus is reduced to the obstinate determination to get home again, without being able to choose the means by which this shall be achieved. Yet it is nevertheless true that one of the main sources of interest in the *Odyssey* is in the drawing of his character—the character of a subtle, adroit man, curious about everything, diplomatic as Achilles never is and as deceitful as the latter is frank, ready to lie from prudence or distrust, and sometimes simply for the fun of it, but enduring, tenacious, unshakeable in his aims and in his fidelity to Penelope, and in the end capable of overcoming a hostile fate.

In the *Odyssey*, Achilles only makes a fugitive appearance, and then as a ghost. By contrast, Odysseus is already one of the principal heroes in the *Iliad*, where throughout he plays a part at least as important as that of Diomedes or Ajax. Moreover, according to the legend, it is he who will inherit the arms of Achilles. Thus the poet has more opportunities of describing his character than that of any of the other heroes. Already in Book ii of the *Iliad* it is he who prevents the flight of the Achaeans. In Book iii, the Trojan Antenor reports the powerful impression his eloquence created when he and Menelaus came as ambassadors to Troy seeking the return of Helen:

When all were standing, Menelaus with his broad shoulders, overtopped the whole company; but Odysseus was the more imposing of the two when both were seated. . . . And when that great voice of his came booming from his chest, and the words poured from his lips like the flakes of winter snow, there was no man alive who could compete with Odysseus. When we looked at him then, we were no longer misled by appearances (III, 210 ff.).

In the councils and assemblies of the *Iliad*, it is the shrewd Odysseus who most often occupies the leading place beside Nestor. In battle, he knows when to give ground if necessary; even, despite his undoubted courage, when to flee. In Book XI, before he is wounded, alone amidst a swarm of enemies he fights like a lion, but the poet shows him in the thick of the fight already debating with himself: 'What is coming to me next? It would be infamy to take to my heels, scared by the odds against me; but even more unpleasant to be caught alone' (404–6). Achilles scarcely weighs the pros and cons. He acts on impulse. Odysseus always ponders and calculates before taking action; he remains cool and even in the most desperate situations his mind never abdicates its authority.

Thus he appears also in the *Odyssey*, just as brave, just as subtle and crafty, a model of intelligence,[1] cunning and constancy. He is seen at his best when, having failed to recognize Athena, (who, disguised as a shepherd boy, is the first person he sets eyes on when he lands in Ithaca), he immediately attempts to hide his own identity and pass himself off as a Cretan. 'He answered her readily enough, but not with the truth. It had been on the tip of his tongue, but loyal as ever to his crafty nature he contrived to keep it back.' But his lies only amuse the goddess who replies with a smile:

What a cunning knave it would take to beat you at your tricks! Even a god would be hard put to it. And so my stubborn friend, Odysseus the archdeceiver, with his craving for intrigue, does not propose even in his own country to drop his sharp practice and the lying tales that he loves from the bottom of his heart (XIII, 291ff.).

Achilles, son of a goddess, is a superhuman being: Odysseus, solely and completely human. In his descriptions of him throughout the *Iliad* and the *Odyssey*, Homer bequeathed to future generations the ideal type of Greek man (if we accept subtlety and a tendency to deception as part of such a character); and perhaps the ideal type of all men (provided one regards as a virtue prudence, which, in cases of extremity, is not above lying).

[1] There is an interesting book by G. Audisio called *Ulysse ou l'Intelligence.*

Agamemnon is represented as the 'king of kings', the 'generalissimo' of the Achaeans, despite the fact that his authority is often mocked at and disputed. The social organization of the Achaeans is of a feudal character, a point clearly seen by Thucydides: 'It was because Agamemnon's power was greater than that of the other chiefs . . .that he was able to unite the expeditionary force' (I, 9, I). Having more vassals and men than the others, he is *primus inter pares*, exercising suzerainty over his turbulent and often intractable vassals. Despite his position, however, his character is not outstanding: he is authoritarian, vain, vindictive and unstable, which sometimes leads him to make catastrophic decisions for which he is roundly chided in the assembly, not only by Achilles and Odysseus, but also by Nestor and Diomedes. In Book XI of the *Odyssey*, his shade is heard plaintively cursing all women because of Clytemnestra's crime.

The aged Nestor 'has seen two generations pass away, and today commands a third;' which simply means that he is a septuagenarian, since the Ancients considered a generation as lasting thirty years. (Herodotus counts three to a century.) Nestor is full of experience and wisdom, and is continually intervening in an attempt to restore agreement between Achilles and Agamemnon. All his one-time physical vigour seems to be concentrated in his tongue, for he makes interminable speeches and, *laudator temporis acti*, delights in the memories of his youth and maturity which he recalls in and out of season. Homer might well have applied to him the sly comment he makes on Priam and the other old men of Troy:

Old age had brought their fighting days to an end, but they were excellent speakers, these Trojan Elders, sitting there on their tower, like cicadas perched on a tree, chirping delightfully (*Iliad* III, 150–2).

In the absence of Achilles, sulking in his tent, the most valiant of the Achaeans are Odysseus, Diomedes and Ajax. Books V and VI especially are full of the exploits of Diomedes, king of Argos and son of Tydeus, who is not even afraid of wounding the gods, for example, Aphrodite, or even Ares the god of war. In the assembly, he criticizes Agamemnon for considering the possibility of giving up the struggle, and restores the courage of the others.

But Ajax of Salamis, son of King Telemon ('the great Ajax', not to be confused with Ajax the Locrian, son of Oïleus) is drawn more individually. It is he who, at the moment of greatest danger, when

Hector is on the point of setting fire to the Achaean ships, puts heart into the resistance. He may be recognized not only by his vast shield, high as a mountain, but by his fighting spirit, which burns more brightly on the defensive than in attack: less mobile than the other warriors, he can hold a whole pack of adversaries at bay. In Book xi of the *Iliad*, Homer compares him successively with a lion retreating step by step before a crowd of huntsmen and dogs, and with a stubborn donkey, who persists in grazing in a field of corn by the wayside, despite the blows that are rained on his back.

Again, in Book vii, we see 'the huge Ajax, rampart of the Achaeans, smiling all over his face', (211–2) as he hurls himself against the Trojans; and in Book ix it would seem that his few and simple words have more power to touch Achilles than all Odysseus' rhetoric. In Book xi of the *Odyssey*, his proud ghost turns away haughtily and bitterly without speaking a word to Odysseus who, by defrauding him of the armour of Achilles, had driven him to commit suicide. This last silent appearance completes in masterly fashion the portrait of Ajax, the formidable hero, taciturn and unlucky, whose smile even has something terrifying about it.

Amongst the Trojans, Hector, the son of Priam and Hecuba, is as bold as Achilles and more straightforward than Odysseus. Clearly the poet's sympathies are all on the side of the Achaeans, for he tends to cover up their setbacks and glorify their slightest successes. Nevertheless, he is always fair to their opponents and speaks highly of Hector, Aeneas and Sarpedon of Lycia. Even Paris, more devoted to Helen than to his fame as a warrior, is shown to be a valiant archer: in Book xi of the *Iliad* he wounds three of the Achaean heroes, and it is one of his arrows that eventually kills Achilles. In Book iii, Hector rebukes him:

Paris, you pretty boy, you woman-struck seducer, why were you ever born? Why weren't you killed before your wedding day? Yes, I could wish it so (39–42).

For Hector himself has a sense of duty and is devoted to his country and his family, as may be seen in the famous conversation with Andromache. Though he has no more illusions than Achilles about the future that is awaiting him, he is nevertheless concerned for the fate of his city, his parents, his wife and his son:

Deep in my heart I know the day is coming when holy Ilium will be

destroyed. . . . Yet I am not so much distressed by the thought of what
the Trojans will suffer, or Hecuba herself or King Priam, or all my gallant
brothers whom the enemy will fling down in the dust, as by the thought
of you, dragged off in tears by some Achaean man-at-arms to slavery. . . .
Ah, may the earth lie deep on my dead body before I hear the screams you
utter as they drag you off (*Iliad* VI, 477 ff.).

Yet this heroic defender of Ilium—a good soldier, good son, good
husband and good father—does not always heed the wise advice offered
him by Polydamas, for he is too high-spirited and greedy of fame.
He even seems to set his own sense of duty above the art of divination,
for when Polydamas tells him of unfavourable auspices, he replies:
'Fight for your country—that is the best and only omen' (XII, 243).

Like Agamemnon, Hector's father Priam is a little overwhelmed
by his kingly responsibilities, but this oriental monarch with his many
wives (Hecuba is no more than the first of them) appears to us full
of a majestic humanity as he begs his favourite son to avoid Achilles
(Book XXII), and especially when he betakes himself to the enemy
camp to persuade the man who has killed Hector to restore his body:

Most worshipful Achilles, think of your own father, who is the same age
as I, and so has nothing but miserable old age ahead of him. . . . Yet he at
least has one consolation, knowing you are still alive. . . . Fear the gods,
Achilles, and be merciful to me, remembering your own father, though I
am even more entitled to compassion, since I have brought myself to do a
thing that no one else on earth has done—I have raised to my lips the hand
of the man who killed my son (XXIV, 486 ff.).

Nowhere in antiquity does supplication attain so noble a level.

In this war poem, which is indeed what the *Iliad* is, Homer nevertheless finds place for a number of moving women characters, particularly Hecuba, Andromache and Helen; while in the *Odyssey*, in
addition to Helen who appears again in Books IV and XV, there are
Penelope and Nausicaa.

Hecuba expresses the feelings of a mother worrying about her son
who is threatened with death, and her despair when events have
justified her fears. Yet there is something slightly conventional about
her, and we are more deeply moved listening to Andromache as she
pleads with Hector:

'You are possessed. This bravery of yours will be your end. You do not
think of your little boy or your unhappy wife, whom you will make a widow

41

soon. . . . You, Hector, are to be father and mother and brother, as well as my beloved husband.' . . . Then Hector handed their son to his wife, who took him to her fragrant breast. She was smiling through her tears, and when her husband saw this he was moved, and stroked her with his hand (*Iliad*, VI, 407 ff.).

Far away in Ithaca, Penelope is, as it were, the sister of Trojan Andromache, like her pledged to her love for her husband and her son. It requires all her strength of character, as well as cunning, to keep the suitors at arm's length. But, like her husband, she knows how to combine constancy and guile; and what majestic dignity she displays, each time she appears in the great hall where they are feasting. But so many vagabonds have tried to deceive her by pretending to bring news of her husband, and when he at last arrives he is so changed and aged by twenty years of wandering on sea and land that she is determined to make absolutely certain that it is really Odysseus: she sends Eurycleia to transport the bed to the marriage chamber, pretending to have forgotten that it cannot be moved, for it was constructed long ago by Odysseus from an olive tree still rooted in the ground: 'this was the manner in which she put her husband to the test'.

Circe and Calypso are goddesses, whose charms are not powerful enough to hold Odysseus, but he has no objection to trying them; in the same way he insists upon hearing the song of the Sirens, for he is avid of experience and wants to know and appreciate everything. As for Nausicaa, she is simply a young girl who, though a princess, does the family washing with her own hands. How could she fail to be moved by Odysseus' clever and flattering speech to her?

Mistress, I throw myself on your mercy. But are you some goddess or a mortal woman? If you are one of the gods who live in the sky, it is of Artemis, the daughter of Almighty Zeus, that your beauty, grace and stature most remind me. But if you are one of us mortals who live upon earth, then lucky indeed are your father and your gentle mother. . . . But happiest of all is he who with his wedding gifts can win you for his home. For never have I set eyes on such perfection in man or woman. . . . Only in Delos have I seen the like, a fresh young palm-tree, shooting up by the altar of Apollo (*Odyssey* VI, 149 ff., and 242–3).

And when Odysseus has bathed and washed himself (at first he is dressed simply and his body is still covered with brine) she admires him, and in her admiration sounds a note of love: 'When first we met

I thought he cut a sorry figure, but now he looks like the gods that live in heaven. This is the kind of man I could fancy for a husband.' Then later, when he is about to depart and she catches sight of him as he comes into the great hall, she bids him farewell in words full of regret, that are almost an avowal of her feelings:

Good luck, my friend, and I hope that when you are back in your own country you will think of me at times, since it is to me before all others that you owe your life (*Odyssey* VIII, 461 ff.).

But it is Helen whose sovran and divine beauty—she is a daughter of Zeus—casts its splendour over so many parts of the two poems. In the *Iliad* she arouses the admiration of the Elders of Troy, whose hearts at least remain young: 'Who on earth could blame the Trojan and Achaean men-at-arms for suffering so long for such a woman's sake? Indeed, she is the very image of an immortal goddess.' And later in the same Book, when Aphrodite insists upon her going to Paris after his defeat by Menelaus, Helen, who begins by chiding him scornfully, ends by coaxing him:

So you are back from the battlefield—and I was hoping you had fallen there to the great soldier who was once my husband! You used to boast you were a better man than the mighty Menelaus. Then why not go at once and challenge him again? . . . But no, do nothing rash, lest you end by falling to his spear! (*Iliad* XII, 428 ff.).

Homer subtly remarks at this point that, as Helen began scolding her lover, 'she turned aside her eyes;' and in a copy of the *Iliad* that belonged to Racine this passage is marked, and there is a note in the margin: 'Helen turns away her eyes as she speaks to Paris because she wants to quarrel with him, for she knows full well that she has only to look at him to become amorous', which is precisely what happens: for a few lines later, when Paris moves towards the bed, she follows him.

In another passage, Hector comes to see her and she shows towards him, in front of Paris, an admiration she never felt for her lover:

Brother, I am indeed a shameless, evil-minded and abominable creature. . . . Since the gods ordained things to this evil end, I wish I had found a better husband, one with some feeling for the reproaches and contempt of his fellow

43

men. . . . Ill-starred couple that we are, tormented by heaven to figure in the songs of people yet unborn (VI, 344 ff.).

She is, too, something of a prophetess and in Book XV of the *Odyssey* she interprets an omen. Like Achilles, but for very different reasons, she is anxious that posterity shall remember her, and indeed foresees that Homer will make her immortal. Writing in the fourth century B.C., Isocrates says: 'Certain of the Homeridae [minstrels who continued the Homeric poems] recount that Helen appeared to Homer in a dream and bade him write a poem about the warriors who fought against Troy. . . . And they maintain that it was thanks partly to Homer's art, *but above all to her*, that this poem was so full of beauty and became so celebrated' (*In Praise of Helen*). Whether or not she was, in fact, the principal source of his inspiration, it is certainly true that both poems are the richer for the divine glow of her beauty.

Later in the *Iliad*, Helen's feelings with regard to Hector are revealed again in her lament over his corpse:

Hector, I loved you far the best of all my Trojan brothers. . . . In all the nineteen years since I left my own country, from you I have never heard a single harsh or spiteful word. . . . So these tears of sorrow that I shed are both for you and for my miserable self. No one is left in the wide realm of Troy to treat me gently and befriend me (XXIV, 762 ff.).

In the *Odyssey*, it is Helen who, at the first glance, identifies Telemachus because of his likeness to Odysseus. To stop her guest weeping, she puts into his drinking bowl a drug she has brought from Egypt that induces happiness, for in addition to being a prophetess she is also something of a magician. Then she recalls her memories of Troy: how one day Odysseus, disguised and unrecognizable, managed to get into the city and how, though she knew who he was, she refused to denounce him to the Trojans:

I rejoiced, for I was already longing to go home again and had suffered a change of heart, repenting the infatuation with which Aphrodite blinded me when she lured me to Troy from my own dear country and made me forsake my daughter, my bridal chamber, and a husband who had all one could wish for in the way of brains and good looks (IV, 260 ff.).

Then, when Telemachus is about to leave Sparta, she gives him a personal gift, a veil embroidered with her own hands: 'Look, it is a keepsake from Helen, for your bride to wear when the longed-for day of your wedding arrives' (xv, 125 ff.). And with what tenderness this woman, who has herself lived through so much, looks forward to the young man's marriage, obviously, though without saying so, wishing his wife may prove more faithful than she herself has been.

Even the secondary, and merely episodic, characters are sketched in so skilfully that they come to life for us: Briseis in the *Iliad*, for example, Eumaeus and Eurycleia in the *Odyssey*. Briseis is Achilles' captive and mistress. In the first Book of the *Iliad*, when Agamemnon's heralds come to summon him, Patroclus hands her over to them on his master's orders, 'and against her will the girl accompanies them'. Discreet as always, this is all that Homer says, yet we are given to understand that Achilles has succeeded in making her fall in love with him although it was he who killed her husband and brothers at Lyrnessos, as she will recall later when she is weeping over the body of Patroclus:

Alas, Patroclus, my heart's delight! . . . When the swift Achilles killed my man and sacked King Myenes' city, you would not even let me weep. You said you would make me Prince Achilles' lawful wife and take me in your ships to Phthia, and give me a wedding-feast among the Myrmidons. You were so gentle with me always. How can I cease to mourn you? (xix, 287 ff.).

The faithfulness of the swineherd, Eumaeus, and the housekeeper, Eurycleia, after their master's twenty years' absence, described in Books xiv and xix of the *Odyssey*, is always intensely moving, as when Eumaeus says:

For I shall never find so kind a master again, wherever I may go, not even if I return to my parents' house. . . . Much as I should like to be back in my own country and set eyes on them again, my longing for them has given place in my heart to overwhelming regret for the lost Odysseus. . . . He loved me and took thought for me before all others. And so, though he is far away, I still think of him as my beloved lord (xiv, 138 ff.).

There is even an anonymous slave girl, charged with the lowly and onerous task of grinding the corn, who appears only for a moment. Yet the poet succeeds in interesting us in her and her lot:

Twelve women had to toil away at these mills, grinding the barley and the wheat into meal for the household bread. At the moment they had all ground their share and gone off to sleep, all except one not so vigorous as the rest,

45

who had not yet finished her task. This woman now stopped her mill and uttered the words that meant so much to her master: 'Zeus, lord of heaven and earth, what thunder from a starry sky! And never a cloud in sight! . . . Let my wish come true. Let this very day see the end of these junketings in the palace' (xx, 105 ff.).

Homer sang first of all of the lives of noblemen and princes, but he did not disdain the rank-and-file like Thersites who though he may be caricatured nevertheless tells Agamemnon some bitter home truths; nor does he forget the hardships of the slaves. Even animals find a place in his poems. There are the fiery coursers that draw the chariots of the princes into battle, like Achilles' horse Xanthos who on one occasion is endowed with the voice and feelings of a human being so that he may predict to his master the death that awaits him (*Iliad* xix). Or again there is Odysseus' old dog:

There lay a dog, who now pricked up his ears and raised his head. Argus was his name. Odysseus himself had owned and trained him before he sailed for holy Ilium. . . . But now, in his owner's absence, he lay abandoned on the heaps of dung from the mules and cattle . . . and full of vermin. But directly he became aware of Odysseus' presence, he wagged his tail and dropped his ears, though he lacked the strength now to come any nearer his master. . . . (But) no sooner had he set eyes on Odysseus after these nineteen years than he succumbed to the black hand of death (*Odyssey* xvii, 291 ff.).

THE ART AND PERSONALITY OF HOMER

The gods and goddesses who appear so often throughout the *Iliad* and the *Odyssey*, either assembled on Mount Olympus or mixing with human beings on earth, experience the same feelings and passions as men and women, but they are distinguished from them by one essential difference: being immortal, they have no fear of old age or death. Their quarrels (for example those between Zeus and his shrewish wife Hera who is always upsetting Olympus with her domestic scenes), their loves (both legitimate and adulterous), even their wounds (cf. those of Aphrodite and Ares in Book v of the *Iliad*), are a sort of inconsequential game. How different, for instance, are the effects of adultery in heaven and on earth: if the deceived husband is Hephaestus, he is merely an object of ridicule and proceeds to avenge himself (*Odyssey* viii); if he is Agamemnon, he is 'cut down like a pig' by his wife's lover (*Odyssey* xi).

Often, the gods present themselves in person to the mortals whose safety or undoing they desire. Sometimes they reveal themselves so that they are immediately recognizable; but more often they take the form of animals, vultures, falcons, swallows, or assume the appearance of a friend or relation, or they may take on some quite anonymous mortal form, as Poseidon does in the *Iliad* (Book XIV), or Athena in the *Odyssey* (Book XIII). All-powerful as they are, they also have the faculty of concealing themselves from mortal sight in a cloud or of hiding a man in the same way from his enemy; and sometimes they confuse both armies by appearing as a phantom who can be mistaken for one of the heroes. Athena conceals herself from Ares by putting on the magic helmet of Hades the 'invisible one' (*Iliad* v).

Why did Homer consider it necessary to bring into play all this heavenly machinery, the memory of which we shall find later in the *dei ex machina* of classical tragedy? In the first place, obviously, because he was a man of his times and had inherited an epic tradition according to which the gods continually intervene in the life of humanity, a time when

> . . . heaven walked on earth,
> Breathing life into a people of gods.

Secondly, he often used the supernatural to explain and enhance the behaviour of men—as Fernand Robert maintains, 'the miraculous in Homer is essentially an expression of human experience.'

In many cases this is true. In the first Book of the *Iliad*, Hera suggests to Achilles that he should summon an assembly of the Achaeans: yet, since the plague had already been raging for nine days, decimating the army, the idea might well have occurred to Achilles of itself. Further on it is Athena who appears to the hero, 'visible to him alone', and persuades him to put up his sword instead of killing Agamemnon before the eyes of the whole army. Again, in Book v of the *Odyssey*, the exhausted Odysseus, though in sight of land, swims along the rocky coast until he finds a sandy haven: 'Had not Athena put the idea into his head, his skin would have been torn to shreds and his bones broken.' In these three cases, and they are not the only ones, divine intervention scarcely does more, in fact, than underline a human reaction. For example, despite his wrath, Achilles might well have had a sudden flash of common sense and resisted the impulse to murder Agamemnon.

In the 'Patrocleia' (Book XVI of the *Iliad*), the case is analogous but not quite the same. In order to enhance the heroism of Patroclus, the poet makes Apollo disarm him before he is struck down by Euphorbos and killed by Hector, but at the same time makes it clear that these events can also be explained in quite human terms. The main cause of Patroclus' death is plainly his own rash folly: he hurls himself almost alone against the Trojan forces, and they, having had time to regroup, surround and overwhelm him. But there is a second cause, not clearly indicated by Homer for fear of diminishing his hero's stature, but which he hints at by suggesting that the Trojans have begun to recognize Patroclus and therefore, despite the armour he is wearing, are no longer afraid that it is Achilles who confronts them: while in line 423 Sarpedon is still unaware of his identity, in lines 538–47, Glaucus at last identifies him by name.

However, in many other places, it seems to me impossible to accept Robert's interpretation. For example, in Book III of the *Iliad*, when Aphrodite disguises herself as an old servant in order to persuade Helen to go to Paris, can it be said that, here, the goddess 'is nothing more than the working of Helen's imagination, a passionate impulse that she tries in vain to resist?' On the contrary, it is clear that Helen is constrained against her will, at a moment when all her wishes, as well as her feelings of remorse, are drawing her towards Menelaus, who has just defeated Paris in single combat.

In the time of Homer, the gods already symbolized the natural elements (in his struggle against the waters of the Scamander, in Book XXI of the *Iliad*, Hephaestus obviously stands for fire), but they were not yet pure abstractions personifying this or that tendency of the human spirit, as they were to become later, after a long process of philosophical elaboration that often turned for confirmation to the Homeric poems.

'Gratuitous' marvels (by which I mean those whose purpose is not to emphasize some particular tendency, or to explain the behaviour of the characters) are also plentiful in Homer. In the *Iliad*, Hera grants the power of speech to Achilles' horse; and she also, in Book XVIII, accelerates the setting of the sun, thus reversing Joshua's miracle in the Bible. The river Scamander, more than half personified (but all rivers were gods) fights in the plain of Troy, first against Achilles, then against Hephaestus. And the blacksmith god makes himself automatons, 'robots', to aid his crippled steps; while the figures on the shield he fashions for Achilles can sing and dance (*Iliad* XVIII). In the *Odyssey* (Book IV), Penelope converses with a shade created by Athena. In Book v, Ino saves Odysseus from the storm by throwing him her magic scarf. Circe is a magician with the power of turning men into swine, and in Book xi Odysseus summons up the shades of the dead.

Both poems are soaked in an atmosphere of marvels and enchantment. But it should be noted that the purely human reactions of the characters are never, on that account, suppressed. Achilles, pursued by the swirling waters of Scamander, remains the same high-mettled, undaunted fighter that we know from the rest of the poem: and Odysseus distrusts the divine spells of Ino and Athena, though they are to his advantage, as he does the traps that are set for him by men, with the same obstinate prudence, the same courage and the same good sense.

In Homer, the miraculous, far from hindering the drawing of character as it does elsewhere, on the contrary enriches its possibilities through the diversity of circumstances in which his heroes find themselves. But clearly, it also has another function: to amuse and enchant the naïve imagination of his audiences.

Despite the almost continuous presence of the gods, despite the repeated invocations of the Muse, the *Iliad* and the *Odyssey* are not, however, religious poems (as has sometimes wrongly been supposed), composed in the shadow of the holy places for purposes of edification. In describing the ornamentation of Achilles' shield, the work of a god, Homer seeks to provide a synthesis of everything essential that he has observed about the life of mankind in peace and in war; yet it is remarkable that no sacrifice, no religious ceremony is depicted there. The poet lived in a religious age, but his rationalist tendencies are indisputable. Otherwise, how could he display that freedom and lack of respect for the gods who take part in his poems which was to shock Plato? To assume that the wanton tale of the loves of Ares and Aphrodite (*Odyssey* viii) must be an interpolation seems to me quite unnecessary; and the episode of Zeus being tricked by Hera (*Iliad* xiv), despite the fact that they are husband and wife, is not so very different in tone. Zeus, who can make all Olympus tremble at a nod of his head, may sometimes behave like a puppet or a bully: nevertheless he remains 'the father of the gods and of mankind'. Critics have often enough expressed surprise at the impiety of Aristophanes and Euripides, but in this respect both poets might well be Homer.

The heroes of the *Iliad* are not afraid to revile and defy the gods, though not often to the point of hurling their javelins at them as

Diomedes does; and Menelaus can exclaim: 'O father Zeus, there is no worse god than you!' In this respect, the comparison with Virgil, who in so many ways imitated Homer, is instructive. Among the many so-called 'Homeric' epithets, which of the heroes of the *Iliad* deserves the one that is always attributed to Aeneas: *pius?* The whole plot of the *Aeneid* depends on 'faith'. Without such faith, Aeneas' journey becomes absurd. Unlike Odysseus who only responds to human motives (nostalgia for Ithaca, his love for Penelope), Aeneas decides to undertake his journey solely on the promise of the gods.

As Mazon has said: 'The truth is, there was never a less religious poem than the *Iliad*. Unlike the majority of great national epics, it is in no way based upon belief.' And one may say as much of the *Odyssey*. Or rather, if these two poems do express a faith, it is faith in man; in man who through his courage and intelligence can learn to control his own unhappy fate.

The epic is first and foremost a story made up of descriptions, and Homer's main theme in the *Iliad* is the exploits of warriors and heroes. There are only two examples of actual single combat, between Menelaus and Paris in Book III, and between Hector and Ajax in Book VII; but since military tactics are still very rudimentary, the fighting as a whole consists of a series of man-to-man encounters. The leaders arrive on the battlefield in their chariots, usually drawn by two horses driven by a squire, but in most cases they fight on foot, while the chariot remains nearby ready to pick them up if they are wounded or defeated. Cavalry is unknown in the *Iliad*, except in similes, for by the time Homer was writing the *Iliad*, four centuries after the Trojan war, mounted horsemen had made their appearance. But the Achaeans themselves were only familiar with 'chariot warfare', analogous to that of Egypt or Mesopotamia.

A whole ritual accompanies the fights between the leaders. Often an engagement is preceded by the exhortation of a god or a comrade: sometimes by an internal monologue expressing the warrior's state of morale. Then the two adversaries address one another, exchanging threats and scathing rejoinders or, if they do not yet know one another (which happens rarely as the war has already been in progress for nearly ten years), they demand each other's names, like Diomedes and Glaucus in Book VI.

Usually each of the warriors carries two spears, or javelins, for throwing, and a sword for in-fighting. The fight begins with the hurling of the spears and continues with swords, or, when these get broken, with whatever happens to be handy, for example, a lump of rock. Achilles, driven back to the ships, snatches up a boat-hook to continue the fight.

Yet despite the general procedure just described, no two fights in the *Iliad* are the same. The details are always different. Homer's public, with their expert knowledge of fighting with spear and sword, must have been delighted by this variety, as well as by the minute and realistic description of the wounds and their exact physical location.

Often the furious warriors, drunk with blood, hotly pursue their victims and indulge in scenes of butchery; Homer's realism never shrinks from cruelty. Thus, in Book XIII, when Teucer kills the Trojan Imbrios, and Hector slays Amphimachos,

the two Ajaxes, disdaining all hazard, possessed themselves of Imbrios' corpse. Like a couple of lions who have snatched a goat from under the noses of the goatherd's snarling dogs and lift it clear of the ground as they carry it off in their jaws through the undergrowth, the helmeted Ajaxes held Imbrios aloft and stripped him of his arms. And in his fury at Amphimachos' death, the son of Oïleus severed Imbrios' head and with a swing sent it whirling like a ball through the crowd to drop in the dust at Hector's feet (197–205).

If such descriptions excite horror, they have first aroused pity, for as Fénelon so well put it in his *Letter to the Academy*: 'Homer never describes a young man about to die in battle without endowing him with a touching charm: he represents him as full of courage and virtue, makes you love him, and involves you in fear for his life; he shows you his father, bowed down with age and alarmed by the danger threatening his beloved child; he makes you see the trembling woman the young man has just made his wife; and you tremble with her. In a sense, the poet deceives you, for he only touches your heart with such grace and tenderness as an introduction to the fatal moment when you will see him you have come to love bathed in his own blood, his eyes closed in eternal sleep.'

The victor nearly always tries to steal his victim's armour, a rich and glorious trophy, but frequently the dead man's comrades intervene and another fight breaks out over the corpse: the longest of these is in Book XVII over the body of Patroclus. In a final speech, the victor boasts of his victory, and showers sarcasms on his dead enemy. Earlier, when Cebriones, Hector's driver, had been killed by a blow

with a stone and fell headlong from the chariot, 'like a diver', Patroclus
had taunted him:

Ha! quite an acrobat, I see, judging by that graceful dive! The man who takes
so neat a header from a chariot on land could dive for oysters from a ship
at sea in any weather and fetch up plenty for a feast. I did not know the
Trojans had such divers (*Iliad* xvi, 745–50).

In Book xxii of the *Odyssey*, Telemachus has the unfaithful servants
hanged and Melanthios is savagely mutilated. These were criminals,
but, if in the *Odyssey* the poet has fewer occasions than in the *Iliad*
to describe such bloody scenes, manners as a whole are almost equally
barbarous.

It has been said that the writer of the *Odyssey* detested the sea.
Certainly he feared its dangers like all the ancients whose frail vessels
could so easily be smashed like toys. The raft built by Odysseus is
completely helpless when Poseidon lets loose the tempest:

A mountainous wave, advancing with majestic sweep, crashed down upon
him from above and whirled his vessel round. The steering-oar was torn
from his hands, and he himself was tossed off the boat, while at the same
moment the warring winds joined forces in one tremendous gust which
snapped the mast in two and flung the sail and yard-arm far out into the sea
(v, 313–8).

Like the battles in the *Iliad*, each of the storms in the *Odyssey* is
described in fresh and striking terms. But the poet also shows us the
sea in its gay and peaceful moods, as when Poseidon skims across it
in his divine chariot:

He clothed himself in gold, picked up his well-made whip, mounted his
chariot and drove out across the waves. The monsters of the sea did not
fail to recognize their King. On every side they issued from their caves and
gamboled at his coming. The sea made way for him in its delight, so that his
bounding horses flew along, and the bronze axle of his chariot remained
dry below (*Iliad* xiii, 27–30).

When the Trojans camp on the field of battle, they light fires that
shine out across the darkening plain like the stars in the sky:

There are nights when the upper air is windless and the stars in heaven
stand out in splendour round the bright moon; when every mountain-top

and headland and ravine starts into sight, as the infinite depths of the sky are torn open to the very firmament; when every star is seen, and the shepherd rejoices. Such and so many were the Trojans' fires (*Iliad* VIII, 554–9).

The description of Achilles' shield, forged by Hephaestus, provides an invaluable sketch of Achaean civilization. Here are two passages, chosen from many:

Next he showed two beautiful cities full of people. In one of them weddings and banquets were afoot. They were bringing the brides through the streets from their homes, to the loud music of the wedding-hymn and the light of the blazing torches. Youths accompanied by flute and lyre were whirling in the dance, and the women had come to the doors of their houses to enjoy the show (*Iliad* XVIII, 490 ff.).

Then Hephaestus depicted a large field of soft, rich fallow, which was being ploughed for the third time. A number of ploughmen were driving their teams across it to and fro. When they reached the ridge at the end of the field and had to wheel, a man would come up and hand them a cup of mellow wine. Then back they turned down the furrows and toiled along through the deep fallow soil to reach the other end. And the field grew black behind them (*Ibid* 541 ff.).

Homer scarcely ever describes the emotions of his characters from the outside. They are expressed directly through the innumerable speeches he puts into their mouths, as we have shown when discussing his portrayal of character. It is these speeches, many of which are admirable—especially those in Book IX of the *Iliad*—that entitle Homer to be regarded as the father of Greek tragedy and eloquence.

As a rule, both narrative and dialogue are objective: by which I mean that the poet almost completely effaces himself, making no attempt to reveal himself through the words or actions of his characters. Yet several exceptions to this rule enable us to catch a glimpse of his personality. This we can only hope to know through his work, because nothing that the Ancients tell us about him can be accepted without caution; to start with, it is extremely doubtful that he was blind.

First, there are the invocations to the Muse or Muses, which occur not only at the beginning of the two poems but also in a number of other places (notably in Books II, IX, XIV and XVI of the *Iliad*). Homer felt himself to be inspired, and invested with the sacred character of the bard. As Odysseus says: 'No one on earth can help honouring and respecting the bards, for the Muse has taught them the art of song and she loves the minstrel fraternity' (*Odyssey* VIII, 479–81). Homer was a master-craftsman but, without inspiration and relying only on his own skill, he knew himself to be incapable of describing so many exploits and adventures: 'I cannot tell everything. For that one must be a god', he somewhere says. And in Book II, before beginning the 'Catalogue of Ships', he invokes the Muses: 'Tell me, you that live on Olympus, since you are goddesses and witness all that happens, whereas we men know nothing that we are not told—tell me who are the captains and the chieftains . . .' (484–6). His humility sprang from a profound recognition of the limits of human nature; his pride, from the conviction that his genius was a gift from the gods.

But even more revealing of the poet's personality are his interventions in the actual course of the story. Often enough, before describing the death of a hero, Homer has already announced beforehand that he is to perish: for example, lines 602–3 and 645 in Book XIII of the *Iliad*, and particularly in Book XVI, referring to Patroclus. Indeed, in Book XI, when Achilles called to Patroclus to go and find Nestor, the poet had already given a warning: 'Patroclus came out, looking like the god of war; and that was the beginning of his end' (603–4). But now, in his emotion, he speaks directly to Patroclus: 'When, like a god from heaven, you leap forth once more, Patroclus, then shall the term of your life be already set!' (XVI, 786–7).

Again and again Homer reveals the profound pity he feels for the fate of his heroes. He is in no way lacking in sensibility, as the cruelty of some of his sanguinary descriptions might perhaps lead one to suppose. In Book XIII he exclaims: 'He would be a hard man indeed, who, seeing their sorry work, delighted in it instead of grieving' (343–6). As Albert Severyns has said: 'By scattering throughout his works these passages in which he deliberately forgoes objective narrative, Homer keeps his audience in suspense, and at the same time provides them with helpful landmarks that enable them to grasp the general architecture of his epic. But, at the same time, he aims to create emotion, to communicate what he himself is feeling.'

Homer is not always grave and serious. He likes a joke, and there are plenty of horse-laughs as well as humour in his poems. Agamemnon says to his brother Menelaus who, touched by a Trojan's prayers, is about to set him free: 'Why are you so chary of taking men's lives? Did the Trojans treat *you* so handsomely when they stayed in your

3. A geometric amphora, *c.* eighth century, from the Ceramic Cemetery (the Dipylon) at Athens, with a funerary cortege and stylized human figures in the central band (pp. 67–8). *British Museum*

4. The Winged Victory of Delos attributed to Achermos, *c.* 550 (p. 94).
National Museum, Athens

house?' (*Iliad* VI, 55–7). Or again, on Olympus, when a domestic scene between Zeus and Hera looks like turning out badly, and the lame Hephaestus, determined to avert trouble, pours out drinks for everyone, suddenly 'a fit of helpless laughter seized the happy gods as they watched him bustling up and down the hall' (*Iliad* I, 599–600). This is Homeric laughter, like that which bursts out amongst the gods when Aphrodite and Ares are caught in their adulterous embrace under the net woven by Hephaestus. Apollo turns to Hermes and asks: ' "And how would you care, though held in those unyielding shackles, to lie in bed by golden Aphrodite's side?" To which Hermes replies: "There is nothing I should relish more. Though the chains that kept me prisoner were three times as many . . . yet would I gladly." And his jest raised another laugh from all the gods except Poseidon who was not amused' (*Odyssey* VIII, 339 ff.).

The whole episode of the cozening of Zeus, in Book XIV of the *Iliad*, is written in a vein of light comedy. At the very moment when Hera is about to achieve her end by her coquetry, and Zeus is imploring her to sleep with him on mount Ida, her prudishness breaks through again: 'No, if it is really your pleasure to do this thing, you have a bedroom. . . . Let us go and lie down there' (340).

In the foot race during the games in honour of Patroclus, Ajax the Lesser, the son of Oïleus, lines up with Odysseus and Antilochos son of Nestor; but suffers a mishap that is recounted with humour and realism:

They were just about to dash up to the prizes, when Ajax slipped in full career. This was Athena's doing, and it happened where the ground was littered with dung from the lowing cattle that were slaughtered by Achilles for Patroclus' funeral. So Ajax had his mouth and nostrils filled with dung, while the much-enduring excellent Odysseus, having caught him up and finished, carried off the silver bowl. The illustrous Ajax took possession of the farmyard ox. Then . . . as he spat out the dung, he remarked to the spectators: 'Damnation take it! I swear it was the goddess tripped me up —the one who always dances attendance, like a mother, on Odysseus' (*Iliad* XXIII, 773–83).

In Book IX, the aged Phoenix reminds Achilles of the care he took of him when he was a child:

I always had to take you on my knee and pamper you, by cutting up titbits from my meat and holding my cup to your lips. You often soaked the front of my tunic with the wine you dribbled from your clumsy little mouth (488–91).

—a homely detail that the fastidious French critics of the seventeenth century were to find 'quite disgusting'.

Nothing throws so much light on the poet's personality as his similes, a number of which we have already quoted. There are some two hundred and forty of them in the *Iliad*, which if they were printed consecutively would amount to eight hundred lines of verse, the equivalent of one of the longer books. In the *Odyssey* they are five times less numerous. These similes are especially valuable because they evoke for us the poet's contemporary world, several centuries later than that described in his poems. For example, the horses in the *Iliad* are always harnessed to chariots, there is no cavalry. But Homer himself was familiar with men riding on horseback and had watched them practising jumping, which he compares with Ajax leaping from prow to prow as he defends the ships (*Iliad* xv). And when Odysseus is in danger of drowning after the smashing of his raft he scrambles on to a beam and straddles it 'like a race horse' (*Odyssey* v).

Homer's similes are derived from many sources, nature, wild animals (especially lions and boars), birds, fishes, agriculture, war, sport and every kind of human activity. Though he was said to have been blind, he had obviously observed every kind of art and craft very closely. When Pandarus' arrow wounds Menelaus in the thigh, the blood runs down his legs 'like the purple dye with which some Carian or Maeonian woman stains ivory to make a cheek-piece for a horse' (*Odyssey* IV, 141 ff.). Sometimes the poetic beauty of these similes makes them unforgettable, as in this description of a dying hero:

Weighed down by his helmet, Gorgythion's head dropped to one side, like the lolling head of a garden poppy, weighed down by its seed and the showers of spring (*Iliad* VIII, 306–8).

The modern reader is often surprised by the extreme freedom of the similes. An association of ideas, a single flash of resemblance, is enough for Homer: thus he compares Patroclus to a little girl crying, as she runs after her mother clinging to her knees; or he speaks of Menelaus as being like a cow that has just calved, because his solicitude for the body of Patroclus is like that of a cow for its newly born calf. And again, a little further on Menelaus is compared to a fly: Athena 'strengthened his shoulders and his knees, and implanted in his breast the daring of a fly, which is so fond of human blood that it returns to the attack however often a man may brush it from his face' (*Iliad* XVII, 570–2).

Often the comparison is developed through a picture that appears to have but little connection with the scene that has suggested it, and yet a single word suffices to bring out the force of the simile. For example, when Odysseus lands on the Phaeacian shore he buries himself under a pile of leaves:

Covering his body as carefully as a crofter in the far corner of an estate *covers* a glowing brand under the black ashes to keep his fire alight and save himself from having to seek a light elsewhere (*Odyssey* v, 488–91).

In Book xv of the *Iliad* there is a simile which better than any other seems to me to reveal the temperament of the poet, his continually alert curiosity (a typical characteristic of the Greek people), his constant desire to learn something fresh, to be somewhere else. To convey the impression of Hera's rapid flight, he compares it to the soaring thoughts of a man who, though he has already seen many countries, continues to plan ever new journeys, and says to himself: 'If only I could go there! Or there!' Certainly Homer envied the gods their ubiquity just as he envied them their knowledge. He would have liked nothing better than to have travelled about the world like Odysseus who 'visited the cities of so many men and knew what was in their minds'. But human life is too short and the facilities too limited: to have done so he would have needed, if not the immortality of the gods, at least their speed and mobility.

Human life is too short—when Diomedes asks Glaucus his name and where he was born, Glaucus replies:

What does my lineage matter to you? Men in their generations are like the leaves of the trees. The wind blows and one year's leaves are scattered on the ground; but the trees burst into bud and put on fresh ones when the spring comes round. In the same way one generation flourishes and another nears its end (*Iliad* VI, 145–9).

But short as it is, life is also weighed down with pain and suffering. When Zeus declares, 'Of all creations upon earth that have strength and movement, none is more wretched than man' (*Iliad* XVII, 446), it is Homer who is expressing his own deepest conviction, the fruit of all his experience. The most profound impression created by a reading of the *Iliad* and, despite one or two shades of difference, of the *Odyssey* also, is that man, the ephemeral creature of a day, can at best experience but little happiness in life, and always accompanied or followed by misfortune. In the final Book of the *Iliad*, when Achilles speaks to the weeping Priam of the two jars in which Zeus keeps the evils and the blessings to be bestowed on mankind, he does not even consider the possibility that Zeus might grant a man nothing but good fortune: it is already a great deal, like Peleus or like Priam himself, to have received from heaven a few years of happiness, for there are many who, throughout their lives, know nothing but misery. This same wisdom Homer puts into the mouth of the young girl, Nausicaa, when she speaks to Odysseus of resignation as being the only attitude for a man stricken by fate:

Sir, your manners prove that you are no rascal and no fool. As for these ordeals of yours, they must have been sent you by Olympian Zeus, who follows his own will in dispensing happiness to people whatever their merits. You have no choice but to endure (*Odyssey* VI, 187–90).

The conclusion of the *Odyssey* is certainly less sombre than that of the *Iliad*. Yet both poems seem to me to be infused with the same feeling: a profound and intense pity. Though Penelope and Odysseus finally come together again, in the twenty years they have been separated they have lost the best part of their lives. And the dangers Odysseus has undergone on his travels were as terrible as those of war, and less glorious. Battered by storms, did he not perhaps regret having survived the Trojan war?

Homer's heroes are not inaccessible to pity, despite their apparent cruelty. If they kill, it is because killing is the rule of war; they do so to avoid being slain themselves, or from hatred of an opponent who has destroyed one of their friends. Yet often enough they pity their dying enemy, thinking of their own death, so likely and so close. So Achilles speaks to Lycaon as a 'friend' at the very moment he is about to strike him down. The gods, too, can be moved to pity, as Zeus is for his son Sarpedon and the heroic Hector at the moment when they are about to die. Yet this pity is without effect; it cannot change the decrees of fate, symbolized by Zeus' golden scales. On the whole, the Olympians' concern with humanity causes more suffering than salvation, for, even more than man himself, the gods are the slaves of their passions and caprices.

It is the poet's own sense of pity that moves us most. It manifests itself, or rather involuntarily betrays itself, in many places. During the embassy to Achilles, the aged Phoenix recounts the following allegory:

Do you know that Prayers are the daughters of almighty Zeus? They are wrinkled creatures, with halting gait and downcast eyes, who make it their business to follow Sin about. But Sin is strong, and quick enough to leave them all behind. Stealing a march on them, she roams the world and brings mankind to grief. *They* come after, and put the matter right (*Iliad* IX, 502 ff.).

This allegory does not only mean that Achilles should forgo his wrath and grant the prayers of the ambassadors. It also expresses one of the deepest feelings of the poet: that, however wretched man's lot may be, he ought at least not to add to his troubles by anger, passion or obstinacy, but should listen to the voice of pity and forgiveness, the only way of modifying a little the harshness of fate. And, if humanity were abandoned by the gods and left to itself, would it be any less unhappy? Zeus' answer is: 'What a lamentable thing it is that men should blame the gods ... when it is their own wickedness that brings them sufferings worse than any that Destiny allots them' (*Odyssey* I, 32–3).

In the midst of the catastrophes decreed by the gods, the best men are capable of great actions, though at the cost of infinite affliction. For the Greek philosophers, Achilles was to become the type of the magnanimous man of action, Odysseus of the magnanimous sage. Both overcame fate by the power of the spirit, but the first by impulse and sacrifice, the second by reflection and endurance. Thus Homer sets before the Greeks the twofold ideal of the hero-sage. In his two poems he exalts the clear-sighted energy of men who, without illusions, struggle with their tragic destinies, with no real and constant help save what they find in themselves, in 'the greatness of their hearts'. Homer admires his characters, but he pities them even more; and it is the pity he feels for them that inspires his most profoundly human accents, those which will doubtless continue to move the generations of mankind as they succeed each other 'like the leaves of the trees'.

59

THE FATE OF THE HOMERIC POEMS

To begin with, the *Iliad* and the *Odyssey* were preserved (and doubtless a number of passages interpolated) by the 'Homeridae', a kind of minstrel fraternity who looked upon the great poet as their patron and even claimed to be descended from him. Cynaethos of Chios who lived in the sixth century B.C. belonged to the fraternity and seems to have been the author of the *Homeric Hymn to the Delian Apollo* which contains the lines:

When a stranger asks of you: 'Whom think ye, girls, is the sweetest singer that comes here, and in whom do you most delight?' then answer with one voice: 'He is a blind man and dwells in rocky Chios: his lays are evermore supreme' (169–173).

Thus, Cynaethos made no bones about passing himself off as Homer, and when Thucydides quoted this Hymn in Book III of his *History* it was to Homer that he attributed it.

How came it that the *Iliad* and the *Odyssey*, written in Ionia, spread to the mainland of Greece? Doubtless it was the Homeridae, and later the rhapsodes, who were mainly responsible. Yet several ancient texts refer to Lycurgus of Sparta and to the Athenians Solon, Peisistratus and Hipparchus. The tradition with regard to the legislator Lycurgus can be dismissed, since he was a legendary figure, but the three Athenians were historical characters of the sixth century B.C.

The vase paintings where we find the earliest representations of scenes from the two poems—Cycladic and proto-Attic pottery—date from the second quarter of the seventh century: thus, around 675 B.C. Homer's work was known in the Aegean Islands as well as on the mainland. In other words, the poems would have reached Athens well before the archontate of Solon (594 B.C.), though it was probably Solon who decided that the rhapsodes should recite only the poems of Homer at the Festival of the Panathenaia, which was already being held before the reorganization of 566.

In the second half of the sixth century, the Tyrant Peisistratus and his son Hipparchus seem to have contributed to the precaution of an Attic recension of the *Iliad* and the *Odyssey*, made necessary by the official recitation of the poems at the Panathenaia. Since then, Homer was regarded as the greatest poet of Greece, or quite simply as 'the poet'. From an early age, the children of Athens and elsewhere were taught to read him, and their minds became soaked in the memory of his poetry: the rôle of La Fontaine's *Fables* in primary education in France provides but a faint analogy with the preponderance of Homer's influence throughout the whole of Hellenic culture.[1] From early childhood, the sensibility and intelligence of the Greeks were moulded by him and for many of them he continued to be their favourite reading.

It is only natural, therefore, that practically the whole of Greek literature, if it does not actually derive from Homer, should at least be profoundly influenced by his work, a rich and inexhaustible spring at which all the writers of Hellas have drunk. In the case of the poets, epic, lyric or tragic, this is immediately apparent, but it is in no sense a paradox to say that the historians, orators and philosophers were also deeply indebted to the Homeric poems. It was to Homer that the Father of History, Herodotus, owed the original plan of his work, which he decided to write 'so that the great and marvellous deeds performed by the Barbarians as well as by the Greeks should not cease to be renowned'. The teachers of rhetoric so much admired the speeches of his heroes that they recommended them to their pupils as incomparable models. As to the philosophers, while at first sight one might expect them to have been as opposed to Homer as truth to fiction, many of them in fact turned to his work again and again to find examples, or at least confirmation, of their theories. Félix Buffière has shown that Greek thinkers, from the pre-Socratics to the neo-Platonists, were continually studying the slightest scraps of his poetry.

From many points of view, the *Iliad* and the *Odyssey*, without being regarded as in any way sacred works, were the Bible of the Greeks, pre-eminently 'the Book'. Not only second-rate poets such as Ion, the chief character in Plato's dialogue of that name, but also authentic philosophers have defended Homer against all attack, even against criticism, by detailed and impassioned apologetics, based on the three exegetical principles: physical, moral and mystical allegory. Even Plato, that prince of 'Homeric atheists', was constantly referring to the two poems, so much so indeed that Jules Labarbe has devoted a whole book to the study of the passages he refers to: *L'Homère de Platon*. As Buffière has said: 'The tireless search to find its own reflection in the mirror of the Homeric poems is one of the constants of Greek thought.'

[1] More nearly comparable is the part played by the authorized version of the Bible in England, at least until the end of the nineteenth century (Trs.).

It must however be added that history and philosophy only reached maturity to the extent that they succeeded in breaking away from Homer's restrictive ascendancy. Thucydides could not restore the Trojan war to its true proportions without convicting the poet of having amplified and distorted reality. Plato, following Xenophanes, was to reproach Homer for having spoken of the gods in unseemly terms, like a bad 'theologian', and excluded his work from his austerely utopian City where fables were not allowed.

Nevertheless, the Greeks remained faithful to Homer. In the fourth century, Xenophon introduced a scene into his *Symposium*, where a young man Nikeratos who claimed to know the whole of the *Iliad* and the *Odyssey* by heart says to the other guests:

Homer, that learned man, dealt with almost every form of human activity in his poems. That is why, if any of you wishes to become capable of running his household or arousing the people or commanding an army, you ought to cultivate my society, since from my thorough knowledge of the poems I am an expert in all these matters (*Symposium* IV, 6).

In the Hellenistic period, Homer's importance for education remained unchallenged. H.-I. Marrou has said: 'In the front rank of the classics, dominating all others, stands Homer. . . . One has only to think of Alexander the Great, taking the *Iliad* with him on his campaigns; or those lost towns on the furthermost boundaries of the Greek world, Marseilles, Sinope, the cities of Cyprus, which in order to assert their loyalty to their Hellenic patrimony in the face of the Barbarians insisted on publishing their own editions of the *Iliad*. Homer dominates the whole of Greek culture. . . . From the primary school onwards his mighty shadow appears on the horizon: "Homer is not a man, he is a god", the children used to copy out in their earliest reading lessons. . . . A mother who asked his teacher how her son was getting on, would be proud to hear that he was already studying the sixth Book of the *Iliad*. Excavations in Egypt have already discovered in their hundreds papyri and ceramic tablets and potsherds containing fragments of Homer.'

In the Roman epoch, an orator of the time of Augustus, Heraclitus, exclaimed: 'From the tenderest age the child just beginning his studies is given Homer for his nurse; barely are they out of swaddling clothes than they are given his poems as pap. We grow up, and he is still close beside us; as we gradually become men, he remains the companion of our youth. But it is in our maturity that he takes possession of our whole being. Never, until old age, do we begin to feel satiated by him. No sooner have we finished re-reading him than we are eager to start again at the beginning. One might almost say that death alone can put an end to our commerce with him' (*The Allegories of Homer* I, 5–7).

Most of the ancient authors referred to Homer as the supreme authority, in the same way as, in the Christian era, men quoted the Bible as the source of all truth, all wisdom and all knowledge. Yet Homer was not a religious poet, although he himself was to become the object of a veritable cult, a kind of Homeric religion, constituting a bond between all Hellenes, more enduring than the city gods who differed from one town to another. Indeed it was through the knowledge and practice of the Homeric poems that Greek culture first took shape.

2

THE ARCHAIC PERIOD

Eighth and Seventh Centuries

Would that I were not among the men of the fifth generation,
but either had died before or been born afterwards. For now truly
is a race of iron.

(HESIOD: *Works and Days*, 174–5)

HISTORICAL BACKGROUND

The first wave of invaders belonging to the Hellenic race, the Achaeans
who occupied Greece in the heroic age, was followed about the
eleventh century by a second wave: the Dorian invasion, known to
ancient tradition as the 'return of the Heracleidae', the sons of
Heracles, who had been driven out after the death of their father. It
was then in the Peloponnese for example, that the three kingdoms of
Argos, Laconia and Messenia were founded, corresponding to the
domains of Agamemnon, Menelaus and Nestor.

These new Hellenes, compared with the Achaeans or 'Mycenaeans'
brought up in the spirit of Minoan Crete, were practically barbarians.
Towards the end of the second millennium B.C. the use of iron had
become common. The appearance of the Dorians in Greece coincided
with the decline of the brilliant Bronze Age civilization and the
beginning of a long period that is sometimes spoken of as the Hellenic
'Middle Ages'. Homer himself lived in this period, but his works
reflect the splendour of Achaean civilization, which was known to
him from tradition and from earlier epics. The period prior to 1000 B.C.
saw the collapse of civilization in Greece, but during the obscure tenth
to eighth centuries a 'renaissance' was gradually beginning to take
shape that was eventually to put an end to the rude Middle Ages—a
renaissance of which the first clear signs were apparent in the seventh
century.

The eighth century, of which unfortunately little is known, was
an age of intense and strenuous ferment. The era of the Olympiads,

64

which until Roman times was the starting point for a chronology common to all the Greek states, began in 776 B.C., the year to which the most ancient victories in the Olympic games were attributed. When we remember that the traditional date for the founding of Rome was 753, we find that the beginning of Greek chronology only preceded that of Rome by a mere twenty years or so. The obscure period of the kings of Rome coincided more or less with the development of Hellenic civilization properly so called: it ended with the institution of the Roman Republic in 509, within a year of the establishment of democracy in Athens by Cleisthenes. It may be, however, that these coincidences were to some extent manipulated by the Hellenistic and Roman chronologists.

It was in the eighth century that the great wave of Greek colonization, begun by the Achaeans but interrupted by the Dorian invasion, started once more; though the Dorians had forced the Achaeans to take to the sea in order to re-establish themselves further away, for example in Cyprus. 'This power of expansion, evidence of the vigour of the Hellenes and their civilization, remains a characteristic and permanent feature of ancient Greece,' says Jean Bérard. And, in fact, colonization was to continue, though on a smaller scale, down to the classical period; and Alexander the Great was to continue it, founding Greek cities as far to the east as his armies succeeded in penetrating.

From about 775 to 675, driven on by the necessity of acquiring more land in order to feed their growing population and to extend their trade, the Greeks founded the Euboean cities on the peninsula of Chalcidice in Thrace: the towns of Cumae, Sybaris and Tarentum on the Italian coast; and Syracuse, Locris, Siris and Gela in Sicily. Between 675 and 500, in a second and more powerful thrust, they colonized the Thracian coast of the Aegean, the coasts of the Propontis and the Pontus Euxinus and, in Africa, those of Cyrenaica and Egypt. In Sicily the towns of Agrigentum, Himera and Selinus were founded and, finally, they extended their conquests as far as Gaul, where the town of Massalia (Marseilles) was built by the Phocaeans about 600 B.C., and the Iberian coast. In course of time, these colonial cities expanded and became the metropolitan centres of new satellite towns, until eventually the Mediterranean, at least its eastern and western ends, took on the appearance of a Greek lake.

In this movement of expansion an important part was, according to tradition, played by the Delphic oracle, though precisely how it is difficult to say. It would seem, however, that the Pythia's prophetic powers were sustained by some kind of intelligence service, based on this centrally situated meeting place of Greeks from every country. For it was also in this period that the great sanctuaries, like those of Dodona and Delphi, both known to Homer, as well as Olympia, were either founded or developed. Around such pan-Hellenic shrines as that at Delphi there grew up 'Amphictyonies', associations of neighbouring states who united to protect their temple and to discuss their common interests; the earliest attempt to form some kind of international organization under the patronage of the gods.

Essentially, Greek religion and its principal gods remained much as they had been in the earlier period, though the various cults became more clearly defined and diversified according to the cities to which they belonged. At the same time, a wave of mysticism began to make itself felt, leading to the practice of divination and the mystery cults mainly associated with Dionysus and Demeter, which was also the source of the Thracian cult of Orpheus, a kind of prophet of the Dionysiac religion; and later of Pythagoreanism.

These developments were accompanied by profound changes in the political and social life of the Greeks. Agriculture, trade and technical skills were steadily improved; and money appeared for the first time, notably in Argolis and the island of Aegina. Monarchy was evolving into various forms of oligarchy in which the big landed proprietors were the real masters, while the small farmers such as Hesiod struggled to make a living out of their small plots of land, continually threatened by the injustice of the wealthy and powerful. Social inequality was becoming more and more unbearable. The poor, forced to borrow in order to survive, were sold as slaves by their creditors if they became bankrupt.

In the seventh century, this social crisis led in many cities to the seizure of power by a 'tyrant' who attempted to found a dynasty, like the Cypselidae of Corinth or the Orthagoridae of Sicyon. In Sparta, the most conservative of cities, the laws later attributed to Lycurgus were to preserve the archaic character of the state even into the classical period, though the authority of the five ephors began to encroach upon that of the two kings.

In Athens, the capital of Attica, which had long been a unified state, kings were replaced by magistrates holding office at first for life, later for a year, who were supervised by the archon and the polemarch. The list of eponymous archons begins with the year 686, but the Eupatridae, or nobles, were the only Athenians who could be appointed to the great offices of state. In the last quarter of the seventh century, by harsh measures of reform that were to become proverbial, Dracon suppressed the interminable quarrels and acts of revenge between the ruling families and insisted that in the domain of justice the clearly defined State Code should be the supreme authority. Thus Dracon may be seen as the precursor of Solon.

ART

The art of these remote times that best enables us to appreciate the development of the technique and manual skill of its craftsmen is pottery. Indeed, throughout the whole of antiquity vessels made of baked clay were in everyday use, fulfilling the function of the glass, porcelain, metal and plastic goods in use today: vessels for carrying water, for keeping wine or grain, perfumes or oil, drinking cups, lamps and so on. But, as with Sèvres porcelain or Delft pottery in our own times, the finest of the vessels made by the potters and painters of antiquity were never intended for everyday use; they were works of art, whose purpose was to decorate the houses of the rich and to give delight by the beauty of their form and colour. In the process of excavation, archaeologists may not always discover statues of stone or bronze, but they seldom fail to have the satisfaction of finding vessels or potsherds of baked clay.

The Cretans, and to a lesser degree the Mycenaeans, left behind them wonderful painted vases, glazed and richly decorated with motifs derived mainly from vegetable and animal life, elegantly stylized fish, octopuses with long, waving tentacles. Accurate dating of the ceramics of the Hellenic 'Middle Ages' is not possible, but we know that until half way through the eighth century all vases were painted in what is called the 'geometric' style, similar to that of the small bronzes from Olympia. This style, which for a long time was despised by critics and amateurs of art, is today becoming fashionable again. Almost invariably the belly of the vase is divided by a series of concentric circles into zones which, like the neck, are decorated with the most varied motifs, both curved and rectilinear. Sometimes birds, animals or men are also represented, but so schematically that the style remains 'geometric'. The upper part of a man's body is simply an inverted isosceles triangle, its point resting on the hips, with the arms springing from its base; but the arms have no modelling and are reduced to simple strokes and the legs are represented almost as sketchily. To help the unskilled draughtsman, faces and feet are shown in profile, the rest of the body full-face.

The production of large geometric vases with human figures seems to have been a monopoly of Athens. It was in the burial ground known as the Ceramic Cemetery that the largest and finest specimens of this style were found, the jars (*pithoi*) with elongated necks, sometimes standing more than six feet high. The entire surface is covered with a variety of decorative motifs arranged in concentric bands, some of which contain rows of animals or scenes with human figures: a dead man surrounded by mourners, a funeral procession, a naval battle.

According to Charles Dugas, 'it was a novelty at this time to attach such importance to the representation of human life. Certainly the geometric vases cannot bear comparison, for beauty of motif, elegance of design or charm of colour, with the splendid Minoan vases; compared with the subtlety and refinement of the latter they produce an impression of barbarism. Yet as one notes the detail of these small and childishly inexpert figures and realizes the painter's effort to reproduce the scenes he has observed, one is impressed by the ingenious curiosity, the spirit of research, that this pottery reveals. The Athenian potters of this period were the first to make man, represented in all the variety of his various occupations, the centre of ceramic ornament.'

And it is true that these Athenian painters of the eighth century already foreshadowed what was to become the distinctive feature of Hellenic art and literature, that is to say, the dominating role of man as 'the measure of all things'. Nevertheless, it is somewhat surprising to find that the age when Homer was producing his consummate poems should only have left behind such relatively mediocre works of art. We have to recognize that there was a considerable time lag between art and literature: turning to the past, to the age of heroes, Homer took over and improved upon the epic legacy of the preceding centuries; on the other hand, the skills of the Minoan and Mycenaean artists having been lost in the confusion caused by the Dorian invasion, an almost entirely fresh start had to be made in the domain of art

However, in the seventh century, a period of artistic effervescence and experimentation, pottery was to make rapid progress under the influence of the East and of its imported skills. About 650, a vase from Argos and another from Eleusis in Attica both depict an episode from the *Odyssey*: the blinding of Polyphemus by Odysseus. Here, the human figure, though still displaying a certain stiffness, is no longer grossly schematized as in the geometric style, but is beginning to take on an appearance of life. And a Corinthian bowl of the same period successfully depicts some horsemen and a man in a chariot taking part in a lion hunt.

To the second half of the seventh century belong the painted earthenware tiles that were used for the metopes of the temple of Apollo at Thermos in Aetolia: a rare, though not unique, example of ancient Greek painting on a flat surface instead of on the rounded surface of a vase. The white figure and the bust of a woman, called Chelidon according to the accompanying inscription, are quite remarkable. (In the legend of Itys, Chelidon was turned into a swallow.)

It was in Athens that the vase painters most rapidly developed their technical skill, as may be seen for example from the Attic amphora depicting Heracles in the act of killing the centaur Nessus on the neck and on the belly the Gorgons flitting over the sea. This vase, which appears to date from the last quarter of the seventh century, already proclaims the marvels of Attic painting to be produced in the following century, with its well-known black figures.

To the archaic epoch also belong a very large number of figurines in terra-cotta, bronze, ivory and lead whose schematized forms have a certain analogy with the geometric style. Many of these figurines come from Crete (where legend has it that Daedalus made the first 'animated' statues); but also from Sparta, Corinth and elsewhere.

In the archaic period, too, Greek architecture began to develop, deriving perhaps from memories of the Mycenaean *megaron*. But we know little of its history, since the oldest buildings were made of perishable materials, mainly wood. In the sixth century and the classical period, these were replaced by new stone buildings. All the more precious, therefore, are the few remains of this ancient architecture that archaeologists have found amongst the foundations of the later temples, such as the ceramic metopes from Thermos which must originally have been inserted in wooden triglyphs.

The oldest Doric temple that is reasonably well-known to us is the temple of Hera at Olympia. This is due to the fact that, instead of having been reconstructed, as the original woodwork decayed, it was gradually replaced by stone. It is a peripteral building, with a façade of six columns. Pausanias, in the second century A.D., recorded having seen several oak columns still standing in the opisthodomos. Most of the wooden columns, however, have been replaced by stone ones, varying in diameter and style according to the periods to which they belong. The different shapes of the capitals indicate the evolution of style from the seventh century to the classicism of the fifth.

Like the first Grecian temples, the earliest religious statues (*xoana*) were also of wood, though from the seventh century onwards these wooden statues were imitated in stone. Amongst the most typical of these 'incunabula' are the female statue at Delos, at the shrine of Artemis, dedicated by Nicandre, a woman of Naxos (as we learn from an inscription on the thigh); and the 'lady of Auxerre', now in the Louvre. In the latter figure, the hair is arranged on either side of the face in two heavy tiers of curls; the right arm is held away from the body, to allow the hand to rest on the breast, but the left arm hangs stiffly at the side, in the position habitually found in the *xoana*, as well as in so many Egyptian statues; the body is flattened and the long robe, hanging straight down without a fold, is only decorated with a few geometrical designs.

HESIOD

About 450 B.C., Herodotus wrote: 'I reckon that Homer and Hesiod lived four hundred years before me, not more.' Elsewhere, in the *Contest of Homer and Hesiod*—a mediocre work, the origins of which may however date from the fifth century—it is clearly assumed that the two poets were contemporaries and could have met. In reality, nothing is less likely, though the interval between them was probably not great. Any precise dating is quite impossible. We have put forward the hypothesis that Homer lived between 850 and 750; and similarly we assume that Hesiod was alive somewhere around the second half of the eighth century.

Both the language and versification of Hesiod derive from the same tradition as Homer's; like the *Iliad* and the *Odyssey*, his poems were written in epic hexametres and, with only slight differences, he used the same formulary style and the same basic vocabulary as Homer. But apart from this formal resemblance, how profound are the differences, the contrasts even, between the two poets!

Homer lived in Ionia; Hesiod in Boeotia, the heart of central Greece. Homer would seem to have had no other occupation than that of poet, or minstrel; Hesiod led the rough and austere life of a poor peasant, cultivating his land with his own hands and his poetic vocation did little to modify this harsh existence. Homer sang of the siege of Troy and noble heroes; Hesiod took as his central theme the 'works and days' of the peasant who, throughout the changing seasons, mixes his sweat with the soil.

It is quite probable that the *Theogony*, which has come down to us as one of Hesiod's works, was in fact by him. In any case, the prologue refers to him by name. Just as Homer began the *Iliad* and the *Odyssey* with invocations to the Muses, so in his prologue the author of the *Theogony* celebrated the Muses of Helicon, that is to say of the mountain in Boeotia on the slopes of which Hesiod lived, in the village of Ascra, not far from the valley of the Muses and the Thespians:

From the Heliconian Muses let us begin to sing . . . (who) one day taught Hesiod glorious song while he was shepherding his lambs under holy Helicon, and this word first the goddesses said to me, the Muses of Olympus, daughters of Zeus who holds the aegis: 'Shepherds of the wilderness, wretched things of shame, mere bellies, we know how to speak many false things as though they were true; but we know, when we will, to utter true things'. So said the ready-voiced daughters of great Zeus, and they plucked and gave me a rod, a shoot of sturdy laurel, a marvellous thing, and breathed into me a divine voice to celebrate things that shall be and things that were aforetime; and they bade me sing of the race of the blessed gods that are eternal, but ever to sing of themselves both first and last (1 and 22–30).

Throughout this prologue one can feel the pulse of a deep religious faith. For the poet, the Muses are clearly not just pale allegorical figures, but powerful goddesses to whom he owes his inspiration and without whom he would simply be another peasant or shepherd. The remainder of the poem, which was very famous in antiquity, recounts the genealogy of the gods, beginning with those primordial divinities, Chaos, Earth and Love (Eros). It is thus a kind of *Genesis*, a rudimentary cosmology and theology, which, unless he happens to be a specialist in the history of religion, is apt to leave the contemporary reader cold. Though clumsy and uneven the poem everywhere breathes a spirit of burning sincerity and, in places, has the note of original and personal poetry. But the *Theogony*, if it was indeed by Hesiod, was certainly written before *Works and Days*, a poem remarkable for quite different qualities, by a man who had reached maturity and whose writing was the fruit of long experience.

All that we know for certain about Hesiod is to be found in *Works and Days*. There we learn that his father, a native of Aeolian Cyme in Asia Minor, was the owner of a coasting vessel and that, having been ruined, he crossed the Aegean sea and settled down in Boeotia:

One day (my father) came to this very place, crossing over a great stretch of sea; he left Aeolian Cyme and fled, not from riches and substance, but from wretched poverty, which Zeus lays upon men, and he settled in a miserable hamlet, Ascra, which is bad in winter, sultry in summer, and good at no time (633–40).

There Hesiod was born. He had one brother Perses with whom he shared his father's inheritance, but Perses, dissatisfied with his share, brought an action against him and the 'kings', that is to say the notabilities and judges of Thespiae, gave judgment in favour of Perses. Hesiod, convinced of his legal rights, believed that they had been bribed by his brother. The latter, however, having fallen into poverty as a result of idleness, sometimes approached Hesiod for help, sometimes threatened him with a new law suit. Hesiod therefore dedicated his poem to him, in order to teach him the love of work and respect for true justice which is not always the same as that meted out by human judges.

Though a seafarer's son, Hesiod detested the sea (as Homer is said to have done). He only once went aboard a ship, and then only for the short journey across the narrow strait of Euripus that separates Euboea from Boeotia. He himself tells us the purpose of his voyage:

For never yet have I sailed over the wide sea, but only to Euboea from Aulis where the Achaeans once stayed when they had gathered a great host from divine Hellas for Troy, the land of fair women. Then I crossed over to Chalcis, to the games of wise Amphidamas, where the sons of the great-hearted hero proclaimed and appointed prizes. And there I boast that I gained the victory with a song and carried off a two-handled tripod which I dedicated to the Muses of Helicon, in the place where they first set me in the way of that song. Such is all my experience of many-pegged ships (647–59).

Thus the sons of a lord of Chalcis in Euboea, Amphidamas, had organized games to celebrate their father's funeral (as Achilles did in honour of Patroclus) and these games included a poetry competition that was won by Hesiod. This passage is almost certainly the origin of the legend described in the *Contest of Homer and Hesiod*, though here there is no mention of Homer.

72

The *Works and Days* opens with an invocation to the Pierian Muses and is followed by a grumbling 'dedication' to Perses: 'Here I shall bring home to Perses some true things.' The construction of the poem is disconcerting because the author shows little skill in handling abstract ideas and his logic is extremely lax. It consists of a poorly organized succession of maxims, allegories and myths, and its various parts are linked by an association of ideas that for the most part remain implicit.

The allegory of the two Erises (Eris was the goddess both of Emulation, which was good, and of Strife, which was bad) is well devised to persuade Perses to keep away from the courts and only to compete with others by his readiness to work hard. (Homer had also written allegories, like that of 'Sin and the Prayers'.)

The myth of Pandora teaches that men should work unceasingly to improve as far as possible the harsh fate imposed upon them by the gods. For Zeus, having been cheated by Prometheus who had secretly given fire to mankind, had made this marvellous woman, endowed her with 'all the gifts' (hence her name) and sent her amongst mankind, who had hitherto been happy, bearing with her a magic jar:

But the woman took off the great lid of the jar, and scattered all these gifts, and her thought caused sorrow and mischief to men. Only Hope remained there in an unbreakable home under the rim of the great jar, and did not fly out for Pandora had already replaced the lid of the jar by orders of Zeus (94–9).

Are we therefore to believe that Zeus intended to deprive men even of hope? Illogical as it may appear, it would seem more likely that hope alone remains in the jar, to be kept in reserve for the use of mankind. As the poet Simonides of Ceos was to say later: 'It is hope and credulity that encourage the vain efforts of mortal men.' Indeed, without hope, without the illusion that in this way they can escape their misery, men would not work. Hope, the one good thing left to them amongst so many ills, is therefore only a snare and a delusion. This is at the very opposite pole of modern optimism: no one has had a more pessimistic conception of the lot of man than Hesiod. In *Works and Days* Pandora is simply the attractive bait that Zeus employs in order to get men to accept her fatal jar: in the *Theogony* where she represents the whole 'second sex', she is herself a punishment inflicted upon mortals, for Hesiod's misogyny is as deep-rooted as his pessimism.

In the Pandora episode we also find the words: 'Ere this the tribes of men lived on earth, remote and free from ills and hard toil, and heavy sickness that bring death to mankind' (90–2). This theme of a 'golden age', as old perhaps as humanity itself, takes us back to the times when Kronos (the Latin Saturn), father of Zeus, reigned in heaven. When this golden race of men, the happiest there ever was, ultimately disappeared from the earth, its place was taken by a silver race, in turn to be succeeded, as a result of still further debasement, by a race of bronze. After this, came the race of heroes, the only one not named after a metal, who perished on the ramparts of Thebes or beneath the walls of Troy 'whither war had brought them in their ships for the sake of Helen of the lovely locks' (164–5). Thus, this myth embodies the memory of at least two historical periods: the heroic age, and the transition from the Bronze to the Iron Age. It is in reference to the latter that the poet says:

Would that I were not among the men of the fifth generation, but had either died before or been born afterwards. For now truly is a race of iron, and men never rest from sorrow and labour by day, and from perishing by night. . . . Yet, notwithstanding, even these shall have some good mingled with their evils. And Zeus will destroy this race of mortal men when they come to have grey hair on their temples at their birth . . . the wicked will harm the worthy man, speaking false words against him. . . . And then Shame and Indignation, with their sweet forms wrapped in white robes . . . will forsake mankind to join the company of the deathless gods (174 ff.).

It is clear that Hesiod conceived the history of humanity as a continuous and irremediable process of decay ordained by malignant gods whose hostility to mankind was far more unrelenting even than that of Homer's gods. And as we watch the two deities Hades and Nemesis flying off in their white veils to Olympus never to return, we can feel the full force and depth of the poet's vision.

Hesiod's morality was based upon experience, an experience both hard and cruel. He expressed it especially clearly in the fable of the hawk and the nightingale. In vain the bird of melody struggles in the savage claws that are bearing her away. The hawk says to her:

Miserable creature, why do you cry out? One far stronger than you now holds you fast, and you must go wherever I take you, songstress though you be. And if I please I will make a meal of you, or let you go. It is a fool who tries to withstand the stronger, for he does not get the mastery, and suffers pain besides his shame (208–9).

The two major themes of the poem, justice and work, are then developed at length, and Hesiod becomes even more didactic as he expounds the proper running of a farm and the different kinds of work in the fields, each with its appropriate season. He describes in detail how to make a plough and other agricultural implements, for in those days a peasant had to rely entirely on his own work and skill. Some of the advice he gives is completely disillusioned:

Do not let a flaunting woman coax and cozen and deceive you: she is only after your barns. The man who trusts womankind trusts deceivers.

Again and again, however, throughout *Works and Days* the great poet reveals himself, especially in passages like the description of the terrible winters in the country around Ascra:

Avoid the Leanaean month, wretched days fit to skin an ox, and the frosts which are cruel when Boreas blows over the earth, across horse-breeding Thrace, stirring up the wide seas, while earth and forest howl. On many a high-leafed oak and thick pine he falls and brings them to the bounteous earth in mountain glens. Then all the immense wood roars, and the beasts shudder and put their tails between their legs. . . . Only through the fleeces of sheep, with their abundant wool, Boreas pierces not; though it makes the old men bent like a wheel. Nor does it blow through the tender maiden, who stays indoors with her mother and is yet unlearned in the works of golden Aphrodite (504 ff.).

This is followed by sensible advice on navigation and maritime trading. And finally the *Works* give place to the *Days*, that is to say a detailed calendar of the days of the month that are lucky or unlucky for various tasks. Reading these curious recommendations, full of ancestral superstitions, reminds one of our old country proverbs and the peasant almanacs of the past.

For anyone who wishes to get an idea of the countryman's life in archaic Greece (and in subsequent periods it has only changed very slowly) the *Works and Days* is a document of exceptional interest. But it was not for this reason that Hesiod became, together with Homer and only a little below him, one of the classic poets whose work provided the spiritual nourishment of Greek youth from their earliest school days. The primary reason was that this peasant from Ascra had a genuine gift for expressing the afflictions of men as they went about their work in peacetime, just as Homer had sung of their sufferings in war and of their travels in distant countries.

THE *Homeric Hymns*

In the *Homeric Hymns*, preludes and mythical tales in honour of the gods of various sanctuaries, we once again encounter the diction, style and versification of the epic poets. They were called 'Homeric' because they were accepted as being the work of Homer, as I have indicated above in respect of the *Hymn to the Delian Apollo* (see p. 60). Thucydides attributed this hymn to the author of the *Iliad*, though it was undoubtedly written by one of the Homeridae, possibly Cynaethos of Chios. That the Greeks possessed hymns belonging to an earlier epoch cannot be doubted, for this kind of religious or liturgical poetry must have been as old as the gods of Hellas, though those that have been preserved do not seem to go back beyond the seventh century. Indeed, some of them were not written until the sixth century.

Homer was only moderately interested in religion, but this was not the case with his 'epigonoi', the Homeridae, who not only continued to weave the endless thread of the Epic Cycle, but also wrote hymns in honour of the gods. Some of these hymns, moreover, may have been commissioned by priests with a view to their being sung as part of the liturgy on ceremonial occasions. The Eleusinian origin of the *Hymn to Demeter*, like the Delian origin of the *Hymn to the Delian Apollo* and the Delphic origin of the *Pythian Suite*, can scarcely be doubted.

In these hymns the mechanical use of the formulary style and clichés of Homer is more frequent than in Hesiod because their authors are much less original. They were not, however, mere imitators. The three hymns I have just referred to, as well as the *Hymn to Aphrodite*, though certainly not the work of great poets, were nevertheless written by skilled versifiers not altogether lacking in talent; they are inspired by sincere belief; and they contain brilliant descriptive and narrative passages that are sometimes full of life and humour. In addition to this, the thirty-four hymns that have been preserved, even the shortest of them (some consist merely of a few lines of prelude), are of great interest for the history of religion.

The *Hymn to Demeter* is pervaded with a religious, almost hieratic, solemnity. It provides a vigorous and clearly arranged account of the Eleusinian myth, starting with the rape of Korê, Demeter's daughter, by Hades the god of the underworld.

Korê was playing with the deep-bosomed daughters of Oceanus and gathering flowers over a soft meadow, roses and crocuses and beautiful violets ... and the narcissus, which the earth made to grow at the will of Zeus ... a marvellous, radiant flower. ... And the girl was amazed and reached out with both hands to take the lovely toy; but the earth yawned there on the plain of Nysa, and Pluto, son of Kronos ... sprang out upon her, and caught her up reluctantly and bore her away lamenting on his golden chariot (5 ff.).

This scene, at first so charming but later becoming dramatic, is followed by the noble picture of Demeter's grief when her daughter is taken from her. She sets out in search of Korê and, quitting Olympus, wanders about the earth, disguised as an old woman.

Here follow local legends of Eleusis in Attica where Demeter stays awhile and is kindly received by the daughters of the king, who conduct her to their mother Metaneira. The goddess who is fasting (as later the candidates for initiation at Eleusis will have to fast) refuses the wine that is offered her, but gives the recipe for the ritual drink of the Mysteries, *kykeon*, a mixture of water, flour and peppermint. The hymn contains a number of other references to the Eleusinian rites.

Metaneira engages Demeter as nurse for her young son Demophon. Without telling his mother, Demeter decides to confer immortality on him (as will be the case with those participating in the Mysteries): one night she puts him in the fire, where Metaneira finds him and utters a cry of alarm. Annoyed by her lack of faith, Demeter abandons the child, then, reassuming the status of a goddess, gives orders for the building of her temple and announces the foundation of the Mysteries:

When she had spoken, the goddess changed her stature and her looks, thrusting old age away from her: beauty spread round about her and a lovely fragrance was wafted from her sweet-smelling robes, and from the divine body of the goddess a light shone afar, while the golden tresses spread down over her shoulders, so that the strong house was filled with brightness as with lightning. And so she went out from the palace. And

Metaneira's knees were loosed, and she remained speechless for a long time (275 ff.).

At last, since Demeter refuses to allow corn to germinate in the ground, Zeus insists upon Hades restoring Korê, who has become Persephone while in the underworld, though the magic properties of a pomegranate seed she has eaten will oblige her to return to spend part of each year with her husband, the lord of the Shades. Mother and daughter greet each other joyfully. Demeter, whose strike has turned out to be a successful piece of blackmail, makes the crops grow once more and entrusts Triptolemos and other heroes of Eleusis with carrying out 'the awful mysteries which no one may in any way transgress or alter': indeed, the Mysteries of Eleusis will remain secret and any divulgation of them will be punishable by death. The hymn ends with the following 'beatitude':

Happy is he among men upon earth who has seen these mysteries; but he who is unititiated and has no part in them has no such lot, once he is dead, down in the darkness and gloom (81–2).

Here, then, we have a poem closely connected with the ceremonies and initiation at Eleusis and with the aetiological myth that is at the heart of them, and with numerous allusions to the rites associated with the Mysteries. But at the same time the poet is aware of the pathetic nature of the rape of Korê and her mother's search for her, and now and then he succeeds in making us share his genuine emotion.

The *Hymn to the Delian Apollo* was certainly intended to be recited at the religious festivals on the sacred island, for it celebrates the birth of the god in Delos. The poem has plenty of charm and freedom, at well as a certain aloofness. Here is the moment of the god's birth:

And as soon as Eilithyia the goddess of sore travail set foot on Delos, the pains of birth seized Leto, and she longed to bring forth; so she cast her arms around a palm tree and kneeled on the soft meadow, while the earth laughed for joy beneath her. Then the child leapt forth into the light, and all the goddesses raised a cry (115–19).

Especially brilliant is the description of the great festivals, the *panegyria*, which brought together crowds of Ionians at the shrines of Leto and her two children, Apollo and Artemis:

Yet in Delos, Apollo, do you most delight your heart; for there the long-robed Ionians gather in your honour with their children and their shy wives, and delight you with their games, and with songs and dancing. . . . Seeing the graces of them all, a man would say they were deathless and unaging if he should come upon them so met together, and would delight in gazing at the men and well-girded women with their swift ships and great wealth. And there is this great wonder besides—and its renown shall never perish—the girls of Delos, hand-maids of the Archer; for when they have praised Apollo and Leto and Artemis, they sing of men and women of past days, and charm the tribes of men (146 ff.).

The 'Pythian Sequel' to this Delian hymn, which may also be regarded as an independent poem—a *Hymn to the Pythian Apollo*—describes the god leaving his native island for Olympus, and then journeying slowly through Greece looking for a suitable place to build his temple. Finally, after some hesitation, Apollo sets his heart on the site at Delphi. He takes possession of the ancient oracle of the Earth by killing the female dragon that guards it, saying: 'Perish!' (*pytheu*), whence were derived his name, Pythian, and also Pytho, the name by which Delphi was known to Homer. Then the god considers how to find priests for his new sanctuary. Seeing some Cretan sailors out at sea, he assumes the form of a dolphin (*delphis*) and, leaping on to the prow of their ship, forces them to put in at Crissa, the port for Delphi, and there reveals his intentions to them: they are to be the first priests of the Pythian Apollo.

The literary merits of this poem are inconsiderable, but the desire to establish a connection between the origin of the Delphic priesthood with the Minoan cults, and the concern to provide fantastic etymologies for the names Delphi and Pytho, are understandable. Here again we are concerned with an aetiological myth, intended to celebrate the founding of the great oracular shrine of central Greece.

The author of the first *Hymn to Aphrodite* begins by praising the cosmic power of the goddess of love:

Muse, tell me the deeds of golden Aphrodite the Cyprian, who stirs up sweet passion in the gods and subdues the tribes of mortal men, and birds that fly in the air, and all the many creatures that the dry land rears, and the sea. All these love the deeds of rich-crowned Cytherea (1–5).

There are, however, three virgin goddesses who are not susceptible to Aphrodite's charms: Athena, Artemis and Hestia, though Zeus himself willingly submits to them. He is determined that Aphrodite herself shall in turn yield to the love she inspires, by desiring the embraces of a mortal man. The hymn recounts at length—not without charm and with many fine touches—how the goddess fell in love with a Trojan, Anchises, a shepherd on mount Ida, to whom she bore a son, the hero Aeneas. This legend, already known to Homer, is developed with wit and, despite the audacity of the theme (which reminds us of Zeus' seduction in the *Iliad*), with a certain solicitude for the majesty of the gods.

The *Hymn to Hermes* is entirely different. It is certainly not lacking in zest and humour; and compared with the hymns to Demeter and Apollo, it has something of the effect of the 'satyr play' which, later on, was to accompany the performance of the tragic trilogies at Athens.

Hermes, the son of Zeus and the nymph Maia, 'cunning and subtle, brigand, thief, master of dreams, wanderer by night', leaves the cave of mount Cyllene in Arcadia, where he was born, on the very day of his birth. He begins by making the first lyre from the shell of a tortoise, then he steals Apollo's oxen from Pieria. To cover up their tracks, he makes the animals walk backwards and, for himself, invents a pair of curious wicker-work sandals. Then he returns to his cradle as though he were an innocent new-born child. Apollo, however, succeeds in finding him and wants to punish him, but Hermes disarms his wrath by making him laugh:

For, as Apollo seized him, he sent forth an omen, a hard-worked belly-serf, a rude messenger, and sneezed directly after. And when Apollo heard it, he dropped Hermes on the ground (294–8).

Here we are closer to the kind of humour that Aristophanes delighted in than to the religious gravity of the *Hymn to Demeter*: again and again we shall find Greek writers mixing the profane and sacred, sheer buffoonery and seriousness, in precisely the same way.

Zeus is called upon to decide between his two sons, but he too allows himself to be made fun of by the mischievous liar Hermes: 'Zeus laughed out loud to see his evil-plotting child well and cunningly denying guilt about the cattle' (289–90). And this curious and entertaining hymn concludes with the reconciliation of the two half-brothers, who exchange their divine attributes: Hermes presents his lyre to Apollo who in return allows him to look after the oxen. We may be sure that in future they will be well protected from thieves!

It is a question whether the epic hexameter, used by Homer, the poets

THE FIRST LYRIC POETS

of the epic cycle, Hesiod and the authors of the *Homeric Hymns*, was
actually invented in Greece or whether it was borrowed from elsewhere. In fact, the natural rhythm of the Greek language is not
dactylic ($-\smile\smile$) nor spondaic ($--$), but rather iambic ($\smile-$) or,
what amounts to the same thing, trochaic ($-\smile$). In any case, it is clear
that when the first Greek lyric poets sought to express their ideas,
impressions and emotions, they resorted to a great variety of rhythms,
amongst which the hexameter is scarcely to be found, except in the
elegiacs, where dactyllic hexameters and pentameters are used alternately.

Plutarch, who was familiar with the whole of Greek literature and
lived at a time when the number of works in existence far exceeded
the comparatively small remnant known to us, helps us, I think, by a
passage in his dialogue *On the Pythian Oracles*, where he is writing as
an historian and literary critic, to understand the birth of lyric poetry:

In those far away times, men were temperamentally endowed with a happy
propensity for poetry. The fervour of inspiration quickly took possession
of their souls, and such was their aptitude that the least external impulse,
the slightest stirring of the imagination, was enough for them to give
expression to it. It was not only astronomers and philosophers who found
themselves drawn to their habitual language, poetry:[1] stimulated by drink
or any lively emotion, under the sudden influence of feelings of grief or joy,
anyone, finding himself among friends, would readily resort to poetic
improvisation. Poetry and love songs played a large part in their festivities
and provided the material for books. When Euripides said: "Eros can make
even a country bumpkin a poet," he did not mean that Eros could confer a
talent for music and poetry on anyone, but that, when this talent was hidden
and inactive, he had the power of arousing and animating it. . . . But, today,
we can no longer, in the words of Pindar,
> Swiftly give utterance, in honour of boys,
> To hymns sweet as honey.'
> (*Moralia*, 405 E).

Such popular and spontaneous poetry is to be found in all countries
and at every period, from ancient Israel to modern Italy; and it was
undoubtedly the source of Greek lyric.

[1] The astronomers, Thales of Miletus and Eudoxos of Cnidus, and the philosophers,
Parmenides, Xenophanes and Empedocles, all wrote in verse.

The myths and legends that provide the basis for epic poetry are still found in the work of the lyric poets, but in this more personal kind of poetry they no longer occupy first place. On the other hand, while the rhapsodes who recited Homer's poems were content to accompany themselves with a kind of monotonous plain-song on the *kithara* (lyre), for the lyric poets music was of primary importance. It is true that this music has been lost and that all we have today are the words, yet it was often the musical accompaniment of these poems that constituted their chief merit, and we know that every lyric poet was first and foremost a musician.

While the inspiration of this new poetry was always personal, when it assumed choral form it could also be of public interest. The Greeks have always enjoyed singing and dancing. From very early times, throughout Hellas, choirs of young men or girls, accompanied by lyres and flutes,[1] took part in religious and civic ceremonies. No festival was complete without them.

The lyric poets expressed themselves, not in the traditional language of the epic, which was an artificial creation, but in their local dialect, for example Aeolic at Lesbos, Ionic at Smyrna or Ceos, and Doric at Sparta. This last town, traditional home of 'fine dancers', played such an important part in the development of the choral lyric that even at Athens, in the tragedies of the fifth century, the words sung by the chorus still retained Doric overtones.

There were many different kinds of lyric, though the same poet might often practise several of them. The personal lyric included the *elegy*, almost always grave and sententious, with a tendency to didacticism;[2] *iambic verse*, above all satirical and intentionally aggressive; and the *Lesbian ode*, expressing passion and the pleasure of the senses. The chief types of the choral lyric were: the *nome*, a liturgical song or hymn; the *paean*, with its grave and noble rhythms; the *prosodion* and the *partheneion*, processional songs; the *hyporcheme*, rhythmically swift and violent; the Dionysian *dithyramb*, a very lively cyclic chorus; the *epinikia*, victory songs in honour of the winners at the public games; and the *enkomia*, songs of praise for times of birth, marriage and mourning.

Terpander of Lesbos was a famous lyre player who mainly

[1] The *aulos* which we refer to by the customary term flute was in fact a reeded instrument, more like our oboe.
[2] It was only much later that the elegy became a literary form restricted to lovers' complaints. The etymology *hé legin* (to say alas) is worthless.

composed *nomes*. He seems to have lived at the beginning of the seventh century, and came to the mainland, notably Delphi and Sparta, where he held an important position as a teacher of music. So little of his poetry has been preserved that he is scarcely more than a name for us, however.

Tyrtaeus was from Aphidnae, but whether this was the town of that name in Attica or Laconia is not known. In any case, he lived at Sparta. His marching songs, a kind of *paean* sung by the soldiers as they attacked the enemy, and particularly his elegies, were well-known. He was above all an 'exponent of energy', the kind of martial energy that was held in honour in a primarily military city such as Sparta:

It is a fine thing to die, a brave man in the foremost rank, falling for his country. . . . Let us fight with all our heart for this land, let us die for our children and not spare our lives. Go to it, you young men, fight in your serried ranks! Let no man give the signal for fear or for flight! Forsake not your elders! It were shame upon you to see before your eyes an aged warrior fallen in the front rank, bald-headed with a white beard, shielding with his hand his sex streaming with blood, his body despoiled by the enemy. O hateful and abominable sight! But, for the young man, everything is seemly, so long as he is decked out in the shining flower of his youth: alive, men admire him and women are in love with him; and, if he dies in the foremost rank, his good looks persist. Stand firm, then, your legs well apart and your feet gripping the earth, and biting your lip between your teeth (*Elegies*, 6–7).

Clearly, in writing this elegy, Tyrtaeus had in mind the passage in the *Iliad* where Homer makes Priam say, referring to his own death: 'Ah, it looks well enough for a young man killed in battle to lie there with his wounds upon him: death can find nothing to expose in him that is not beautiful. But when an old man is killed and dogs defile his grey head, his grey beard and his privy parts, we plumb the depths of human degradation' (XXII, 71–6). This concern for the plastic beauty of the human body, even in death, is itself a significant indication of the profound aesthetic feeling of the Greeks.

In the elegies of Mimnermus of Colophon, we find an inspiration as different from that of Tyrtaeus as were the pleasure-loving Ionians from the austere Spartans. Mimnermus was a flute player who lived in the second half of the seventh century, and may have been known to Solon. When Mimnermus wrote: 'If only, when I am sixty, I could meet death and the Fates without illness and without sorrow', Solon replied that, in his opinion, it would be better to say 'at eighty' than 'at sixty'. Mimnermus had a horror of old age: again and again he repeats 'Better to die than to grow old!' There was a legend that Priam's brother, Tithonos, had received from Zeus the gift of immortality, but not of perpetual youth: 'Poor wretch!' commented Mimnermus 'the gods have granted him an eternity of misery.' The themes he preferred to sing of were the delights of youth, love and pleasure:

What life or pleasure can we know without golden Aphrodite? Would I might die when I lose the taste for secret loves, for their delightful and voluptuous gifts, the fine flowers of youth, beloved of men and women! (*Elegies*, I, 1–2).

Yet he knew all too well that the best period of a man's life lasts but a short while, and there is often an air of melancholoy sadness about his *carpe diem*. Like Homer, whose work he knew well, he compares man's ephemeral life with that of the leaves of the trees, that so soon fall to the ground and die:

Like the leaves that the flowery springtime puts forth in the sun's warmth, we delight in the flower of our youth for a fugitive moment. But soon the black Shades close in upon us, one bringing the sadness of old age, and the other, death. Too soon the fruit of youth goes rotten: hardly can it endure the fullness of the daytime. And once that bound is past, life becomes worse than death. . . . When the hour of his youth is gone, he who was lovely once is only an object of pity, even for children and friends (*Ibid.*).

The anguish of growing old, which haunted so many later poets, was never, perhaps, expressed with more force and simplicity.

ARCHILOCHOS

The Greek colonists did not always live in such distant countries as the shore of the Black Sea or those of Gaul and Spain. In the first quarter of the seventh century the rocky island of Paros, whose marble had not yet been exploited and whose inhabitants kept themselves alive on a niggardly diet of cereals, figs, and fish from the Aegean, sent some of its people to colonize Thasos, another island not far from the Thracian coast, which, with its rich soil, its woods and gold mines, seemed to the Parians to be a kind of Eldorado. The leader of the colonists was called Telesicles. He was the father of

Archilochos, but the poet never attempted to conceal the fact that he himself was a bastard, his mother being the slave girl Enipo. While this did not prevent Archilochos from enjoying the rights of citizenship, it deprived him of any hope of inheriting his father property, thus condemning him to a life of poverty.

Like all young Hellenes, Archilochos was brought up on Homer and Hesiod. His poetic gifts seem to have been precocious, and they gave rise to a curious legend, known to us from an inscription on the memorial dedicated to him by the people of Paros in the third century A.D., and recently discovered and published by a Greek scholar, N. M. Kontoleon. The monument formed part of a shrine to the Muses, or *Mouseion*, like those to Homer at Chios, to Hesiod on mount Helicon and to Mimnermus at Smyrna.

One moonlight evening, the young Archilochos, a simple ox-herd, was bringing a cow to town to sell. On the way he met a group of girls, but while he stood joking with them, suddenly both cow and girls disappeared from sight and in their place he found a lyre that had been placed at his feet. The symbolism is clear: the young women were the Muses and they had taken his cow in exchange for the lyre. The inscription goes on to recall Hesiod, to whom the Muses had also appeared at the threshold of his poetical career; and refers to the *Homeric Hymn to Hermes*, where the connection between shepherds and musicians or, as used to be said, 'between the crook and the lyre', is explained.

Archilochos told his father about his strange adventure, and the latter, having to go to Delphi to consult the oracle about the affairs of the city, took the opportunity of asking Apollo about this personal problem. The Pythia replied:

> One of your sons, Telesicles, shall become
> An immortal poet upon earth, he who shall first
> Salute you on your return to your own country.

And, naturally, when Telesicles landed at Paros, the first person to greet him was Archilochos!

Despite this legend, which seems to associate Archilochos with the poets of the epic period, his poetry was to prove very different from that of Hesiod or of the Homeridae. Today, alas, nothing remains of it but a few wretched fragments, enough however to let us catch a glimpse of the poet's rich and original personality.

Since the people of Paros were of Ionian origin, it was the Ionic dialect that formed the basis of Archilochos' poetic language. He continued to use the elegiac metre, but he also borrowed the rhythms of popular tradition, the iambic trimeter and the trochaic tetrameter; while in his *epodes* he employed combinations of a more sophisticated and varied couplet. His *Hymn to Heracles* begins:

To thee, lord Heracles, famed conqueror, hail, and to thee, Iolaos, both valiant warriors! To thee, famed conqueror, Heracles, all hail! (*Fragment* 298).[1]

This hymn was the best known of all, and the refrain *Tenella Kallinike* became a proverbial mode of address, which is often to be found in the comedies of Aristophanes.

Many of the citizens of Paros having perished in a shipwreck, amongst them one of the poet's brothers-in-law, he wrote a 'consolation' in the form of an elegy, which would be banal but for the couplet that was to shock Plutarch's moral sense:

> Since weeping will not cure my grief,
> Pleasure and feasting cannot make it worse (*Fragment* 5).

He was too frank and open-minded to care much about good taste or the conventions. To a courtesan, whose nickname, Pasiphilê, means 'dear to all', he wrote another couplet: 'Fig tree of the rocks, where many rooks delight to feed, How sweetly, Pasiphilê, you make your guests at home' (*Fragment* 11).

But it was with Neoboulê, the daughter of a well-known Parian citizen, that Archilochos fell in love, and he sang of his passion for her in burning words:

Hair and breast steeped in perfume, she would awake desire in an old man. . . . Wretched am I, unable to breathe, overwhelmed with desire, and the gods stabbing me to the bone with hideous suffering. . . . Now am I tamed by the longing that turns the bones to water: no longer am I moved by feasting or the delights of poetry. . . . O that I could seize Neoboulê in my arms , fling myself upon this burning wine-skin, thrusting belly against belly and thigh against thigh! (*Fragment* 38).

[1] This and the following references are to the edition by F. Lemerre and A. Bonnard, published in Paris (Trs.).

5. The temple of Hera at Olympia, c. 530 (pp. 69–70)

6. The Athenian Treasury at Delphi, *c.* 500 (pp. 121–2, 123)

Perhaps this last desire was prior to the rupture between them, for her father, who had promised his daughter to Archilochos in marriage, eventually changed his mind; whereupon the poet became furiously angry and from then on pursued both father and daughter with his bitter taunts. In one of his epodes he says to Neoboulê: 'No longer is your body in the freshness of its bloom; your skin has begun to fade, and the plough of old age is digging its furrows there' (*Fragment* 89), and he descends to the coarsest insults, comparing his one-time betrothed to an old lioness in search of young lovers, and describing her as a 'fat whore'. While of the father he says: 'What notions have got into your head, old Lycambos? Who has muddled your wits? Once you were a man of good sense: but now your fellow citizens gloat over you . . . You have broken your solemn word. . . . By Zeus, I may have been robbed of my wedding feast, but this man shall pay for all he has done to me.'

The poet also took his revenge in fables, a kind of poetry that Hesiod had essayed, but which Archilochos put to quite different purposes. In these he compares himself to a fox, and the 'sage Archilochos' cunning fox' passed into a proverb: we even find it in Plato's *Republic*.

Disappointed in love, still as poor as ever, Archilochos decided to become a soldier and set off for Thasos where the new city had to defend itself against its powerful neighbours. But, for all that, he did not forgo his calling as a poet: 'Though I have become a servant of mighty Ares, I remain a master in the charming domain of the Muses.' If he fought, it was first and foremost to ensure himself a living: 'It is on my lance that I depend for my ration of black bread and my wine of Ismaros, and it is on my lance that I lean as I drink it' (*Fragment* 8).

But in Archilochos' eyes military glory was an empty dream, and he always preferred a live dog to a dead lion: 'Once a man is dead, no one respects him any more, and he is forgotten by fame. . . . All that we have for the dead is our insults' (*Fragment* 7). Nor does he attempt to conceal the fact that on one occasion he threw away his shield so that he could run away more easily:

Today my shield is the pride of a Seian.[1] Despite my intentions, as soon as I found a suitable bush, I quit our admirable army. But I saved my life.

---

[1] The Seians were a tribe in Thrace where the Parian colonists of Thasos often campaigned.

Why should I worry about an old shield? All the worse for it: I can buy myself a new one, just as good (*Fragment* 117).

Obviously, we have come a long way from Achilles and Hector, and all the other heroes of the Trojan war. Yet this free and lively zest for life seems to have been prized by the ancients (who knew the whole of his work, not the poor fragment that remains today) almost as highly as Homer and Hesiod, as we may see from Plato's *Ion*.

From the social point of view, also, a new spirit can be sensed in his poetry. Though it may not be possible to find, in the few fragments that have been preserved, any formal protest, nevertheless one feels that this illegitimate son, condemned to so hard a life, was always opposed to the privileges enjoyed by the rich and powerful, like Lycambos. André Bonnard, however, was perhaps exaggerating when he spoke of Archilochos 'as the first mouthpiece of the efforts that were to lead to the collapse of the old aristocracies, to the flowering of the human being within the framework of popular sovereignty in the cities, and finally to the new struggle against tradition that the earliest philosophers, inspired by rational ideas, were to undertake.'

The poet who once threw away his arms to save his life, perished, it is said, in a battle between the armies of Thasos and Naxos, somewhere around 640, that is to say, about the date of Solon's birth in Athens.

3

TOWARDS DEMOCRACY

Sixth Century

I have given the people all the powers they need, neither
diminishing nor increasing their rights beyond measure.

SOLON: Elegy

HISTORICAL BACKGROUND

The sixth century still belongs to the archaic epoch, and is indeed a
continuation of it; yet after the long preparation of the seventh and
eighth centuries it was also a period when rapid developments were
taking place in every sphere of life, political, literary and artistic.
It was then, too, that science, philosophy, drama and literary prose
made their appearance for the first time. This sudden and vigorous
growth retained certain elements from the past, but, facing towards
the future, it was also the prelude to the triumph of democracy and
classicism.

Like the preceding century, it was notable for the continued Greek
colonization of the Mediterranean and the setting up of tyrannical
regimes in a number of cities. It was then, for example, that the
Milesians founded several towns on the Cimmerian Bosphorus, such
as Panticapaeum, the modern Kerch. It was also the age of Polycrates,
who thanks to Herodotus is today the best known of the 'tyrants',
and of Peisistratus of Athens who was almost contemporary with him.
Several of these tyrants it is true, considerably increased the strength
of their cities and governed with a wisdom and sense of proportion
not always to be found in the 'demagogues' of the fifth century.
Pittacus of Mytilene, a city in Lesbos, who was looked upon as a
tyrant, reformed the government, but resigned his authority as soon
as he considered his task to be completed. A contemporary of Solon,
he deserves to be reckoned with him amongst the Seven Sages of
Greece.

But it is the political and social developments in Athens that are

89

best known to us. At the beginning of the sixth century, Athenian society, despite the achievements of Dracon, was still disturbed by the oppressive measures imposed by the Eupatridae on the lower classes who were beginning to organize themselves for revolt. To put an end to their bloody uprisings, the parties finally succeeded in reaching agreement about the choice of an arbiter to reform the government; and in 594 Solon was appointed archon with supreme authority.

Solon's personality dominates the whole period, and as he was not only a statesman but also a great poet, part of whose writings have been preserved, we shall return to him later. Here, it need only be said that his social, political and economic reforms were of decisive importance for the whole future of Athens. Despite the intervening period of tyranny that was to separate him from Cleisthenes, it was Solon who, cautiously but definitively, led his countrymen towards the ideal of justice and equality. Yet wise as his reforms were, they could not completely eliminate the causes of party strife and his old age was darkened by prophetic signs of further tyrannical government. In 530, shortly before his death, Peisistratus seized the Acropolis.

From many points of view, however, Peisistratus who admired Solon's achievements was to pursue the same aims by different methods. In Aristotle's opinion he administered the State 'as a citizen, rather than a tyrant', with a genuine understanding of the public weal, and kindly moderation. By undertaking the provision of public buildings on a large scale, he gave a considerable impetus to the development of the arts, since architects, sculptors and a large number of craftsmen were involved in their construction. It was he and his son Hipparchos, surnamed *Philomousos*, Lover of the Muses, who instituted the Homeric recitations at the Panathenaia (see p. 60), and also the first dramatic performances at the Dyonisia. Towards artists, poets and scientists both father and son behaved like enlightened and generous patrons. Finally, by the boldness of his foreign policy, it was Peisistratus who laid the basis for Athenian domination, particularly in the Hellespont and the Aegean.

Shortly after 530, Peisistratus died in his bed, of an illness—an unusual and admirable end for a tyrant! He was succeeded, as in a monarchy, by his eldest son Hippias, who shared authority with his younger brother Hipparchos until, in 514, the latter was killed by Harmodias and Aristogeiton. Though the primary motive of this murder was homosexual jealousy (Hipparchos had made advances to the handsome Harmodios, Aristogeiton's lover), it was later to be celebrated as a great patriotic achievement, and the action of the 'tyrannicides' was attributed solely to their love of liberty.

After his brother's assassination, Hippias became hardened and began to rule as a real tyrant. His foreign policy met with setbacks and eventually the noble Athenian family of the Alcmaeonidae who were living in exile at Delphi persuaded the Oracle to urge the Spartans to undertake the liberation of Athens. Sparta obeyed the orders of the Pythian Apollo and in 510 Hippias was driven out of Athens by a foreign army which was supported by a number of noble emigrés as well as the liberty-loving people. Thus the way now lay open for the institution of a genuine democracy, such as Solon had only partly foreseen. The task was accomplished in 508 (a year after the traditional date of the establishment of the Republic in Rome), by one of the Eupatridae who had gone over to the popular side: Cleisthenes, the grandson of a tyrant of Sicyon.

The whole territorial organization of Attica was now profoundly modified by a new division of the urban and rural *demes*, which were henceforward grouped into ten tribes, while the older divisions simply disappeared—much as in France, at the time of the Revolution, the ancient provinces were replaced by departments. The Council, or Senate, now consisted of five hundred members—fifty from each tribe—and like the old Council of the Areopagus, was made up of archons who had completed their term of office, and was subject to the supreme authority of the Assembly (*ecclesia*), in which every free Athenian was entitled to a seat; every Athenian, that is to say, who was born of Athenian parentage and inscribed on the register of a *deme*. Finally, in the hope of preventing any reversion to tyranny, Cleisthenes instituted the curious procedure of *ostracism*, which gave the people power to banish, for a period of ten years, any citizen who was suspected by a majority of the *ecclesia* of aspiring to absolute power.

The revolution led by Cleisthenes opened a new era for Athens; and indirectly, for the whole of Greece. For, though all the cities did not adopt a democratic regime, many of them now began to look to Athens as the prototype of civil liberty and, especially after the battles of Marathon and Salamis, to imitate the institutions of the city which had taken the lead in the victorious resistance to the invaders.

ART

Ionian pottery of the sixth century, with its 'oriental' influences and its strings of animals arranged in bands reminiscent of the 'geometric' style, underwent considerable development and diversification, particularly the splendid *hydriae* found at Caere in Etruria. One of these has an entertaining illustration to the *Homeric Hymn to Hermes*: on the left in a kind of cave covered with branches are the cattle stolen from Apollo, while on the right the baby Hermes is asleep in his cradle, beside which stand a bearded man and two women engaged in animated discussion and gesticulating energetically. Another *hydria* from Caere, not so well made and badly mutilated, shows Nestor nominating the ambassadors who are to visit Achilles, a scene from Book IX of the *Iliad*.

Many of the vase-painters of this period had a predilection for scenes from the epic poems, as may be seen from the famous 'François Vase' in Florence, a large, black-figured *crater*, or mixing bowl. For this the painter, Cleitias, chose as his principal subject the marriage of Thetis and Peleus, a scene comprising almost two hundred and fifty figures, whose identities are indicated by upwards of a hundred inscriptions. Here, white is used in a number of places, especially for the faces and arms of the women and goddesses. Though still somewhat stiff and awkward, it is a splendid example of the art of the miniaturist, displaying an extraordinary realism even in the smallest details.

To the third quarter of the century belong the vase paintings of Execias, like the amphora showing Achilles and Ajax playing at dice, and another on which the Dioscuri are represented with their mother Leda and their human father Tyndareus. These two works, as well as several others, are of admirable workmanship.

Towards the end of the century, the painter Nicosthenes began to employ new techniques, such as covering the natural clay with white slip in order to throw the black figures into stronger relief. Such experiments foreshadowed the later red-figured vases of the fifth century.

After the shadowy beginnings of the eighth and seventh centuries, architecture now burst into full flower. The tyrants were intent upon beautifying their towns and they also increased the number of utilitarian projects, especially those concerned with the provision of water, so rare and precious a commodity in Greece: Peisistratus transformed the spring of Kallirrhoe into a monumental fountain with nine mouths, while Polycrates employed Eupalinos of Megara to build the famous aqueduct of Samos, which flowed through a tunnel nearly a thousand feet in length. But, above all, the whole of Hellas was now covered with a series of magnificent temples, built of tufa, limestone or marble.

The severe and masculine Doric order was dominant in Greece itself, and even appeared on the Asian coast, at Assos, across the water from Lesbos. Corinth built its temple of Apollo; Argos, the temple of Hera. At Delphi, the Alcmaeonidae undertook the reconstruction of the ancient temple of Apollo, which had been destroyed by fire in 548, giving it a marble façade; while at Marmaria, the temple of Athena Pronias was also rebuilt. A number of 'treasuries', temples in miniature, were also built in the various pan-Hellenic sanctuaries, like that of Megarus in the Altis, the sacred grove of Olympia; or those of Sicyon, Cnidos and Siphnus in the Delphic sanctuary of Apollo.

On the Acropolis at Athens, Peisistratus began to build a temple a hundred feet long (and therefore called the *Hecatompedon*) which at the time of Hippias' overthrow was still not completed and which was later burnt down by Xerxes. In the lower town, Peisistratus also undertook the ambitious construction of the huge *Olympeion*, which was only to be finished, seven centuries later, by the Emperor Hadrian. But the best preserved of these sixth-century temples are to be found in Sicily and southern Italy, above all at Selinus and Paestum.

In Asia and the coastal islands the Ionic order triumphed. Here, the more slender and ornate columns rest on a base and are crowned by elegant voluted capitals; and, compared with the robust virility of the Doric columns, present an almost effeminate appearance. The most famous temples of Ionia, both for their size and their rich ornamentation, were the Artemesion at Ephesus and the great temple of Hera at Samos.

Temples and treasuries were decorated both with sculpture in the round (cult statues, caryatids and acroteria) and with bas-reliefs (friezes and pediments). In the course of the sixth century, the art of sculpture made even more astonishing progress than painting and architecture. At Delphi, the art of the Argive school may be seen in the statues of Cleobis and Biton, the sons of a priestess of Hera at Argos, whose story was later to be told by Herodotus. The arms of the two young men are held close to their sides, but they are tensed with the effort of drawing a chariot. In representing the powerful muscles of these robust athletes, the artist still relied on partly archaic methods, such as the incised line outlining the chest.

At Delphi, too, better than elsewhere, it is possible to trace the evolution of a style that was to lead to an ever truer and more lively representation; from the Sicyon metopes, through the Cnidos caryatids to the Siphnos carvings. The stylization inseparable from archaism gives these works, in which the effect of awkwardness and stiffness is only gradually eliminated, a powerful originality. Taken as a whole, the most remarkable of the three works is the frieze of the Siphnos treasury, especially the *Gigantomachia*, which reveals an art already sure of itself, full of sturdy vigour, as well as a tendency towards ostentation.

While the statue of Hera discovered at Samos still resembles a column, and is clearly derived from the ancient *xoana* that were carved from tree trunks, the Winged Victory at Delos, also dating from the first half of the sixth century, reveals an entirely new attempt to represent in stone the movements of flight and of running.

The influence of Ionia, at that time more civilized and refined than Greece itself, became the preponderant one throughout Attica. At Athens, in the Museum of the Acropolis, the visitor is at first disconcerted by the rigid figures and harsh polychromy of the archaic pediments, like the one representing the struggle between Heracles and the Triton, but the marvellous Ionic *Korai*, also polychromatic, immediately delight him. These young girls, with their rather fixed smiles, seduce us by the supple modelling of the flesh, the minute carving of the abundant hair that falls over their shoulders and breasts, and the elegant draping of their thin tunics and the heavy folds of their cloaks.

Lastly, two recent discoveries, made in 1952 and 1959 prove that in the second half of the sixth century the Greek bronze moulders had attained an even more astonishing mastery than the carvers in marble. The famous Vix mixing-bowl, found in France near Châtillon-sur-Seine, is 1 m. 64 cm. in height and weighs about 450 lbs. The handles are sumptuously decorated with two Gorgons' busts, ending in serpents' tails, and the neck, with a frieze of alternating hoplites and four-horsed chariots; while there is also a remarkable figure of a woman that was originally on the cover. The second discovery, the *kouros* from Piraeus, is a splendid nude Apollo, 1 m. 90 cm. in height, of which Jean Charbonneaux has said: 'When one remembers that the

Apollo of Piombino, 1 m. 15 cm. high and dating from about 490 B.C., has hitherto been regarded as the oldest of the great Greek bronzes, one appreciates the full importance of a statue that is not only considerably larger but also some thirty to forty years older.'

SOLON

Unless Tyrtaeus was born in Attica, which is not certain, Solon was the first of the Athenian poets and writers, and the two hundred and fifty odd lines of his poetry that have come down to us enable us to form a pretty good idea of his vigorous talent and rich personality.

Born about 640, of a noble but impoverished family, Solon, who is the subject of one of Plutarch's most valuable *Lives*, actually belonged to the middle class, a fact that was to prove of advantage to him in his role of arbiter between the Eupatridae and the *thetes* or proletarians. From his youth he travelled widely, partly to acquire knowledge, partly to make money by maritime trade. But he appreciated material wealth at its true value, considering as equally happy both 'the man who possesses masses of gold and silver, fertile wheatfields, horses and mules, and he who has only his natural vigour—a healthy stomach, strong flanks and sound feet—and, in due course, the beauty of a boy or a woman; thus is happiness complete' (Bergk: II, 24, *Fragment* 14, 1–5).

Clearly, he was a sage who did not despise the pleasures of life; and, as a poet, he sometimes gave free reign to his sensuality, not disdaining 'boys in the flower of their youth' and 'longing for the sweetness of thigh and lip' (*Fragment* 25, 1). However, as he grew older, he foreswore 'Grecian love' and was content to love women, wine and poetry: 'Today, I delight in the works of the Cyprian, of Dionysus and the Muses, sources of man's delight' (Bergk: II, 26, *Fragment* 20). And Plutarch assures us that, 'having escaped from the tempests of homosexual loves, he established himself in the calm waters of marriage and philosophy' (*Amatorius* 751 E), a rare enough combination in Greece, where philosophy so often set up house, so to speak, with pederasty.

Back from his youthful journeys, we see him at first as an ardent and militant patriot. Athens, at war with Megara, had been obliged to give up the island of Salamis, and any attempt to renew hostilities was forbidden by a decree, on pain of death. Solon secretly composed an elegy of a hundred lines on the subject, and then, feigning madness and dressed in a fantastic costume, went into the streets to proclaim his poem which began: 'I come as herald from friendly Salamis, to sing you a song by way of a speech' (Bergk: II, I, *Fragment* 2, 1–2). His burning words, it would appear, persuaded the Athenians to abrogate the decree and once again to declare war which ended with the re-conquest of Salamis from the Megarians. Whereupon, in order to establish Athens' 'historical claim' to the island more firmly, he is said to have forged a couple of hexameters and inserted them in the 'Catalogue of Ships' in the *Iliad*, (see p. 9).

But when, in 594, his countrymen elected him Archon, it was to home affairs and legal reform that he primarily devoted himself. This provided him with further opportunities of using his lyre as a weapon to spread his ideas and defend his laws, for many of his poems, though not lacking in bold imagery and real poetic drive, are more like pamphlets or propaganda leaflets. When certain Athenian 'realists' mocked him for failing to seize the occasion of his archontate to make himself tyrant, this is how he expressed this outlook:

Solon is neither wise nor cunning, for he has refused the fine gifts the gods offered him. The fool did not know how to draw in his net when it was full: he lacked both the wit and the courage. Otherwise, in return for being rich, powerful and tyrant of Athens for but a single day, he would have consented to be flayed alive on the morrow, though his race had perished with him Bergk: II, 33, *Fragment* 23, 1–7).

Had anyone but he been granted supreme power, he says elsewhere, 'he would not have held back the people nor been content till he had churned the cream to make butter for himself. But I stood firm, like a boundary stone between two armies' (*Fragment* 25, 6–7). This is borne out by Aristotle: 'Solon stood out against both parties and, at a time when he could have become tyrant by allying himself with which of them he cared to choose, he preferred to make himself detested by both, so long as he could save his country and furnish it with sound laws' (*Constitution of Athens* XII, 2).

His policy of the golden mean we find expressed in these lines:

I have given the people all the powers they need, neither increasing nor diminishing their rights beyond measure. As for the mighty, envied for their wealth, I have been at pains to do them no injustice. Both parties have

I covered with my stout shield, preventing either from winning an unfair victory (Bergk: II, 5: *Fragment* 25, 6–7).

An even prouder note is struck in an iambic poem in which he prides himself that, by abolishing debt, he had at once saved the Athenians, who had become little better than serfs, and freed the country itself:

Did I stop short, then, before achieving the aim for which I united my people? She best may bear witness before the tribunal of Time, venerable mother of the Olympian gods, the black Earth, from whom I tore up the landmarks set on every side: yesterday but a slave, today she is free. I have brought back to Athens, to this country founded by the gods, many a man who had been sold into slavery or driven into exile; many who had wandered so long in foreign lands that they had forgotten their mother tongue. . . . And all this have I done solely by the power of the Law. . . . Putting forth all my strength, I have bestirred myself on every side, like a wolf beset by a pack of hounds (*Fragment* 24, 1–27).

Having established his code of laws, for the next ten years Solon once again lived far away from Athens. During this time he appears to have travelled in Egypt, Cyprus and, perhaps, Lydia, always curious like Odysseus 'to visit the cities of mankind and to know their minds'. Returning to his own country, he must have realized sadly that once again civil strife was beginning to raise its head and could only lead to the victory of Peisistratus. He lashed his countrymen for their cowardice in refusing to defend their liberties: 'You let yourselves be fascinated by the tongue and speeches of a knave. Alone each of you steps warily as a fox, but once you get together you have nothing but an empty mind' (*Fragment* 8, 5–8).

When the tyranny was ultimately established, he did not bow before it, but continued to address his stinging reproaches to the people of Athens: 'Only your cowardice is the cause of your wretched lot: don't try to blame the gods. These men, you have yourselves protected and puffed up, forging this shameful slavery for yourselves' (*Fragment* 8, 1–4). Though already an old man, he never ceased to be interested in everything that was going on: 'In my old age I am ever more eager to learn.' He died in his eighties, admired on every side: even Peisistratus is said to have respected him.

Thus Solon put every aspect of himself into his poetry, his intransigeant patriotism, his love of liberty, his ideals adapted to men's potentialities (which earned him his place amongst the Seven Sages of Greece), his curiosity and open-mindedness, his robust loyalty, and also the frank enjoyment of the pleasures of the senses that makes him so living and highly coloured a personality.

SAPPHO

Sappho (or, in her native Aeolian dialect, Psappho) was almost contemporary with Solon: she reached the height of her powers at the end of the seventh and the beginning of the sixth centuries. She was the only great poetess of ancient Greece, for Corinna of whom practically nothing is known now appears not to have been the contemporary of Pindar as was previously believed, but to have lived in the Hellenistic era.

By the mere fact of her sex and her genius, therefore, Sappho is an exceptional figure in Greek history. Strabo was to speak of her as a 'wonder'; in an epigram in the *Anthology*, attributed to Plato, she is referred to as the 'tenth Muse'; while the Ancients regarded her poetry as belonging to the first rank, alongside that of Homer—a judgment that is not belied by what little of it remains.

Like Terpander, who before her time had brought renown to the lyric school of Lesbos, she was born in one of the towns on the island, either Eresos or Mytilene, and belonged to the aristocracy. In Aeolia, the way of life was certainly very different from that of Greece itself: it may be assumed that women were allowed far greater freedom than in Athens, and that the daughters of the rich and noble families were as well educated as the men, but in special schools reserved for girls. Sappho, it would appear, was herself in charge of a kind of residential college for girls, that reminds one of Madame de Maintenon's establishment at Saint-Cyr, though its aims and principles of education were certainly quite different.

Sappho married and had a daughter Cleis. She was banished from Lesbos where civil war was rife and went to Syracuse, but her exile does not seem to have lasted long. She lived to a considerable age, for in one of the fragments that has been preserved, she complains of the drawbacks of growing old. Her unrequited love for the handsome Phaon and her suicide by throwing herself from the Leucadian rock, are purely legendary. Though in Plato's *Phaedrus*, Socrates calls her 'the lovely Sappho', she probably owed her reputation for beauty to the splendour of her poetry and her power of evoking love, since the oldest accounts describe her as being small and swarthy. But her unattractive appearance concealed a fiery spirit and an incomparable musical and poetic genius.

Here is the *Prayer to Aphrodite*, the only complete poem of hers that has come down to us:

You of the sparkling throne, O immortal Aphrodite, daughter of Zeus, hatcher of plots, I beseech you, my queen, let not loathing or grief afflict my heart.

Come to me now, you that listened to my voice in the past and came at my behest, leaving the golden dwelling of your father

And harnessing your chariot: and your fine swift sparrows drew you round the darkling earth, beating their multitudinous wings, and, from the height of heaven, drove straight through the ether,

Till suddenly you were here. Then you, O blessed one, your immortal face lit up with a smile, asked me what was this new tribulation, why once again had I cried out to you,

And what burning desire was ravaging my crazy heart: 'Who is she that you beg once more, me, the Persuader, to fetch for your loving? Who is it, my Sappho, that is wronging you?

'Speak: if she flees from you now, soon she shall pursue you; if she rejects your gifts, she shall offer you her own; if she does not love you now, she soon shall, even if it be against her will.'

So, once again, come to me, free me from my bitter longing, grant me my heart's desire, and, in this battle, stand once more at my side (Rheinach-Puech ed.: *Fragment* 1).

In this poem, certain mannerisms and the conventional use of mythology perhaps slightly veil the passionate sincerity of the feeling, but in the famous *Ode* it bursts forth in all its nakedness:

> In my eyes he is the equal of the gods,
> He who sits close at your side,
> Savouring the sweetness of your voice
> And the charm

Of that laugh that pierces my heart,
Till it beats in my very lips.
I have only to see your face,
And my voice cracks.

My tongue goes dry in my mouth,
Fire burns beneath my skin,
And my ears grow suddenly deaf,
My eyes blind.

My whole body is drenched with sweat,
I tremble from head to foot;
My cheeks turn green as the grass,
And I feel I shall die.

(*Ibid.* 2)

This poem, in which the physical effects of passion are expressed
in a manner at once so striking and so simple, was as famous in antiquity as the finest passages from the *Iliad* or the most renowned
choruses of Sophocles and Euripides, and many Greeks knew it by
heart. Thus Plutarch, in his *Dialogue on Love*, speaking to his young
friend Daphnis who has just become betrothed to Lysandra, says
lightheartedly: 'My dear Daphnis, if Lysandra has not made you
completely forget your old loves, why not recall to mind those lines
of the lovely Sappho, where she describes how, at the sight of her
beloved, she loses her voice, her body feels on fire and, growing
suddenly pale, she is overwhelmed with bewilderment and dizziness,'
—and, thereupon, Daphnis at once recites this ode (*Amatorius* 763 A).

These same lines, imitated in Rome by Catullus and Lucretius,
were quoted by the author of the *Treatise on the Sublime* to whom we
owe their preservation; and they were also frequently translated into
French in the sixteenth and seventeenth centuries, notably by Boileau.
Racine, too, was undoubtedly familiar with them, for he makes
Phèdre say:

Je le vis: je rougis, je pâlis à sa vue;
Un trouble s'éleva dans mon âme éperdue;
Mes yeux ne voyaient plus, je ne pouvais parler:
Je sentis tout mon corps et transir et brûler.

I saw him: I flushed and grew pale at sight of him.
Bewilderment rose in my distracted soul;

My eyes no longer saw, and I could not speak:
I felt my whole body burn and grow chill.

Several fragments enable us to form some idea of the establishment that Sappho directed. It was a kind of 'sorority' (*thiasoi*), dedicated to the Muses, the Graces and Aphrodite, in the same way that Plato's Academy was later placed under the patronage of Athena, Eros and the Muses, for in antiquity every cultural organization also had a religious character. Sappho herself called her college 'the house of the servants of the Muses'. Now, music (*mousikê*), the art of the Muses, included not only music and the dance, but the whole of scientific, literary and artistic culture. Thus dedication to the Muses, as well as to Aphrodite and the Graces, already implied a considerable programme of study. Yet, though Sappho's pupils learned music, dancing and poetry, it was not with a view to becoming professionals, but in order to develop their personality, for most of them, like Sappho herself, would eventually marry.

The poetess was therefore a teacher who considered that the best education was one inspired by love. Socrates was to take more or less the same view, but while he insisted that this love should remain purely of the spirit, it is by no means certain that this was so with Sappho and her lovely pupils. 'What did the Lesbian Sappho teach, if not love?' Ovid was to ask. And certainly the Ancients scarcely leave us in any doubt as to the intimate nature of the passion felt by 'masculine Sappho, lover and poet', as Baudelaire calls her; and since they could read the whole of her work, and not just the fragments known to us, they were in a better position than us to form an opinion.

Gyrinno, Atthis, Anactoria, Gongyla, Arignota, all these girls flit like delicate and charming shadows through her poems, dazzling her with their beauty:

The sight of Anactoria, with her graceful walk, the radiant glow of her face, delighted me more than all the chariots of the Lydians, and their warriors in their armour charging on foot. . . . (*Ibid.* 27, 15–20).

Come back, I beg of you, Gongyla, that I may see you in your milk-coloured tunic. O what longing floats upon your beauty ! Whoever sets eyes upon her, thrills at her coaxing. And I, I rejoice, for it is the Cyprian goddess herself who thus reproaches you, she whom I call upon in my prayers. . . . (*Ibid.* 36)

The moon has gone down, and the Pleiades also; it is the middle of the night. The hours draw out, and here on my bed I lie alone. . . .

O that this night might last the length of two. . . . (*Ibid.* 74)

You have done well to come: I have been longing for you. Like a spring of water you well up in my soul, aflame with desire. Welcome, my Gyrinno! (*Ibid.* 46)

The erotic quality of these lines is scarcely to be doubted. First and last, love is Sappho's central theme, and she associates it with the forces of nature and everything in the universe, for these are inseparable for her from the emotion and torment she experiences. Water, fire, flowers, the sun and the stars are constantly evoked in her poems, linked with the delight and suffering of the heart by subtlely concealed associations, that already impart to her poetry an accent of modernity.

OTHER LYRIC POETS

The name of Alcaeus is inseparable from that of Sappho. Born like her of a noble family in the island of Lesbos, he was her exact contemporary and we know, moreover, that he knew her. There is little likelihood, indeed, that their meeting, as depicted on a splendid vase dating from about 480, a *calathos* now in Munich, was only a legend. Alcaeus was in love with Sappho, but she rejected him. He declared his love in a poem of which only a few words have been preserved: 'Purest Sappho, of the violet locks and tender smile. . . . I long to speak to you, but shame prevents me' (*Fragment* 64). To which Sappho replied in another poem, refusing him: 'If the desire in your heart was for goodness and beauty only, if your tongue had never spoken an evil word, shame would not veil your eyes' (*Fragment* 160). Sappho was married and the lovers she took were not young men.

Alcaeus wrote hymns to the gods: to the Pythian Apollo, Hermes, Athena, Aphrodite and Eros. But his most personal poems were inspired by the experiences of a restless life, in which politics, war and adventure, as well as pleasure, all had a part. Like Sappho he was exiled, but more frequently and for longer periods it would seem: and for a time he retired to Egypt. Having actively participated in the civil wars between the cities of Lesbos during the troubled period that preceded the government of Pittacus (see p. 89ff.), he refused the amnesty offered by this generous tyrant, and remained irreconcilably opposed to him. He did not return to Lesbos until after Pittacus' abdication.

Alcaeus also fought in the war against Athens, when she was disputing the Lesbian claim to Sigeum in the Troad. We know of this from Herodotus: 'During an encounter in which the Athenians were winning, the poet Alcaeus took to his heels and escaped from the battle, leaving his arms in the hands of the Athenians, who hung them on the wall of the sanctuary of Athena at Sigeum. Alcaeus wrote a poem about this, which he sent to Mytilene: in it, he described to a friend, Melanippos, what had happened to him' (*Histories* v, 95).

In several of the fragments of his work that have been preserved, Alcaeus' bitter invective expresses the violent feelings of a party politician. On the death of the tyrant Myrsilos, he joyfully exclaimed: 'Now let us drink our fill and get drunk, for Myrsilos is dead' (*Fragment* 55)—an unusual funeral oration. Nor did he spare Pittacus: 'This peasant's son, Pittacus, everyone joins in acclaiming him, and now they have set him up as the tyrant of our comely and ill-starred city' (*Fragment* 110).

But it was not only to celebrate the death of a hated tyrant that Alcaeus used to drink: he found excuses for carousing all the year round:

Come, let us drink, for the sun is at its zenith. . . . Zeus hurls down rain, the heavens unleash winter, and the rivers are frozen over. Bring winter to its senses by lighting the fire, and then let us fill our cups to the brim with wine and set soft pillows beneath our heads (*Fragment* 62).

I hear the footsteps of the flowering spring. Quick, quick, mix me a bowl of wine with a dash of honey (*Fragment* 91).

Moisten your throat with wine, for the summer's star has risen: this is the hard season of the year, when the heat makes everything thirsty. Hidden amongst the leaves, softly the cricket chirps, and from the shade of its wings freely scatters its clear song, while the sun spreads its flames over the earth, drying up everything. The thistle is in flower: this is the time when women are filled with longing and men languish, when Seirios drains the strength from your mind and slackens your knees (*Fragment* 111).

Though parts of this last fragment are borrowed from Hesiod's *Works and Days*, Alcaeus' tone is usually extremely personal; and whether he is writing of the black hair and eyes of the young boy Lycos, or describing the beauty of a woman's body, his verse takes on a rich sensuality, for like so many Greeks he enjoyed the beauty both of women and young men.

The poet Stesichoros owed even more to Hesiod, but above all to Homer. His real name was Teisias, and his pseudonym means 'Chorus master'. He was probably born at Himera in Sicily. His best known poems were hymns, not in honour of the gods, but of the heroes, and were sung by a choir to the accompaniment of a lyre but without dance movements. In them he celebrated the adventures of the great mythological and epic heroes in a new and original manner. From several points of view, Stesichoros may be regarded as a forerunner of Pindar.

In the *Geryoneis* the poet describes Heracles sailing in the golden cup of the Sun in search of Geryon's oxen, and other hymns were called *Cerberus*, *Scylla*, the *Boar Hunt*, the *Capture of Ilium*, the *Return* and the *Oresteia*. But it was the *Helena*, with its famous palinode, which gave rise to the curious legend recorded by Plato in his *Phaedrus*. Socrates, believing himself to have spoken ill of love, considered that 'a palinode was necessary in expiation' and declared that he must first purify himself after the example of the poet Stesichorus. The latter, 'having had his eyes put out for maligning Helen, was not, like the blind Homer, unable to explain his misfortune. Inspired by the Muses, he understood the cause of his affliction, and hastened to write these lines: "No, there is no truth whatever in this story! No, you never embarked on the well-laden ships; nor were you welcomed within the Trojan ramparts!" And as soon as he had finished this palinode, Stesichoros immediately recovered his sight' (*Phaedrus* 243 a–b). Thus Stesichoros forestalled Euripides who in his tragedy *Helena* was also to maintain that the daughter of Zeus had never been to Ilium and that for ten years Greeks and Trojans had simply been fighting over her ghost.

Alcman was born at Sardis in Lydia but like Tyrtaeus he spent most of his life in Sparta and wrote in the Doric dialect. His best known poems were choral lyrics, *partheneia*, hymns intended to be performed by choirs of young girls. The short fragments that we still possess suggest that his poetry was graceful and intimate, though rather commonplace, a long way from the fire of Sappho or the audacity of Alcaeus. It is only in certain descriptions of nature, somewhat reminiscent of Hesiod, that he approached greatness:

Everything is asleep: the mountain tops and their depths, headlands and streams, and the swarming reptiles that feed on the black earth, and the whole tribe of bees and the monsters of the sea; even the birds on their great wings have succumbed to sleep (Bergk: *Fragment* 60).

With Arion, who may have been a disciple of Alcman, we find ourselves back in the island of Lesbos, for he seems to have been born there, at Methymna. He played the lyre and mainly wrote Dionysian *dithyrambs*, a kind of choral lyric from which tragedy was eventually to develop.

He travelled a great deal and, like Alcman, spent some time at Sparta, but lived mainly at Corinth at the court of the tyrant Periander. Thence he made a journey into Italy, whence, having made a lot of money, he returned to Greece in a Corinthian ship. It was then that he experienced the miraculous adventure recounted by Herodotus (*Histories* I, 24): having been granted the favour of singing a farewell song and still wearing the splendid costume of a lyre player, he leapt into the sea, where a dolphin, charmed by his music, picked him up and bore him on its back to cape Taenaron. . . . We are not necessarily obliged to believe every word uttered by the 'father of history', though in this case he adduces as evidence 'a small bronze *ex voto* of Arion, that could be seen at Taenaron, representing a man astride a dolphin'.

Anacreon was born at Teos, an Ionian city in Asia Minor, and reached maturity in the second half of the sixth century. He lived at Samos, at the same time as another poet, Ibycos of Rhegium, under the patronage of Polycrates; and also in Athens, where, at the court of Peisistratus' son Hipparchus, he was a friend of Xanthippus the father of Pericles. He was a typical court poet, agreeable, frivolous and brilliant, and he succeeded in maintaining his sprightliness and gaiety into old age, dying at the age of eighty-five. Asked one day why he did not write hymns to the gods like the poets of the past, but instead to beautiful youths, he replied: 'Because they *are* our gods.'

Indeed, Eros was Anacreon's favourite god: 'I sing of tender Eros with his flowery crowns, master of the gods and tamer of men.' And the capricious god mocks at those whose hearts he touches: 'I love and I love not: at one moment I am full of desire, then suddenly I feel none.'

He delighted to linger 'within the budding grove' of young girls, to one of whom he addressed this graceful appeal:

Why do you look at me askance, my little Thracian mare, breaking away so swiftly? Do you take me for a clumsy rider? I could harness you perfectly, I tell you, turning you at the end of the stadium with a touch of the reins. Grazing in the fields, light as the wind you rear and cavort; but what you need is a skilled horseman, who would break you in (*Fragment* 75).

Having been turned down by another girl, he good-humouredly commented:

Golden-haired Eros threw me a purple ball and invited me to play with the young girl in embroidered sandals, but she, born in lovely Lesbos, seeing my white hair, only mocked me, and turned away, open-mouthed, to another man (*Fragment* 14).

When he wanted to, Anacreon could write with savage humour. One of his principal butts was a certain Artemon, his successful rival for the favours of the beautiful Eurypyle:

Now the fair-haired Eurypyle no longer disdains the illustrious Artemon. Once he used to go about, hiding his bloody head in a coarse hood, with wooden ear-rings, and a dirty second-hand shield of ox-hide on his back; and many a time he's been tied to the whipping post and put to the wheel, his back scarred with weals, beardless and bald. But, today, this son of Kykos gets into his chariot, wearing golden ear-rings and carrying an ivory parasol like a woman (*Fragment* 21).

Anacreon was so well-known that, like Alcaeus and Sappho, he is often to be found depicted on vases, and it may well be that the lines I have just quoted inspired the artist of the amphora in the Louvre (G 220) which on one side shows the portrait of a man playing the lyre and on the other a bearded man carrying a parasol.

In fifth-century Athens there were many readers who appreciated the beauty of these Ionian and Aeolian poets. In his *Thesmophoriazousae* Aristophanes for example says: 'To think that those famous poets, Ibycos, Anacreon of Teos and Alcaeus, whose lyrics have so sweet a savour, wore women's *mitrai* and led sensual lives after the fashion of Ionia.' Indeed, such was Anacreon's renown that he has been repeatedly imitated. A whole collection of poems inspired by him, the *Anacreontica*, has come down to us; and many of these vivacious, witty odes—*To his Lyre, The Silver Cup, Love and the Bee*—were later to serve as models for English and French poets, notably the members of the *Pléiade*. This imitation at second remove, so to speak, is the finest homage that could be paid to a poet whose original work time has so badly mutilated.

The collection of elegies by Theognis of Megara differs in every respect from the *Anacreontica*. It contains nearly fourteen hundred lines, but as these include recognizable passages from Solon, Mimnermus and Tyrtaeus, it is impossible to determine exactly which parts are the authentic work of Theognis himself.

However, the lines addressed to Cyrnos are undoubtedly his. Cyrnos was a young man of noble birth whom Theognis sought to prepare for life by describing to him his own experience, but the elegies reached a much wider public, for they were sung to the accompaniment of the lute at the banquets of the *hetairai* which served as meeting places for the aristocracy.

Theognis was a doctrinaire and fanatical politician. He had been horrified by the popular revolt that took place about the year 570 during his youth at Megara. In his eyes, the democrats stood for everything that was bad, and his first advice to Cyrnos was to shun them like the plague. He could not refer to them without hatred and invective, while those born into the aristocracy he looked upon as repositories of all the virtues, provided they did not marry beneath them:

'Look, Cyrnos: we select true-bred rams, donkeys and stallions to mate with pure-blooded females, yet there are men of quality who do not scruple to marry women simply for their wealth, with the result that good blood is mixed with bad (183 ff.).

Theognis was a hard, bitter and disillusioned man. He forbade hope and preached vengeance, and his didacticism was cold and pedantic. Yet to his pupil Cyrnos he always spoke like a father, with a tenderness comparable to that of Sappho for her lovely young girls:

Do not be content to love me only in words, while your heart and thoughts are set on others. Either love me with sincere affection, or hate me frankly. . . . I feel you have not the least consideration for me, but treat me like a child, deceiving me with your speech (87 ff.).

Some of his couplets were to become famous, like the completely banal: 'O loveliest and most charming of boys, come close to me for I have something to say to you' (1365), the first few words of which we find inscribed on a Tanagra cup, apparently spoken by the bearded man who reclines on a banqueting couch.

Despite his celebrity, it is doubtful whether 'dull Theognis' was in any real sense a poet. Plutarch, whom one might have expected to approve of him as a moralist, certainly did not think so: he regarded him as a versifier, dressing up pedestrian ideas in rhythm like a man who rides in a ceremonial chariot because he is too pretentious to go on foot.

Of all the Greek lyric poets before Pindar, Simonides of Ceos was the one who most nearly approached formal perfection. Born a little before 550 in Ioulis, the tiny capital of the little Ionian island of Ceos, not far from Attica, he went to Athens and there, like Anacreon, was patronized by Hipparchus. When the latter's murder resulted in the dispersal of all the artists and poets he had surrounded himself with, Simonides went to live in Thessaly, at the courts of Crannon, Pharsalus and Larissa. Eventually, in the time of the Persian wars, already in his eighties, he retired to Sicily to the court of Hieron tyrant of Syracuse where he met his nephew Bacchylides and Pindar. He died at the age of eighty-nine.

He was a court poet and he demanded high payment for the poems he was commissioned to write. There is a story that Anaxilas, the tyrant of Rhegium, having won a prize at the Games with a team of mules, ordered an *epinikion* from Simonides, but only offered him a small fee. This the poet refused, on the grounds that the mules, having been sired by mere donkeys, were unworthy of his art: but as soon as Anaxilas raised his offer, he at once wrote a hymn to them, describing them as 'daughters of swift mares'.

Of the innumerable poems he wrote in the course of his long life —epigrams, dithyrambs, paeans, hyporchemes, epinikia and threnodies —only about a hundred lines have survived. He was regarded as a past master in the difficult art of the funeral epigram: two elegiac couplets were enough for him to bring out sharply the outstanding characteristics of a man's life or death. In honour of the soothsayer Megistias, killed at Thermophylae at the side of Leonidas, he composed this epitaph:

Beneath this monument lie the remains of the illustrious Megistias who fell beneath the blows of the Medes on the banks of the Spercheus. A prophet, he clearly foresaw his fate, yet would he not abandon the Spartan leaders (Bergk: *Fragment* 94).

In his poetry, Simonides succeeded in expressing his kindly, smiling wisdom with great charm. As we know from Plato's *Dialogues*, what cultivated Athenians especially looked to him for were those happy turns of phrase in which he brilliantly summed up a whole aspect of human experience in a few expressive words. For example, in one of his elegies, seven couplets of which have been preserved, he resumed the famous lines from the *Iliad* on the rapid succession of human lives which like the leaves of the forest fall and renew themselves every season. He also had a notable gift for enduing a mythical tale with genuine feeling, as when he described Danaë being thrown into the sea with her young son Perseus:

In the well built chest, tossed about by the furious winds and pounding waves, Danaë, pale with fear, her cheeks bathed in tears, clasped Perseus in her arms, and said: 'O my little one, what wretchedness I suffer! But you, you sleep in my arms, and your childish heart is at peace in this fearful dwelling, fastened with nails of bronze, in the midst of threatening night. Wrapped in your purple quilt, you take no notice of the huge waves breaking above your pretty head, nor of the howling wind. Did you but know the danger you are in, your tender ear would be attentive to my words. But sleep, my little one, sleep! O that the sea and our great calamity might also sleep! Show us your mercy Zeus: and, if I have spoken too boldly, forgive me for the sake of my child' (*Ibid.* 37).

THE BIRTH OF TRAGEDY

In his *Life of Solon*, Plutarch tells us that in his latter years 'Thespis was beginning to act tragedies, and the novelty of the spectacle attracted the crowd, though they had not yet been thrown open to competition. Solon, who by nature liked to hear whatever was new in order to learn from it, and who in his old age was more given to leisure and amusement, and even, indeed, to music and wine, went to see Thespis, who, in the manner of the ancient poets, acted in his own plays. After the performance he questioned him, and asked if he was not ashamed to tell such gross lies to so many people. To which Thespis replied that he saw no great harm in speaking and acting in play, as he did. . . .' (*Solon* 29, 6–7).

From this it is clear that Thespis must have already begun to be known about 560, though it was not until about 534, towards the end of Peisistratus' tyranny, that the city Dionysia and tragic contests were first instituted.

Greek tragedy developed out of the dithyramb, a kind of choral lyric, which explains why the songs and dances of the chorus were to be of such importance in the plays of Aeschylus, Sophocles and Euripides. In a certain sense, the Greek theatre goes back to the 'epic drama': in Homer the narrative is frequently interrupted by the speeches and monologues of the characters, and even more often by dialogue. Yet tragedy did not develop directly from the epic: it arose through the intermediary of lyric poetry, its true origin being the dithyrambs of Arion, a poet who himself owed much to Homer.

Moreover, the Greeks had always had an instinct for mime. The most ancient of the religious festivals were gradually supplanted by scenic displays representing some episode from the legends of the gods or heroes: thus, at Delos, the *Stork Dance* recalled the twisting and turning of Theseus in the Cretan labyrinth; and the *Septerion* at Delphi enacted the struggle of Apollo with the serpent Python and the god's subsequent purification at Tempe. The dithyramb was sung and danced by the chorus around the altar of Dionysus, the *thymele*, which was retained in the theatres of the classical period, in the circular *orchestra* where the tragic chorus danced and sang.

The decisive innovation, traditionally attributed to the Athenian Thespis—originally he belonged to the *deme* of Icaria near Marathon —was to transform the speaker of the prologue to the dithyramb, who announced and commented on the theme of the choral song, into an actor, *hypokrites*. This single actor would play a number of parts in succession in which he responded to the chorus. Alternately god, hero or messenger, he would repeatedly return to the stage, each time introducing some new subject and thus allowing the chorus to vary their songs. Dramatic action was still embryonic, but it already existed.

If Horace's *Ars Poetica* is to be relied upon, the actor, not yet wearing a mask but with his face smeared with wine dregs, represented the feasts of Dionysus that were connected with the wine harvest; and Thespis used to transport his earliest tragedies by chariot from town to town throughout Attica before presenting them in Athens. Thespis himself probably took the part either of the actor or of the leader of the chorus, the *coryphaeus*; and he was certainly not the only tragic poet to perform the multiple functions of impressario, author, stage-manager, ballet master and actor.

Either in the time of Thespis or a little later, it became the established custom to present three episodes from the same legend in succession.

Just as the actor played a variety of parts, so the chorus would represent different groups of people, for example the companions of Laios, then those of his son Oedipus, then those of Eteocles or Polynices, Oedipus' sons. Each of the three episodes eventually became a tragedy, and together they formed a connected trilogy. This was followed by a fourth play, more directly related to the legend of Dionysus, god of the dithyramb and of the theatre, in which the chorus consisted of the attendants of Dionysus, the Satyrs. This was later to become the 'Satyr play' which extended the dramatic trilogy to a tetralogy. The meaning of the word *tragoedia* (goat song) is obscure, but perhaps it may best be explained by the goat that was anciently sacrificed to Dionysus.

Plutarch says that, in Solon's day, 'the novelty of the spectacle attracted the crowd'. And indeed, even if Thespis was a much inferior poet to his successors Phrynichos and Aeschylus, tragedy must have produced the effect of a wonderful innovation and a quite new art form. Unlike the Homeric rhapsodes or the cyclic choruses, action was here directly interpreted by men, behaving and speaking as if they themselves were the gods or heroes of the story, thus creating the illusion of the theatre.

It would scarcely be an exaggeration to compare the invention of tragedy with that of the cinema; at least such a comparison helps us to appreciate its radical novelty. Jacques Lacarrière has said: 'The tragic stage was to become a universe in itself, charged with its own intense reality, oppressive or liberating at the will of the dramatist. The spectators at Aeschylus' *Oresteia* in 458, who fled at the appearance of the Erinyes on the stage, were reacting in much the same way as those who, twenty-five centuries later, were to react to the first cinema. These two arts, based exclusively on illusion, of the image on the screen or the actor on the stage, were to impress the public above all by their unexpected power of suggesting reality better than reality itself.'

THE BEGINNINGS OF PROSE

Plutarch regarded the first appearance of literary prose in Greece as a phenomenon closely connected with the general evolution of society and its mode of life. Indeed, after describing the origin and development of lyric poetry in archaic times, in words that I have already quoted (see p. 106), he went on:

The use of language is like the circulation of money: its function, too, depends on habitual and familiar use, and its value changes according to the times. Once the common currency of language was poetry, rhythm and song; then history and philosophy themselves fell within the domain of music and poetry. . . . But changes that occurred in the order of things and in the outlook of men modified their way of life. Banishing what was superfluous, custom suppressed elaborate hair-styles and golden hairpins, did away with long flowing tunics. . . . Simplicity replaced luxury, and men began to see the absence of studied elegance and affectation as a higher form of ornament than ostentatious over-refinement. Language underwent the same transformation, the same stripping down: history abandoned the chariot of poetry, and by learning to walk on foot in prose succeeded in distinguishing truth from legend. In the same way, philosophy chose to enlighten and instruct rather than to dazzle, and pursued its enquiries only in prose (*De Pythiae Orac.* 406B ff.).

It was during the sixth century, and first of all in Ionia, that this parallel development in manners and in literature took place. Of course, the art of the Muses continued to be practised by poets, both epic and lyric, as well as by the new tragic dramatists. But it was in this period that the first prose-writers appeared, although certain chroniclers or historians, as well as some of the philosophers, maintained the old practice of writing in verse.

The same evolution is to be seen in a minor literary form, the fable. From the earliest times, the Greeks delighted in expressing their experience of life in the form of fables in which the animals are gifted with speech. We have already seen both Hesiod and Archilochos doing this in their stories of the Nightingale and the Hawk, and the Eagle and the Fox (see pp. 74 and 87 above). In the sixth century such fables multiplied and took the form of short prose tales which were attributed to Aesop who soon became a legendary figure. According to Herodotus, Aesop had been a slave in the household of Iadmon the Samian at the same time as the famous courtesan Rhodope. The fables that he invented and told in the course of his journeys earned him a considerable reputation, but they also made him enemies. Thus the people of Delphi were so offended by his irony that they falsely accused him of sacrilege and put him to death; though later they had to pay blood-money to Iadmon's grandson.

The *Aesopian Miscellany* that has come down to us contains over three hundred and fifty fables, but it is quite impossible to tell which of these were in fact by Aesop. What is certain, however, is that

Aesop enjoyed a special prestige at Athens where a statue was erected in his honour; and Aristophanes often alluded to his fables in his comedies. In Plato's *Phaedo*, Socrates who was condemned to death in 399 is said to have had a dream while he was in prison, in which he heard a god ordering him 'to write poetry'; and as he knew many of Aesop's fables by heart he applied himself to turning them into verse.

Originally, Aesop seems to have come either from Phrygia or Lydia; but in any case from Asia. The first philosophers and the first historians, too, were almost all Ionians, born in the towns along the coast of Asia Minor or on the nearby islands. We have already drawn attention to Ionia's influence on Attic art in this period (p. 94). But she was not only the mother of literature and the arts: she also laid the basis of the science that was to become our Western science, our intellectual heritage; this was the first fulfilment of, the key to, the miracle of Greece.

Thales of Miletus, one of the seven Greek sages and a contemporary of Solon, was both a scientist and a philosopher. As a scientist he was able, it seems, to estimate the distance of ships out at sea from the top of a tower, and a number of famous theorems were attributed to him. He was also said to have predicted the eclipse of the sun in 584, and came to be looked upon as the typical philosopher: one day when he was walking along with his eyes fixed on the stars, Plato tells us in the *Theaetetus*, he fell into a well and was laughed at by a charming Thracian servant girl. At the same time, he seems to have had plenty of common sense: as a politician he sought to unite the Ionian cities in a federation to resist the Persian invasion; as a business man, having one winter foreseen an abundant olive harvest, he rented all the presses in the neighbourhood cheap, and then, later on, let them out again at a profit to the peasants who were unable to cope with the glut of olives.

As a philosopher, Thales was not satisfied with the explanation of the creation of the universe provided by the ancient theogonies such as Hesiod's. He set out to discover the first principle of life and reached the conclusion that water was the promordial element. His knowledge of astronomy is open to dispute: his famous prediction of the solar eclipse was not very exact and it was probably based on empirical notions borrowed from the Chaldeans. But as a philosophical *physicist*, concerned, that is to say, with the nature (*physis*) of the universe, he was certainly one of the first to try to synthesize contemporary knowledge in order to provide a complete explanation of

113

the *cosmos*. Such an intellectual undertaking was at that time doubtless premature, but it denotes the mental energy and curiosity which are the basis of all philosophy. Thus it was also in Ionia, at Miletus, that philosophy, another invention of the Greek mind, was born.

Pythagoras, a native of Samos, left his country when he was about forty years old, possibly to escape the tyranny of Polycrates, and established himself at the other end of the Greek world, at Crotona in Italy, where disciples flocked to hear him. The philosophical school he founded became a veritable Church, for he achieved what was later to be the dream of Auguste Comte: he was as much concerned with practical conduct and morality as with pure speculation. The 'Pythagorean way of life' entailed rules as rigorous as those of Christian monks: his disciples ate their meals in common, and practised severe abstinence as well as self-examination.

As a result of the religious and mystical character of Pythagoreanism, its founder soon became a legendary figure: as the son of Apollo or Hermes, he was supposed to have descended into hell and then returned to earth, like Heracles and Theseus; he had a golden thigh; and was gifted with ubiquity and also, of course, with the power of prophecy.

The justification for naming a theorem after Pythagoras was certainly greater than in Thales' case, for he appears to have considerably advanced the study of arithmetic and geometry. But just as the first astronomers were also astrologists and the first chemists alchemists, so for the Pythagoreans the science of numbers was bound up with mystical contemplation. Unlike Thales, however, they were mathematicians first and foremost, and it was in the harmony expressed by the relations between numbers that they discovered a kind of substance or active cause, which they declared to be the principle of the universe.

In succeeding centuries, Pythagoreanism became more and more mixed up with another mystical trend, Orphism, whose completely legendary founder was supposed to have been the Thracian minstrel, Orpheus, the prophet of Dionysus, who could calm and enchant the whole of nature with his lyre, including wild beasts and the waves of the sea. The Pythagoreans were also musicians: they studied the science of sound, the intervals of which can be numerically measured, and thus founded the acoustic theory of harmony; and they also believed in the religious and cathartic power of melody. Plato was to be deeply influenced both by them and by the Orphics.

Xenophanes, like Mimnermus, was born at Colophon and like him was also a poet since, as I have said, many philosophers continued to express their ideas in verse as indeed Parmenides and Empedocles were still to do in the fifth century. Xenophanes himself tells us that he travelled throughout the length and breadth of Greece, as the itinerant sophists were to do later, and that at the age of ninety-two he was still active.[1]

He wrote elegies like Mimnermus, but of his long poem *On Nature*, in epic hexametres, we have only a few short fragments. What is most striking about him is the nobility of his religious feeling and the acuity with which he criticized polytheism; in this sense he may be regarded as a direct precursor of Plato. He was a convinced monotheist: 'Amongst gods and men, there exists but one god, the supreme god, who, neither in body nor in spirit, resembles mankind' (Ed. Diels: *Fragment* 23). And in his *Silloi*, a kind of satire, he adds:

Homer and Hesiod attributed to the gods all the things that are a shame and a reproach amongst men: adultery and deception. . . . If oxen, horses and lions had hands and could paint like men, the horses would represent the gods as horses, the oxen as oxen: in short, we should have images of the gods resembling the whole animal species. . . . The Ethiopians say of their gods that they are flat-nosed and black; the Thracians, that they have blue eyes and red hair (*Ibid.* 11–12 and 15–16).

It is clear that criticism of traditional religion began early amongst the Greeks: already in the sixth century B.C. an Ionian philosopher considered that the gods, far from having created mankind as Hesiod thought, were pure inventions of the human imagination. But this acute criticism did not result in atheism, since Xenophanes continued to worship a supreme being. One is reminded of the words Corneille puts into the mouth of Polyeucte:

> La prostitution, l'adultère, l'inceste,
> Le vol, l'assassinat, et tout ce qu'on déteste,
> C'est l'example qu'à suivre offrent vos immortels.

[1] We have already noted, and shall frequently do so again, examples of the remarkable longevity of the ancient Greeks for many of the writers were entitled to be called *macrobioi*. The average expectation of life was certainly much lower than it is today on account of the high rate of infant mortality, but it would be a mistake to conclude from this that people grew old at an earlier age than in the century of penicillin and surgical progress.

Adultery, prostitution, incest, theft,
Assassination, all we most detest,
These are the examples offered by your gods.

With Heracleitus of Ephesus we return to prose. This proud and lonely philosopher, disdainful of the crowd, often misanthropic, came to be known as 'the dark one' on account of the extreme concision with which he clothed his originality of mind and profound intuitions.

As water was for Thales the primordial element, so for Heracleitus it was fire, undying and always changing:

This world, which is the same for all creatures, was not created either by gods or by men: it always has been, is and will be. Between all things and fire there is exchange, and between fire and all other things (Ed. Diels, *Fragment* 30).

A remote forerunner of the Stoic physicists, he seems to have believed in a periodical destruction of the universe by fire, *ekpyrosis*: 'As we move on, the fire will judge and will condemn everything' (*Ibid.* 66). In his view, contradiction and the unity of opposites are the very condition of becoming: 'War is the king and father of everything' (53) 'Everything is in flux' (91) and 'One cannot bathe twice in the same stream' (91), because the water will have changed. We should not trust our senses, but only reason: the apparent variety of things is an illusion, since 'Everything is one', but this unity is not stationary, as Xenophanes believed, but on the contrary pure motion. The profound harmony existing between all things is only revealed by reflection: 'The invisible harmony is worth more than that which is seen.' Night and day are but two faces of the same reality: 'The crowd takes for its master Hesiod, the great scholar who was incapable of distinguishing night from day; but indeed they are one and the same thing' (*Ibid.* 57).

These few fragments (some hundred and twenty-five of them have been preserved) enable us to catch a glimpse, not only of the originality and vigour of Heracleitus' thought, but also of the driving force of his swift, abrupt and subtle style.

Like philosophy, history also 'abandoned the chariot of poetry'. For Plutarch, the first historians were quite simply the poets of the epic cycle and Homer himself, who, though they undoubtedly embellished the exploits of the heroes, could not have invented them, since the war of Troy was an historical fact. It was in Ionia, in Miletus, the same town as Thales, that the first prose writer, or *logographos*, was born: Hecataeus, the man who foreshadows Herodotus.

As a matter of fact, his 'historical' work, the *Genealogies*, though actually written in prose, was more like a mythological poem. In it he recounted the legendary tales of Deucalion, of Hellen and his sons, of Heracles and the Heracleidae; as well as of such foreign heroes as Aegyptus, Danaus and Cadmus. With such vague and dubious material to work on, Hecataeus made a genuine attempt to sort out the true from the false, as may be seen from his opening words: 'Thus speaks Hecataeus of Miletus: I write of these things as they appear to me to be true, for the accounts of the Greeks are various and, in my opinion, ridiculous' (Ed. Müller: *Fragment 33*).

Thus Hecataeus firmly intended to apply the spirit of criticism, but in these fabulous realms what could he do but choose from the various versions of a myth the one that seemed to him to be the least improbable? When, seven centuries later, Plutarch wrote the *Life of Theseus* and proclaimed his intention of 'forcing fable to submit to reason and to assume the bearing of history', he was simply following the same road that Hecataeus had been the first to take—a road which perhaps leads nowhere. In the Preface to this same *Life*, Plutarch also says: 'In their atlases, historians push the countries they know little of to the edges of their maps.' For him, as for all the ancients, history and geography were inseparable, comprising a single science, *Historia*, the two aspects of which were complementary and could not be dissociated: the study of countries and the study of facts. That is why, for example, Herodotus devoted the whole of the second Book of his *Histories* to a description of Egypt.

Hecataeus seems to have been a far better geographer than historian, in the limited sense of the word. His *Description of the World* filled two whole books, one on Europe and the other on Asia, for in those times Africa, or Libya, was regarded as part of Asia. This first 'world geography' was based on the author's own numerous travels and personal observation, but evidently he also included notions he had picked up from all over the place, with the result that this part of his work, too, is not devoid of fable: for instance, he repeats the legendary account of the battle between the Pygmies and the Storks in Upper Egypt. A map was included in the *Description*, one of the attractions of which was the accounts of such curious animals as the phoenix, the hippopotamus and the crocodile.

When, later, Herodotus came to speak of these animals, he reproduced whole phrases from his predecessor almost word for word.
Plagiarism may well be the most spontaneous form of admiration,
but one cannot help regretting that Herodotus should have indulged
in a practice very common in antiquity and by no means unknown
amongst writers today: that of naming a colleague when criticizing
him, but borrowing from him anonymously. He refers to Hecataeus
when he makes fun of him for claiming to be descended from a god,
but when he speaks of Egypt as 'a gift of the Nile' he omits to mention
that he owes this singularly happy phrase to Hecataeus.

7. The Apollo of Piraeus, *c.* 525, a hollow-cast bronze *kouros* (youth) discovered in 1959 (pp. 94–5). *National Museum, Athens*

8. Head of Apollo from the west pediment of the temple of Zeus at Olympia, 465–457 (p. 123). *Olympia Museum*

4

THE TRIUMPH OF DEMOCRACY
First Half of the Fifth Century

Beneath this stone lies Aeschylus the Athenian, son of Euphorion,
Buried in the fertile soil of Gela;
Well-known for his prowess in battle,
As the wood of Marathon and the Medes bear witness,

Epitaph from *Vita Aeschyli*

HISTORICAL BACKGROUND

The sixth century had witnessed both the development towards democracy in Athens and, in Asia, the founding of the Persian empire, which was to last until the time of Alexander the Great. The reign of the great conqueror Cyrus, who subdued the kingdoms of Assyria, Babylon, Media and Lydia, was more or less contemporary with the tyranny of Peisistratus, from 560 to 530. His son Cambyses conquered Egypt and was succeeded in 521 by Darius, the son of Hystaspes, who launched the first Persian expedition against Greece.

This confrontation of Asia and Europe in the Persian Wars was to influence the whole of the first half of the fifth century: it was the Greeks' ultimate victory that enabled Hellas, and above all the Athenians the chief architects of victory, to attain full political, as well as artistic, intellectual and literary maturity after the growing pains of the sixth century. It was this mature civilization that constituted the classical age.

Already before the opening of the fifth century Cyrus had overrun all the Greek towns of Ionia, with the exception of Miletus which succeeded in concluding a treaty of alliance with him. But in 499, at the instigation of the Milesians and despite the wise advice of Hecataeus, the Ionians revolted. Confronted by the power of the Persian Empire, they appealed for help to the other members of their race, the Hellenes of Greece itself. Athens sent twenty triremes; and Eretria, a town in Euboea, another five. In 498 the Athenian hoplites took part in the capture of Sardis, the capital of Lydia, and possibly in the burning of the temple of Cybele which provided the Persians with an excuse for savage reprisals.

But Darius' satraps reacted and in 494 Ionia was once more subdued and punished. As the instigator of the revolt, Miletus was taken by storm and destroyed. For a long time to come the brilliant artistic and literary achievements of the Greek cities of Asia Minor whose civilization had hitherto surpassed that of Greece itself was at an end.

The intervention of Athens and Eretria in Asia, however, had aroused Darius' resentment and he regarded this as an admirable pretext for invading Hellas and adding it to his empire. In 491 he sent emissaries to the Aegean islands and the cities of the peninsula to lay claim to 'land and sea' in token of submission. Faced by the question of whether or not Greece was to become a Persian satrapy, Athens and Sparta gave their answer in the traditional manner, by executing the great king's ambassadors. In September of the following year this led to the unsuccessful landing at Marathon where ten thousand Athenian hoplites, with the help of another thousand from Plataea, drove the Persian army back into the sea (the Persians had relied for advice on Peisistratus' son Hippias, exiled from Athens in 509). Amongst those who fought at Marathon were the poet Aeschylus and his brother Cynegiros who lost his life there.

In 485 Darius died. He was succeeded by his son Xerxes who began to prepare for a great invasion, overland by way of Thrace as well as by sea, which would reverse the setback at Marathon. Meanwhile, thanks to the foresight of Themistocles and the silver from the Laurium mines, the Athenians were also feverishly increasing the size of their fleet. In 480, despite the heroic resistance of Leonidas and his Spartans at Thermopylae, Xerxes entered Athens, almost deserted by its inhabitants, and set fire to the temple of Athena on the Acropolis in revenge for the burning of the sanctuary of Sardis. But the Greek fleet, led by the Spartan Eurybiades and inspired by the Athenian general Themistocles, defeated the Persian navy in the bay of Salamis, a battle in which, once again, Aeschylus took part. Beaten at sea, Xerxes retreated precipitately through Thrace, leaving behind in central Greece an army under the command of Mardonios which was defeated the following year at the battle of Plataea.

Scarcely had she freed herself from this terrible threat when Hellas went over to the offensive: a Greek fleet landed at Mycale, in Asia opposite Samos, and cut another Persian army to pieces. Then the

Athenian contingent, led by Xanthippus the father of Pericles, besieged and took the city of Sestos, on the Hellespont, thus establishing the first outpost of the Athenian Empire on the Straits (478). At this point, Herodotus' account of the war comes to an end. The islands of Thasos, Samos, and Chios retained their independence, but it was not yet possible to free the continental cities of Ionia from the Persian yoke.

In Sicily, about the same time as the battle of Salamis, Gelon, tyrant of Syracuse, defeated the Carthaginians at the battle of Himera, thus driving back the Barbarians from the West, as Athens, Sparta and some thirty other cities had driven back those from the East. Henceforward, following its destiny, Hellenism was able to breathe more freely throughout the whole Mediterranean, apart from Asia.

To meet the eventual contingency of a renewed Persian offensive, the Athenian Aristeides, surnamed the Just, set up the maritime Delian League, thus assuring his country the hegemony of Greece at the expense of Sparta. In 468 Cimon, the son of Miltiades and leader of the aristocratic party, destroyed a Persian fleet off the coast of Pamphylia, at the mouth of the river Eurymedon, thus justifying the 'tribute' that the other members of the League, as allies (and, indeed, before long as subjects) of Athens, paid to the imperial city as insurance against the Persian threat. It was not, however, until about 450, at least if the 'peace of Callias' was an historical fact, that hostilities between Greece and Persia were officially ended.

About the year 461 Cimon was ostracized, thus leaving the field open to the leaders of the democratic party, Ephialtes and Pericles, who were pursuing the policy initiated by Cleisthenes. The last political prerogatives of the aristocratic Areopagus then passed to the popular assembly: payment of officials (*misthophoria*) and more widely based admission to the magistracy enabled all free-born Athenians to participate in the administration if they so wished. Democracy was in full spate. After the assassination of Ephialtes, Pericles became the undisputed leader of Athens whose influence was now extended over many Greek towns and over the majority of the islands in the Aegean.

ART

The defeat of the Persians was the occasion for many valuable donations to the sanctuaries in gratitude for the help of the gods. The Athenian Treasury at Delphi, a small Doric temple, completely built of marble with two columns between the *antae*, which has been reconstructed by French archaeologists, dates almost certainly from the years following the battle of Marathon in 490, and, not, as was at one time maintained, from the last decade of the sixth century.

After the battle of Salamis, the Athenians were first concerned to strengthen the walls of the city and could not immediately undertake the reconstruction of the temples of the Acropolis destroyed by Xerxes: this was to be accomplished after 450 by Pericles and Pheidias. The most characteristic and best known temples of the first half of the fifth century are those at Aegina and Olympia.

On the island of Aegina, the new temple of Aphaea, a goddess later to be assimilated with Athena, was a Doric peripteral building, with six columns in front and twelve at each side, which has been remarkably preserved as far as the architrave. The columns and walls are of local limestone, while Pentelic marble was used for the pediments and roof. Inside, a double colonnade with superimposed orders divides the *naos* into three naves, and also carries lateral galleries that were reached by wooden stairs.

The vast temple of Zeus in the pan-Hellenic sanctuary of Olympia, built of fossil-bearing stone, is not nearly so well preserved, but even its ruins are majestically imposing. This Doric building, peripteral and hexastyle like the temple of Aphaea, but twice the size, rises from an enormous substructure of volcanic rock. In the *naos* may still be seen the remains of the tall plinth of blue stone from Eleusis, on which used to stand the colossal statue of the god, made by Pheidias of gold and ivory.

In this period, sculpture and painting were developing still more rapidly than architecture. At the end of the sixth century the marble caryatids of the Acropolis and the great bronze *kouros* in the Piraeus (see p. 94) still bore the characteristic imprint of archaic art: the strictly full-face pose, with the weight borne equally on the two legs (when one of these is advanced, it is always the left one), neck and head unbendingly erect, and the expression of the face either rather fixed or lit up by a stereotyped smile. With the first half of the fifth century, the breaking away of Greek art from archaic conventions came to a head: the human figure is freed from all hieratic stiffness; the artist has become capable of expressing harmoniously the varied attitudes and movements of real life. As in the fable of Pygmalion, the statues and vase portraits no longer appear to be static but are alive and full of the movement of living people.

This transformation can be seen for the first time in the architectural sculpture on the three monuments we have just mentioned: the Athenian Treasury, and the temples of Aphaea and Zeus. At Delphi, the Athenian metopes recount the exploits of Heracles and Theseus, particularly their battle with the Amazons, who originally came from Asia—a transparent allusion to the struggle against the Persians. The admirable metope representing the goddess Athena and Theseus has a religious, almost mystical, feeling. In these unfortunately mutilated sculptures, as de La Coste-Messelière has pointed out, 'classicism, but newly born, is throwing off its swaddling clothes: why should we be surprised, then, if it does not immediately display its full liveliness and strength? At the Athenian Treasury, we can follow from one metope to the next precisely this struggle towards liberation: Attic art is already committed to its triumphant advance towards the Panathanaic Way; for the last time archaism serves as the starting point but the starting point for a great forward leap.'

The same may be said of the carvings on the two pediments at Aegina which, dating from about 480, represent, around the central figure of Athena, the struggle of Heracles and Telamon against Laomedon of Troy, and the battles of the warriors of the *Iliad*, both mythical allusions to the confrontation of Europe and Asia. A wounded soldier, half reclining, and a Heracles resting on one knee to draw his bow, are both lovely and harmonious figures, but the composition as a whole is somehow lacking in ease and variety, and expresses a too determined striving for symmetry. All the figures on these pediments were originally coloured.

So, too, were the carvings on the pediments and metopes of the temple of Zeus at Olympia, which, some twenty years later in date, approach even closer to classic perfection. One of the pediments represents the preparations of Pelops for the chariot race against King Oenomaus of Pisa, the father of Hippodamia; the other, the struggle between the Centaurs and the Lapiths. Here, the admirable figure of Apollo, right arm outstretched, dominates with its Olympian calm the violence and tumult of the struggle. The pediments originally illustrated the exploits of Heracles; and, in the Louvre, one can still see Heracles presenting Athena with the birds from lake Stymphalis, and struggling with the Cretan bull: the first scene is tranquil and majestic, the second full of the energy of combat, the hero's body cutting across that of the bull, regardless of symmetry.

Where the sculptures are detached from the background of the tympanum they are almost completely in the round. Of the bronze group of the tyrannicides, Harmodios and Aristogeiton (see p. 90), ordered by Athens in 477 to replace that carried off by Xerxes, we have only copies, but we do possess the admirable statue of the Auriga, or Chariot Driver, found at Delphi. This is bronze, 1 m. 80 cm. high, standing in a votive chariot, which was donated by Plyzalus, tyrant of Gela, in 478 or 474 to commemorate a victory in the Pythian hippodrome. The Auriga is shown at the moment when, having carried off the victory, he is making a triumphal turn round the stadium to receive the plaudits of the crowd. The elegant folds of his tunic, suspended from his shoulders by a cord and girdled at the waist, fall to his feet. As F. Chamoux says: 'The Auriga is the contemporary of Aeschylus, Pindar and Bacchylides. He belongs to a period of sincere faith and bears the stamp of it. By his somewhat rigid stance, his almost haughty reserve, he evokes the austere nobility of the great choral lyrics. One might almost suppose he was actually listening to a hymn.'

The marble votive bas-relief of a melancholy Athena, helmeted and leaning on her spear, dates from about 460. It is also a gravely religious work, but if it is true that the stele in front of the goddess proves that it was dedicated by an athlete, it, too, is connected with the games. The enigmatic and admirably carved triptych of the 'Ludovisi Throne' probably belongs to the same period.

Amongst the great Greek sculptors the first who is more to us than a mere name was Myron, an Athenian belonging to the *deme* of Eleutherae. Towards the middle of the fifth century he carved a group, very different from that of the tyrannicides, which represents Athena and Marsyas and illustrates the invention of the flute. But better known, thanks to the copies of it that still exist, is his famous Discobolos: the first statue in which the human figure is shown, at the full stretch of its physical powers, with such rhythmical grace and superbly balanced harmony.

As regards pottery, the first half of the fifth century corresponds pretty much to the severe style of the red-figured vases, that is to say, the period of the greatest masterpieces, many of which are signed: thus the bowl of Geryon and the Antaeus *crater* are signed by Euphronios; the bowl showing the exploits of Theseus, by Douris; and the sack of Troy bowl, by Brygos. It was also the time of those marvellous paintings of Ganymede and his cock, the Maenads in ecstasy, the naked girl at her toilet, Aphrodite bestriding a goose, and so on.

The influence of large-scale painting was at this time very noticeable also among the vase painters. About 470, Polygnotus of Thasos, who was already well-known for his huge paintings on the walls of the treasury of Cnidos at Delphi, described by Pausanias as representing the sack of Troy and scenes in Hell, settled in Athens. He brought with him conceptions and techniques that were quite new in painting, especially as regards the representation of figures on different planes and the striking rendering of facial expression. Polygnotus' work, like that of all the great painters, has utterly disappeared, but we find a reflection of it in such ceramic works as the *crater* of the Niobidae or the bowl of Penthesilea. In the first, Apollo and Artemis, the two archers, are shooting their arrows at the children of Niobe. The depth of background and the different planes are indicated by wavy lines, which, before the knowledge of perspective, created the illusion of depth. Forcibly but without excessive realism, boys and girls, stricken to death, are shown in every kind of attitude that could express the despairing weakness and cruel suffering of their last moments.

The Penthesilea bowl is even more moving. The Amazon, coming to the aid of Priam, is confronting Achilles, and at the very moment that he plunges his sword into her breast their eyes encounter one another. Achilles recognizes her as a woman who is worthy of him, his equal, a creature of noble breeding. He is overwhelmed with a sudden, immense love for her, but it is too late: life is already draining from her body, and the hero is overwhelmed with a terrible grief, as he realizes he has just killed the woman he loves but who will never be his.

BACCHYLIDES

The mother of Bacchylides was a sister of Simonides of Ceos (p. 108). He was born at Ioulis, a city on the island of Ceos, and probably received his earliest instruction in the lyric art from his uncle. Banished from Ceos, perhaps as a result of a democratic uprising by the party supporting Athens, he settled in the Peloponnese, but before this he had already sent a triumphal ode to Hieron of Syracuse. The Sicilian tyrant, who liked to surround himself with poets and artists, summoned him to his court, where he found himself at the same time as Simonides and Pindar.

Since Pindar, at the end of his *Second Pythian Ode* which is dedicated to Hieron, alludes to 'envious rivals', it has been supposed from antiquity that he was referring to the two Cean poets. And it is indeed possible that the association of the three poets gave rise to feelings of emulation, perhaps to quarrels. Writers are often quick to take umbrage, even the greatest of them, and dislike seeing colleagues whom they regarded as their inferiors treated as equals. *Genus irritabile vatus....*

Until 1897 nothing was known of Bacchylides' work beyond a few short fragments. But in that year the discovery of an Egyptian papyrus made available some twenty poems, some of which were well preserved, though the majority were badly mutilated. They consisted of *epinikia*, odes written in honour of victors at the games, like Hieron, heroic hymns similar to those of Stesichorus, paeans and dithyrambs. Bacchylides also wrote songs to be sung at banquets, and love songs.

Two of the poems that have been best preserved were inspired by the legend of the Athenian hero, Theseus. *Ode* XVII, *The Striplings*, perhaps a paean, was, as the two last lines clearly indicate, sung at Delos, on the occasion of a pilgrimmage from Ceos to the sanctuary of Apollo. Probably, therefore, it was a youthful work, written before his exile. He tells how, on board the ship that was taking the young Athenian men and women as tribute to the Minotaur, Theseus quarrelled with King Minos because the latter dared to lay hands on one of the Athenian girls. In order to bring back proof that he was the son of Poseidon, Theseus thereupon plunged into the sea where he was received by Amphitrite and eventually returned safe and sound to the ship, wearing a marvellous robe and crown. Here are the lines describing Theseus' journey beneath the sea and Amphitrite's welcome.

Swiftly the ship was sailing, driven forward by the breath of Boreas, when suddenly, seeing the hero plunge into the sea, all the youth of Athens began to tremble; and tears streamed from their eyes, for they feared some dread disaster. But swiftly the sea-dwelling dolphins bore the great Theseus to his father's palace, lord of the horses. There, as he approached the divine dwelling, the sight of the Nereids made him quiver with delight. . . . And there, too, in the delightful palace, he beheld his father's beloved wife, Amphitrite of the great eyes, a venerable goddess. She clothed him in a robe of purple, and upon his curling locks set a crown of sombre roses that crafty Aphrodite gave him for a wedding gift (*Ode* XVII, 1 ff.).

A lovely bowl by the Athenian potter Euphronios (see p. 124) illustrates this scene from the legend: one sees the youthful Theseus in his short linen tunic before a seated Amphitrite; Tritons and dolphins indicate that they are in the depths of the sea; and between them stands Athena, wearing her helmet and armour, as a symbol of the divine protection that surrounds the young hero.

Ode xviii, perhaps a dithyramb, is called *Theseus* and was written for the Athenians. It is a lyric dialogue between a chorus and Aegeus, the father of Theseus, and shows very clearly how choral poetry could give rise to tragedy (see p. 110). Aegeus has just been hearing of the amazing exploits of a young hero (whose name is unknown and is nowhere mentioned in the dialogue) during a voyage from Troezen to Athens. The dramatic interest of the work lies in the fact that the uneasiness of Aegeus, before he recognizes his son, suggests that he will treat him with hostility, and on Medea's advice, try to poison him. Here are one or two passages from the poem:

Chorus: O king of holy Athens, prince of the subtle Ionians, what new song of war has the bronze mouthed trumpet uttered? Are the frontiers of our country assailed by the furious leader of a hostile army?

Aegeus: But a moment ago a herald arrived, whose feet have trod the long road from the isthmus. He tells of the invincible deeds of a valiant knight... I am afraid! What may be the end of such exploits?

Chorus: Who may this hero be? From what country does he come? What kind of clothing does he wear? ...

Aegeus: Two men only, they say, attend upon him. He wears his sword slung from his splendid shoulders. . . . Though he is still but a child, who knows what tricks Ares may be up to? War and strife, when bronze clashes upon bronze? They say he is come in search of shining Athens (*Ode* xviii, *passim*).

Pseudo-Longinus, in his *Treatise on the Sublime*, says of Bacchylides that he was 'a faultless poet, who wrote brilliantly and with perfection'. In fact, his style is fluent, limpid and ornate. But although his Odes are bathed in a steady, gentle light, they have none of Pindar's sudden lightning flashes. One can well imagine the latter's annoyance if his contemporaries really regarded this versifier as his equal, for between him and Bacchylides is the gulf that separates genius from talent.

PINDAR

Hesiod was born in Boeotia, but his father was an immigrant from Aeolis: Pindar belonged to an aristocratic family whose roots were firmly planted in Boeotian soil. He was born in 518 in a village near

Thebes, and always regarded himself as a Theban. The Athenians were only too ready to make fun of the Boeotians whom they looked upon as an obtuse and slow-witted people with a weakness for food, though like most such collective prejudices this one contained only a very slight element of truth. Indeed many Boeotians were amateurs of art and cultivated music and poetry, the flute being especially esteemed by them. One of the most famous sanctuaries of the Muses was on the slopes of Mount Helicon.

Pindar was a precocious poet, his *Tenth Pythian Ode* having been written in 498, when he was only just twenty. It was no accident that this early work should have been in honour of a victory won at Delphi, for not only was Phocis, where the sanctuary of the Pythian Apollo was situated, in the extreme west of Boeotia, there was also a natural affinity between the majestic serenity of the Apollonian cult and the grave, religious spirit of the poet. The Delphic priests were to load Pindar with honours and privileges and the Pythia even ordained that part of the money offered to the god should be set aside for him.

In 480, the year of the battle of Salamis, Pindar was approaching his forties. When all his fellow Boeotians, except the Plataeans, sided with the Persian invaders (to such an extent, indeed, that in the following year, they allowed themselves to be massacred at the battle of Plataea by those Greeks who were fighting for their independence and liberty) what was his reaction? From the earliest times it has been alleged that he was inclined to collaborate with the Persians, and the following passage from one of his *hyporchemes* has been quoted as evidence of his pacifist leanings: 'War is a pleasing enough thing for those who know nothing of it, but those who have experienced it feel a strange trembling of the heart at its approach' (Puech Ed., *Fragment 3*).

Be that as it may, once the barbarians had been defeated and driven out, Pindar celebrated the liberation of Greece and the courage of her people, particularly in the *First Pythian Ode* and the *Fifth* and *Seventh Isthmian Odes*. Scarcely an heroic attitude, perhaps, though it was the one also adopted by the Delphic priests: the oracle of Apollo which at the time of Xerxes' invasion advised the Greeks to bow beneath the inevitable yoke, later glorified the architects of the Hellenic victory. Simonides of Ceos, the Ionian, displayed a bolder and more steadfast patriotism than the Dorian Pindar.

Like all the well-known poets of the time, Pindar travelled widely.

He frequently visited Delphi, Olympia, the Isthmus of Corinth and Nemea for the Games, and must have been present at many of the victories celebrated in his *epinikia*. We have already mentioned his visit to the court of Hieron of Syracuse, probably about 476, when he wrote his first three *Olympian Odes* and dedicated them to Hieron and Theron of Agrigentum. Like Hieron, the latter was tyrant of his city, and Pindar was doubtless on terms of personal friendship with both of them.

Pindar had a lofty and dignified conception of his status as a poet, regarding it as his right to address the great ones of the world as equals, with complete frankness and without any hesitation about telling them unpleasant truths. When he praised them, he was always ready to add advice, warnings and even criticism, and in the *Fourth Pythian Ode* he displays the same attitude towards King Arcesilaus of Cyrene. Whether he himself personally visited Cyrene is unknown, but it is quite possible.

In the second half of his life, from 480 onwards, such was his fame that he received invitations from all sides, not only from tyrants and kings, but also from cities. He certainly went to Athens, since he wrote a dithyramb in honour of the city, for which he was rewarded with the privileged title of *proxenos*, as well as a gift of ten thousand drachmas; the democracies, also, prided themselves on their munificent treatment of poets. But there can be little doubt that he felt more at home in the aristocratic city of Aegina, the rival of Athens, then at the height of its prosperity, and where a superb temple had just been erected to its goddess, Aphaea (see p. 122): of the forty-four triumphal odes that have come down to us, eleven were dedicated to the people of Aegina. Only the Sicilians, with fifteen dedications, were more favoured.

When the poet was present at a festival where one of his works was to be performed, he himself rehearsed and conducted the chorus; otherwise, he entrusted the task to a choir-master, *didaskalos*, selected by himself.

Pindar was married and had a son and two daughters; but he was also a pederast in his youth. He was in love with Thrasybulus, and right at the end of his life, with Theoxenos. In a eulogy written for the latter, he admits: 'The beauty of boys in the freshness of youth wakes the fire in my heart' (*Enkomion* IV, 5–7). According to tradition, he was eighty years old when, in 438, he suddenly died, in the theatre at Argos, his head resting on Theoxenos' shoulder.

Pindar excelled in the lyric forms, and we have fragments of his hymns, paeans, dithyrambs, partheneia, hyporchemes, eulogiae, skolia and threnodies. But the only poems that have come down to us intact (if indeed it is permissible to use the word, when the music is of course lost) are the *epinikia*, or triumphal odes, grouped together in four Books, each relating to one of the great pan-Hellenic Games: the Olympian, Pythian, Nemean and Isthmian.

Despite the revival of the Olympic Games in our own times, it is difficult for us to realize the importance that these periodical athletic contests had for the Greeks. Nowhere else was their intense feeling of *philotimia* (love of honour and glory) so abundantly manifested. The fame of a victor at the Olympia or at the Pythia (of an Olympionikos or Pythionikos, as they were called) reflected distinction upon his whole country. The victors, gods of the stadium or the hippodrome, though the prize they received at the Games was purely honorary (a crown of laurel leaves), were subsequently loaded with the most substantial gifts by their grateful and enthusiastic fellow citizens. The Athenian Olympionikoi were housed and fed at the expense of the State, in the Prytaneum. One town, it is said, even pulled down part of its walls so that the victor might make his entry through a gate that had never before been used.

While in the fifth century it had not yet become the custom to put up statues to a country's great men and generals, the Olympionikoi were entitled to erect their own effigies in bronze or marble in the Altis of Olympia. To celebrate their success, they could also invite a poet to write an ode which would then be publicly performed during the course of the official ceremony.

Of the odes of Pindar, some refer to victories won in the hippodrome, chariot races (*quadrigae*), in which four horses or mules were harnessed abreast, and ordinary horse races, which were regarded as the noblest of all since they were only open to those who were wealthy enough to own a stud of horses. For this reason, the *epinikia* in honour of such victories are to be found at the beginning of each of the four Books. His other odes are dedicated to the winners of events contested in the stadium: these included foot races (once round the stadium, about 200 yards; the *diaulos*, twice round; the *dolichos*, six times round; or races in which the competitors had to carry a hoplite's shield); wrestling; boxing; the *pankration*, a mixture of the two; and, finally, the *pentathlon*, which included running, jumping, wrestling, and discus and javelin throwing. For the boys there were only three types of contest: running, wrestling and boxing.

Pindar's Style

In the Pindaric odes, one looks in vain for the kind of technical descriptions and picturesque details of the various sports that are to be found in Book XXIII of the *Iliad*, or in late Hellenistic poems. Pindar was content to describe the contest in a few short, dry phrases, in order to devote himself to praise of the victor and, especially, of his country and family (as an aristocrat he firmly believed in the inheritance of talent); while not omitting to mention either the gods as the givers of victory, or the particular festival that had provided the athlete with the opportunity to distinguish himself.

Such are the principal themes of the *epinikia*. Yet almost always at the heart of the ode (unless it is an unusually short one), there is some legend of the gods or heroes, which he evokes rather than recounting it in the epic manner. In his swift, concise fashion the poet selects two or three episodes from the story, which he takes for granted will be known, and proceeds to project them in brilliant relief. Then, as a rule, he concludes with religious and moral observations on the human lot, one or two grave utterances, and an allusion to his own genius, which is, so to speak, his personal signature.

If, today, these odes produce in the reader's mind an impression of disorder, confusion and obscurity, this is due in the first place to Pindar's very personal poetic style (we are a long way from the limpid clarity of a Simonides or a Bacchylides): the vocabulary is extremely individual; the style, lively, abrupt and full of contrast; the phrasing may be long drawn out, or suddenly contracted, according to the effect the poet is aiming at. But our real difficulty arises from the fact that the structure of the odes derives not so much from logic as from music; and since the melodies have been lost, we cannot adequately appreciate the movement, the inflection, of the poem. It is rather like having the libretto of an opera without the score. All that the philologist can do is to study the extremely varied and scholarly prosody, and note that most of the *epinikia* of any length have a strict metrical form: they consist of triads, forming a *strophe*, an *antistrophe*, which is an exact rhythmical replica of the *strophe*, and an *epodos*, in which the same metrical elements are arranged in a different manner.

The clearest and most characteristic example of the Pindaric manner is the brilliant prelude to the *First Olympian Ode*:

Though water be the first of all the elements,[1] yet gold, sparkling like a

---

[1] According to Thales of Miletus water was the essential element of the universe (see p. 113).

flame in the night, overshadows all other treasure with its proud opulence. Would you sing of the Games, O my heart? Then seek not in the desert of the noon-day sky a star more dazzling than the sun, nor hope to celebrate a contest more glorious than Olympia's (*Olymp.* I, 1–10).

Wishing to emphasize the primacy of Olympia, the poet compares it to gold amongst all earthly objects, and to the sun amongst the stars. These images of gold, of light, and of vivid colours like purple, occur frequently in his work, but they should not just be seen as simple and commonplace comparisons: gold, light, purple represent sacred principles, and have a religious significance.

The poet then speaks of Hieron, and of the songs with which the guests at his hospitable table are entertained. And he continues:

Come! Take down the Doric lyre that hangs on the wall, if indeed your soul has been freed of care by the thought of Pisa and of Pherenicos, who, without touch of spur, sped along the banks of the Alpheus, bearing his master to victory, the lord of Syracuse who delights in horsemanship. For the fame of Hieron shines bright in this country of heroes, founded by Pelops the Lydian, he whom the mighty Poseidon, the earth-shaker, once fell in love with, when Clotho drew him forth from the pure cauldron, his shoulder splendid with the gleam of ivory (*Ibid.* 17 ff.).

Pisa was a town near Olympia, which for long enjoyed the presidency of the Games; Pherenicos ('he who carries off the victory') was the name of Hieron's horse, which had won the race. But these few words about him speeding along the banks of the Alpheus (a river near Olympia) are the only reference to the race, for, recollecting that Pelops once reigned in Olympia, the poet immediately passes on without any transition to the legend of this hero, a native of Lydia in Asia Minor, a legend that is closely connected with the origin of the Olympic Games: it was to Pelops' tomb in the Altis, the sacred grove of Olympia, that pilgrims came to worship. Pelops was Poseidon's favourite, who loved him as Zeus loved Ganymede. According to the usual version of the story, Tantalus, the father of Pelops, had invited the gods to a feast, and offered them as one of the dishes his son's body, cut up and boiled. The gods, realizing what it was, decided to restore the child to life, but not before Demeter had already eaten one of his shoulders, which Clotho therefore replaced with an ivory one. Having evoked this myth, however, in the second triad of the *Olympic* Pindar dismisses it as blasphemous:

For man should attribute to the gods nothing but noble deeds: that is the safest way. Thus, son of Tantalus, I mean to speak of you otherwise than those that came before me. . . . Yet I would not refer to any of the gods as cannibals. That I refuse, for rarely does a blasphemer escape punishment (*Ibid.* 35 ff. and 53–4).

And the poet boldly proceeds to correct and re-write the story of Tantalus and Pelops, by omitting everything that seems to him unworthy of the divine majesty.

Here we may recall Xenophanes' criticisms of traditional mythology (see p. 117). But Pindar is no philosopher, and his much less radical reservations apply only to certain particularly scandalous tales. He is a poet with profound religious convictions: but he is also a theologian, who having thought much about the heavenly myths, is not afraid to modify them if they conflict with his conception of divinity. He is fully conscious of his creative power as a poet and claims the right to make use of mythological material in his own fashion.

According to him, if Tantalus was condemned to suffer in hell, it was not because he had killed and cut up his own son, but for having stolen from the gods the nectar and ambrosia that could make men immortal. In other words, like Prometheus who stole fire from heaven in order to give it to mankind, Tantalus was a courageous benefactor of humanity, victimized by divine jealousy. But, in thus maintaining the gulf that separates them from mortals, the gods were only doing what they were obliged to do; and Pindar failed to realize that, by thus modifying the myth, he was perhaps creating a less flattering image of the gods than that which emerges from the old version, according to which Tantalus was punished for a monstrous crime. The moral he draws from the fate of Tantalus is that nothing can be hidden from the gods: 'He who hopes to conceal from the gods but a single one of his acts deceives himself.'

In the third, and the beginning of the fourth and last, triads, he then goes on to describe the famous 'race of kings', prototype of the Olympic chariot races, in which Pelops, as a result of defeating Oenomaus, king of Pisa and father of Hippodameia, carried off the young princess as his bride. In the prayer he addresses to Poseidon before this exploit, Pelops gives vent to his feelings:

Great deeds are not for cowards. Death comes to all men. Why skulk in darkness, then, remote from all that makes life worth the living, till an obscure old age consumes us? No, I will face the contest (*Ibid.* 82 ff.).

Like all the Greek poets, Pindar often draws upon Homer, and here he must have in mind the passage in the *Iliad* where Sarpedon the Lycian says to Glaucus: 'Ah, my friend, if after living through this war we could be sure of ageless immortality, I should neither take my place in the front line nor send you out to win honour in the field. But things are not like that. Death has a thousand pitfalls for our feet; and nobody can save himself and cheat him. So in we go, whether we yield the glory to some other man or win it for ourselves' (Book XII).

Pindar concludes the poem with the hope that Hieron may one day also win the chariot race, and promises that when he does he will again write a hymn in his honour. His final words are:

For surely the Muses hold in reserve for me a mighty shaft. Many degrees of greatness are there: for kings, its highest pinnacle. So look not upon me with envy! May you walk always upon the heights, while I in days to come, still the companion of the victors, make known my genius amongst the Greeks of every land (*Ibid.* 112 ff.).

In the prelude to his *Sixth Olympian Ode*, composed in honour of Agesias of Syracuse, Pindar compares his poetry to nobly designed architecture:

To support the splendid portico, let us set up columns of gold, as though we were building a magnificent temple. And as the work grows, we will give it a façade that will shine from afar. Since our hero is a Victor at the Games, priest of the prophetic altar of Zeus, one of the founders of illustrious Syracuse, shall he want, then, for a hymn? (*Olymp.* VI, 1 ff.).

Even more impressive is the prelude to the *First Pythian Ode*, dedicated to Hieron after his victory in 470 in the chariot race at the Delphic hippodrome. It is in praise of music, and the poet immediately sweeps us up on to Olympus:

O golden lyre, immemorial apanage of Apollo and the violet-haired Muses, at the sound of your voice the dancers' rhythmic tread opens the festival, and the singers obey the signal as your trembling strings sound the first notes of the prelude in the ears of the chorus. You have power to put out the fire at the point of the thunderbolt; perched on the sceptre of Zeus, the eagle succumbs to sleep, till on either side his swift wings droop, this king among birds; above his beaked head a dark cloud floats, softly closing his eyelids; and now he arches his supple back in sleep, lulled by the magic of your notes. And even stern Ares, forgetting the harsh iron of his spears, lets sleep sink softly on his soul . . . Then he who lies in hideous Tartarus, hundred-headed Typhon, enemy of the gods, trembles (*Pyth.* 1, 1 ff.).

This Ode, consisting of five triads, is possibly Pindar's masterpiece. Typhon, the monstrous giant overthrown by Zeus, was supposed to have been imprisoned in Tartarus, beneath the volcanic region that stretches from Vesuvius to Etna; whenever he turned over, there was an eruption. Now, Hieron had recently founded a town to which he had given the name Etna and Pindar seized the opportunity of describing a volcanic eruption such as he himself may well have witnessed:

There from the mountain sprang, spewed out from the abyss, the purest springs of unapproachable fire. All day these torrents spread their flood of burning smoke; and in the darkness, a red flame rolled towards the sea, dragging with hideous din great blocks of fallen stone into the depths (*Ibid.* 21 ff.).

In the fourth triad of the same Ode, Pindar recalls, in praise of the tyrants of Syracuse, sons of Deinomenes, the victories of Himera, where Gelon had defeated the Carthaginians in 480 (see p. 121), and of Cumae, where Hieron had defeated the Etruscans in 474. To the Greeks, the Carthaginians and the Etruscans were the barbarians of the West, as the Persians were of the East, which is why Pindar here associates the two victories:

I beseech you, O Zeus, grant that the Carthaginian may stay at home in peace, and that the war-cry of the Etruscan may be stilled, for did not they see, at Cumae, their insolence weeping for the loss of their fleet? They know how they suffered when the chief of the Syracusans brought them to heel, when he flung the prime of their youth from the prows of their swift ships, thus delivering Greece from the threat of bitter slavery. For Salamis I will seek my reward in the gratitude of the Athenians, at Sparta I will speak of the battle fought at the foot of Cithaeron[1]—where twice the Medes with their curved bows met disaster—but not without first having laid at the feet of Deinomenes' sons the hymn they have earned by their valour (*Ibid*, 1, 71 ff.).

If Pindar felt it necessary to modify certain of the myths, like that of Pelops, it was to make them conform with his own religious beliefs

[1] The battle of Plataea.

135

For him, the gods were all powerful; nothing could escape their grasp and nothing good could be achieved without their help. In the *Second Pythian Ode* he said:

God alone shall accomplish everything in accordance with his hopes: God, who outsoars the eagle in its flight and overtakes the dolphin in the sea, bends the proud man to his will, while to others he bequeaths imperishable glory (*Pyth.* II, 49 ff.).

This might almost be a verse from one of the Hebrew psalms: its inspiration seems to spring from an acceptance of monotheism. But the truth is that all Greeks, whether poets or philosophers, were equally at home with the multiple gods of polytheism or the conception of a single divine essence: to them, their innumerable divinities appeared as different emanations of a single supreme principle. Though Pindar's gods have the same names as Homer's they are by no means identical with them. Zeus still occupies first place, but his son Apollo is no longer the cruel god who inflicts sickness and death with his arrows; he has become 'philanthropic', the friend of mankind. He, is omniscient, and it is impossible to imagine him being misled, as Zeus is in the *Iliad* by the feminine wiles of Hera; or even to think of teaching him anything. In the *Ninth Pythian Ode*, Apollo asks the Centaur Chiron to tell him about the birth of Cyrene, the nymph he has just fallen in love with, and the Centaur replies:

What strange caprice moves you to speak so craftily, you who can neither lie nor deceive yourself? Do you, O king, ask me how this girl was born? You who know the dread term of all things, each twist and turn they take, who can count the leaves the earth thrusts forth in spring, and the grains of sand in sea and river, stirred by the waves and the winds' breath—you, who can clearly see the future and all its causes (*Pyth.* IX, 42 ff.).

Pindar's greatest fear is to speak ill of the gods, to commit blasphemy. His odes contain many prayers as when Pelops prays to Poseidon. Reading him, one is continually aware of a profound faith, a spirit of contemplation and worship. He frequently expresses his ideas about morality and the human condition; and here, too, while accepting traditional views, he at the same time seeks to rid them of impurities and to infuse them with spirituality. In the *Eighth Pythian Ode* he exclaims:

Ephemeral creatures that we are! Who shall say what each man is, and is not? For man is but the shadow of a dream. Yet if the gods bestow upon him but a gleam of their own radiance, bright flame surrounds him and his life is sweet (*Pyth.* VIII, 95 ff.)

Pindar is less pessimistic than Homer or Hesiod. Realizing like them how brief, fragile and cruel a thing human existence is, he still thinks it possible for men to experience some happiness here on earth, provided always that the gods show them favour. For him, this happiness is called youth, beauty, love, wealth, power and, above all, fame. But the joys of life are always short-lived and uncertain, in a sense accidental, since they depend solely upon the gods who may prove to be capricious. In the end it is unhappiness that prevails: and, indeed, the *Eighth Pythian Ode*, from which the above optimistic lines are taken, is above all, to use the words of one of the scholiasts, 'a lamentation upon human existence'.

As to the further question—whether man, this ephemeral creature committed to death, may expect happiness in the beyond?—here again, when we remember the answer that the shade of Achilles gave to Odysseus (see p. 36), Pindar appears to be less pessimistic than Homer. This is almost certainly due to the extent to which Pindar was influenced by Orphic mysticism and 'the fine hopes' of the Pythagoreans. For him, Orpheus was the son of Apollo; and in the following passage he is clearly referring to his Orphic beliefs:

All men who have had the energy, during their triple sojourn in this world and the next, to keep their souls pure of all evil, shall follow to the end of the path of Zeus that leads to the castle of Kronos. There, where the Islands of the Blest are cooled by ocean breezes, from the splendour of golden flowers, some on the branches of magnificent trees springing from the earth, some nourished by the water, shall they weave themselves garlands and crowns (*Olymp.* II, 75 ff.).

Yet the reader who confined himself to the *epinikia* would have but an incomplete idea of Pindar's poetry. True, it is there that one finds the inspired and always gravely serious poet, the prophetic seer conscious of his mission, concerned to raise the minds of all those who attended performances of his genuinely liturgical odes towards the transcendent, omnipotent and omniscient gods. But a style of sustained nobility, an eloquence that occasionally tends towards over-emphasis, can become wearisome, unless every now and then the poet

allows himself and his reader to relax a little, even perhaps to smile.
And this is something that Pindar himself well understood. The
Thirteenth Olympian Ode was written in honour of Xenophon of
Corinth, who had won the foot race and the pentathlon. Now this
athlete, being a devout man who did not rely only on the strength
of his muscles, had made a vow that, if he returned from Olympia
victorious, he would offer to the Aphrodite of his town a troop of
holy prostitutes. He carried out his vow and when the time came for
him to present his gift and to offer the appropriate sacrifice to the
goddess, Pindar composed a second poem, this short *scolion*, or
drinking song:

O hospitable girls, hand-maids of Peitho[1] in opulent Corinth, you who
make the altar smoke with the golden tears of incense, how often do your
thoughts turn towards Aphrodite, the celestial mother of love? In the eyes
of the goddess, my children, the tender fruit of your youth that you gather
upon your delectable couches is blameless; for what necessity demands
cannot be wrong. But what will the lords of the Isthmus[2] have to say, I
wonder, when they find that for the prelude to my honey-sweet song I
have chosen to sing of public women! . . . O Cyprian queen, see how
Xenophon, grateful to you for having granted his prayer, has brought to
your sanctuary fifty girls sworn to your service (*Enkomion* III, Ed. Puech,
IV, 188–9).

AESCHYLUS

Between the Theban Pindar and the Athenian Aeschylus, there are
many similarities that we shall shortly be discussing. In the same
way that Theseus came to be regarded as the real founder of Athens,
while Cecrops and the other kings that preceded him were forgotten,
so Aeschylus may be seen as the true creator of Attic tragedy. Before
him, however, there had been Thespis (see p. 109ff.) and, more
important, Phrynichos, who, though his work was properly speaking
lyrical rather than dramatic, was certainly a poet of talent.

Phrynichos, an Athenian like Thespis, still had only one actor,
though this actor took several different parts in succession and carried
on a kind of dialogue with the Chorus, like Aegeus in the dithyramb
by Bacchylides referred to above (p. 127). There was scarcely any action

[1] Peitho is the personification of Persuasion or Seduction. She was one of the goddesses
attached to Aphrodite.
[2] Probably the magistrates who presided at the Isthmian Games which were held
near Corinth.

in his plays, but long after his death the sweet harmony of his songs was remembered by the Athenians: Aristophanes frequently praised him: in the *Birds*, for instance, he says of him that he 'worked at his heavenly songs like a bee making honey'.

The subjects of most of his tragedies were taken from ancient legend, as may be seen from the titles that have come down to us: *Alcestis, Antaeus, The Danaides, Tantalus, Troilus* and *The Women of Pleuron* (which probably dealt with the story of Meleager). But Phrynichos also initiated a quite new development of tragedy, seeking inspiration in contemporary political and military events.

I have mentioned earlier that Miletus, the intellectual and artistic capital of Ionia as well as its strongest city, was captured and ruthlessly punished by the Persians (p. 120). Not long afterwards, in Athens, Phrynichos produced a tragedy, *The Capture of Miletus*, which profoundly moved the audience: they 'burst into tears', says Herodotus. But, when they recovered from this immediate reaction, the Athenians, annoyed at the poet for drawing attention to a disaster for which they felt themselves to be at least partly responsible, imposed a fine on him.

However, this did not induce Phrynichos to give up writing on contemporary themes, for four years after the battle of Salamis he put on *The Phoenician Women*: the women of Sidon who formed the Chorus, wives and mothers of the Phoenician seamen who had proved to be the Greeks' most redoubtable opponents, bewailed the defeat of Xerxes in such melodious and moving songs that they continued to be popular in Athens throughout the whole of the fifth century. Here, too, there can scarcely have been much action, since right at the beginning, while arranging seats for the ministers of the great king, a eunuch announced the result of the battle in a prologue.

The Phoenician Women may be seen as a rough sketch for the *Persae* of Aeschylus, since the latter went out of his way to pay tribute to his predecessor at the beginning of his own tragedy: its first line, 'Behold most of the Persians have already set forth for Greece!' being taken almost word for word from the opening of *The Phoenician Women*.

Aeschylus was almost exactly a contemporary of Pindar, having been born of a noble family in Eleusis in 525 B.C. Like the Theban poet he was a believer, interested in theology and inclined to reflect upon the gods and the fate of humanity. Like him, too, he wrote in a grave and noble style, difficult and often rather abrupt. And, again like him, he seems to have been fully aware of his own genius and to have been of a proud and passionate disposition: at least so he is described by Aristophanes in the *Frogs,* though the latter was not born until after his death and could therefore only speak of him in the light of his work or from hearsay.

The special distinction of Aeschylus in Aristophanes' eyes was the fact that he had fought at Marathon, that he was a Marathonomachos, a man who had belonged to the great and noble period when Athens herself was covered in glory and the strictly brought up Athenians were decent law-abiding men, ready to fight for their country like heroes; a period full of old-fashioned ideas of nobility which Aristophanes and his contemporaries admired, while at the same time regarding some of them as slightly ridiculous.

Aeschylus had, in fact, fought not only at Marathon but also at Salamis, being thirty-five years old at the time of the first battle, and forty-five at the time of the second. His epitaph, quoted at the beginning of this chapter, may perhaps have been written by himself, but in any case it indicates that, in his time, an Athenian's behaviour as a soldier was more highly esteemed than any literary merit, for there is no reference to his poetic activity, though his ninety tragedies contributed so much to his country's fame.

He made his first appearance in the theatre when he was twenty-five, and it was not until sixteen years later, in 484, that he gained the prize. His early years must therefore have been difficult and hard-working. In 472 he achieved a second victory, this time with the *Persae;* and it was probably then that he was invited by Hieron to put on this tragedy in Syracuse, for the victory of Salamis that it celebrated was as important as those of Himera and Cumae. Amongst the poets at Hieron's court Aeschylus must have met Simonides, Bacchylides and Pindar; and it was while he was in Sicily that he wrote a tragedy in honour of Etna, the town that Hieron had recently founded (see p. 135).

In 468, after his return to Athens, he had the disappointment of seeing Sophocles carry off the prize for the first time, though in the following year he had his revenge with the Theban tetralogy (of which only the *Seven* has come down to us) and ten years later saw the triumph of the *Oresteia.* But by that time Cimon having been exiled in 461, Ephialtes and Pericles were already initiating their democratic reforms; and Aeschylus was a member of the Eupatridae. Once more he set out for Sicily, and there before long (455) he died, almost seventy years old, at the city of Gela.

Of Aeschylus' ninety tragedies, only seven remain, less than one in ten. Three of these, *Agamemnon*, the *Choephoroe* and the *Eumenides* comprise the connected trilogy of the *Oresteia* and deal with successive phases of the same legend and its chain of murders. Three others, the *Suppliants*, the *Seven Against Thebes* and *Prometheus Bound*, certainly belonged to similar trilogies, though the other two tragedies have in each case disappeared. The *Persae*, however, was performed between two of the lost tragedies, the *Phineus* and *Glaucus of Potniae*, the theme of which bore no relation either to each other or to the *Persae*. Thus it would seem that although Aeschylus had a predilection for the connected trilogy, the scope of which was well suited to his genius, he also wrote at least one 'free' trilogy. Whether Phrynichos had composed connected trilogies is not known, but it seems unlikely that either the *Capture of Miletus* or the *Phoenician Women* formed part of such composite works. As the successors of Aeschylus soon abandoned this grandly impressive form, he may possibly have been the only writer to have adopted it.

None of Aeschylus' satyr plays have survived.

In the tragedies, Aeschylus began by introducing a second actor, and later, in imitation of the young Sophocles, a third. For the *Suppliants*, the *Persae* and the *Seven*, only two were required, though each of them had to play several parts in succession. For example, in the *Persae*, the important parts of Atossa and Xerxes were taken by the *protagonist*, those of Darius and the messenger by the *deuteragonist*, which is why Atossa cannot welcome Xerxes on his return; and in the same way, in the *Suppliants*, Danaus is unavoidably absent when the Herald arrives, since both parts were played by the same actor.

In its opening scene, the *Prometheus* seems to demand the simultaneous presence of three actors: the god Hephaestus, with the help of Cratos and Bia (Power and Strength) is chaining Prometheus and binding him to a rock. Bia, who remains silent, is simply a walking-on part, but both Cratos and Hephaestus have to speak; and though, while the three executioners are on the stage, Prometheus says nothing, once they have withdrawn, he utters the 'cosmic' prayer: 'O holy air and swift winged winds, O river-waters and the multitudinous smile of the sea's waves, O earth, mother of all creatures, and you, O sun, from whom nothing is hidden, behold what a god has been made to suffer at the hands of gods' (*Prometheus* 89 ff.). It has been suggested that, at this point, the protagonist must have taken the place of a lay-figure, but, as Maurice Croiset remarked, 'not everyone would have been prepared to accept such a lay-figure'. At the same time, throughout the rest of the play, only two actors are required.

Each of the three parts of the *Oresteia*, however, demand three. In the *Choephoroe*, for example, the protagonist played the part of Orestes, the deuteragonist those of Electra and Clytemnestra, and the tritagonist those of Pylades (this is not simply a walking-on part: he has to speak lines 900–2), the servant, the nurse and Aegisthus. By giving the parts of Clytemnestra and Electra to the same actor, Aeschylus made it impossible for mother and daughter to appear together, whereas both Sophocles and Euripides, in their *Electras*, were to make a great point of the confrontation of the two women.

The anonymous author of the *Life of Aeschylus* says: 'He was the first to heighten tragedy by more effective action, and to introduce an elaborate stage setting that would impress the audience with the magnificence of the spectacle by using painted scenery and machines, altars and tombs, trumpets, ghosts and the Erinyes. He dressed his actors in huge trailing robes with long sleeves, and, to make them taller, increased the height of their buskins.' Moreover, like the lyric poets, Aeschylus was also a musician: the choral song and the monody with flute accompaniment both played an important part in all his tragedies, and there was also dancing. His plays were therefore comparable with our opera, but an opera of which the libretto, which alone remains to us, bears all the marks of one of the greatest poets of all time.

Recently, attempts have been made to prove that the *Suppliants* was one of Aeschylus' later works. However that may be, of all the tragedies that have been preserved, it is the one with the most archaic structure, the nearest to what we may imagine the dramatic poems of Phrynichos to have been; the lyrical element is still predominant and the protagonist whose fate is at stake is the Chorus. The action of the play is simple, linear and elemental: in response to the long prayer of the Danaides, Pelasgos, king of Argos, at last appears; but he cannot make up his mind to declare himself their protector against the sons of Aegyptus, who want to carry them off in marriage, because he is not convinced of the justice of their cause. 'The great scene between Pelasgos and the Chorus,' says Paul Mazon, 'which takes up almost the whole of the first part of the play, has the naïve gravity, the pious intensity, of an Italian primitive.' In the end, however, Pelasgos gives in to the pleading of the Suppliants; another example of the irresistible religious force of prayer in antiquity, like Priam's, in Book XXIV of the *Iliad* (see p. 41). The Herald sent by the sons of Aegyptus violently demands the surrender of the Danaides, but thanks to Pelasgos' firm refusal he goes away empty-handed; not, however, before his threats have announced the other, lost, plays of the tetralogy: the *Egyptians*, the *Danaides* and the satyr play, *Amymone*.

The profundity of Aeschylus' thought would be clearer to us if all four of these plays, but especially the three tragedies, had been preserved. Nevertheless, from the *Suppliants*, it seems fairly clear that he approved the refusal of the Danaides to let themselves be married by force, while at the same time blaming them for expressing their horror of men and rejection of physical love. By so doing they were guilty of pride (*hybris*), and also of violating the laws of nature which express the will of the gods; a crime for which they are eventually condemned to infernal punishment. He was to return to this theme of the sanctity of marriage in the *Oresteia*, and in the *Eumenides* he says: 'A law more powerful than any oath protects the marriage bed for there men and women are joined by fate' (217–8).

Paul Mazon's observation, that 'in this drama, though the principal character is a Chorus of young girls, there is no trace of feminine charm', is fully justified. And in the *Frogs*, Aristophanes was to make Euripides say to Aeschylus: 'There's certainly not much Aphrodite about you!'—or, in other words, little tenderness. But this was typical of the hard, virile men of Marathon: for them, marriage was a sacred institution in which personal feelings counted for very little, and love (*eros*), since it could only exist between equals, was necessarily homosexual. There was certainly more warmth of feeling in the *Myrmidons*, a lost tragedy in which Aeschylus portrayed the friendship of Achilles and Patroclus as passionate love.

In the *Persae*, the Chorus is not composed of women as it was in Phrynichos' *Phoenician Women*, but of counsellors of the Great King, the Faithful, who were better able to understand the historical importance of events. In 476, Themistocles had been the Leader of the Chorus in Phrynichos' play celebrating the battle of Salamis; in 472, Aeschylus chose as his Leader of the Chorus the young Pericles, then only about twenty years old, who must certainly have been interested in the success of a tragedy in which contemporary politics played such an important part.

The play opens with the Faithful expressing their concern at being without news either of the army or of the king. Throughout the play the Persians always refer to themselves as the 'barbarians', and the gods they invoke are Greek gods; at the same time, Aeschylus delights in recording the sonorous names of the Persian lords, 'Amistres, Artaphernes, Megabates and Astaspes', and the prodigious richness of their costumes and armour. All this created for the Greek spectator the sense of wonder that exoticism always arouses, as well as a sense of superiority at having defeated so wealthy and powerful an enemy.

In the next scene, Queen Atossa, wife of Darius and mother of Xerxes, comes to consult the old men of the Chorus about an ill-omened dream she has had during the night. Aeschylus fully appreciated the dramatic effect of warnings conveyed in dreams; and how many dramatic authors have made use of the device since! Then the Messenger arrives and announces disaster: 'Persians, the whole army of the barbarians has perished!'—an exaggeration, since the forces commanded by Mardonios were still intact in central Greece. Then, turning to Atossa, he quickly reassures her with the news that Xerxes is still alive, at which she, more mother now than queen, exclaims: 'So daylight breaks the gloomy spell of night!' And the Messenger proceeds to give an account of the battle of Salamis, even down to the number of ships engaged on both sides, which is much more coherent and detailed than that of the historian Herodotus. Whereupon the Chorus laments:

Truly, this is the hour when the whole of Asia groans, knowing herself emptied of her people. Xerxes it was who led them forth, alas! Xerxes it was, alas, who lost them! With his sea-going galleys, Xerxes has brought all to ruin, alas! . . . Foot soldiers and seamen, like a huge flock of birds clothed in sombre blue, the ships bore them forth, alas! The ships, alas, have lost them! The ships grappled by disaster, the ships and the strong arms of the Ionians (*Persae*, 548 ff.).

The Queen calls upon the Chorus to summon up the shade of Darius, so that the old King may advise them in their extremity; and what follows is an extraordinary scene of black magic. The Chorus performs a violent ritual mime, punctuated with strange words and shrill onomatopoeia, and in response to the magic power of this savage incantation Darius appears from his tomb. This is a moment of intense emotion. Sixty-five years later, in the *Frogs*, Aristophanes was to recall how it still lingered in the memory of the Athenians; and even today, when the play is adequately performed, the effect is deeply moving.

Aeschylus purposely overlooks the fact that the first maritime expedition against Greece, which had been led by Darius, had foundered at Marathon. He presents him as a wise and moderate ruler, who condemns his son for 'pride' (*hybris*) and taxes him with being mad because, by risking his ships at sea, Xerxes had overstepped the bounds the gods had set to the Persian empire. Darius also foretells the future: his son's difficult retreat through Thrace and the battle of Plataea, where 'the Dorian spear will drown the earth with a rich libation of blood'. The contrast between the Greek spear and the Persian bow is a theme that runs through the whole play.

Finally, we see the pitiable arrival of Xerxes himself (it follows almost immediately after that of the Messenger, but such contractions of time were a theatrical convention) and the defeated King and his Counsellors withdraw to the palace of Susa, howling, rending their clothes and tearing out their beards in the wretchedness of their grief. What a sight for the victorious Greeks! Like the Danaides, Xerxes had tried to break the fetters imposed upon humanity by the gods; and, like them, for doing so he was cruelly punished.

The case of Eteocles in *Seven Against Thebes*, first performed in 467, is less clear. In this play, whose warlike and patriotic spirit must have appealed to the Marathonomachoi—'chockful of Ares', Aristophanes called it—Eteocles is certainly made to suffer for his fratricidal hatred of Polynices, a crime against the blood bond. But to an even greater extent he is the victim of the curse Oedipus has laid upon his two sons and, to go back still further, of the evil destiny that has pursued the Labdacidae ever since the time when Laios, the father of Oedipus, disobeyed the oracle of Apollo. Originally, the *Seven* was the third tragedy of a trilogy, and was preceded by the *Laios* and the *Oedipus*, while the satyr play that followed was called the *Sphinx*, but none of these has survived.

Eteocles is a character of great nobility,[1] and his manly resolution and ardent patriotism are emphasized by contrasting them with the timid and spineless lamentations of the Chorus of Thebans. He knows it is his destiny to perish, but he dominates his fate by sheer strength of character, the essential feature of every Greek hero from the time of Homer's Achilles onwards. He is determined to save Thebes, even at the cost of his life; and, in fact, he does so.

[1] It is perhaps true, as Paul Mazon maintains, that he is 'the finest character in the whole Greek theatre', if one is only referring to male characters, but Sophocles' Antigone and Euripides' Alcestis may be considered more exemplary.

His one moment of weakness, which he quickly overcomes, is when he realizes that he has to fight against his brother:

O crazy race, so bitterly hated by the gods! O house of Oedipus, and mine, so steeped in tears! Today, alas, a father's curse must be fulfilled, and neither weeping nor self-pity will avail (*Seven Against Thebes*, 653–7).

In this long scene, the Messenger's description of the seven enemy chieftains who are besieging the seven gates of Thebes has a remarkable power and variety, but here, as in the *Suppliants*, there is very little action: the tragedy is only brought to life and sustained by the character of Eteocles. At the end, the bodies of the two brothers are laid on the stage and the Chorus chants a solemn dirge over them.

In all his plays, Aeschylus, at once poet and theologian, is always, preoccupied with the motives underlying the actions of the gods, both upon earth and in heaven. In this respect *Prometheus Bound* is especially significant since its whole action takes place in the world of the gods. Prometheus, being an Immortal, is thus a god like all the other characters in the play: Hephaestus, Cratus, Oceanus and his daughters (the Oceanides who form the Chorus), Io, the daughter of the river god Inachus, and Hermes, not to mention Zeus himself who, though he does not actually appear on the stage, is the motive force of the whole play. What is at issue here is a struggle between the gods, like that of the 'Theomachia' in the *Iliad*.

This amazing play presents Zeus as an abominable tyrant, for Hephaestus and Hermes merely carry out his orders; the first with sad resignation, the second with cynical zeal. By contrast, the tortured Prometheus, the benefactor of mankind upon whom he has bestowed the gift of fire and of civilization, appears as the spokesman of justice who is unjustly punished—I almost wrote, crucified. Moreover, the episode of Io, though quite foreign to the main theme, is related to it by the fact that it too illustrates Zeus' injustice.

But in order that there shall be conflict and therefore matter for tragedy, it is necessary that Prometheus should not only be the victim: even when he is bound to the rock he must also have a weapon he can avail himself of. In fact, he possesses a terrible secret: he knows the name of the goddess (Thetis), whose marriage to Zeus, if consummated, would cost the lord of the world his throne, for it had been foretold that the son she would bear him would prove stronger than his father. But despite Hermes' insistent demands, Prometheus obstinately refuses to reveal the secret, and amidst the rolling of thunder, the rock to which he is chained is shattered. The last words he speaks are almost the same as his first, quoted above (p. 141): 'Behold what a god has been made to suffer at the hands of gods.'

If *Prometheus Bound* had simply been one play on its own, it would appear to be, first and foremost, a vehement protest against the injustice of the supreme god. And in this respect, it is important to note the arrogance displayed by Prometheus: though in deceiving Zeus he was inspired by the best intentions, his attitude subsequently hardened into one of haughty revolt, rejecting any kind of compromise. Thus Prometheus also, like the Danaides and Xerxes, was guilty of the sin of *hybris*. But *Prometheus Bound* was only the first part of a connected trilogy which continued with *Prometheus Unbound* and the *Fire Bearer*, both lost. We know, however, that in the second tragedy Zeus' son Heracles shot his father's eagle as it was feeding on the liver of the Titan, and that in gratitude the latter disclosed the terrible secret to Zeus and was therefore pardoned. The effect of this reconciliation was to establish Zeus as a just god, which at the beginning of his reign he certainly had not been. Thus, while drawing upon the ancient *Theogonies* such as Hesiod's, Aeschylus at the same time modified them in order to introduce his own moral convictions. The Greek gods were immortal, but they were not eternal nor immutable since they were born of time: Zeus himself was the son of Kronos. They, like men, were therefore capable of development, and in this extremely 'theological' trilogy Aeschylus' purpose was to show that, through his conflict with Prometheus, the greatest of the gods had learnt to become just.

Of all that remains to us of Aeschylus' work, the *Oresteia* is beyond question the pinnacle of his achievement. This connected trilogy, which was first performed in 458, when Aeschylus was sixty-nine years old, has come down to us complete, and only the satyr play that should have followed it, the *Proteus*, is lost.

The first part, *Agamemnon*, opens in an apparently light-hearted atmosphere: almost at once, the sentry posted by Clytemnestra on the terrace outside the palace sees the signal fire announcing the fall of Troy. But mixed with the feeling of satisfaction we become aware of a sense of anguish, at first muted, then gradually intensifying until at last it becomes stifling. Already there is something disquieting in the sentry's words: 'A great ox stands on my tongue, but if the walls of this palace could speak, they would tell the whole truth' (*Agamemnon*

36–8). What he is referring to, as will soon become clear, is Clytemnestra's hatred of Agamemnon and her love for the usurper Aegisthus. The Chorus of old men of Mycenae dare not rejoice at the good news: for can it really be that victory over the Trojans marks the end of the misfortune of the Atreidae? Does not the blood of Iphigenia still cry out for vengeance? In sacking Troy, have not the Achaeans been guilty of crimes and sacrilege?

To this last question, the Herald who has been sent ahead by Agamemnon gives an overwhelming answer: the triumph of the Achaeans had been accompanied by every kind of excess and impious *hybris*. At the very moment when the king is about to appear, the Chorus chants:

Justice smiles beneath the smoke-stained roof, honouring those whose lives are pure. But from palaces bedecked with gold, if ruled by a polluted hand, she averts her eyes. . . . Yet it is she, Justice, who alone leads everything to its appointed end (774 ff.).

Thus, in one sense, Clytemnestra will be carrying out a just sentence, ordained by the gods, for Agamemnon is guilty of a serious crime and must die. To bring this home visually to the audience, Aeschylus conceived the admirable stage device of the purple carpet. Such carpets were specially kept for those religious festivals at which the statues of the gods were carried in procession, and Clytemnestra orders the servants to unroll one of them before the gates of the palace; then she cunningly sets about persuading Agamemnon to enter his own house by 'this purple road'. Clearly, she is anxious for him to condemn himself by a display of pride that will prove that he considers himself the equal of the gods. The wretched man half suspects a trap and at first refuses; but eventually he consents. As he enters the palace, he recommends to his wife's care the captive he has brought back from Troy in his chariot. It is Cassandra.

When Clytemnestra, with false humility, invites her to enter the palace, Cassandra remains standing in the chariot, motionless as a statue, and maintains a silence as proud as that of Prometheus chained to the rock. But immediately Clytemnestra has left the stage, she cries out twice: 'Alas! O heaven and earth! Apollo! Apollo!' Then, in an extraordinarily effective scene, she abandons herself to prophetic frenzy: as she flings herself about, uttering hoarse cries, she actually *sees* the future, which she describes in short, broken phrases:

O unspeakable horror! What do I see? Is it the infernal net? . . . Look, trapped in a veil, the cow has snared the black-horned bull. She strikes, and he sinks into the brimming bath.

The crisis passes, and more calmly she goes on to prophesy her own fate:

She it is, the two-footed lioness that slept with the wolf while the noble lion was away, she it is who will kill me, wretch that I am (1072 ff. *passim*).

Then she snatches the prophetic fillets from her brow and flings them to the ground, and with lowered head hurries into the palace where she knows she is to be stabbed to death: 'This house stinks of murder and spilt blood.' And suddenly from within, the death cries of Agamemnon are heard, proving that her prophecy has come true.

Thanks to the rotating stage, known as the *ekkyklema*, the audience could now see inside the palace, where the two bodies were laid out side by side, while nearby Clytemnestra, still holding the bloody sword in her hand, proclaims her pride in this double murder with horrifying cynicism:

His blood sprayed me with its black drops, sweet to my heart as the dew with which Zeus feeds the germ within the bud. . . . Here lies Agememnon, my husband, slain by my hand. And the work is well done, for thus it had to be (1390 ff.).

As the Chorus indignantly protests, a long debate ensues which, since it provides Aeschylus with an opportunity to express his ideas fully, Clytemnestra makes no attempt to cut short. Agamemnon is the victim of the ancient curse that hangs over the race of Atreus and Thyestes, but, at the same time, also of his own sins, the worst of which, in the eyes of Clytemnestra, was the sacrifice of Iphigenia, though she also reproaches him for his faithlessness to herself—to her, the adulterous wife,—with Chryseis and Cassandra. Since it is Clytemnestra, his wife, who has killed him, the vengeance satisfied by this first murder calls for still further vengeance: 'The race is riveted to misfortune.' Confronted with this threat from the Chorus, for a moment Clytemnestra weakens, but the appearance of Aegisthus revives all her old audacity. The Chorus Leader names the future avenger: Orestes. Furious, Aegisthus begins to threaten him, at which the Chorus Leader exclaims: 'What? So bold? Must the cock show off to his hen?' But Clytemnestra has now recovered her calm assurance: 'Pay no attention to their idle barking,' she says. 'You and I, masters of this house, know full well how to restore order' (1671–3).

One can see that, like the Danaides, like Eteocles and Prometheus, Agamemnon is at the same time both in the right and in the wrong: in the right as regards the atrocious Clytemnestra, in the wrong as regards the innocent Iphigenia whom her mother believed herself to be avenging. It is as though his sins were the embodiment of the curse that hangs over his whole race like some kind of 'original sin' and from which were to spring all the murders committed by successive generations. In this doomed family, crime engenders crime, vengeance cries out for vengeance. Will there ever be an end to the chain of horrors?

In *Agamemnon*, this question is clearly posed, but it is not answered until the third part of the trilogy. The second, the *Choephoroe*, enacts the vengeance that has already been foretold. In the centre of the stage is the tomb of Agamemnon, dominating the whole play and, in a sense, its protagonist. Right at the beginning, Orestes appears, having been reminded of his oath by the Chorus in *Agamemnon*: the oracle of Apollo had ordered him, as soon as he reached the age of manhood, to avenge his father by killing Clytemnestra and Aegisthus. Almost at once Electra appears with her serving women, the Choephoroe or libation-bearers, who form the Chorus, to lay funeral offerings on her father's grave which has hitherto been neglected. She has been sent by Clytemnestra who has been frightened by a dream (like Atossa). Electra finds a lock of hair that Orestes has left on the grave and sees his footprints. Presently he comes forward and in a moving scene brother and sister recognize each other. They climb up on to the funeral mound and, kneeling and striking the ground with their fists, pronounce an incantation like that of the Persians at the tomb of Darius. Here, however, the dead man's ghost does not appear; though he is to aid them by sending 'Justice to fight on their side'.

From this point, events follow one another swiftly. As a result of two theatrical devices, on the part of Orestes and the Chorus, the double murder is carried out inside the palace. But while Aeschylus does not allow the audience to see the actual matricide, the moments immediately preceding it are portrayed in a brilliantly dramatic scene: hearing that Aegisthus has already been killed, Clytemnestra comes

9. The François vase, *c.* 570. A black-figured crater by Ergotimos, decorated with scenes of the marriage of Peleus and Thetis, painted by Cleitias (p. 92). *Archaeological Museum, Florence*

10. Red-figured crater, *c.* 475, depicting the episode in the Theseus legend which forms the subject of Bacchylides' *Ode* XVII (p. 126). *Civic Museum, Bologna*

out of the palace calling for an axe and almost runs into her son
carrying a drawn sword in his hand. She flings herself on her knees,
pointing to the breast that once suckled him and begging for mercy;
for a moment Orestes hesitates, but when Pylades reminds him of
Apollo's injunction, he drags his mother into the palace and kills her
too.

Here, as in the parallel scene at the end of *Agamemnon*, the revolving
stage enables the spectators to see the two dead bodies, with their
murderer beside them. But Orestes is much less sure of himself than
his mother was at a similar moment. He attempts to justify the deed he
has committed, but his mind reels under its burden of remorse: he
imagines he sees the Erinyes, 'his mother's maddened bitches', who will
pursue him for ever like Gorgons, blood dripping from their eyes and
snakes writhing in their hair. And he sets out for Delphi, hoping to
find sanctuary there with the god who has driven him to murder.

We shall come back to the *Choephoroe* later, when comparing it with
the *Electra* of Sophocles and of Euripides, for it so happens that the
three plays, in which each of the great tragic writers deals with the
same story in his own way, have all come down to us.

In the *Eumenides*[1], we follow Orestes to Delphi. The Pythian
priestess is praying before the temple of Apollo, which she presently
enters. But almost immediately, uttering a cry of horror, she returns
to the stage: she has seen Orestes, his blood-stained sword still in his
hand, clasping the *omphalos*, the sacred navel-stone of Delphi, and
accompanied by a hideous troop of Erinyes, who eventually follow
her out of the temple. At the original performance, it is said, so
horrible was their appearance that some of the spectators sprang
from their seats in fright and began to leave the theatre.

Apollo wants to drive the Furies from his sanctuary, and another
theomachy ensues not unlike that in *Prometheus*: but this time the
conflict is between the young god of light and purification and the
goddesses of night who represent the ancient law, according to which
the murder of anyone related by blood demands ineluctable vengeance.
(The Furies had not pursued Clytemnestra, because she was not
related by blood to the husband she had killed.) Now her ghost
appears—alive or dead she figures in all three parts of the trilogy—
lashing them on, inciting them to pursue Orestes. Apollo's argument
is that the marriage bond, 'sealed by Zeus and Hera, goddess of

---

[1] Both the Eumenides and the Erinyes refer to the redoubtable avenging goddesses
whom we know as the Furies.

Hymen', is as strong as the ties of blood (see p. 143), and that therefore Clytemnestra was guilty, whereas Orestes, since he was acting in obedience to the gods, is innocent.

In this play, unity of place and of time are not observed, since the second part takes place in Athens and, in the interval, Orestes is supposed to have spent a long time wandering about the world 'wearing out' the stain of guilt. It is Athena herself who solemnly summons the Council of the Areopagus to try Orestes and she ostentatiously casts her vote in his favour. The reason she gives for doing so is unexpected: being herself motherless (she was born from the forehead of Zeus) she is on the side of the father, that is, of Agamemnon. And Apollo himself, as Orestes' advocate, supports this singular argument: 'The mother is not the child's begetter, she only nurses the seed implanted in her. The true begetter is the man who quickens her: she but a stranger who protects the shoot' (*Eumenides*, 657 ff.); and in proof of this he points to Athena, the goddess born without a mother. Aeschylus' contemporaries, deeply imbued with the sense of masculine superiority, would have been only too ready to accept this argument.

The tribunal is equally divided, for and against Orestes, but he is aquitted, thanks to the casting vote of Athena, the president. He sets out for Mycenae, pledging eternal friendship to Athens on behalf of his descendants, the Argives. As for the Erinyes, abandoning their role of ferocious law-givers, a sanctuary is created for them on the hill of Ares where the Areopagus is held, and there, transformed into the Eumenides, the 'kindly Ones', they become the protectors of flocks and harvests. Actually, the name Eumenides is simply a euphemism, like the word *euonymos*, which was always used superstitiously to denote the 'left', a word as 'sinister' in the eyes of the Greeks as it was to the Romans.

Thus peace is achieved between the Erinyes and the gods of Olympus, between the ancient code of law, that is to say, and the new and more clement one. Since this was due to Athena and her favourite city, one may imagine how flattering the ending of the trilogy was to Athenian patriotism, while at the same time it reminded the Argives of the gratitude they owed to the city of Pallas. Yet at the very moment when Aeschylus was paying tribute to the Areopagus, Ephialtes and Pericles had already taken steps to restrict the prerogatives of this aristocratic body: the poet's political attitude would therefore seem to be pretty clear.

Aeschylean tragedy was a tremendous dramatic spectacle, arousing in the audience feelings of uneasiness, fear, anguish and terror. But, by the conclusion of the trilogy, the conflict, in which, as in the epic, the gods often participated (sometimes, indeed, as in *Prometheus*, dominating the whole play), was resolved, and the discordant voices of the antagonists were hushed.

The Attic theatre grew out of lyric poetry, which it managed to absorb without destroying. Like Pindar, Aeschylus, being a great lyric poet, was also a musician. Here we have to rely on tradition, which speaks highly of his musical gifts, for all the evidence on which to base a judgment has disappeared. But we do have, in all the seven tragedies that have been preserved, the words of the Chorus; and in these lyrics there is little of suavity or tenderness. The laments of the Danaides are in no sense elegiac: they are cries of hatred, revolt and terror. In *Prometheus*, it is true, the Oceanides display more gentleness and feminine grace, for the unjust suffering of the tortured god moves them to compassion. But the Chorus of the Erinyes is terrifying and their songs are filled with violence and savage cruelty. The poet who could speak of 'the multitudinous smile of the sea's waves' rarely smiled himself, and when he did one is reminded of Ajax, the terrible hero of the *Iliad*, whose smile was a frightening grimace. The lyrics of Aeschylus are distinguished by their force and brilliance: they do not charm, they strike and dazzle.

In the *Frogs*, Aristophanes makes Euripides criticize Aeschylus for his pompous and over-emphatic style, especially for his vocabulary with its neologisms and long composite words, 'pegged together' as he says. Yet, in the same comedy, he is also praised for being 'the first of the Greeks to have created phrases splendid as towers and raised the level of tragic poetry'. From the point of view of style, he was indeed one of the boldest of innovators, and it was he, much more than Phrynichos who established the noble, sometimes slightly mannered, language of tragedy. Yet this nobility of style is in no way to be confused wth the affectations of the French writers of the *grand siècle*; when Racine, for example, would write two lines of periphrasis rather than mention such a 'vulgar' word as 'shirt'. With Aeschylus, there is nothing in the least academic in the sustained loftiness of his style and inspiration, nor did it exclude a robust realism. The Chorus' comparison of Aegisthus to 'a cock with his hen' at the end of *Agamemnon*, quoted above, could not conceivably have been written by either Corneille or Racine.

In Book IX of the *Iliad*, Phoenix says to Achilles whom he had brought up as a child: 'You often soaked the front of my tunic with the wine you dribbled from your clumsy little mouth'. In the *Choephoroe*, Aeschylus goes much further than Homer when he makes Orestes' nurse say:

My precious Orestes! Didn't I take him from his mother the moment he was born and wear myself out nursing him? And how he used to cry! Why, he'd keep me on the go for nights on end. But when children are too young to have any sense, you've just got to treat them like puppies and put up with their tantrums. While they're still in their swaddling clothes you can't expect them to let you know every time they want to eat or drink or go on the pot—they can't help it if their little bellies work. Really, you'd need to have second sight! And Lord knows how often I was too late, and had to wash all his napkins through. But there, if you want to be a nurse, you may as well make up your mind to be a laundress as well (*Choephoroe*, 748–60).

Here, it is clear, Aeschylus is amusing himself by making the nurse speak like a woman of the people[1], adapting style and content to the character.

His work abounds with imagery, for the most part forceful and expressive. Like Pindar, he is responsive to the splendour of sunlight and the glitter of gold, as may be seen especially in the *Persae*. Often, the boldness, even the apparent incoherence, of his metaphors is disconcerting. Queen Atossa expresses her fear 'lest our wealth should become so overweening that it overthrows the edifice of our happiness and turns it to dust' (*Persae*, 162–3); and in the same play Darius says: 'Excess of pride brings forth a crop of errors, whose harvesting yields naught but tears' (821–2). Are these to be regarded as examples of preciosity and bad taste? Or is it not rather that the poet is striving to compress into a few words the wealth of imagery that spontaneously bursts upon his imagination?

It is often said that men who actually take part in a battle only remember those minute details of it that directly concern themselves, like Fabrice at the battle of Waterloo, in the *Chartreuse de Parme*. Yet Aeschylus, who had been one of the hoplites at Salamis, manages to give a most dramatic, lively and admirably composed account of this great encounter, without allowing himself to get bogged down in

[1] As Shakespeare does in *Romeo and Juliet* (Trs.).

detail. At the same time, some of the most striking scenes are brilliantly observed and described. He had seen with his own eyes the corpses of the Persians floating in the sea, prevented from sinking by the great folds of their oriental clothing, and he makes the Chorus say, as they listen to the Messenger's story: 'At your words, alas, I can see our loved ones, their lifeless bodies borne up by their woollen mantles, being endlessly tossed and soused by the heaving waves' (*Persae*, 274–7).

The dominating idea in all his plays, as in Herodotus' *Histories*, is that of Nemesis, that is to say, of the gods' jealousy. As Homer says 'Between mankind and the gods there lies an abyss'; and for mortal men to attempt to cross this abyss, either from pride or love of glory, was both impious and dangerous. Xerxes and Agamemnon, the barbarian and the Greek, were both guilty of this sin of *hybris*. 'With their speechless tongues,' says Darius, 'the mounds of dead upon Plataean soil shall proclaim in the sight of men, even to the third generation, that mortals should not strive to outstrip their human lot' (*Persae*, 818–20). Originally, before Socrates gave it another meaning, the Delphic maxim 'Know thyself' meant 'Know the limits of human nature; never forget the need for moderation and justice.' And 'Nothing in excess' was another Delphic saying. Men must always be conscious of their essential weakness. The Chorus of Oceanides says to Prometheus: 'What help did you expect from these creatures of a day? Did you not see the feeble impotence, like that of dreams, that dogs the footsteps of the human race?' (*Prometheus Bound*, 546–50)—lines that echo those of Pindar in the *Eighth Pythian Ode* (see p. 137).

Like Pindar, Aeschylus was a faithful follower of the Pythian Apollo, as the *Eumenides* abundantly proves. Is it possible that this supplement to conventional religious belief, which Pindar seems to have found in Orphism, had reached Aeschylus through initiation in the Eleusinian mysteries? He was born at Eleusis; and, in one of his serious moments, Aristophanes makes him offer up this solemn prayer: 'O Demeter, you who have nourished my soul, let me prove myself worthy of your mysteries' (*Frogs*, 786–7). There is no direct evidence, however, that he was actually initiated; and Mazon, for example, thought that he was not. 'Nor is this at all surprising,' he says. 'For Aeschylus was a religious, rather than devout, man; one, moreover, who prided himself on his aloofness from his fellows: "I think in solitude, apart from other men," he proudly claims in one of the choruses of *Agamemnon*.'

Justice, of which Nemesis is the guardian, lay at the very centre of Aeschylus' thought, as it was later to form the subject of Plato's profoundest reflections in the *Republic*. But the poet's principal concern was with justice as it existed in the world of the gods, for he was a theologian rather than a philosopher. Are the gods themselves just? this was the question he posed in the trilogy of Prometheus. And the conclusion he arrived at was that, if the greatest of the gods had not always been just, at least he eventually became so. As a believer, he was convinced that the divine will was founded in reason and that though this might sometimes appear to be obscure, it was the duty of the pious, upright man to try to understand it, and to act in accordance with it. Though Orestes did indeed kill his mother, in the end he was absolved of his hideous crime because, in committing it, he was obeying the gods.

This was the teaching of Aeschylus, for, as Aristophanes says, he always regarded his tragedies as a means of 'teaching the people'. Despite their sombre magnificence, despite the terrible destiny they seem to offer to mankind, they are nevertheless essentially optimistic: Prometheus, the benefactor of humanity, is ultimately reconciled with Zeus; in the person of Orestes, the doomed race of the Atridae eventually finds peace and the remission of its sins.

The faith from which this strong and lucid optimism sprang was not blind, but tirelessly sought for confirmation in the ancient myths; and it was only achieved after a long and bitter spiritual quest. It is the kind of optimism one would expect from the generation of the Marathonomachoi, the men who, through struggle and sacrifice, had defeated the enemy invaders and assured the glorious destiny of Athens and of Greece.

HERODOTUS

The historian of the Persian Wars in which Aeschylus fought was Herodotus, a Greek from Asia. He was born at Halicarnassus in Caria in 485 of a well-known family that must have been related to indigenous stock, since his father's name, Lyxes, is not Greek. His family were politically opposed to Lygdamis, the tyrant of Halicarnassus and a vassal of the Persian king, and as a result much of Herodotus' youth was spent in exile at Samos. Having reached the age of manhood, however, he returned to his country and with other exiles helped overthrow Lygdamis. Later he paid long visits to Athens, during one of which he gave public readings of his work, for which he was handsomely honoured by the Council.

At various times, Herodotus undertook long journeys which took him to Egypt and Cyrene, to Syria and Babylon, to Colchis, Olbia, Paeon and Macedonia. In those times, apart from merchants, few people travelled so far as this, though Solon had 'toured' the world with a view to educating himself. Herodotus had a more specific reason for doing so: to prepare for his life-work by making notes of everything that he saw and heard on his travels. Everywhere he went he found Greeks, or people who could speak Greek, and these he questioned about the history and customs of their country.

Thus he had already visited the greater part of the Orient then accessible to a traveller when, in 443, Pericles appealed to men from all over Greece to take part in a great pan-Hellenic colonial enterprise: the foundation of Thurii, the new Sybaris, in southern Italy. Herodotus jumped at the opportunity of visiting the western Mediterranean, which was as yet unknown to him, and eventually became a citizen of the new town, which is why some of the manuscripts of his *Histories* refer to him as Herodotus of Thurii, instead of Halicarnassus. He would seem to have died about 425.

As I have pointed out above (p. 117), with reference to Herodotus' precursor, Hecataeus, the Ancients did not distinguish between history and geography. *Historiai*, the title of Herodotus' work, actually means 'Researches' or 'Investigations' and is just as much applicable to the study of countries and customs as to that of facts and events. The opening words of his *Histories* are:

Herewith Herodotus of Thurii makes known the results of his enquiries, in order that time may not efface the memory of men's achievements, and that the great and wonderful exploits of barbarians as well as Greeks may always be renowned; and, in particular, to explain the causes that led the Greeks and barbarians to make war upon one another.

Like Homer, therefore, Herodotus set out to celebrate 'great and wonderful exploits' and in this sense his *Histories* are a continuation of the epic tradition. The one great difference is, that the heroes he chose to write about were not warriors of an age many centuries earlier than his own, but men of the immediately preceding generation. The danger of making mistakes was thus diminished, and historical truth could, in principle at least, replace epic invention. But Herodotus does not immediately plunge into an account of the Persian wars. That only begins with Book VI by which time his work was more than half completed. Subsequently, his *Histories* were artificially divided into nine books, and each of them was given the name of one of the Muses.

His purpose was, then, to discover 'the causes that led to the Greeks and barbarians making war upon one another'. But since the principal cause was Persian imperialism, the lust for conquest that haunted the mind of Darius and, after him, of Xerxes, his researches into what led up to this great clash between Europe and Asia provided an opportunity for describing the creation of the empire. Thus the first five Books are in fact a history of the Persian empire up to the time of Darius, though they also contain a number of long digressions devoted to descriptions of the various countries conquered, or unsuccessfully attacked, by the Persians, together with an account of the customs of their inhabitants: Medes, Lydians, Babylonians, Massagetae, Egyptians, Ethiopians and Scythians. Of these, the account of Egypt is the most important and occupies the whole of Book II.

There are even passages in which Herodotus tells us whatever he had been able to discover about countries the Persians had never attempted to conquer. In Book IV, for example, where he refers to Cyrene, he describes at length the tribes that inhabited the interior of Africa, and even attempts to justify this digression by asserting, against all probability, that a Persian expedition had been dispatched with a view to subjecting the whole of Libya to the Great King.

It would seem likely that when Herodotus first embarked on his enterprise, he had not yet fully worked out the ultimate form that his work was to take. It may have been that, to begin with, he thought of writing a 'Description of the World' like Hecataeus, or perhaps an 'Account of the Persian Empire'; and that with this in mind he accumulated a vast amount of material in the course of his reading and travels. Later when he decided to write a history of the Persian Wars and the events immediately preceding them, he felt reluctant to sacrifice his collection of notes and therefore included an account of all the countries he was acquainted with. Besides, it should not be forgotten that the Ancients' conception of book-making was very different from ours. In those times, books consisted of rolls of papyrus or parchment (*volumina*), so that it was almost impossible to add notes and appendices. Greek, and Latin, authors were therefore obliged to include in the body of the text all those comments and casual observations that would today be relegated to the bottom of a page or the end of the volume.

Herodotus was not one of those writers like Sir John Mandeville or Chateaubriand who boast of having explored a country when in fact they have scarcely set foot in it. He never lies. When some region is only known to him by hearsay, he honestly says so.

For Hecataeus there had been only two continents. For Herodotus there were three, Europe, Asia and Libya (Africa), though in effect he treats them as one, for, as he says, he 'could not well understand why, since there was but one world, men should have given it three different names.' He laughs at Hecataeus for supposing, as Homer had done, that the earth was 'a perfectly round, flat disk, as if it had been cut out and then surrounded with the Ocean stream,' and goes on: 'Now, for my part, I know nothing of an Ocean stream; Homer, I think, or some earlier poet, must have invented the name and introduced it into poetry' (II, 21–2). One might be tempted to see in this an example of the positive and rigorous methods of Thucydides. Yet the fact is that Herodotus himself also regarded the world as a disk, not a sphere; and all he was disputing was the fact that it is perfectly round. As to whether it was completely surrounded by water, he admits his ignorance. In the north there was the land of the Hyperboreans, and as for the south, he knew that in the sixth century the Pharaoh Necho II (whom he calls Necos) had given orders for a voyage round the world: starting from the Arabian Gulf, some Phoenicians had sailed round Africa and then, after passing through the Pillars of Heracles (the Straits of Gibraltar), had returned to Egypt. 'On their return,' Herodotus says, 'they recounted that after sailing round Libya they had seen the sun on their right hand. This fact does not appear to me to be at all credible, but perhaps it will appear so to others' (IV, 42). This time, Herodotus' scepticism was mistaken, since the position of the sun at noon does change after the equator has been crossed.

Here we can already begin to appreciate Herodotus' 'method' which consists in scrupulously recording everything he hears, while at the same time maintaining his personal opinion if any particular assertion strikes him as incredible.

Herodotus was curious about everything, and he tried to understand everything. For example, the phenomenon of the periodical flooding of the Nile, which makes Egypt the 'gift' of the river, profoundly intrigued him. He was unable to solve the problem, or the related one of the sources of the Nile, but having expounded and discussed all the solutions that had been suggested he puts forward his own. This is in fact worthless, yet it is only in this way, by feeling one's way forward and advancing successive hypotheses, that science has made progress.

To his avid imagination, the world offered innumerable marvels (*thaumata*) and prodigies (*terata*); and these two words frequently recur throughout his work. Many of his descriptions of exotic animals which Aristotle was later content simply to repeat were fantasies of his imagination. According to him, the camel's hind legs each had two thighs and two hocks. Such was the fecundity of the female hare that she was able to carry three litters simultaneously, conceived at different times and all in different stages of growth. In contrast, the lioness never had more than a single cub at a time, which tore the mother's womb with its claws when it was being born. Yet, when he was told about the fabulous phoenix, he suspended judgment.

Thus he displays an amazing combination of intellectual honesty and puerile naïvety. 'The *Histories* of Herodotus,' Bonnard has said, 'contain a strange mixture of scientific probity and credulity. He honestly seeks the truth and is at enormous pains to pursue it to the ends of the earth. But at the same time he still delights in marvels, as do all immature peoples, and the more of them he can discover the better he is pleased. For the Father of History, history's greatest achievement is the discovery of marvels supported by reliable evidence. It is almost as though he would have liked history to be a kind of fairy story, but a fairy story that could be proved to have really taken place.'

Herodotus was also interested in natural history, as well as cosmography, physical geography and pretty well everything else, but it was to human geography and ethnography that his attention was mainly directed. The fact that he was a Greek meant that man always occupied the centre of his mind. He was always amazed by the wonderful achievements of human intelligence and industry and, as Sophocles was to say, the greatest marvel of all was man himself.

Whether at the Egyptian pyramids or in Babylon, Herodotus made the most careful measurements of everything he saw, and noted down every detail; and his errors were minimal, mainly about such things as the height of the pyramids which he could of course only estimate. He describes the long and complicated process by which the bodies of the Egyptians were embalmed and mummified, without omitting anything. He knows where the Arabs found incense, cinnamon and gum resin; he has also heard of cotton, but as there was no word for it in Greek he calls it 'the wool that comes from trees'. In Iran, in the neighbourhood of Susa, he refers to a well, from which asphalt, salt and 'a black oil with a strong smell' were obtained, evidently petroleum (VI, 119).

He was particularly interested in noting customs that differed most from those of the Greeks. Of the Egyptians he says:

They do everything in the opposite way to other people. With them it is the women who sell in the markets and undertake petty trading; the men remain indoors, weaving. It is the women who stand up to urinate; and the men who squat. They relieve themselves in their houses and eat in the streets (II, 35).

When he discusses the variety of customs in different countries, one might almost be listening to the voice of Montaigne or Voltaire:

If all men were asked to choose from the diversity of customs and to point to the most seemly, each of them would, upon ripe consideration, select those belonging to his own country; so deeply are men convinced, each in his own mind, that their own customs are the best of all. King Darius summoned certain Greeks amongst his followers and asked them under what circumstances they would be prepared to eat the bodies of their own relatives; to which they replied that they would not do it at any price. Whereupon Darius summoned some Indians, known as Callatiae, who do eat their relatives; and in the presence of the Greeks, who could understand what was said thanks to an interpreter, he asked them under what circumstances they would agree to burn their bodies; they cried aloud and besought Darius not to utter blasphemy. Such is the strength of custom, and, in my opinion, Pindar was speaking the truth when he declared in one of his poems that 'custom is queen over the whole world' (III, 38).

Herodotus enjoyed savage stories of murder, mutilation and torture: his writings are full of them, especially Book IV, where he speaks of the Scythians and the sanguinary rites associated with their royal funerals. He had a particular taste for scabrous, repulsive and obscene details. The inhabitants of the islands of the Araxis copulate with their wives in public like animals. Amongst the Agarthyrses, the women are held in common. On the day of their wedding, the wives of the Nasamons had to give themselves to all the guests. The Gindanian women proudly wore on their ankles as many bangles as they had had lovers. In Lydia, all the girls first became prostitutes in order to amass a dowry. The inhabitants of Mendes in Egypt venerated a goat god: 'Not long ago, a remarkable thing happened; a he-goat had intercourse with a woman, and this was treated as a public exhibition' (II, 46). He obviously takes pleasure in describing how the Scythians and the Amazons copulated (IV, 113), and in recording a curious recipe for making a horse whinny (III, 87). He also claims to know that the sperm of Indians and Ethiopians is black.

Herodotus treats psychology in a very summary manner. In his account of the Lydians, he makes no attempt to explain Candaules' curious insistence upon displaying his wife naked, and in general he is very little concerned to understand the motives and characters of historical figures. For example, with regard to Themistocles and Miltiades he accepts contradictory traditions, with the result that his portraits of these great men are extremely vague.

He has been accused of being immoral, but it would be truer to say that he often appears to be amoral. Cleverness, even when it was associated with cruelty and theft, always seems to him worthy of admiration. This is apparent, for example, in the very improbable story of the two brothers who stole the treasure of Rhampsinites, a real *Thousand and One Nights* story: the pharaoh, unable to think of any other way of discovering the thief than by putting his daughter in a brothel, ended up by giving her to him in marriage 'as the man who knew most about it, the Egyptians excelling all other peoples in this respect, and he all other Egyptians. . . .' (II, 121). Herodotus in no way blames Themistocles for putting public money in his own pocket. Indeed, he fully accepts the world of Hermes and Odysseus where sharp practice and trickery were practised with impunity.

Herodotus himself distinguished three different stages in his historical work: observing, listening and reflecting—on which a critic has commented slyly that 'it was clearly with the two first that he was most concerned.' And, indeed, his critical sense, though obviously not to be denied, was subject to curious lapses. His qualities were those of a reporter or chronicler rather than of an historian, and the man that has been called the Father of History was above all an excellent story-teller.

Nevertheless, advances in our knowledge of antiquity, and especially in archaeology and anthropology, have in general confirmed his statements. While he was in Cyrene, enquiring into the sources of the

Nile, he heard that the Nasamons, in the course of exploring central Africa, had encountered a race of dwarf Negroes. For a long time, this account was dismissed as one of his typical stories: then, in the second half of the nineteenth century, explorers in equatorial Africa discovered the dwarf Negrillo tribes. With regard to Book II especially, the development of Egyptology since Champollion's time has made it possible to check Herodotus at a number of points, and almost always he has been proved to be right. His chronology of Egyptian history, however, remains indefensible. Yet, as regards the events of the past, what else could he do but rely on what he was told? He claims to have obtained his information from Egyptian priests, but he may have mistaken illiterate hangers-on of the temples for members of the priesthood.

In his descriptions of events, Herodotus displays all the qualities of a skilled and copious narrator. He is always clear and, in spite of frequent digressions, easy to follow; and he has a wonderful knack for describing the outstanding occasion, knowing just how to sustain interest. His language, which is literary Ionian, often displays Homeric touches. His phrases, related by juxtaposition rather than grammatically, flow with the limpid fluency of a slow, calm river. Sometimes, however, he is encumbered by his sheer excess of information, none of which he is prepared to sacrifice, with the result that now and then he fails to see the wood for the trees. The battle of Salamis is a case in point; he describes a series of individual encounters, but tends to lose sight of the general shape of the battle as a whole, which is much more clearly described by Aeschylus in the *Persae*. Here the historian, though on his own ground, proved inferior to the poet.

Herodotus' credulity reaches its height whenever there is any question of oracles, especially those of Delphi. Like Pindar and Aeschylus (he was familiar with the work of both poets and quoted them by name),[1] he professes the greatest reverence for the Pythian Apollo and his priests and never thought of questioning any information he obtained from them. His whole account of Croesus, in particular, appears to have been inspired by 'Delphic propaganda'. He cites innumerable oracles, always with complete faith in the Pythia's predictions, many of which were certainly invented after the events they claimed to have predicted.

Having opposed the tyranny of Lygdamis in Halicarnassus, Herodotus had his own ideas as to the best form of government. Tyranny,

---

[1] Pindar in III, 39 and Aeschylus in II, 156.

whether that of Polycrates at Samos or of Peisistratus at Athens, he rejected with horror, but he seems to have admired the Spartan oligarchy and the Persian monarchy as much as the democracy of Athens. In Book III, in defiance of all probability, he makes some Persian lords discuss with Darius the relative merits of monarchy, oligarchy and democracy (III, 80–2). The opinions they express presumably reflect the current arguments that he had heard when such matters were being debated in Greece.

Both Pindar and Aeschylus believed in Nemesis. Herodotus also considered this divine jealousy to be the cosmic force that was responsible for the fall of empires. At Samos, where he had spent several years of his youth in exile, he had collected numerous stories about the fate of the well-known tyrant Polycrates. Too successful in everything he undertook, Polycrates sought to appease Nemesis by the sacrifice of a valuable jewel that he was particularly fond of: he threw it into the sea, but the ring was found by a fisherman in the belly of a fish and returned to him—Nemesis had refused his offering and Polycrates died on the crucifix. Croesus and, finally, Xerxes are in turn represented as victims of Nemesis, because they allowed their pride and lust for power to distort their judgment. 'Those whom Zeus would destroy, he first makes mad.'

Usually, in Herodotus' view, human destiny comprises more evil than good. This is the meaning of the fate of the Argive twins, Cleobis and Biton, whose statues have been found at Delphi (see p. 93): they had performed an act of signal piety; yet the goddess Hera, whom their mother served as priestess, rewarded them with precocious death: 'Those whom the gods love die young.' In matters of religion, Herodotus often maintains a prudent silence, for fear of upsetting his readers by revealing an act or belief appertaining to one of the 'mysteries' and therefore protected by the laws of secrecy. This was the one subject on which he tells less than he knew.

Towards the Boeotians, who had betrayed the Greek cause by forming an alliance with the Persians, Herodotus showed himself to be a severe critic. And it was for this reason that Plutarch wrote a whole treatise on the *Malignity of Herodotus*, accusing him especially of excessive sympathy for the barbarians. In fact, Herodotus was completely free from malignity, though it is quite true that he showed no sign of hostility on principle, or of prejudice, towards the barbarian races. He even emphasized, before Xenophon, the Persians' moral qualities, their hatred of lying. Having been born in Asia, in a country owing fealty to the Great King, he had none of the prepossessions of an Athenian or a Spartan with regard to the 'hereditary enemy' to be hated whether one knew them or not. Thus he was not lacking in impartiality, one of the first requirements for an historian. Yet, precisely because he, better than anyone else, understood the barbarian world, he was acutely conscious of what specifically differentiated the Greeks: the fact that they prized their liberty more than their lives.

In Aeschylus' *Persae* there is the following exchange between Queen Atossa and the Leader of the Chorus on the subject of the Greeks: 'And what chieftain acts as head and master of their army?—They are not slaves, nor subject to any man.—How then did they resist the enemy's invasion?—Well enough to have destroyed Darius' mighty and magnificent army' (241-2). These lines are almost echoed in Herodotus' imaginary conversation between Xerxes and the exiled Spartan Demaratos. Xerxes asks:

'How could a thousand men, even ten or fifty thousand, stand up against such a mighty army as mine, if they are all equally free and do not accept the command of a single man?' To which Demaratos replied: 'Though the Spartans are free, they are not free in everything: they have one master, the law, which they fear more than your subjects fear you, and they carry out every bidding of this master. Now, he always gives the same orders: Do not run away from the battlefield, however mighty the enemy may be, but stand firmly at your posts, ready to conquer or die' (VII, 103 ff.).

This passage has the very accent of Tyrtaeus.

Herodotus' *Histories* opened up for the Greeks a vast perspective of the world: it gave them, or at least developed in them, a sense of the relativity of habits and customs; it broadened their outlook, often restricted to the petty limits of their tiny states, to include the whole cosmos that was then known to man. At the same time, it helped to strengthen the national feeling of Hellenism against the barbarians, not merely because it described the victories that had been won over the Persians, but also because it consciously exalted the Greeks and their ideal of proud independence as one of the conditions of life.

THE PHILOSOPHERS

As a result of settling in Crotona in southern Italy, then known as Greater Greece, Pythagoras of Samos (see p. 114) had sown there the seeds of Ionian science and philosophy, and they were to grow rapidly. Both Parmenides and his disciple Zeno were born there in the city of Elea and grew up under the influence of Pythagoreanism.

The actual date of Parmenides' birth is unknown. According to the prologue of Plato's *Parmenides*, the sixty-five year old philosopher, 'of a noble and handsome bearing with his white hair', visited Athens with his disciple Zeno, then in his forties, in order to take part in the festival of the Panathenaia, where they met Socrates, still quite a young man. Socrates had been born in 469 and his encounter with the visitors from Elea may well have taken place in 450, in which case the date of Parmenides' birth would be somewhere around 515. This would make him an almost exact contemporary of Pindar. Evidence from another source, however, suggests that Parmenides was already alive in 540, and Plato's chronology is scarcely ever to be relied upon; many of the accounts in his *Dialogues* are fiction. In any case, Parmenides' poem, *On Nature*, was certainly written in the first half of the fifth century, possibly about 480.

This work is in epic hexameters, like the poem of Xenophanes of Colophon, and has the same title (see p. 115). Moreover, Parmenides' ideas were undoubtedly influenced by those of Xenophanes. Considerable fragments of this poem have come down to us, including the fine prelude, which is almost worthy of Pindar:

The mares that draw my chariot have brought me to the end of my desire, their galloping feet have borne me along the pathway of the Goddess who is the Sage's guide. Thus was I led hither, my chariot drawn by cunning horses; and young virgins pointed the way for me. The axles grew hot in the wheel's hub, and cried out like the sound of a flute; two pairs of wheels, drawn by the fierce energy of the horses, drew me towards the radiance of the daughters of the Sun as they left the dwelling of Night, and their hands drew back the veils that were upon my eyes. There stand the gates that open the way from Night into Day. A great beam is set above them, and the threshold is made of stone; thrusting up into the air, they are closed by mighty doors, and Dikê the terrible stands guard over their iron bolts (*Fragment* 1).

Then Dikê, that is to say Justice, welcomes the poet:

Youth, O you who were conducted by the immortal Charioteers, you who have reached our dwelling-place with a single bound of your horses, I salute you, for it is no perverse fate that set you upon this journey, remote though it is from the roads familiar to mortals! If you are come, it is because the destiny of the Just urged you on. Therefore it is decreed that you shall know all things: Truth's sincere heart which persuades, and also the opinions of men, fallacious as these are. For these too must be known to you, if, in studying all things, you mean to form a true judgment of the sensible world (*Ibid.* 8).

There is a question, here, of a divine revelation, which to begin with consists of a solemn affirmation of being: 'They are one and the same thing, thinking and being.' But it is easy to stray from the path of truth under the influence of opinions that consist of nothing but uncertainty and false appearances; and this is the road that is followed by 'the demented crowd, for whom being and non-being, what is at once the same and not the same, constitute the law' (*Fragment* 8). Unique being is eternal:

How is it possible that one day being shall perish? How could it have come into existence? To suppose that it was created is to deny its existence, and all the more so if one supposes it to have come into existence on a particular day. Thus, the idea of its being created is impossible, and of its being destroyed, unthinkable.

Being is both indivisible and continuous, both without motion and immovable:

When it finally completes its existence, it attains perfection: it is like the harmony of a perfect sphere, every point on which is equi-distant from its centre. For it is necessary that being should not be here greater, and there less. . . . It is in all things inviolable. From its centre to its uttermost limit, its existence shines, homogeneous and sovran (*Fragment* 10–11).

In the second part of his poem, Parmenides returns to the world of appearances, of phenomena, which is the world of opinion, not of knowledge:

You shall know the nature of the air, and the constellations that shine in it; the flame of the sun's pure orb, the hermetic workman, and its origin; and the wandering work of the round-eyed moon, and its nature. You shall know the heavens which enfold everything (*Fragment* 17).

Parmenides then goes on to repeat a number of details from the old *theogonies*, especially the one bearing the inspiring name of

Orpheus. Eros, the love that denotes sexual attraction, 'was created before any of the other gods'. Moreover, the two sexes are unequal: On the right, in the fecund womb, boys; on the left, girls.' Now, the right side is the side of light; the left, or 'sinister' side, that of darkness. Pythagoras had already declared: 'The good principle created order, light and men; the evil principle gave birth to chaos, darkness and women.'[1]

Clearly, philosophizing in verse is a chancy business, poetry and dialectics are not easy bed-fellows; which is the reason why Aristotle, Plutarch and Cicero all considered Parmenides' poetry to be mediocre, —though it was not to prevent Lucretius from being a great poet.

By his grasp of ontological reality, however, Parmenides did much to clear the way for the philosophy of ideas, in the same way that his distinction between truth and opinion foreshadowed the distinction that Plato was to establish between knowledge and conjecture. He was not an idealist philosopher, for whom matter had no reality, for eternal being, as he conceived of it, seems to have had physical consistency; its spherical form was surely an image of the *cosmos*? All Greek metaphysicians were to some extent to claim kinship with the Eleatic philosopher whose works show him to have been both a poet and a skilled dialectician.

His principal disciples, Zeno of Elea and Melissos of Samos, had no talent as writers. Zeno's famous paradoxes in defence of Parmenides' thesis of being, in which he sought to prove the impossibility of motion and plurality, are well known. The arrow only appears to fly through the air, the swift-footed Achilles can never catch up with the tortoise, because, in theory at least, the distance between them can be infinitely divided. As for Melissos, the fact that he was born in Samos proves that the influence of the Eleatics extended as far as Ionia, the exact reverse of what had happened with the teachings of Pythagoras: thus the West was repaying the benefits it had received from the East. Another example of this unity of the Greek world throughout the Mediterranean was the gold tripod that Gelon of Syracuse presented to the Delphic oracle after the battle of Himera in 480; for the tripod, with its statue of Victory, was the work of a Milesian goldsmith.

Melissos was not only a philosopher. Like a later follower of Pythagoras, Plato's friend Archytas of Tarentum, he was also a gifted

[1] Simon de Beauvoir is justifiably shocked by this sentence which she ridicules by using it as the epigraph of her book *The Second Sex*.

strategist and statesman: in 441, he directed the defence of Samos against the Athenians with such skill that Pericles became alarmed.

Like Parmenides, Empedocles also wrote in epic hexameters, and indeed his amazing personality imperiously demanded the prestige of poetry. Since the Pythia proclaimed her oracles in verse in the name of Apollo, god of the Muses, then Empedocles, an authentic philosopher who regarded himself not only as a god, but also as prophet, sage and worker of miracles, would also write in verse.

He was born at Acragas (Agrigentum) in Sicily at the beginning of the fifth century, of a rich and noble family, which included—supreme distinction—several victors in the Olympic Games. In his hymns of purification (*Katharmoi*) he presents himself to his readers without any false modesty:

O, my friends, who inhabit the great city that hangs above the waters of the Acragas with its golden banks, you who live at the summit of the citadel, men intent upon good, whom no evil has besmirched, I salute you. Behold it is I who come, for ever delivered from death, an immortal god, whom all men venerate as is fitting. My head is encircled with wreaths, and for me the flowers of the garlands burst into flower. No sooner do I and my disciples enter a flowering city than I am overwhelmed with honours, and men and women innumerable follow me, enquiring of me the road that leads to riches and calling upon me to utter oracles; while those whom the knives of pain have long since pierced, seek to know from me the saving word that is proof against sickness (ed. Diels: *Fragment* 112).

In his poem *On Nature*, he bequeaths his philosophical system to his disciple Pausanias:

Hear, then, Pausanias, O son of the wise Anchites. . . . Men have but a brief glimpse of life, men who with their swift destiny are as smoke blown and lost in the wind, the playthings of every impulse. But you, since your steps have brought you as far as this, you shall know all that mortal mind can grasp (*Ibid.* 8).

In the system of Empedocles, Heracleitus' every-changing present is combined with Parmenides' unchanging being. According to him, nothing is either created or destroyed, the four elements (fire, earth, air and water) have existed from all eternity. Originally indistinguishable, they were contained within a sphere, the *Sphairos*, which was sustained by Love (*Philia*), but subsequently dissolved by Hatred

(*Neikos*). The struggle between these two opposed cosmic forces continually created beings, and then destroyed them in order to create new beings out of the same elements, which, though susceptible of an infinite variety of combinations, themselves remained unchanged. Even the gods were not immune from this process of flux and reflux: they lived longer than men, but in the end they died (which is logical, since in a polytheistic system the gods are born at a given moment of time).

The following are one or two characteristic examples of his thought:

Nothing that is mortal has either a beginning in birth, nor an end in death that carries off everything, for the elements only come together and, once they have been mixed, are again dissociated. Birth is simply the name men have given to a moment in this continual rhythm of things (*Ibid.* 8).

My words shall tell of things in their double aspect: for sometimes what is one has grown from what is multiple, and, on the contrary, sometimes the multiple was born of the division of what was one. . . . Change never ceases its perpetual becoming, for either Love is drawing all towards unity or Hatred is disjoining and putting asunder what Love has joined (*Ibid.* 17).

In the past, I was already both boy and girl, both bush and bird, a dumb fish in the sea (*Ibid.* 117).

And in words of genuine poetry he speaks of

the strength hidden in men's limbs, that we call Love or Joy or Aphrodite, by which are achieved the thoughts of lovers and the entwining act of desire.

As in the case of Pythagoras, it was not long before legend seized upon this more than life-size figure, who, not content with being a great philosopher and a great poet, had proclaimed himself to be a god. It was said that he had not died, but had disappeared in a storm (like Romulus), or else had been flung into the crater of Etna, and that all that could be found of him was one of his sandals, thrown out during an eruption.

THE BIRTH OF COMEDY

From the philosophers to the comic poet Epicharmos, of whom we shall shortly be speaking, is but a short step, since Diogenes Laertius refers to him in his *Lives of the Philosophers*.

Like tragedy (see p. 109ff.), comedy was born from the cult of Dionysus. It developed out of the wild tumult of the *komos* (from which the word *komoedia* is derived), a burlesque procession in honour of the god of wine, in which cheerful and half-drunk revellers, after a copious feast, roamed about, shouting out coarse jokes at the passers-by. At the head of the procession, a phallus was borne as a standard. In the *Acharnians*, Aristophanes shows Dicaeopolis organizing such a ceremony, though on a small scale, and himself singing the Dionysian hymn: 'Phallus, joyful companion of Bacchus, night-bird, adulterer, lover of little boys. . . .' (263 ff.), while his daughter performs the office of *kanephoros* (basket-carrier), and his slave carries the image of the phallus. It was these revellers who eventually became the Chorus of the comedy, of which, as in tragedy, one, though later several, actors took the part of Coryphaeus or Leader. Unlike tragedy, however, comedy did not first arise in Attica, but among the Dorians first at Megara, and later in Sicily.

Epicharmos was the first writer who provided comedy with a story, a dramatic plot. He was born at Cos in the second half of the sixth century, but when only three months old was taken to Sicily by his parents, who settled at Megara Hyblaea. Later, during the reigns of Gelon and Hieron, he lived in Syracuse, where he may have met Simonides, Bacchylides, Aeschylus and Pindar. He died at the age of ninety.

The subjects of his plays, of which the titles of more than twenty are known to us, were taken either from mythology—*Alcyoneus, The Wedding of Hebe, The Cyclops, Philoctectos, Chiron, Boeseiris*— or from everyday life—*The Peasants, The Fleecers, Riches, The Man of Taste, Pots and Pans, Hope, The Woman of Megara*. In the second group, Epicharmos gave free rein to his brand of popular realism. Unfortunately we possess such minute fragments of these plays that it is impossible to reconstruct the plot of a single one of them, and they only give us the briefest glimpse of the author's style and inspiration.

In *Hope*, a sponger thus describes his superficially cheerful, but actually wretched, existence:

I have dinner with anyone who will put up with me—it's just a question of inviting myself: or with someone who can't stand me—in which case an invitation is superfluous. At table, I'm as witty as can be, make everyone laugh and sing the praises of my host. . . . As soon as I've eaten and drunk all I can, I clear off. But no slave's provided to accompany me with a lantern. Then, stumbling around, I wander about all night alone; and if I run into a night watchman, I consider myself lucky if I get off with a few cracks over the head. And when at last I get home, fagged out, I curl up on the floor, but can't get to sleep till the good wine begins to work (ed. Kaibel, *Fragment* 35).

The human sympathy and compassion that this account displays, point forward to Menander rather than to Aristophanes. Again, in the same play, Epicharmos speaks of a rake 'draining the cup of life at a single draught' (*Ibid.* 34); and in *Boeseiris*, describing Heracles having a meal, he says:

Why, just to watch him eating is enough to make you die of fright: what with the dull rumbling in his throat, the crashing of his jaws, the grinding of molars, the squeaking of canines, the whistling through his nose and the twitching of his ears (*Ibid.* 21).

While of the aged heroine in *The Woman of Megara* he says: 'In front she's flat, but her back's as sharp as a skate's: she's as dried up as a scorpion, and her skull's as bony as a stag's' (*Ibid.* 90). One is reminded of Archilochos' mordant caricatures, or of Homer's description of Thersites.

Here is a scrap of dialogue, in which one man is telling another about the results of a good banquet:

Well, you begin with the usual sacrifice, and then sit down to dinner; and after you've eaten, everyone starts drinking.
    That sounds all right to me.
    Yes? But, you see, the drinking sets you singing; and from singing you fall to arguing; and the argument leads to a law suit; and the law suit results in a sentence: and so you end up in the lock-up, with irons on your legs and a fine to pay (*Ibid.* 148).

Epicharmos was certainly witty, and his style was brilliantly vivacious. His plays, like those of Menander and Euripides later on, were full of moral maxims: 'Wariness and sobriety are the soul of wisdom' (250), or 'To get married is to stake everything on the throw of a dice' (280). Some of his sayings have an almost metaphysical ring: 'The mind sees, and the mind hears: as for the rest, men are blind and deaf' (249). And he even goes as far as to introduce philosophical arguments into his plays:

Take any number you like, odd or even, and add one to it or repeat it twice: do you think it will still be the same number?
    Of course not.

Well, in just the same way, if you take an arm's length, and either add to it or subtract from it some other length, the first length will no longer exist.

Quite so.

Right! Then apply the same principle to men: one grows larger, the other smaller; they are all continually changing. And it's just the same with you and me: yesterday we were one thing, today we are another, and by tomorrow we shall be something else. So it all goes to prove that we never remain the same (170).

These ideas were clearly derived from Heracleitus. The person that is being addressed is content simply to agree, like those with whom Socrates argues in Plato's *Dialogues*. In this sense Plato's works are also comedies, and it is easy to understand why he thought so highly of Epicharmos, rating him well above the Athenian comic poets whom he considered to be too coarse, and not far beneath Homer.

If Diogenes Laertius regarded Epicharmos as one of the Pythagorean philosophers, it was doubtless because he accepted as authentic certain works that were falsely ascribed to him. Yet it is only the rich who find it easy to borrow, and assuredly Epicharmos had a mind that was open to philosophical ideas.

In Athens, comedy does not seem to have flourished until after the Persian Wars. The most important of Aristophanes' predecessors, who were doubtless inspired by Epicharmos, were Magnes, Cratinos and Crates; but almost all we know about them is what is to be found in the *Knights* of Aristophanes. This play, which was performed in 424, like all 'ancient' comedy, has a *Parabasis*, a kind of entr'acte, in which, while the actors are off stage, the *Coryphaeus* speaks directly to the audience on behalf of the author. This explains why Aristophanes was reluctant to produce his comedies under his own name (prior to the *Knights*, he always adopted a pseudonym):

For a long time now he has noticed your fantastic attitude with regard to age: he has seen how you dropped his predecessors as soon as they began to grow old. He saw what happened to Magnes directly his hair began to turn white—a man who, again and again, carried off the trophy from all his rivals in the theatre: in your eyes, whatever he did was wrong—whether he strummed, or flapped his wings, or Lydianized himself, whether he dyed himself the colour of a frog or simply buzzed,[1] it made no difference....

[1] An illusion to the comedies of Magnes, the *Lute Players* the *Birds*, the *Lydians*, the *Gnat*, the *Frogs*. Two of these titles, the *Birds* and the *Frogs*, were adopted by Aristophanes.

Eventually, he remembered Cratinos, who had once made a name for himself with such a flood of praise that it swept everything before it, tearing up oaks and plane-trees in its course, not to mention your quibbling, and sweeping them away with their roots in the air. At banquets, the only songs that were sung were the *Well Heeled Goddess* or the *Slick Couplet Fakers*. . . . so much was he the rage. But now, when you see him reduced to talking twaddle, you haven't the slightest pity for him. . . . And what about Crates? Just think what an outcry he's had to put up with from you, and what rebuffs—a man who, for next to nothing, used to give you the best show of your lives, and could crack the wittest jokes without a trace of a smile (*Knights*, 518 ff.).

The best of these three poets was Cratinos, and it is possible to form some idea of one of his comedies, the *Bottle*. In it, having been reproached by Aristophanes for drunkenness, he set out to prove that drink had not affected his talent. He represented himself in the play as the husband of Comedy, who was always complaining because he neglected her for his mistress, Drunkenness, and finally took him to court. This was the theme of the play and to judge from such fragments as have survived, it seems to have been carried through with staggering zest. In any case at the great festival of Dionysus in 423 it took first prize, while Aristophanes, with the *Clouds*, only came third, that is to say, last.

Following in the footsteps of Archilochos, Cratinos pilloried the vices of his time, and was not afraid of attacking those in power; even Pericles did not escape his gibes. He was disgusted by the new sloppiness of behaviour, by the debauches of the rich, and the general weakness for every kind of superstition and foreign cult. He may have 'chastised with a smile', but a smile that disarms can also wound and kill, and it was Cratinos, more than any other writer, who paved the way for Aristophanes.

5

IMPERIALISM AND THE DECLINE OF ATHENS
Second Half of the Fifth Century

Our city has become the school for all Greece.
Pericles, according to Thucydides.

HISTORICAL BACKGROUND

Up to the time of the Persian Wars, the preponderant influence in Greece, the *hegemony*, was exercised by the Spartans: as late as 479, at the battle of Plataea, it was the Lacedaemonian Pausanias who commanded the Greek army. The decisive part played by Athens at Marathon and Salamis, and especially the creation of the Delian League which turned the Aegean into an 'Athenian sea', put an end to this hegemony: from then on, thanks primarily to the strength of her fleet, Athens became more powerful than land-bound Sparta. Yet Sparta was by no means content to see herself relegated to second place and watch Athens striving to dominate Greece by progressively transforming her 'allies' into subjects: in 465 Thasos revolted and succeeded in carrying on resistance for two years. This was the underlying cause of the intestine struggle, the Peloponnesian War, that was to ravage and weaken Hellas after her defeat of the Persians, first from 462 to 446, and again, more seriously, from 432 to 404.

The first Peloponnesian War lasted sixteen years. The ostracism of Cimon, leader of the aristocratic party which had traditionally been friendly with Sparta, and the alliance of Athens with the Peloponnesian city of Argos, marked the rupture between the two camps. While Athens was dispatching an expedition into Egypt to support a local revolt against Persian rule, a great coalition, soon to include her ancient rivals Corinth and Aegina, was being formed against her. As usual, Boeotia was to become the battlefield: in 457, Athens was defeated at Tanagra, but two months later took her revenge at the battle of Oenophyta. Aegina capitulated, and was forced to pay tribute.

175

In 454 the treasury of the Delian League was transferred from the sacred island of Apollo to the Acropolis in Athens; a measure that appeared to the allies as an intolerable appropriation by Pericles of the tribute that they paid. From then on the number of revolts and defections within the Athenian empire rapidly multiplied and were put down with increasing harshness. In 447, still in Boeotia, the Athenian sustained a serious defeat at Coroneia, but before long they had defeated Euboea and Megara which had attacked them without warning. In the following year this first war was brought to an end by a peace that was concluded for thirty years.

In fact, however, it was to last for less than half that time, from 446 to 432. Athenian imperialism, on the initiative of Pericles, continued to extend its sway by peaceful means such as the project for a pan-Hellenic Congress (a piece of political and religious propaganda to persuade the Greeks to offer the first fruits of the harvest to the goddesses of Eleusis) and the proposal to found a colony at Thurii by building a new Sybaris, an undertaking in which Herodotus took part. Thanks to the tremendous wealth that thus accrued to the federal treasury, it then became possible for Pericles to launch a great programme of public works, notably the construction of the Parthenon and other buildings on the Acropolis.

Yet the subject towns of Athens considered themselves to have been slighted: Samos revolted in 442, and despite the energetic resistance it put up under the leadership of the philosopher Melissos (see pp. 168–9) was severely punished in the following year by Pericles who was accompanied on this expedition by Sophocles as one of his generals. A renewal of the war against Sparta seemed inevitable. Thucydides, a lucid and perspicacious historian if ever there was one, was not mistaken: the real causes of the Second Peloponnesian War were not the engagement at Corcyra, nor that at Potidaea (in which both Sophocles and Alcibiades took part), nor Athens' decree against Megara, but, in the first place, Athenian imperialism, victorious and aggressive;[1] and, in the second, the determination of the Spartans and their allies, especially the Corinthians, to end this domination and 'set Greece free'.

Hostilities were to cover two ten-year periods: the 'War of Archidamos' from 431 to 421, and the 'War of Deceleia' from 413 to 404.

[1] Today democracies are considered to be more pacific then totalitarian regimes; in antiquity this was not at all the case. Athenian democracy was a great deal more warlike than aristocratic Sparta.

During the first of these, King Archidamos of Sparta, almost every spring, laid waste the countryside of Attica, which, in accordance with Pericles' plan, was deserted by its inhabitants. At the same time, the Athenians, shut up within their impregnable city which was connected with the Piraeus by the Long Wall, refused any engagement on land, but sent their fleets to ravage the coastal regions of their enemies. In 429, largely due to the over-population of the city, the great plague killed one in three of the Athenians and amongst them Pericles himself.

Mytilene, on the island of Lesbos, was the next city to revolt and was savagely punished. From Pylos, the Athenian Cleon carried out an unexpected raid that resulted in the capture of a hundred and twenty Spartans: the enemy immediately sued for peace, but it was refused. At Delion in Boeotia (where Sophocles and Alcibiades once again found themselves among the combatants), the Athenians were beaten. In Thrace, the leadership of Thucydides (the future historian) failed to prevent the loss of Amphipolis; for which he was banished. In 422, not far from the same city, the Athenian Cleon and the Spartan Brasidas, 'the hammers of war' as Aristophanes calls them, were both killed and their death made possible the conclusion of the 'peace of Nicias' in 421.

What followed, however, was less a period of genuine peace than a kind of cold war. In 415, carried away by the fiery temper of Alcibiades, and without adequate preparation, the Athenians plunged into the Sicilian expedition which proved disastrous for them—the losses they sustained being comparable with those caused by the plague in 429.

By 413, open hostilities had again broken out between Athens and Sparta, the 'War of Deceleia'. On the advice of Alcibiades, who had been banished from Athens and taken refuge in Lacedaemon, this city in Attica was fortified by the Spartan army, which was thus able continually to harass the Athenians. From that moment, the latter were thrown on to the defensive. The revolution of 411 in which Antiphon lost his life, the return of Alcibiades to the political scene (who despite his treachery was regarded by the Athenians as their last hope), the sombre events that followed the naval victory off the Arginusae islands, all these episodes eventually led to the irreparable disaster of Aegospotami, where the last Athenian fleet was destroyed by the Spartan Lysander with the financial backing of the Persians. In 404, Athens was besieged and forced by famine to surrender.

Her fortifications were dismantled to the music of flutes and her defeat was hailed throughout Greece as the end of oppression. It was certainly the beginning of a new era.

ART

In his *Life of Pericles*, Plutarch maintains that the great statesman undertook the building of the monuments of the Acropolis for two reasons: to bequeath to posterity a lasting memorial of the power and magnificence of Athens and to ensure full employment for the poorest citizens of his own generation. Thus these vast projects were inspired by a kind of State socialism and their fulfilment involved the participation of the various bodies of craftsmen enumerated by Plutarch: 'carpenters, sculptors, smiths, stone-cutters, gilders, ivory-workers, painters, inlayers, carvers, porters and waggoners, rope-makers, weavers, saddlers, surveyors and miners, not to mention the great crowd of labourers'. And he continues:

The monuments sprang up, imposing in size and inimitable in their beauty and grace. The workmen strove to outdo one another in the perfection of their craftsmanship, but the most wonderful thing was their speed of execution. All these undertakings, any one of which would have seemed to demand several successive generations for its completion, were finished within the term of one man's political career. . . . Admiration for the monuments of Pericles was all the greater because, in addition to the speed with which they were erected, they were built to endure. No sooner were they finished than they already displayed the beauty of age, yet today they still have the freshness of buildings that have just been completed. There is upon them a kind of youthful bloom that preserves them from the hand of time, as if they had been tended by the breath of life, a spirit that old age cannot harm.

When Plutarch was writing this, the Propylaea, the Parthenon and the Erectheum had been in existence for scarcely five hundred years. They remained more or less intact until 1687, when the Parthenon, which the Turks had turned into a powder magazine, was blown up by the Venetians; and Morosini's vandalism was continued by Lord Elgin in the early nineteenth century. In our own day, the restoration or 'anastylosis' of its colonnade makes it possible to appreciate the magnificent proportions of the temple of Athena Parthenos.

Compared with the temple at Aegina, or even that at Olympia, its

178

immediate predecessors (see p. 122), the Parthenon, built completely of marble and sumptuously decorated, marks the ultimate perfection of religious architecture in Greece. It was completely built, and all its sculptures were carved, in the short interval of peace from 446 to 432. The Propylaea, the entrance gates to the Acropolis, were begun in 437. The small Ionian temple of the Aptera Victory, or Athena Nikê, was projected during the lifetime of Pericles, but not completed until after his death, during the war against Archidamos, about 425; while the Erectheum, whose curious plan is explained by the religious memories it enshrines, was begun in 421, shortly after the peace of Nicias.

In addition to these outstanding monuments, the second half of the fifth century also saw the construction or completion of several other buildings that would have been the glory of any city less powerful and less devoted to the arts than Athens. It was then that the Pseudo-Thesion, still dominating the Agora and the best-preserved of all Greek temples, was finished; and the temples of Asclepius and Dionysus, with the theatre of the Odeion, were built on the slopes of the Acropolis. . . . It was then, too, that the Telesterion at Eleusis, the building used for initiation into the mysteries, was enlarged according to a new plan; at Rhamnous a temple was built in honour of the great goddess Nemesis; and on the promontory of Sunium the temple of Poseidon, the ruins of which still dominate this stretch of coast. Towards the end of the century the fine circular temple to Athena Pronaia, the enigmatic *tholos*, was built at Delphi.

Though most of the architects of these Greek buildings are as unknown to us as the men who built the romanesque and gothic cathedrals, the names of Ictinos, Callicrates, Mnesicles and Coroebos were traditionally handed down as those of the men mainly responsible for the monuments on the Acropolis and at Eleusis, and were recorded by Plutarch and other writers. But the supreme organizer of all these vast undertakings, the man who occupied the position of a kind of Minister of the Fine Arts, was Pericles' friend, the sculptor Pheidias. It was he who conceived and executed the gold and ivory statue of the Olympian Zeus (see p. 122) and the colossal statue of Athena, some forty feet high and also of ivory and gold, which stood at the end of the *naos* of the Parthenon, on a plinth that was itself more than six feet high. The ivory was used for the goddess's face and arms, the gold for her raiment and helmet; in her right hand she carried an image of Victory, and her left hand rested on a richly carved shield; inside, in addition to the elaborate timbering of the armature, was a system of air and water channels designed to preserve this extra-ordinary work. Standing in the shadow of the immense temple this prodigious statue must once have had the impact of some divine apparition, an epiphany of the daughter of Zeus, the ideal of Athens incarnate.

The Athena Parthenos, as well as the Athena Polias, or Promachos, which used to stand in the open not far from the Parthenon, have both disappeared, but much of the splendid sculpture of the temple can still be seen: the pediments on the east side, with Athena issuing fully armed from the forehead of Zeus, and on the west, her quarrel with Poseidon; the external frieze, Doric, with various mythological combats reproduced on the metopes; and, above all, the internal frieze, Ionic in style and therefore unbroken, in which Pheidias and his assistants represented the procession of the Panathenaia, the great festival in which, every four years, the religious and civic fervour of the Athenian people expressed and renewed itself. Comparable with this is the slightly earlier bas-relief from Eleusis of the young hero Triptolemos being blessed by Demeter and Korê, in which the artist succeeded in conveying the religious atmosphere of the Mysteries through the solemn nobility of the sculpted figures.

While Pheidias was the most gifted of the Athenian stone-carvers, his genius should not be allowed to eclipse the fame of the Peloponnesian sculptor, Polycleitus of Sicyon. To him we owe the two exquisitely proportioned statues of athletes, the Doryphoros and the Diadumenos, based on the 'canon' of Polycleitus, which prove how far Peloponnesian sculpture had advanced since the Delphic figures of Cleobis and Biton described above (p. 93).

In the last quarter of the fifth century, the Caryatids that support the tribune of the Erectheum so gaily and apparently effortlessly, and especially the splendid bas-reliefs on the balustrade of the Athena Nikê, represent a development of Pheidias' austere and noble art towards a new ideal of gracefulness and elegance that already foreshadows the work of the fourth century, especially that of Praxiteles. Admirable as they are, the Victories leading a heifer to the sacrifice with their intricate draperies blowing in the wind, or the Victory taking off her sandal, her clinging tunic emphasizing rather than concealing the lines of her figure, already suggest an almost excessive virtuosity; their sheer technical skill, that is to say, tends to absorb the whole of our attention.

The influence of this superb flowering of art, particularly of Attic architecture, spread throughout the Greek world. Ictinos, one of the architects of the Parthenon, also worked in the Peloponnese, where, at Bassae, in the lovely countryside around Phigalia, he designed the temple of Apollo Epikourios, an essentially Doric building which nevertheless contains, in the interior of the *naos*, ten Ionic pillars attached to the walls by buttresses and one isolated pillar that is a prototype of the Corinthian order. At Xanthos in Lycia, on the outermost confines of Hellenism, the statue of the Nereids, despite its many indigenous features, shows traces of Attic influence at the very end of the fifth century.

The vase painters, who in the previous period had been under the influence of Polygnotus of Thasos, now turned to sculpture for their inspiration. To begin with, as they sought to imitate the impressive naturalness and dignity of Pheidias, the severity of the red-figure style gave way to a greater freedom, and towards the end of the century, competing with the technical skill and elegance of the new sculpture, they adopted a more flowery style. The only ceramic painter of the period that we know by name was Aison, whose signature appears on a cup representing the exploits of Theseus. The inside medallion shows the hero as a youth; a splendid athlete, full of nervous energy, who has killed the Minotaur and is dragging his body from the labyrinth, while Athena looks on. On the outside are depicted six of the other Labours of Theseus, the various figures in which display an admirable ease and freedom of movement. Another cup medallion that has something of the majesty of Pheidias shows Themis, in the role of Pythia, bestowing upon Aegeus the famous oracle he had asked for in order that he might beget an heir. Separated by a Doric pillar representing the temple, the graceful prophetess bowed over the high tripod and the sturdy, bearded figure of the hero confronting her, make a solemn, admirably proportioned composition. In Munich there is a *stamnos* with a painting of a soldier saying farewell, in which one can sense something of the spirit of the Panathenaian frieze; it has the same purity and simplicity of line, the same reserved grace of attitude and expression, the same controlled intensity of feeling.

This was also the best period for the white-based vases which offer us a clearer impression of the painting than those with red or black backgrounds. Many of these are funerary vases, and represent the dead man or woman in a pose as noble and calm as the stele of Hegeso; and one of the best of them shows a warrior, standing before the seated figure of his wife as he bids her farewell.

A characteristic work in the 'flowery' style is a *hydria*, painted and signed by the potter Meidias. In one lively scene the Dioscouri are carrying off the daughters of Leucippus, while another, more peaceful, shows Heracles in the garden of the Hesperides. The figures in their clinging garments are full of grace, yet both the poses and the treatment of the drapery already betray a tendency towards mannerism.

SOPHOCLES

At the time of the battle of Salamis, it has been said, Aeschylus was fighting, Sophocles was singing, and Euripides was being born. In this case Sophocles would have been born in 496, at the village of Colonos near Athens, for we know that at the age of sixteen he was chosen to play the lyre as leader of the chorus of youths who sang the paean in honour of the victory of Salamis. Thus, from the date of his birth, we might have included him in the last chapter, for he was ten years older than Herodotus, but all his surviving tragedies, with the possible exception of the *Women of Trachis*, appear to have been written after 450. When he died in 406, he was ninety years old.

The whole of his long life seems to have been one of happiness and joy, success and triumph. He was good-looking and extremely talented, not only as poet and musician, but also as dancer, actor and virtuoso. As a young man, dressed as a girl, he took the part of Nausicaa, playing ball with her companions as in Book VI of the *Odyssey*;[1] and he also played the ancient bard Thamyris who as a lyre player was said to have rivalled the Muses. He had been well educated and brought up, for his father owned an establishment for the manufacture of arms and was very well off.

As a dramatic poet he was even more prolific than Aeschylus (he is said to have written a hundred and twenty-three plays) and he won the first prize for tragedy more often than his predecessor, without once having been placed third, that is to say, last. Yet Sophocles made no attempt to avoid his civic and religious duties. In 443 he was a member of the college of treasurers that administered the tribute paid by the towns belonging to the Delian League. In 441 he was appointed general and took part as a colleague of Pericles in the punitive expedition against the island of Samos; and he was a general for a second

---

[1] Though women were allowed in the theatres, all the parts, even of women characters were played by men.

11. The Penthesilea bowl, *c.* 460, a red-figured kylix in whose decoration is reflected the painting technique of Polygnotus of Thasos (p. 125). *Antikensammlungen, Munich*

12. Bas-relief by Pheidias, *c.* 440, found at Eleusis, depicting Demeter, Triptolemos and Kore (p. 180). *National Museum, Athens*

time under Nicias. In 413, after the disaster in Sicily, though already over eighty, he was one of the commissioners (*probouloi*) responsible for taking emergency measures for the protection of the city.

In other respects, he was the very type of pious, god-fearing man, and a devout believer. He was a member of a religious order that honoured the memory of the great figure of medicine, Amynos; and in 421, when the Athenians had the statue of Asclepius brought from Epidaurus, it was Sophocles who took it into his house until a sanctuary had been built to receive it. For this, the members of the brotherhood of Amynos bestowed upon him the surname of Dexion, the Welcomer, and later, as though he were a hero, dedicated a chapel to him in the sanctuary of Asclepius and Amynos. Sophocles composed a paean in honour of Asclepius.

He married an Athenian woman and had a son by her, Iophon, who became a tragic poet like his father. But, like his friend Pericles, he also fell in love with a foreign woman, Theoris of Sicyon, who bore him a bastard, Ariston, whose son became Sophocles the Younger; his favourite grandson and also a writer of tragedies. The tradition that because of this preference Sophocles was brought before the courts by his family as suffering from senility and squandering the family fortunes is probably only a legend.

Having himself been a handsome youth, he remained very susceptible to masculine beauty throughout his life. He was already past fifty when, at a banquet in Asia in the course of the expedition against Samos, he amusingly scored off a prig, by making up to a young cup-bearer and boasting of being a better general in love than in war. His tender feeling for boys elicited from his colleague Pericles the stern rebuke: 'A general, Sophocles, should keep his eyes pure, as well as his hands.' But this did not prevent him from being robbed of a valuable cloak by a male prostitute when he was already sixty-five years old, an adventure that led to an exchange of scathing witticisms between himself and Euripides.

This freedom of behaviour in no way conflicted with his devotion to the gods (whose morals were in any case scarcely edifying), since religion and sexual morality were then regarded as two entirely separate spheres. It was certainly not on religious grounds that Pericles, who himself appears to have been something of a libertine, had reproached him; what concerned him was the human and civic dignity of a magistrate whom his city had entrusted with an important official position.

Easy going, extremely sociable and readily approachable, Sophocles had many friends, who must have included, in addition to the statesmen Pericles and Nicias, the historian Herodotus. Very different from Aeschylus, he was naturally lively and lovable. In the *Frogs*, Aristophanes makes Dionysus say of him: 'He gets on as well with Hades as he used to do with everybody here on earth.' He died in 406, just in time to avoid the humiliation of the fall of Athens at the end of the Peloponnesian War.

His tragedy *Oedipus the King* ends with these lines: 'For mortal men, it is their last day they should think about. Call no man happy till he has lived his life to the end without misfortune' (1527–30). Shortly after his death a comic poet wrote in allusion to these lines: 'Happy Sophocles! He has died after a long life. He was as lucky as he was gifted. He wrote plenty of tragedies and his end was a good one, for he never knew the meaning of misfortune' (Phrynichos: *Fragment*). It is clear that, in the eyes of his contemporaries, Sophocles was the perfect example of a happy man.

This imperturbable happiness is reflected in his work. Aeschylus' genius still showed traces of archaism: his lofty pride, his abrupt, harsh style. Sophocles, who reached the age of manhood at the very moment when the defeat of the Persians was assured, was able to enjoy the fruits of victory in peace and never had to brace himself for the strain of war; he is calmer, more serene; his tragedies are the purest example of Attic 'classicism'.

This view might perhaps have to be modified, however, if all his plays had been preserved, especially those written during the first half of his life. He was awarded the first prize in 468, at the age of twenty-eight. Plutarch tells us that he himself used to speak of having written in three distinct styles: at first he imitated the 'grandeur' of Aeschylus; then he adopted an 'incisive' and 'highly wrought' manner that was perhaps somewhat precious; and finally he achieved a more natural tone, admirably adapted to the characters in his plays. This third style is the only one we know, for the seven tragedies that have survived all come from an anthology, produced in the Roman period mainly for teaching purposes, and they all belong to the second half of his career.

They are, in the most likely order of composition: the *Women of Trachis*, *Antigone* (first put on in 441), *Ajax*, *Oedipus the King*, *Electra*, *Philoctetes* and *Oedipus at Colonos* (a play written right at the end of his life when he was almost ninety and not performed till 401, five years after his death). One of his satyr plays, *The Sleuths*, has also survived in a very mutilated form.

The subjects of these plays, like those of Aeschylus, are taken from the cycle of Troy (*Ajax*, *Electra* and *Philoctetes*), and the Theban cycle (*Antigone*, *Oedipus the King*, *Oedipus at Colonos*); to which Sophocles added another, the *Women of Trachis*, from the Heracles cycle. None of his tragedies was inspired by contemporary military or political events, like Aeschylus' *Persae*, and he scarcely alludes to contemporary events, as Euripides was fond of doing. At the very most it might be said that when Theseus, at the end of *Oedipus at Colonos*, welcomes Oedipus with the pity due to his misfortunes, he is in a sense staking a claim, on behalf of Athens, to the gratitude of the Theban enemy: Oedipus promises that his body, buried in Attica, will protect the country 'from the ravages of the children of earth', that is the sons of Cadmus. Now, at the time when the aged Sophocles was writing this play, Thebes was the bitterest enemy of the Athenians.

The innovations that Sophocles introduced into the art of tragedy were less important than those of Aeschylus. It is said that it was he who first used a third actor, the *tritagonist*, and we have already seen how Aeschylus hastened to imitate him in this in the *Oresteia*; he broke away definitively from the connected tetralogy; and lastly, while diminishing the relative importance of the lyrics sung by the Chorus, he increased the size of the latter from twelve to fifteen singers.

What was genuinely new in the plays of Sophocles compared with those of Aeschylus was their greater emphasis on the development of individual character. Like his great predecessor, he believed in the gods, but it has been said that he was perhaps 'more devout than religious'. True, he makes the gods appear on the stage: Athena at the beginning of *Ajax* and the deified Heracles at the end of *Philoctetes*. But fate and the gods now leave more freedom to human action: their influence though it still makes itself felt, is more remote, thus allowing Sophocles to lay greater stress on the power of man's will. His characters are no longer simply the playthings of the gods, like Orestes in the *Choephoroe*, whose actions are determined by Apollo. As professor Snell has said, they are 'lonelier than those of Aeschylus. Oedipus, Antigone and Ajax are conceived as "acting" men; they act in accord with definite ideas of their own—but in the Sophoclean context that means that they act in deliberate opposition to the world around them. In the

end action turns into self-destruction'. [1] This development was to be
carried to its logical conclusion by Euripides.

All Sophocles' protagonists display a clear-sighted, firm and
unshakeable will power, and it is this that constituted the real action
of the plays, an action in which external events are few. In *Ajax* the
only thing that actually happens is the hero's suicide; but what
interested Sophocles, what he was so splendidly capable of describing,
what gives the tragedy its essential pathos, were the alterations of
fear and hope that are experienced beforehand by Ajax's friends,
especially the moving character of Tecmessa.

The most striking example of this inflexible will power is Antigone
herself. Piety and her love for her brother Polyneices have convinced
her she must bury his body, despite the orders of King Creon and the
certainty of death if she is discovered. Already at the beginning of the
play her mind is firmly made up and nothing can make her change it.
Against Creon, who represents civic authority, the established order
and the written law, she pits her religious and moral conscience,
defending the inalienable liberty of the human individual against the
State. When Creon angrily says to her: 'So, you have dared to disobey
my laws,' she makes the unforgettable reply:

Yes, for it was not Zeus who decreed them! It was not Justice, seated beside
the infernal gods, who imposed such laws upon men, and little did I think
your interdict so powerful that it could permit a mortal to break the un-
written but unswerving laws of the gods. These do not date from today or
yesterday, and no man knows when first they were decreed. How can I,
then, for fear of what may come, expose myself to the anger of the gods?
Did I not know already that I must die, whether you forbade me or no?
But to die before my time, I here proclaim, for me is not amiss. Living as
I do amidst immeasurable misery, should I not be content to die? It is no
grief to me to suffer death. But grief it would have been to allow the body
of my mother's son to lie unburied after death. For that I should have
suffered: not for this. To you, no doubt, mine seems a madman's act.
Yet may it prove that he's the madman who takes me for mad (*Antigone*,
449 ff.).

For Creon, as for all ancient society, an enemy of the city is not
entitled to any consideration or pity: 'Even a dead enemy can never
be a friend.' To which Antigone superbly answers: 'It is love, not
hatred, I would share' (552–3), a cry that anticipates the higher

[1] B. Snell; *The Discovery of the Mind*, p. 109.

morality of centuries later: 'But I say unto you, you shall love your enemies.'

Yet Antigone is not so blinded by her purpose that she fails to realize what she is renouncing by her acceptance of death. To defy Creon, she can insist, like Socrates before his judges: 'For me death is a blessing', but alone with the old men of Thebes, who form the Chorus, she lets herself go and sings a long threnody for herself. As she is about to enter the subterranean vault, her 'bridal chamber' as she calls it, her last words are:

Robbed of mourning tears, without friends or husband, here am I in my misery, dragged along a road that lies open before me. Alas, no more shall I behold the splendour of the holy sun. None shall lament my fate, no friendly lips utter a groan (*Ibid.* 876–82).

But though she is now experiencing all the horror of being utterly abandoned, she does not weaken or flinch. Not for a moment does she dream of submitting to Creon to save her life. And yet Sophocles understood that the bravest hero may tremble at the thought of death, though still confronting it courageously. Antigone arouses our pity as well as our admiration because her spirit, though it cannot be broken, is still susceptible to human weakness.

The better to bring out her character, Sophocles cleverly contrasts her, right from the beginning of the play, with her sister Ismene. Similarly, in *Electra*, he introduces Chrysothemis as a foil to the heroine. Both Chrysothemis and Ismene are gentle timid girls who could never reach the heights attained by their sisters. They try to dissuade them from their terrible purposes and, though admiring them deep within their hearts, they tenderly reproach them. It is as though they said: 'It is enough that we admire you, do not ask us to imitate you.' But neither Electra nor Antigone can conceal their scorn. In the same way, in order to reveal the character of Creon, Sophocles contrasts him, on the one hand, with his son Haimon, Antigone's betrothed who kills himself beside her dead body; and, on the other, with Teiresias, the blind seer, who appears in all his spiritual majesty. The principal effect of almost every peripeteia in Sophocles' plays is, indeed, to reveal one of the characters in a new light, to provoke in him reactions that will expose his deepest feelings; their purpose is not so much dramatic, as psychological.

This comes out very clearly in *Electra*. The subject of the play is the same as that of Aeschylus' *Choephoroe*, but how differently the two poets approach their theme. The Greek tragic poets felt no hesitation about dealing with the same stories as their predecessors, because they felt themselves capable of investing them with new life. Orestes, who in the myth is simply an instrument of the gods, was not a suitable protagonist for Sophocles, and he therefore brought Electra to the forefront, as his title indicates. Aeschylus had made it impossible for Electra and Clytemnestra to confront one another (see p. 142); for Sophocles, the long scene between mother and daughter afforded an opportunity for a closer study of their characters. It is in this pitiless scene that Electra most completely reveals herself:

> You killed my father to become the slave of the coward you now live with . . . You sleep with the murderer. . . . In you I see his mistress, not my mother . . . O that Orestes might come to consummate our revenge upon you, since I, though willing, am not strong enough. Go then, proclaim before the world that I am nothing but a wicked, scolding, shameless daughter. And if I am expert in the role, it is my blood that speaks (*Electra*, 560 ff.).

When the traveller, who is in fact Orestes, pretends to be a messenger come to announce Orestes' death, it gives Electra the opportunity first to utter her grief and tenderness in broken, heart-rending phrases, and then, when at last she learns the truth, to express her delirious joy: 'O beloved voice, so you have come to me. . . . I clasp you in my arms' (*Ibid.*, 1224 ff.).

At the end of *Electra*, Sophocles does not, like Aeschylus, show us Orestes, seeing, or believing he sees, the terrible avenging spirits, the Erinyes; and, similarly, in *Antigone*, it is the calm and noble Teiresias who foretells the future, not the half-crazed Cassandra. Such god-sent madness aroused in him a sense of estrangement and mistrust, and such irrational and excessive behaviour was beyond the compass of his art. Yet, when it comes to physical suffering of a purely human kind, which Aeschylus scarcely attempts to show on the stage, he describes it with profound insight: the dying Heracles at the end of the *Women of Trachis*, or Oedipus tearing out his eyes at the end of *Oedipus the King*.

Of all Sophocles' plays, *Oedipus the King* is the one with the most minutely contrived and the most moving plot. Severe critics have pointed out certain improbabilities of detail, though none that cannot be justified by theatrical convention. Its theme is like that of a detective novel, in which a ruthless detective is ultimately forced to the terrible conclusion that he himself is the murderer he has been looking for. Here again, the peripeteia of various kinds serve to release the reactions of Orestes, providing him with an opportunity to give expression to his changes of feeling.

In *Oedipus at Colonos*, the protagonist once again recovers the majestic gravity of the opening scenes of *Oedipus the King*, but it is no longer that of the king clothed in his purple robes; it is the majesty of a man who has endured misfortune, exile and grief, nobly and with dignity. Georges Méautis professes to see in Oedipus, and all the other Sophoclean heroes, men predestined by fate who, having passed through the 'dark night' of suffering, attain supreme wisdom, become, indeed, saints.[1] This, clearly, is an exaggeration. When, in *Oedipus at Colonos*, Oedipus utters the terrible curse that is to result in his two sons fighting one another to the death (as happens in Aeschylus' *Seven Against Thebes*), it is impossible to maintain that he has achieved ultimate serenity, has overcome all feelings of anger and hatred. Nevertheless, the Ancients did understand the purifying power of grief; and, as he nears his end, Oedipus takes on something of the prestige of holiness, which is accentuated by his mysterious disappearance. Yet there remains a profound difference between the pagan hero or sage and the Christian saint, for, as Pascal says, the latter belongs to 'a different order'. When the poet confronts Oedipus first with Creon and then with Polyneices, it is in order to probe his character to its depths, to reveal the violence and bitterness that remain despite all the blows of fate he has endured.

Deianeira, in the *Women of Trachis*, is of all Sophocles' protagonists the one who least understands what it is she wants, though eventually she does make up her mind to send Heracles the fatal tunic. But the poet cannot be said to have explored the nature of her jealousy very deeply; it was Euripides who was to make a truly original study of this passion in *Medea*. Possibly, however, the *Women of Trachis* was written before Sophocles had attained his full stature as a dramatist.

The psychology of his secondary characters is never neglected by Sophocles. Neoptolemos, in *Philoctetes*, is an attractive young man, loyal and upright, a worthy son of the Achilles of the *Iliad*, hating lies 'more than the gates of hell'. Doubtless, when drawing this character, Sophocles had in mind the idealized figure of a young

[1] Georges Méautis; *Sophocle, essai sur le héros tragique* (Albin Michel, 1957).

Athenian, 'handsome and good' (*kalòs kagathós*). Out of a sense of obedience, Neoptolemos at first agrees to play the odious role forced upon him by Odysseus with regard to the sick and wounded hero, Philoctetes: the latter, having made off with the bow and arrow of Heracles, without which an Achaean victory is impossible, has to be persuaded to return to Troy. Eventually, however, disgusted by all the deception (which Odysseus regards as second nature, whether in himself or in others) his feeling of compassion for Philoctetes makes him revolt and he reveals the truth to him.

There could scarcely be a more insignificant part than that of the guard in *Antigone*, who surprises the heroine in the act of disobeying the king's orders, and takes her before him. Neither his fear of Creon's threats, nor his delight when he escapes punishment, prevents him from feeling pity for Antigone:

> She never denied it. Yet somehow I can't help feeling both glad and sorry at the same time: to be rid of the whole business would be a good thing, but to bring misfortune on your own folk is a pretty dirty trick. Still, all things considered, the way I see it is, it's your own life that matters more than anything else (*Antigone*, 434–40).

For Antigone, on the contrary, it was precisely this 'anything else' that was of more concern than her own life.

In Sophocles' *Electra*, Clytemnestra is more complex, and therefore truer to life, than in Aeschylus' version, where she is all of a piece, a relentless criminal, without scruple or remorse. In both plays, however, she makes use of exactly the same arguments to justify her crime: the sacrifice of Iphigenia, and Agamemnon's infidelity to herself. Yet, when Sophocles shows her attempting to convince Electra of the justness of her cause by appealing to her sense of feminine solidarity, she is clearly ill at ease:

> This father you still weep for, of all the Greeks he alone dared to sacrifice your sister to the gods, yet in begetting her he suffered none of the pain I did who brought her forth (*Electra*, 530–3).

What the poet implies is that Clytemnestra, however deplorable as a wife, may yet, as a mother, have felt a genuine affection for her children. In the souls of all his characters, even of those whose behaviour it would be hard to defend, good and evil are inextricably

mixed as they are in real life, where human beings are seldom wholly
good or wholly bad. Unlike Euripides, Sophocles never portrays
men or women in whom cowardice, meanness or egoism excludes all
decent feeling, and this was why he was able to express the opinion
(subject of so many examination questions!) attributed to him by
Aristotle: 'I show men as they ought to be, Euripides only as they are.'
Yet, in reality, it is Sophocles who shows the deeper understanding
of human nature, because he refuses to portray any man simply as a
monster.

In the main, Sophocles' women characters are much more alive
and attractive than those of Aeschylus. He could never have created
the character of Antigone unless he had been convinced that there are
women capable of greatness and nobility; and he seems also to have
felt compassion for woman's position in society, which he conceived
to have been the same in the heroic age as it was in his own. When
Creon says to Antigone: 'While I still live, no woman shall lay down
the law to me', he is defending not only his kingly majesty, but also
his belief in male superiority. And, on this issue, it is clear that the
poet is on the side of the young girl.

Deianeira bewails her unhappiness as a wife: our youth ripens in a place
apart, where neither the heat of the sun, nor rain, nor winds can come to
vex us; far from all suffering, our lives unfold in innocent delight; until the
day comes when the maiden takes the name of wife. And then she, too,
must share the cares of night, always in fear for her husband or her children
(*Women of Trachis*, 144–50).

And again, in the lost tragedy, *Theseus*, a woman says:

Often, when I think of what our woman's nature is, I feel how small a thing
we are. . . . As soon as we reach our youth and our minds begin to awake,
we are sent away from home to be sold, far from the gods of our fathers,
far from those who brought us into the world, to live among strangers
(*Theseus*, ed. Nauck, 251 ff.).

The tragedies of Sophocles differ from those of Aeschylus in that
the catastrophes that overwhelm his heroes are of their own making,
not ordained by the gods. And their suffering is all the greater in
that they are almost always struck down at the very moment when they
believe themselves to have escaped the menace of fate: it is so with
Oedipus in *Oedipus the King*, with Clytemnestra in *Electra*, with Creon

in *Antigone*. The sudden and complete reversal of fortune, the instantaneous collapse, signifies the end of all their efforts and all their hopes. Though the sense of terror he evokes is perhaps not so powerful as in Aeschylus, the feeling of pity is more intense.

Sophocles' style is less majestic than Aeschylus', but it is better adapted to discussion, to the passionate interchanges that take place between his characters; he does not disdain rhetoric, but his use of it is discreet and confident, and he does not, as Euripides too often does, abuse it. While his lyrics lack the abounding vigour of Aeschylus', they are more concentrated, and also more restrained in tone, Apollonian rather than Dionysian. Two characteristic choruses may be found in the *Antigone*. In the first, which celebrates the greatness of mankind, civilization is seen, not as a gift from the gods as in *Prometheus*, but as the invention of man, the creator, if not of his own destiny, at least of the conditions governing his life on earth.

Many are the marvels in this world, but none greater than that of man himself. What other creature can cross the louring sea when the winds and the storms blow from the south, making his way through the hollows of the mighty waves, beneath the open abyss. . . . Words, thoughts swift as the wind, dreams from which cities are born, all these he has taught himself. . . . (*Antigone*, 332 ff.).

The second is a hymn to the power of love, which according to Empedocles (see pp. 169–70) was one of the two great cosmic forces, from which all living things are constituted:

Love, O invincible Love, you who swoop down upon our flocks, and you who keep watch, alert in the fresh cheeks of girls. . . . Whether amongst the gods or short-lived men, there is none who can escape you, and your touch is enough to drive us mad. . . . Here, truly, it is desire that triumphs, desire that is born of the maiden's glance, hastening to her husband's bed, desire that is among the mightiest laws, among the masters of the world, Aphrodite, the invincible one, who makes sport of everything (*Ibid.*, 781 ff.).

Right at the end of his long life, in *Oedipus at Colonos*, Sophocles sings the praises of the little Attic town where he was born:

This is white-walled Colonos, where more than anywhere else the tuneful nightingale delights to sing, in the depth of the green embowered valleys. He lives in the dark-leaved ivy, inviolable arbour of the god, whose dense screen protects him from sun and wind alike. . . . Here, as each morning breaks, watered by the heavenly dew, great bunches of narcissus bloom, the antique crown of two great goddesses, and saffron's golden gleam. . . . And in these parts, as nowhere else, the grey-green olive grows, our children's nurse, the tree that neither young nor old dare harm or rob (*Oedipus at Colonos*, 670ff.).

Sophocles, the friend of Pericles the 'Olympian', truly belonged to the generation that, developing the heritage handed down by the Marathonomachoi, made of Athens 'the school of Greece'. Like the sculpture of Pheidias, his tragedies have the serenely noble stamp of classicism, of an art, that is to say, that has attained its fullest maturity.

THE PHILOSOPHERS

It is probable that Sophocles and Anaxagoras knew each other, since they were both friends of Pericles. The three men were exact contemporaries, all having been born at about the beginning of the fifth century.

Anaxagoras was not an Athenian: he came from Clazomenae, an Ionian town in Asia Minor, but he was the first philosopher to make his home in Athens, which throughout the rest of antiquity was to be the most celebrated city of philosophers. There he lived for at at least thirty years, from 460 to 430. At the beginning of the Peloponnesian War the Athenians, dissatisfied with Pericles' government, took legal proceeding against those near to him, like Aspasia and Pheidias. Nor did they overlook Anaxagoras: accused of impiety, he was forced to leave the city in order to save his life; he retired to Lampsacos where he died, more than seventy years old. It was at Athens, however, that he published his prose work, called, like those of his predecessors, *On Nature*, a few fragments of which still exist.

His philosophical system is related to the ideas of both Parmenides and Empedocles. In his view, 'the totality of things is eternally equal to itself'; Being remains always identical with itself; only the appearances that it assumes vary. 'The Greek are wrong when they speak of "being born" and of "dying". For things are not born, neither do they die, but being already in existence they combine and then separate again.'

These 'things already in existence' are not the four elements of Empedocles, but the minute particles from which the elements are formed, and they are infinitely divisible (differing in this respect from the indivisible atoms of Democritus), 'for there are smaller ones without end, since it stands to reason that Being cannot cease to be.' Here his arguments recall those of Zeno.

The essential originality of Anaxagoras was that he substituted for the quality of the cosmic forces posited by Empedocles (love and hate) a single motive principle which he called mind (*nous*). It is mind that organizes the world, just as, by giving the initial 'push', it was mind that first caused the primitive and chaotic mass to emerge from the state of inertia. It is 'infinite and absolute master: alone, it is in itself and for itself.' It is a directing intelligence, a kind of world spirit.

This lofty philosophy, disdaining the beliefs and superstitions of the common herd, appealed to Pericles; and since he himself was aloof and proud, his enemies put it about that he looked upon himself as the supreme principle, and nicknamed him 'the mind'.

It is perhaps not surprising that Anaxagoras should have been accused of impiety, since he denied the divinity of the sun and moon, declaring them to be simply material bodies, and scarcely believed in divination, that essential part of ancient religion. Plutarch describes him arguing before Pericles with the soothsayer Lampo, about a ram that had been born with only one horn. Lampo insisted that the prodigy had a prophetic meaning, but the philosopher, 'having cut open the ram's skull, showed that the brain was not in its usual place, but was shaped like an egg and had slipped from the cranium to the spot whence the roots of the horn emerged' (*Life of Pericles*, 6). This anatomical explanation of the phenomenon was a challenge to the whole principle of prophecy; and Anaxagoras may be regarded as one of the founders of rationalism.

Democritus, the founder of materialism, went much further than Anaxagoras in his rejection of accepted ideas, and the notion of mind as the organizing principle of the world must have seemed to him simply another invention, like the gods of polytheism. This forerunner of Epicurus was born about 460, ten years or so after Socrates, and is said to have been more than a hundred years old when he died. Like his teacher, Leucippus, he was from Abdera in Thrace, a country that had hitherto played little part in the intellectual life of Greece. Indeed, the people of Abdera had a reputation for being even more stupid than the Boeotians, although the sophist Protagoras was also born there.

Like almost all Greek philosophers except Socrates, Democritus travelled a great deal: he had argued with the priests of Egypt and of Chaldaea, and had even been as far as India to talk to the *gymno-sophists* (the 'naked sages'), who in Greek eyes were the outstanding representatives of the mysterious wisdom of the East. He wrote sixty works, the title of which are known to us from a list drawn up by Diogenes Laertius. This indicates that Democritus had a mind of universal scope: he was interested not only in philosophy, but also in philology, literary history, music and the natural sciences; and like Anaxagoras he dissected animals. Cicero and Plutarch, who thought little of Parmenides' poetry, considered Democritus to have been a great prose writer, and Dionysus of Halicarnassos compared his style to Plato's.

The fact that only a few fragments of this impressive and highly esteemed body of work have survived has been attributed to the hostility towards the 'father of materialism', first on the part of the Platonists and later of the Christians. But the large-scale disappearance of ancient literature is so general a phenomenon that such an hypothesis is unnecessary. Indeed, what is really astounding, what is really hard to explain, is that Plato's works should have survived in their entirety.

It was Democritus who first introduced to the world of ideas the concept, and the name, of the atom. According to him, this ultimate, indivisible particle of matter could provide the explanation of everything. The whole universe, including the gods, was composed of atoms, which collide or combine and then fly apart again in empty space. Today, some of his deductions from this fundamental intuition appear naive and childish: he thought that the sensation of hearing and seeing were the result of streams of atoms, 'simulacra', that detached themselves from objects and flowed into our ears and eyes. But may this not have been a presentiment, as it were, of sound and light waves? Unlike Xenophanes, he did not throw doubt upon the inspired art of divination. According to him, the human soul itself is a material object, being composed of extremely subtle and mobile atoms; and in the case of madmen, and of prophets in a state of trance, their souls attain a peculiarly high temperature and susceptibility, which gives them a special aptitude for receiving the 'simulacra' emanating from other creatures and from the universe as a whole. When these streams of 'simulacra' originate from those higher, though still material, beings, the gods, the prophetic soul receives from them a revelation of truth that is hidden from normal men. This was his explanation of poetic, as well as prophetic, inspiration; and, despite their opposition to Democritus' materialism, both Plato and Aristotle were to revive this theory and borrow freely from it.

Though this great thinker could not completely free himself from the beliefs of his time, he was conscious of the limitations of knowledge 'Do not attempt to know everything,' he wrote, 'unless you wish to remain ignorant of everything.' His theory of atoms proves him to have been a precursor of genius. True, the atom he conceived of as indivisible has now been split, but his deterministic and mechanistic conception of the universe closely resembles the hypotheses that have made possible the prodigious developments of modern science. It was Democritus who laid the basis for positive scientific research and the picture of the universe which we have today is essentially that of Democritus: an inconceivable number of particles, scattered through infinite space in continual motion.

Both Anaxagoras and Democritus dissected animals (the dissection of human bodies was prohibited in ancient times by religious scruples), and thus made some progress in biology. The organ they knew most about was the liver, on account of its special importance to the sooth-sayers, whose prophecies were based on the inspection of the entrails of animals offered in sacrifice. It is permissible, therefore, to include the physician Hippocrates amongst the philosophers. Just as every historian in antiquity was also a geographer, so every 'lover of knowledge' included within the scope of his enquiries the whole of nature and all living creatures. All pre-Socratic philosophers were also physicists and physiologists, and Plato in his *Timaeus* and Aristotle in all his writings were to continue this tradition. In ancient Greece as in renaissance Italy, where men like Leonardo or Pico della Mirandola investigated every field of knowledge, specialization, which for us has become a necessity, had not yet begun to restrict the intellectual horizon of outstanding minds. Moreover, Plato maintained that the Hippocratic method, being based on knowledge of 'the nature of the universe', resembled his own dialectical approach (*Phaedrus*, 270 c-d).

Hippocrates was the contemporary of Democritus. He was born in the island of Cos in 460 and his family were Asclepiadae, members of a religious body that worshipped Asclepius (the Aesculapius of the Romans), the son of Apollo the Purifier and the god of medicine. He practised his profession throughout the whole of Greece and died at a very advanced age in Thessaly.

Although it is impossible amongst the huge collection of Hippocratic treatises to distinguish with certainty the master's works from those of his disciples, there is no doubt at all that Hippocrates was the great founder both of rational medicine and of medical humanism. The art of medicine was already known in the time of Homer—indeed, he had insisted that 'a single doctor was worth several men'—but treatment was purely empirical, except for the religious suggestion practised in the sanctuaries of Asclepius, and certain diseases, such as epilepsy or 'the king's evil', were attributed to divine or demonic possession, only to be cured by exorcism.

'With the coming of the Hippocratic age,' the surgeon René Leriche has said, 'observation became systematic and precise. Despite the poverty of anatomical teaching and the ignorance of physiology, the school of Hippocrates built up a genuine pathology as a result of etiological research, based on careful study that sometimes amazes us by its precision. Hippocrates insisted upon a systematic examination of the patient and an investigation of all the factors that might assist in prognosis. Abandoning the religious conception of illness, he directed his attention towards life, thus creating the only method that could lead to genuine knowledge, the method of observation.'

As for the Hippocratic oath, it was so far ahead of its time in the feeling of respect that it expressed for every human being, whatever class he belonged to, that it remains entirely relevant today.

THE SOPHISTS

Originally, the word 'sophist', like the word 'demagogue' (leader of the people), had no pejorative significance. On the contrary, it was used to designate a learned or clever man who excelled in some branch of art or learning: in this sense, a doctor or a skilled craftsman was a Sophist. Many of those we call Sophists were genuine philosophers; others, the majority, were preoccupied with the art of speech, of eloquence; some even claimed to know everything and to be capable of teaching it. It was this exaggerated pretension that led Plato to criticize them and eventually robbed the title of sophist of its original prestige.

All the sophists were teachers, but teachers who were continually 'on tour', travelling from town to town, and accompanied by a veritable court of respectful disciples who hung upon their every word. Like the rhapsodists, they surrounded themselves with impressive pomp and wore robes of purple. As soon as they arrived in a town, they would give public lectures to exhibit their talents and learning and to attract new disciples. For the young, their arrival was a thrilling experience, as may be seen from the opening of Plato's *Protagoras*, where one of Socrates' young friends seeks him out early in the morning to announce the great news 'Protagoras is here!' and to ask him to introduce him to the master.

Since their fees were high, only the wealthy could afford to be taught by the sophists, and the best known among them amassed considerable fortunes. To what did they owe their tremendous success? The local teachers, in Athens, for instance, only offered elementary instruction in grammar, arithmetic and music: the whole field of what today comprises secondary and higher education was provided by the sophists. It was they who supplied the young men with a general background of ideas and trained them in the art of oratory, thus preparing them for leadership, especially in democratic cities like Athens where success in politics largely depended upon the ability to speak well in public: the popular assembly, which was the ruling body, placed its confidence only in those who were able to please and persuade them by their speeches.

In addition to this, the sophists brought with them an atmosphere of novelty. With the utmost freedom, they popularized the most daring philosophical ideas and criticized traditional religion, and they had no hesitation about raising such issues as the organization of the government and of society. They were the inaugurators of the 'century of enlightenment' which not everyone approved of; many of the older and more mature citizens were shocked by their audacity and this naturally delighted the younger generation.

The eloquence of Themistocles and Pericles owed nothing to rhetoric, which was not yet taught in Athens at the time when they were starting their careers. It was in Sicily that the art of oratory was born, in the first half of the fifth century. Its originator, Corax, had a pupil Teisias, from whom he claimed payment for his lessons. Teisias thereupon proceeded to prove how well he had assimilated his master's teaching by refusing to pay, supporting his refusal by the following argument: 'Either you have successfully taught me the art of persuasion, in which case I can easily persuade you that I owe you nothing; or you have failed to teach me anything, in which case also I owe you nothing.'

This anecdote shows that, right from the beginning, one of the essential aims of rhetoric was to sustain an unjust cause with specious arguments or, as we still say, with 'sophisms'. One of the characters in Aristophanes' *Clouds*, Strepsiades, sends his son to the sophists to learn how to swindle his creditors. 'Provided you pay them,' he says, 'these gentlemen will teach you how to speak so that you can win any lawsuit, whether just or unjust' (*Clouds*, 98–9). Now, the teaching of the orators was based on the notion that, in any argument, there are two conflicting theses, one strong and the other weak; the aim of rhetoric being to ensure victory for the weak thesis. But Strepsiades is such a blockhead that he gets everything muddled up. 'With them, he goes on, 'there are two kinds of logic, strong and weak. Of these, the weak one wins by supporting the unjust cause' (*Ibid.*, 112 ff.). And we then have to listen to a lengthy polemic between True Logic and False Logic, the former personifying the old way of life before the cursed invention of rhetoric, the latter standing for the collapse of all moral standards.

The rascal Teisias took as his pupil another Sicilian whose fame was to overshadow that of his teachers: Gorgias of Leontini. Born about 485, Gorgias was a contemporary of Herodotus, but he lived to be over a hundred. In 427, his native town sent him as ambassador to Athens, where he became an immense success.

As a philosopher, Gorgias was a radical sceptic. In his chief work, which has the significant title *On Nature or the Non-existent*, he set out to prove three successive propositions: that nothing exists; that, if anything does exist, it cannot be known; and that, if anything is knowable, knowledge of it cannot be communicated to anyone else. Holding such ideas, it is not surprising that Gorgias soon gave up philosophy, where he obviously had nothing more to say, for rhetoric. He wrote a manual on the art of oratory and a number of set speeches (*Pythian* and *Olympian*) in which, addressing himself to the Greeks assembled for the festivals of Delphi and Olympia, he urged upon them the necessity for peaceful agreement. There are also fragments of a Funeral Oration he wrote, and various Eulogies.

The sophists were much given to composing this type of eulogy (*enkomia*) as an intellectual pastime: to show off their skill in handling paradox, they preferred to take as their subjects men and women who had very little to recommend them. This was the case with *The Enkomion of Helen* and with *The Defence of Palomedes*, a greater liar and trickster even than Odysseus, both of which have survived.

Gorgias' principal merit is that he created an artistic prose style, subtle and melodious, in which the short sentences, much less condensed than those of Isocrates, achieve a brilliant effect through the use of studied antitheses, rhythmical phrasing and internal rhymes and assonance. Thucydides' elaborately abstract and brilliant style owes much to his influence. His gift for form can be judged from the two short speeches that have survived, and also from the entertaining, but faithful, imitations of his style that Plato introduces in the *Gorgias* and in the *Symposium*, where the poet Agathon is made to speak like a devoted disciple of the Sicilian rhetor.

Protagoras of Abdera was also born about 485. So famous did he become that he was able to charge ten thousand drachmas for a course of lectures (at a time when the daily wage of a workman was two drachmas). According to Plato, he was paid ten times as much as a sculptor like Pheidias. He often visited Athens where he met Pericles; and it was there, when he was seventy years old, that he was charged with impiety and like Anaxagoras forced to flee. He perished in a shipwreck about 411.

The work that led to his accusation began with these words:

As to the gods, I can say nothing: whether they exist or whether they do not. There are many things that prevent us from knowing this: firstly, the obscurity of the question and secondly, the shortness of human life.

And he also declared that 'Man is the measure of all things' (*Fragments* 3 and 1). His agnosticism was akin to the scepticism of Gorgias.

As regards language and the art of speaking, Protagoras was primarily a grammarian and logician. He taught his disciples to use words with precision and to construct seemingly irrefutable arguments. In Plato's *Protagoras* he undertakes to lecture on the subject: Can virtue be taught? He begins by appealing to myth, goes on to make a set speech, and then comments on a passage of poetry. He is clearly well satisfied with himself and enjoys hearing himself speak, but apart from this Plato does not attempt to make fun of him, and the ideas he puts into his mouth are both just and reasonable.

Prodicos of Ceos also visited Athens several times as ambassador. He lectured on morality and on literary style. In the *Clouds*, despite the general attack on the sophists, Aristophanes has one of his rare words of praise for him, referring to his 'knowledge and wisdom'. It was Prodicos who invented the well-known fable of Heracles at the cross-roads of Vice and Virtue. Socrates considered his morality, even if not based on reason, to be sensible and practical, and sent him some pupils. As a stylist, he seems to have insisted to the point of pedantry on distinguishing between words of similar meaning, and in the *Protagoras* Plato makes fun of him for this by making him say: 'In a discourse of this kind, the audience should display, not in-difference, but impartiality, which is by no means the same thing. . . . For my part, I urge you to make concessions: discuss, but do not dispute—which is by no means the same thing' (*Protagoras* 337 ff.). Nevertheless, his effort to establish a precise use of language certainly had its uses; and from several passages in Thucydides and Isocrates it is clear that they were influenced by his 'method'.

Hippias of Elis prided himself on knowing everything: there was no branch of science or art he was not familiar with and he even went so far as to claim that he made his own clothes and shoes. But his eloquence seems to have been so utterly empty of meaning that it brought discredit on the name of sophist. The Athenian Antiphon, however, was a man of a very different stamp; an orator and politician as well as a sophist. Attempts have been made to distinguish two authors of the one work bearing his name that has come down to us, Antiphon the Orator, and Antiphon the Sophist; but it was almost certainly by one man.

Born about 480, Antiphon was condemned to death in 411 during the 'clean-up' that followed the collapse of the government of the Four Hundred. We learn from Thucydides that he was the principal inspirer and organizer of this revolt of the oligarchy. When the aristocrats belonging to Cimon's party were defeated by Pericles they had not been disarmed. Forced to take refuge in secret societies (*hetairiai*) they watched from the shadows, and the slightest set-back to the ruling democratic party was enough to re-awaken their hopes and stimulate a fresh outbreak of plots. One of these conspirators was Critias, who in 404 became the leader of the Thirty Commissioners appointed by the Spartan occupation forces. A disciple of Socrates and the sophists, he wrote tragedies and historical works, and in his play, *Sisyphos*, he put forward the idea that the gods had been invented, by a 'clever and cunning man' in order to frighten criminals and evil-doers, thus using fear to improve men's morals.

Antiphon was a teacher of rhetoric who published a series of model speeches and arguments in his *Exordia* and *Perorations*, now lost, and in his *Tetralogies* which have survived. The latter consist of groups of four imaginary speeches, two for the prosecution and two for the defence; and three of his actual cases have also come down to us, all dealing with homicide. Unfortunately, however, we do not possess the speech he made in 411 when defending himself, which, in Thucydides' opinion, was not only his best but 'the best that has ever been made up to the present time'. Thucydides continues:

In ability, Antiphon was not inferior to any Athenian of his day, and his talent for conceiving and expressing ideas was unsurpassed. He did not speak in the Assembly, nor, except when forced to do so, in the courts, since the crowd distrusted him because of his reputation for eloquence. But those who had to defend themselves, either before the people or before judges, found in him the most helpful of counsellors (VIII, 68).

SOCRATES

Though most of the sophists went to Athens in search of reputation and fortune, they were not born there. Socrates, however, like Antiphon, was an Athenian born and bred. To many of his fellow citizens, certainly to Aristophanes, Socrates was simply another sophist. Since no prophet is honoured in his own country, many Athenians who were prepared to tolerate sophists coming from abroad found it hard to put up with a man whom they were continually meeting in the streets of their own city; and they made no attempt to conceal their feelings. Yet Socrates never demanded payment from his pupils.

His position, indeed, was unique. Since he wrote nothing and despised books, it might even be considered questionable whether his name should be included in a history of literature. Yet his amazing personality was to dominate the whole literature of Greek philosophy throughout the succeeding centuries to such an extent that its history falls naturally into two parts; 'pre-Socratic' and 'post-Socratic'. Thanks to the principles he established and to the thinkers who accepted his authority, above all Plato and Aristotle, his influence extends far beyond antiquity, down to our times.

Yet what do we know of him? Two of his disciples in particular,[1] Plato and Xenophon, have described him, but their portraits differ considerably. Which of them are we to believe? For my part, I have not the slightest hesitation. Plato, an original thinker who created his own philosophical system, put many of his own ideas into the mouth of Socrates; Xenophon, essayist and historian, an intelligent and

---

[1] Many others, like Antisthenes and Aeschines the Socratic, wrote dialogues in which Socrates appears as the teacher, but their works are only known to us from fragments.

cultivated man but no more of a philosopher than you or I, carefully noted everything he saw and heard. I prefer to rely on him.

Socrates was born at Athens in 469, into a lower middle-class family, his father being a stone-carver and his mother a midwife. As was customary he learned his father's trade and was thus able to earn a modest living, but it was not long before he gave himself up entirely to his vocation, philosophy. At a time when practically all intellectuals were great travellers, he never left Athens and its immediate neighbour-hood except to fulfil his military duties: from 432–430 he took part in the siege of Potidaea, where he astonished his companions by his resistance to the extremes of heat and cold and proved his courage by saving the wounded Alcibiades; during the retreat from Delion in 424 he showed such coolness and resolution that none of the enemy dared attack him.

As far as possible, Socrates held aloof from public life, but at some time or other every citizen had to play his part in the administration of the State. In 406, when he was both *bouleutes* and *prytaneus*, he resolutely opposed the popular feeling against the generals of the Arginusae, at considerable cost to himself. Two years later, he opposed the oligarchic power of the Thirty again at the risk of his life. Chosen with four other citizens to arrest an Athenian of Salamis whom the Thirty wanted to kill in order to confiscate his property, Socrates was the only one who refused to obey this unjust order, and he stayed at home. Fortunately for him, this regime of terror was almost immediately overthrown.

He was married and had three sons. His wife Xanthippe was a difficult woman, a misfortune that Socrates used to joke about with his friends, maintaining that he had purposely chosen a bad-tempered wife, since this made it easy for him to put up with other people. In fact, Xanthippe had other qualities which he appreciated.

It was not the oligarchic government but the restored democracy that in 399 condemned him to death on a charge 'of failing to honour his country's gods, seeking to introduce new ones, and corrupting the youth'. This was the same charge of impiety that had already been brought against Anaxagoras and Protagoras: the cities of antiquity, even Athens, were totalitarian in their outlook, and religious toleration was unheard of. According to Xenophon, the essence of Socrates' reply to his judges was that, having reached the age of seventy, he was afraid that his physical strength was declining with old age, and that by condemning him to death they would therefore be doing him a service. The tone of Plato's *Apology* is quite different and, though many of the opinions there attributed to Socrates were doubtless expressed by him, one cannot help wondering whether Plato, a hagiographer of genius, was not already seeking to glorify the memory of his teacher, as he was to do later in the *Phaedo*.

Cicero says that Socrates 'brought philosophy down from the sky to earth'. By this he did not at all mean that Socrates sought to substitute rational understanding for religion, but simply that, unlike earlier philosophers who studied the physical universe in an attempt to discover a first principle (fire, water, the elements or mind), Socrates devoted his attention to the nature of man himself. He accepted the Delphic utterance, 'know thyself', as an invitation to man to examine his own soul before presuming to penetrate the mysteries of the universe. In this way, man would become conscious of his own ignorance. 'The only thing I know,' he used to say, 'is that I know nothing.'

For him, however, this intellectual humility was only a starting point: he was very far from accepting the agnosticism of Protagoras. In his view, the philosopher must devote himself whole-heartedly to the pursuit of truth by submitting himself to the rigorous discipline of dialectic, that is to say of free discussion; which, incidentally, afforded wonderful scope for Socratic 'irony'. The study of any problem must be based on precise definitions and, in order to avoid the mistakes due to haste and inexactitude, must proceed step by step.

'No one is willingly evil.' Moral weakness is the result of faulty judgment. Inherently, men only desire what is good, but they are often mistaken in their view of what is good. Their first duty, therefore, is to improve themselves by achieving greater clarity, by establishing order and harmony within themselves, by purging their souls of everything that can disturb this harmony: passion, ambition, the desire for money. Man's real wealth is only to be measured by adapting his needs to his resources: he, Socrates, who owned practically nothing, was better off than the wealthy Ischomachos, whose way of life involved him in considerable expense. Temperance is a necessary condition of happiness.

Man is a social animal and, as such, his actions should be dictated by justice and friendship. The unjust man, even if he is successful, is at heart, and despite all appearances, more to be pitied than the just man who is persecuted. The egoist, too, is bound to be unhappy. Socrates based all human relations on friendship. He himself was always looking for new friends, devoting himself, as he said, 'to the pursuit of young people', he even professed to be a 'procurer' because of his continual efforts to establish relations of confidence, affection and mutual help between the people he knew.

In reality, he was a severe moralist. This boon companion, who on occasion could drink more than anyone else without getting drunk, who joked about the ugliness of his face and the size of his belly, who, when surrounded by friends, loved to sing and laughed at everything under the sun, showed no indulgence towards certain aspects of contemporary behaviour. He unequivocally condemned the practice of homosexuality with boys, an issue on which Plato palpably mis-represents him. And he was also the first philosopher, perhaps influenced by Pericles' mistress Aspasia whom he admired for her cultivated intelligence, to proclaim the equality of the sexes, an idea that ran contrary to the whole Greek tradition.

Did he consciously set out to destroy people's belief in the gods? Personally, I do not think so. His was not a narrow-minded rational-ism; mystery he accepted, aware that human reason could not explain everything in the world. Certainly he condemned superstition and interpreted religious myths with the utmost freedom, but he was neither a blasphemer nor atheist. Moreover, he believed in divination and used to advise his followers to consult the Delphic oracle if they were worried by having to take some important decision. He also referred frequently to his inner voice, his 'daimon', which forbade him to do certain things.

The reason he was charged with being anti-religious was that the authorities were determined to identify him, dishonestly, as Aristo-phanes had already done in 423 in *Clouds*, with those sophists who advocated radical scepticism. In fact, in attacking him, the democrats were attacking the teacher of the aristocrat Alcibiades and others who held the same opinions. He seems to have been severely critical of Athenian nationalism and of the democratic imperialism of Themis-tocles and Pericles, which, though it had increased the military strength of Athens, had not improved the morals of her people but, on the contrary, had merely made them prouder and more grasping. His trial in 399, allegedly on religious grounds, thus had a considerable political undercurrent and the chief prosecutor was one of the best-known leaders of the democratic party, Anytos. He was found guilty by a majority of only thirty votes out of a total of five hundred. How serenely he accepted his unjust sentence is well known: he refused to escape from prison, despite his friends' efforts to persuade him and the plans they had prepared; and eventually he drank the hemlock. He died an honest man, and his death was as exemplary as his life.

EURIPIDES

Euripides studied the teachings of the sophists, and throughout his work one is conscious of the influence of contemporary rhetoric and the new ideas that were in the air. He was, as Nestle stresses by the title of his book, The Poet of the *Aufklärung*.

He was born in the island of Salamis in 480, but nothing is known about his family. Aristophanes makes a number of references to his mother having sold vegetables in the market, but if he came from so poor a background[1] it is hard to understand how he could have afforded the expense of studying under Protagoras and Prodicos, and could later devote himself entirely to poetry. Besides, he knew Socrates and Anaxagoras and frequented their circle. He is said to have married twice, both times unhappily: 'The carryings-on you impute to other men's wives, you're now suffering from yourself,' Dionysus says to him in the *Frogs* (1048). His unsatisfactory marriages seem to have made him a misogynist.

He was twenty-five years old when he made his first appearance in the theatre, in 455, the year of Aeschylus' death, with the *Daughters of Pelias*, a tragedy taken from the story of Medea. Unlike Sophocles, he rarely won the first prize, only five times in all, though he wrote ninety-two plays, which means that he must have competed on twenty-three occasions.

Euripides was a favourite target for the comic poets: from the *Acharnians* (425) to the *Thesmophoriazusae* (411), not to mention the *Frogs* which appeared after his death, Aristophanes pursued him unmercifully. The portrait he paints of Euripides is that of a proud and lonely man of letters, isolated from the world and shut up in his study, dreaming and meditating all day 'with his feet up'. And, in fact, we have no evidence that Euripides took any part in public life. Morose and gloomy by nature, he lived a retired life and would appear to have been of a generally misanthropic temperament rather than in any special sense a misogynist. Eventually, upset by the

---

[1] It is true that money can be made by retail trade, but in Athens women who worked outside the home were looked down upon: they only did so if they were forced to by financial difficulties.

attacks of the comic writers and disappointed by his lack of success, he left Athens, as Aeschylus had done before him, and ended his life abroad. In 408 he went to Thessaly, and then to Macedonia, whose king, Archelaos, was creating a reputation as a philhellenist by surrounding himself with Greek artists and writers. He died at Pella at the age of seventy in 406, the same year as Sophocles, leaving three sons, the youngest of whom also wrote tragedies.

Though of the three great tragic poets Euripides was the one who enjoyed least success during his lifetime, after his death his plays were in greater demand than those of either of the others. The fact that they were performed so frequently doubtless explains why, today, we still have more works by him than by Aeschylus and Sophocles combined: eighteen tragedies (including *Rhesus*, his authorship of which has sometimes been denied, though without adequate reason) and a satyr play, the *Cyclops*. In his tragedies he considerably widened the range of his subjects, taking them not only from the Trojan and Theban cycles (*The Trojan Women, Hecuba, Helena, Iphigenia in Aulis, Iphigenia in Tauris, Electra, Orestes, Andromache, Rhesus* and the *Cyclops* from the former; and from the latter, *The Suppliant Women* and the *Phoenissae*), but also from the cycles of Dionysus (the *Bacchae*) and of Heracles (*The Madness of Heracles* and the *Heracleidae*, as well as from the local legends of Athens (*Ion, Hippolytus*) and of Thessaly (*Alcestis, Medea*).

To suit his dramatic purposes, he modified these stories much more freely than his predecessors had done, sometimes in an almost casual way. In the lost *Antigone*, he made Creon's son help the daughter of Oedipus in her pious law-breaking; a god then saves the two lovers from Creon's anger, and they are married; whereupon a god appears, and announces that they will have many children—or at least a son, Maeon. Here, as Weil observes, 'by devoting so great a role to love, Euripides gave fresh life to the story, though completely altering its meaning.'

In the established myth of Medea, it was the people of Corinth who killed her children, because of their anger at her having caused the death of their king and his daughter. It seems to have been entirely Euripides' idea to make Medea herself kill them, but it was an invention of genius. In *Helena*, he took his theme from the palinode of Stesichoros (see p. 104): deceived by the gods, it was only Helen's image that Paris carried off to Troy, she herself having been taken by Hermes, to the court of Proteus in Egypt. Thus we first discover Helen in the island of Pharos, off the Egyptian coast, where in due course Menelaus also arrives, having been driven off his course by a storm on his way home from Troy. By this time Helen is trying to escape from the advances of Proteus' son, Theoclymenos, who has just succeeded his father. She and Menelaus meet and succeed in escaping by tricking Theoclymenos with the help of his sister Theonoë and Helen's brothers, the Dioscouri. One can see from his how, in Euripides' hands, tragedy tended to become a kind of dramatized novel.

Some of his tragedies have very little plot. *The Trojan Women* is simply a succession of moving scenes, a long threnody, in which Hecuba laments over the fall of Troy and its terrible consequences: the sharing out among the Achaean chieftains of the captives, especially Cassandra and Andromache, and the death of Astyanax. Others have two distinct plots, roughly linked together, as, for example, in *Hecuba*, where the subject of the first part is the sacrifice of Polyxenes, and of the second, Hecuba's revenge upon Polymestor, who has killed her son Polydoros. Or, again, in *The Madness of Heracles*, where the hero first saves his wife and children, threatened with death by the tyrant Lycos; then, suddenly transformed into a sanguinary brute, kills them in a fit of madness. Moreover, in some of Euripides' plays the plots are so involved and complex that it is easy for the audience to get lost. In *Orestes*, whose theme is similar to that of Aeschylus' *Eumenides*, Helen arrives unexpectedly, in advance of Menelaus. She cuts off a lock of her hair to lay on Agamemnon's tomb, but Electra, by this time condemned to death, has the presence of mind to say, 'See, it is only the end of the tress she has cut, lest her beauty should be spoilt' (*Orestes*, 128 ff.). In the end, Electra and Orestes, who have been condemned to death by the democratic assembly of Argos for murdering the king and queen, succeed in organizing a plot and seizing the palace. The *Phoenissae* is even more bewildering. The title of the play recalls one by Phrynichos, but the subject is quite different. It is taken from the Theban legend, and the Chorus consists of 'Phoenician' women, probably Carthaginians (Carthage was a colony of Tyre), whose exotic dress must have had a spectacular effect. The story of Oedipus is resumed by Jocasta in a prologue, but the action of the play then proceeds to condense the whole sequence of events comprised in Aeschylus' *Seven Against Thebes* and in Sophocles' *Oedipus the King*, *Antigone* and *Oedipus at Colonos*. It becomes almost a dramatic précis of the whole Theban cycle.

In the *Persae*, Aeschylus had paid tribute to his predecessor

Phrynichos by reproducing a line from his play. Euripides, on the contrary, openly criticized the work of his predecessors, especially that of Aeschylus. Thus, in the *Phoenissae*, he makes Eteocles say: 'To name all the chiefs would take too long, since the enemy is already encamped beneath our walls' (751 ff.). And similarly, in *The Suppliant Women*, Theseus says: 'One thing I will not try to tell, lest I make a fool of myself: which men, in the course of the battle, fight which, and who slays whom. To pretend to know were folly' (846 ff.). In both cases he is obviously and maliciously alluding to the long scene in *Seven Against Thebes*, where Aeschylus enumerates and describes at length the leaders assembled at the gates of the city. In *Electra* he goes even further, poking fun at the signs by which brother and sister recognize each other in Aeschylus' *Choephoroe*: a lock of hair, footprints, a piece of embroidered cloth. When an old man points out these clues to Electra, he makes her reply:

How should the hair of a woman resemble a man's? . . . A brother's footprints could not match a sister's, his must be larger. . . . If he still wears the cloak that I embroidered for him as a child, it must have grown as fast as he (527 ff.).

If one compares this passage with the text of the *Choephoroe*, one discovers that Aeschylus says nothing about the stuff embroidered by Electra being a garment. Euripides' criticism is therefore dishonest. It is, moreover, dramatically most improbable, but presumably it amused the audience.

In other respects, too, *Electra* contains significant innovations as compared with Aeschylus' *Choephoroe* (see pp. 150–1) and Sophocles' *Electra* (p. 188). In Euripides' play, Electra has been forced by Aegisthus to marry a simple, but noble-minded peasant, who out of respect for the princess has refrained from consummating the marriage. Thus the whole action takes place in the country, in an atmosphere of rustic romance. Electra adopts the role of a frugal housewife, concerned nevertheless to provide a fitting meal for her guests, Orestes and Pylades. In order to lure her mother to the cottage where Orestes is waiting to kill her, she pretends she is with child and that her labour pains have begun. This is not far from 'bourgeois' tragedy: the fact that Electra has married beneath her might almost be seen as symbolical of the lowering of the tone of tragedy that occurred between Sophocles and Euripides.

When, in the *Cyclops,* he makes the audience laugh at Polyphemus' expense, Euripides is simply following the rules, since this was a satyr play, the only one to have survived intact. For it was a mixed form, neither tragedy nor comedy, and the Chorus of lubricious and cowardly satyrs who accompany Dionysus give a spice of farce to the story, which is taken from Book IX of the *Odyssey*. When, however, in *Alcestis*, Heracles is made fun of as a gross drinker and eater, a drunken glutton, it is more surprising. Admetus, the servant, is shocked by this guest, who drinks his wine undiluted and then, drunk and wreathed with myrtle, 'starts roaring at the top of his voice'. True, according to the Argument, *Alcestis* was intended to take the place of the satyr play. Nevertheless, the noble devotion of Alcestis, whose death takes place on the stage, and Heracles' heroism in rescuing her from Thanatos, or Death, are a theme for tragedy. It would seem, therefore, that long before Shakespeare and the Romantics, Euripides was prepared to mix comedy and tragedy in the same play.

Yet Aristotle speaks of Euripides as 'the most tragic' of all the dramatic poets. Doubtless, he meant that, more than either Aeschylus or Sophocles, Euripides appealed directly to the emotions of the audience, used all possible means to arouse terror and pity. A fallen king, for example, would be shown dressed in rags, like Telephos and, in the *Archarnians*, Aristophanes makes fun of the collection of old clothes that Euripides was supposed to keep at home. He contrives scenes of suspense, as when Ion fails to recognize his mother Creousa until he is on the very point of killing her; or again, in *Aegeus*, where Theseus is only recognized by his father as he is about to drink from the poisoned cup; or, in *Cresphontes*, where Merope picks up the axe to behead her son, and actually speaks the words, 'Let justice be done. My own hand shall strike the blow,' while the audience is kept on tenterhooks, wondering whether anyone is going to tell her that Cresphontes is her son. He even went so far as to exhibit on the stage the suffering of children, those of Alcestis at their mother's deathbed, or Medea's, whose cries are heard as their mother kills them.

For the exposition of his plays, Euripides relied on the convenient, but artificial, means of the Prologue. Where Aeschylus and Sophocles plunge straight into the action of the play, Euripides first announces his theme in a lengthy monologue, spoken by one of the characters, or sometimes by a god, without any regard to the requirements of drama.

In the *Phoenissae*, it is Jocasta who speaks the prologue; in *Alcestis*, it is Apollo; while in *Hippolytus*, the goddess Aphrodite, having first announced herself—'Great and famous is my name, amongst mortals as in heaven: I am Cypris the goddess'—goes on to explain how she will avenge herself on Hippolytus, who disdains her.

As to his denouements, they often take the form of a divine epiphany, the god appearing *ex machina* (*apo mechanes*), standing high above the stage on the *theologeion*. This device was also used by Sophocles in *Philoctetes*, but Euripides employs it much more frequently: *Andromache* ends with the intervention of Thetis, *Helena* with that of the Dioscuri, *Orestes* with that of Apollo; in *Ion*, *The Suppliant Women* and *Iphigenia in Tauris*, it is Athena who appears; while in *Medea* it is the heroine herself who is raised above the stage in her magic chariot—a conclusion that is criticized by Aristotle as unworthy of an otherwise admirable tragedy.

It has often been said that Euripides secularized tragedy, in the sense that his characters are motivated by purely human passions, and not, as in Aeschylus, by the will of the gods, nor by a sense of duty based on religious conviction, as in Sophocles. But, since the great majority of Athenians remained believers, it may well have been that Euripides was anxious to satisfy them and therefore introduced the gods, at the beginning and end of his plays, in this artificial manner. Yet the whole Olympian machinery is quite obviously tacked on to plots which, in themselves, have little to do with religion. The madness of Orestes is no longer, as it was in Aeschylus, given objective reality by the presence of the Furies, whom Euripides scarcely believed in. When he does see the 'avenging bitches' it is during an attack of nervous depression, brought on by remorse; they are simply an hallucination, and Electra behaves like an intelligent and devoted nurse. His recovery is due, not to an act of exorcism carried out by the Delphic Apollo with the blood of a sacrificial pig, but to the kind of treatment that might be prescribed by a psychiatrist. It was not for nothing that Euripides was the contemporary of Hippocrates.

He was also the great portrayer of passionate love, itself a form of mental illness. In the *Frogs*, Aristophanes criticizes him for his delight in stories of adultery and incest, and for writing plays about women like Phaedra, Sthenoboea and Canace. In *Aeolus*, the heroine has intercourse with her brother Macaraeus. Sthenoboea, the wife of Proetos, falls in love with the young and virtuous Bellerophon; when he rejects her advances, she slanders him to her husband whom she forces to kill him (a story similar to that of Joseph and Potiphar's wife). The tragedies of *Aeolus* and *Sthenoboea* have been lost, but we still have *Hippolytus*. Phaedra, overwhelmed by her love for Hippolytus, kills herself, but leaves behind a letter incriminating him; and it is Theseus' belief in his guilt that leads to the death of Hippolytus, despite his innocence. Racine's *Phèdre* is certainly different from Euripides'; in his version, she has become a Christian and a Jansenist, but the essential features of her character were certainly taken from the Greek poet.

As Sappho did before him (see p. 100), Euripides describes the physical manifestations of love-sickness. Phaedra says:

Lift me up, raise my head. I feel as though the joints of my wretched limbs were broken. Hold my hand, maidens. Take off this fillet, it crushes my head, and let my hair fall free. . . . O that I might slake my thirst in pure spring-water, and lay me down beneath the poplars in some wooded meadow! (*Phaedra*, 198 ff.).

But Euripides' masterpiece is unquestionably *Medea*. He had already been attracted to the legend of the sorceress of Colchis, and one of the plays in his first trilogy was the *Daughters of Pelias*. In the character of Deianeira (*The Women of Trachis*), Sophocles had dealt with jealousy, but without penetrating very deep: here, Euripides makes an unforgettable analysis of the passion. Medea is a barbarian, to whom Jason owes his life and his capture of the Golden Fleece: she has borne him two children, but now he has forsaken her in order to marry a younger woman of royal blood, Glaukê, the daughter of Creon, king of Corinth. Medea is 'raging like a lioness'. Exiled by Creon, she pretends to submit, manages to delay her dismissal by a trick and employs the time to plan her terrible revenge. She sends Glaukê as a wedding gift a deadly magic garment, a kind of shirt of Nessos, and as a result, after suffering hideously, the young woman and her father die. But to avoid 'becoming the laughing-stock of her enemies', she is above all determined to wound Jason in his most sensitive spot, by killing their two sons. This was, as I have pointed out above, a brilliantly dramatic modification of the original legend. At the very moment when she is preparing to carry out this abominable act, however, she feels a great surge of love for the children, and in a tremendous monologue gives vent to the emotion rending her mind, the struggle between her will and her divided heart. At first, in the presence of her sons, her words are full of tragic ambiguity:

O children, my children, for you there will be a city, a home where you will always live, robbed of your mother, while for me there can only be my misery to live with. . . . Never again, from that other life, shall your dear eyes behold your mother. Woe, woe! Why do you look at me like that, my sons? Are you trying to smile at me for the last time? O, what am I to do? Seeing the light in my children's eyes, my heart fails me. I cannot! No, I cannot! Farewell, my purpose. . . . Must I, to harm the father, grieving for his children, double and redouble my own grief? No, not with this hand. Farewell my purpose. But this is weakness. Shall I make myself a laughing-stock by letting my enemies go unpunished? Am I, then, such a coward?

Then she sends the children away, and continues:

My hand shall not falter. But not you, my heart, not you shall commit this crime. Let them be, O wretched heart, spare them, for even if they are far away they will still bring you joy. No! by the avenging spirits of Hades! Now is no turning back; the deed is fated.

She calls the children back to her:

Come, my sons, give me your right hands and let me hold them. O dearest hands, O lips I love, the form and noble features of my children! Go, go away. I've no strength left to look upon my sons: I am borne down by evil. Too well I know what horror I intend, but passion overwhelms my mind, worst cause of man's worst ills (*Medea,* 1021 ff.).

This last phrase, with its terrible lucidity, might serve as epigraph to the whole of Euripides' work, in which passion predominates over all other feelings. Where Sophocles' Antigone arouses admiration and pity, the character of Medea inspires horror and compassion: she knows that her determination to injure Jason can only result in her own unhappiness, but she is inflexible in her purpose and, in the end, jealousy and pride triumph over her love for her children and her concern for personal happiness.

The spectators do not actually see the murder of Medea's children, nor those of Aegisthus or Clytemnestra, though in *The Suppliant Women* Evadne's suicide actually takes place on the stage. Usually, as

Madame de Romilly has shrewdly observed, 'rather than exhibiting the brutal pathos of actual deeds, Euripides prefers to dwell insistently upon the suffering that results from them; he does not confront us directly with the deed itself, but makes it live again through the prism of the emotions.'

Euripides relied much more than Sophocles on the resources of rhetoric and the subtleties of language. He was fond of creating a sense of tragic ambiguity which, as we have just seen in Medea's speech, can be extraordinarily effective; other examples are the scenes between Agamemnon and Iphigenia in *Iphigenia in Aulis* and between Heracles and Admetus in *Alcestis*. But the device he especially favoured was *stichomythia*; those prolonged dialogues in which two characters vie with one another in a series of tense, single-line epigrams. Aeschylus and Sophocles had also used this device, but Euripides abused it. Again, his work abounds in long speeches expressing his personal opinions on every kind of subject, full of pithy maxims derived from his experience of people and of life. This is why so many passages from his lost plays, often of considerable length, have been preserved in the writings of other ancient authors; for instance, the argument from *Antipoe*, in which Zethos supports the case for a life of action against Amphion, who defends the contemplative life, devoted to art and the things of the mind.

These speeches, it must be admitted, though interesting in themselves, nevertheless slow down the action; and sometimes when the author is too obviously substituting his own views for those of his characters, fail to move us. When Orestes, expatiating on the noble character of the peasant who has married his sister, exclaims: 'There is no sure sign of virtue, for in the natures shared by men all is disorder' (*Electra*, 367), it is the beginning of a long tirade on the relative moral worth of the various classes in society, in which it is all too clearly Euripides, rather than Orestes, who is speaking. Another example is the passage where Hippolytus addresses Zeus, attributing to the whole female sex the perverted passion he has discovered in Phaedra:

If it was your purpose to propagate the human race, why did you entrust the means to women? Better it would have been for men to buy their children's seed for gifts of gold or silver or weight of bronze, placed in the temples, and thus have rid their homes of the whole brood of womankind (*Hippolytus*, 618 ff.).

13. Red-figured calathos, *c.* 480, depicting the meeting of Alcaeus and Sappho (p. 102). *Antikensammlungen, Munich*

14. The monument of Lysicrates at Athens, *c.* 334 (pp. 248, 316)

And he then proceeds to develop his thesis of woman's perversity at length, point by point, like one of the oratorical exercises the sophists used to set their pupils. Such lapses in taste are not uncommon in Euripides.

Living shut away in his study, the poet was, however, in touch with the political and military events of the time, and he frequently alludes to them. In several of his plays he flatters Athenian patriotism, particularly in *The Suppliant Women*. This has nothing in common with Aeschylus' tragedy except the name, for it deals, not with the Danaides, but with the mothers of the heroes slain before Thebes: Theseus, a just and pious king, insists upon Creon handing back the bodies, a theme treated by Aeschylus in the *Eleusinians*, though somewhat differently. Now, in 424, the Boeotians, having won the battle of Delion (see p. 177), had in fact refused to restore the Athenian dead. Thus Euripides is purposely choosing a subject bearing on current events, and he makes the Theban herald say:

The town from which I come obeys but one man. We have no orators, stirring up the mob, flattering them, twisting them in every direction to serve their own interests; men whom the crowd worships one day, and condemns the next; men who, to hide their mistakes and escape the punishment they deserve, are quick to slander others (*Suppliant Women*, 410 ff.).

Here, the reference to Cleon and the other Athenian demagogues is unmistakable.

In *Andromache*, Menelaus of Sparta and his daughter Hermione are represented as vile and wicked creatures, utterly devoid of human feeling. The aged Peleus attacks Menelaus in this furious speech:

You a man? You miserable coward, born of impure stock! You, who let a Phrygian rob you of your wife, leaving your house unlocked as if the hussy were an honest woman! Why, she was only too glad to go, for how can anyone in Sparta hope to have a decent wife, when instead of keeping your girls at home, you let them go about with naked thighs and short skirts, and race and wrestle with the young men? Ask Helen, who forsook your home and your bed for the charms of a foreign wastrel (*Andromache*, 590 ff.).

Such words must have been well received by the Athenian audience, since only recently a Spartan army under Archidamos had laid waste their vines and olive trees (see p. 177).

Not all the allusions, however, are so easily established, and in using them to establish the dates of plays which are in doubt, scholars have sometimes been led astray. It would certainly be rash to assume that the description of Phaedra's illness in *Hippolytus* was a reference to the famous plague of 429: what she died of was not the plague, but love.

With regard to religion Euripides' attitude was equivocal, doubtless from a sense of prudence, for tragic poets were not immune from charges of impiety. One of the lost plays, *Menalippus the Sage*, began with the words: 'Zeus, whoever Zeus may be. . . .'[1] This line caused a scandal, and Euripides was obliged to modify it when the play was put on again. But even the alteration remains ambiguous, for it can mean either 'Zeus, since you are wise. . . .' or 'Zeus, assuming that you are wise. . . .' But his work also contains formal declarations of atheism, as, for example, in another of the lost plays, *Bellerophon*:

They say there are gods in heaven. But this is not so, unless in our folly we are prepared to believe in ancient tales.

However, since these words were spoken by Bellerophon in a moment of impious pride that was later to be punished, Euripides could claim to be merely adapting the words to the character. Nor could anybody pretend to be shocked when Polyphemus says:

To be able to eat and drink all day long without doing yourself any harm, that is all Zeus means to sensible men. And as for those who complicate human life by inventing religious rites, let them go and hang themselves (*Cyclops*, 336–40).

Yet, though Euripides may not have believed in the gods, he was nevertheless the author of the *Bacchae*, a play that is throughout alive with the spirit of mysticism, and where human reason submits to the divine power of Dionysus. To a lesser degree, *Ion* is also steeped in the religious atmosphere of the Pythian sanctuary. In the character of Hippolytus, Euripides presents a typical devotee of Orphism, full of fervid devotion for his divine companion, the goddess Artemis— 'Look, wretched man, she is there, your beloved goddess!'—and the

---

[1] The chorus in Aeschylus' *Agamemnon*, l. 160) uses almost literally the same words, but in this context they clearly express the poet's embarrassment at the variety of Zeus' manifestations, whereas Euripides is throwing doubt on his very existence.

exchange between Artemis and the dying Hippolytus breathes a profound and tender piety. It would seem that Euripides was but little attracted by the cold religion of the city gods, consisting as it so largely did of an exchange of mutual services, prayer and sacrifice in return for the divine favour: *do ut des.* For him both his religious life and his conception of the deity take a personal form: God, the guarantee of spiritual life, reveals himself within each individual conscience.

There is a similar ambiguity about Euripides' social ideas. He was one of the first Greeks to question the legitimacy of slavery, going so far as to say: 'The souls of many slaves are freer than those of free men.' The position of women, also, was looked upon as inferior. Yet though Euripides is often regarded as a misogynist, and his plays certainly contain plenty of passages comparable to Hippolytus' speech quoted above, at the same time many of his portraits of girls and women show them in a wholly admirable light: Iphigenia, Polyxena, Evadne, Alcestis and, in the lost tragedy *Protesilaos*, Laodamia. Already Sophocles had expressed compassion for the sad lot of women but Euripides goes considerably further. Perhaps he had heard Socrates expound the 'paradox' of the theoretical equality of the sexes: in any case, many passages written by this supposed hater of women sound like vindications of womanhood. Not only does Medea exclaim:

Of all creatures that live and think, it is we women who suffer most. . . . They say we live safely at home while the men fight in the wars. A crazy argument! Why, I'd rather thrice take my place in the front line with my shield on my arm than once give birth to a child (*Medea*, 230 and 248 ff.).

But, in the same play, the Chorus sings:

All things will change. I, a woman, shall win fame and renown; and the hour will come when the prestige of women is no longer weighed down with evil report. Then shall the songs of the poets cease to revile me with slander (*Ibid.*, 415 ff.).

As Weil perceived; 'It was to his studies of the aberrations of the female heart that Euripides owed his ancient and persistent reputation as a misogynist, but, despite Aristophanes, this is more apparent than real.'

For us, Euripides remains the great poet of the passions of love and jealousy, conceived of as irresistible forces, capable of destroying in those they assail every trace of shame or pity. As Phaedra's nurse says:

When she attacks with violence, Cypris is irresistible, but gently she approaches him who yields to her; and those who show themselves mighty and proud she will seize upon, and inflict dire outrage upon them. She haunts heaven's heights, she dwells in the waves of the sea, Cypris of whom everything is born. Life she sows and love she grants, and we on earth owe our whole being to her (*Hippolytus*, 443 ff.).

As the poet of love's universal power, Euripides was the precursor of the Alexandrian writers; the Theocritus of the *Sorceresses*, the Callimachus of *Acontius and Cydippe*, the Apollonius of Book III of the *Argonauts*. His poetry is akin to that of the Hellenistic period also in the quality of its lyricism, graceful rather than forceful, and occasionally showing a tendency towards preciosity. The Chorus of Women in *Hippolytus* chants:

Eros, O Eros, whose eyes distill desire, inspiring sweet longing in the hearts you pursue, press me not beyond bearing. . . . Vainly, all in vain, on the banks of Alpheus, or in Apollo's Pythian shrine, shall Hellas pile high the slaughtered bulls, if to Eros, lord of mankind who bears the key to Aphrodite's charmed enclosure, we do not pay homage. . . . (*Hippolytus*, 525 ff.).

One has only to compare this with the Chorus on the same theme from *Antigone*, quoted above (p. 192), 'Love, O invincible Love. . . .,' to feel how much the lyric gift of Sophocles differed from that of Euripides, which was closer to that of Anacreon and Simonides.

In some of his Choruses there are even traces of the sophist, as for example in *Alcestis*:

I who have dwelt in the Muses' garden, who have soared towards the heights, many teachings have I studied, yet no power have I found as strong as Necessity. Neither the words of Orpheus, inscribed on the Thracian tablets, nor the herbs that Apollo bequeathed to Asclepius are remedy against it. . . . She is the only goddess whose image or altar man may not approach: she is deaf to our prayers (*Alcestis*, 962 ff.).

Sometimes Euripides puts into the mouths of his characters the most eloquent monodies, for example Alcestis, Electra and Ion. The latter, a kind of sacristan in the sanctuary of Apollo at Delphi (he must have suggested to Racine certain features of his Joas), is sweeping the approach to the temple and says:

O you, my servant, cut from the loveliest of laurels, who before the temple sweep the altar of Apollo. . . . Each day, from the sun's swift rising, with you will I purify the court of my god. Hail, all hail! Blessed is Leto's son. It is splendid, O Apollo, this service I do you before your temple, your prophetic dwelling. Glorious is my task, since I offer my strength at the feet of the immortal gods. Never shall I weary of this holy labour, but praise the god who sustains me, Apollo, my god and my benefactor (*Ion*, 112 ff.).

Lacking the power of Aeschylus and the nobility of Sophocles, the artistry of Euripides is also less perfect: too often one is conscious of the dramatist's tricks of the trade; philosophy and rhetoric sometimes detract from the poetry. Yet the man who could create such characters as Medea, Phaedra and Alcestis was indisputably a major poet. Inadequately appreciated by his contemporaries, Euripides was to become for later generations one of the best known classic writers after Homer: musicians often played the melodies of his Choruses,[1] and every cultivated man repeated his maxims and knew whole speeches from his plays by heart.

THUCYDIDES

Thucydides was, like Euripides, a disciple of the sophists; like him, too, he was a free-thinker and a stylist. His *History* begins as follows:

Thucydides of Athens wrote the history of the war between the Peloponnesians and the Athenians. He began the task when the signs of war first appeared, having foreseen that it would assume considerable proportions and exceed all previous wars in scope (i, 1).

Thus, in 432 when the Peloponnesian War began, Thucydides must already have been old enough to appreciate the importance of what was happening. Moreover, in 424 he was appointed general, for which

---

[1] One of the Delphic inscriptions of the second century B.C. records that at a Pythian festival music taken from Euripides' *Bacchae* was performed.

he would have had to be not less than thirty. Thus he was probably born some time before 460, at about the time when Pericles was beginning his political career.

He was probably the grandson of Miltiades, since the name borne by his father, Oloros, was the same as that of a king of Thrace, whose daughter had been married to the victor of Marathon. In this case, the historian belonged to an aristocratic family on which Miltiades' son, Cimon, had conferred even greater honour. Such a background would explain his conservative tendencies: these did not prevent him from doing justice to the democrat Pericles who was himself of noble birth, but to the newcomer, Cleon, he showed little favour. His inheritance of gold mines, near Strymon in Thrace, enabled him to enjoy a position of independence and material comfort: he was able to attend the lectures of the sophists and, later on, to devote himself to prolonged research in preparation for his work. He was acquainted with Anaxagoras, Antiphon, Gorgias and Prodicos.

In 430 he fell victim to the plague. Six years later, having been appointed general, he arrived at Amphipolis too late to prevent the Spartan Brasidas from seizing the town. The Athenians, always ready to blame their unsuccessful generals, arrested him and condemned him to exile, where he was to remain for twenty years until the end of the Peloponnesian War in 404. This period of banishment proved to be an advantage from the point of view of his work. He settled at Scaptesyle in Thrace, near his gold mines in Mount Pangaion, but much of his time was spent in travel. As an exile, he was able to gather information freely from the enemies of Athens; and his enforced leisure allowed him to devote his time to working on his history. He did not succeed in completing it, however, for it ends with his account of the year 411, and this eighth and last Book would seem not to have been revised or corrected by him. Neither the circumstances nor the exact date of his death are known, but he probably survived into the early years of the fourth century.

Born before 460, Thucydides was only some twenty years younger than Herodotus, yet his conception of history was entirely different. Though there was scarcely a generation between them, the gulf separating their whole mental outlook was even deeper than that between Sophocles and Euripides. Thanks to the philosophers and the sophists, the evolution of ideas in the fifth century was amazingly rapid, and by the end of it they had attained an almost prodigious maturity.

The Preface to Thucydides' *History* opens with an account of ancient Greece, usually known as the 'archaeologia'. He surveys the past in order to prove that he had realized from the start that the Peloponnesian War, by reason of the forces involved and the variety and extent of its theatre of operations, was of far greater significance than any that had preceded it, even than the struggle against Troy or the war with Persia. He therefore sets out to exalt his theme, as he had been taught to do by the sophists, by means of rhetorical hyberbole (*auxesis*), yet the arguments he uses always denote a rational approach, a rigorous method of ascertaining and interpreting the facts that is closely akin to that of his contemporary, the physician Hippocrates. Twenty-four centuries before Marx, he explains social and political history in terms of economics:

The inhabitants of the coastal regions now began to acquire greater wealth and adopted a more settled life [compared with the nomadic existence of the more ancient peoples]; some of them even, conscious of their increasing wealth, surrounded their cities with walls. Moreover, yielding to the desire for gain, the weaker were prepared to submit themselves to the stronger, while the most powerful of them, thanks to their greater resources, were able to persuade the smaller cities to accept their authority (i, *viii*, 3).

Where Herodotus had been, like Homer, primarily concerned to celebrate noble deeds, Thucydides, in the manner of modern historians, sought to extract from epic poetry the kernel of truth contained in it. For example, he says:

In my opinion, the reason Agamemnon was able to unite the forces of the Greeks was that he disposed of greater power than the others, not because the suitors of Helen whom he led were bound by the oath they had sworn to Tyndareus. . . . Indeed, it was he who brought the greatest number of ships, besides those he was able to provide for the Arcadians, as was pointed out by Homer, if his information is to be relied upon (i, *ix, passim*).

The reserve displayed in the final sentence is typical of the hesitant and cautious way in which Thucydides makes use of evidence provided by the poet. Yet, as late as the Roman period, an historian of Strabo's standing was prepared to accept Homer as an infallible authority.

Thucydides goes on to point out that, though Mycenae, Agamemnon's capital, was doubtless only a small city, we should beware of being misled by appearances. If Sparta were one day to be destroyed, we should be amazed that the ruins of so mighty a city appeared so mediocre, 'whereas, if Athens were to suffer the same fate, we should assume from outward appearance that it had been twice as powerful as it in fact is' (I, *x*, 2). The archaeological excavations carried out in Athens during the nineteenth century fully confirmed Thucydides' view: those at Sparta were disappointing.

If the siege of Troy lasted for ten years, it was because the Trojans were never confronted at one time by more than a part of the superior forces of the Achaeans. The latter, being short of provisions, were obliged to carry out raids in Asia Minor and the neighbouring islands, as we know from Homer (see pp. 16–17). Here again, as with the strength of the Greek army, he explains the course of the war in economic terms.

When we are considering the past, he says, 'it is difficult to accept every piece of evidence that presents itself' (I, *xx*). And he proceeds to give three examples of historical mistakes, two of which had been made by Herodotus, though he does not mention his predecessor by name; he leaves it to the informed reader to discover that for himself. He continues:

One should hesitate before believing either the poets who adorned and amplified their theme, or the chroniclers who wrote them with a view to pleasing their hearers rather than establishing the truth (I, *xxi*).

Here, he obviously has in mind Hecataeus and Herodotus, both skilled spinners of agreeable tales; the Ancients, it seems, almost always read aloud, and we know that Herodotus used to give public readings of his work in Athens.

There is only one respect in which Thucydides adopted the procedure of ancient, rather than modern, historians: that is, his habit of attributing to statesmen, generals and ambassadors speeches obviously composed by himself, in which he puts into practice the arts he had learnt from the orators. But he justifies this quite straightforwardly:

With regard to the speeches made by various individuals, either just before the war or when hostilities had actually broken out, it has been difficult to reproduce even their general tenor with any accuracy, either for me when I heard them personally, or for those who reported them to me: I have written, therefore, what it seems to me the speakers would have said in the circumstances, keeping as closely as possible to the general sense of what was actually said (I, *xxii*, I).

What he does not mention is that, for him, these speeches were a convenient means of revealing not only the characters and motives of the men who made them, but also the inter-relation of events, at least as understood by him; in other words, his own philosophy of history. For Thucydides' lucid and penetrating mind had deeply pondered the historical process, the problem of cause and effect, as well as the psychology of the leaders and of the crowd. As Madame de Romilly has said, 'Thucydides' speeches are interspersed with generalizations, from commonplace maxims to profound political analyses. And the latter help to sustain the narrative. . . . Human development has its laws; and by studying its various crises it is possible to discover affinities that lend themselves to classification, thus providing a sounder basis for future action.'

Moreover, Thucydides is careful to explain the method he adopted in his effort to arrive at the truth.

As regards the incidents of the war, in describing them, I have not thought it right to rely upon the reports of the first comer, any more than upon my personal opinion; either I took part in them myself, or I have enquired about them from others with the greatest possible attention to detail. To establish the truth about them has been a laborious task, for even those who have actually witnessed an event present different versions of it, depending upon their sympathies with one side or the other and on their powers of memory. For the reader, the absence of marvels in my account will perhaps diminish its attraction, but those who wish to understand clearly both the events of the past and those which, in all human probability, will occur in future in the same or a similar manner, will consider it useful; and for me that will suffice. Indeed, what I have written is not simply a rhetorical exercise for the moment, but a possession for all time (I, *xxii*, 2–4).

From this, it is possible to appreciate the depth and the scope of Thucydides' aim: by writing the history of the greatest war yet known (the 'great war', unfortunately, has always been the most recent one) to provide for future statesmen 'a possession for all time', a storehouse of wisdom to which they can turn for useful lessons. Paul Valéry was not alone in rejecting the view that our knowledge of the past is valid in respect of the future, but Thucydides accepted it wholeheartedly. He had faith in the power of reason. He believed in the necessary succession of cause and effect in the evolution of humanity. Without underrating the part played by chance, he was convinced that the fate of nations was determined by their leaders. But if the work of the historian is to have this permanent value it is essential for it to be firmly based on the rock of established fact, continually checked and verified by an impartial mind. Did Thucydides achieve this lofty ideal, which would seem to be accessible only to pure intelligence? Apart from a few questions of detail, I think we are justified in saying that he did. Thanks to him, in any case, there is no other period of Greek history that has been so brilliantly illuminated for us as these twenty years between 432 and 411.

Geography occupies a much smaller place in the work of Thucydides than in that of Herodotus. Nowhere does he describe a country, its monuments and customs, merely for pleasure, gratuitously. The purpose of all such descriptions, for instance the harbours of Sphacteria or Syracuse, with their roadsteads and fortifications, is simply to clarify the narrative and enable the reader to understand the situation. Always, in his work, the historian takes precedence over the geographer; geography simply appears as the auxiliary, the handmaid, of history.

Unlike his predecessors, and most of his successors, Thucydides was always at the greatest pains to establish the correct chronology of the events he described. In this respect the difficulties were considerable, for the Greeks had not yet adopted the habit of reckoning the passage of time from the Olympiads. In each city, the dates of public transactions were only to be derived from the name of the magistrate then in office, while the names of the months varied from town to town. The method adopted by Thucydides, therefore, was to establish the date of the beginning of the war by reference to a number of simultaneous happenings: the number of years that the priestess of Hera at Argos had exercised her function, the names of the first Ephor at Sparta and of the reigning Archon at Athens, both annual appointments. Succeeding years he spoke of as the first, second, third and so on, of the War; while within each year he distinguished between the winter season, lasting about four months, during which military operations were normally suspended, and the summer season of eight months, which he further subdivided: the beginning of spring, the shooting of the corn, the setting of the ears, the ripening, the harvest, the gathering of the grapes, and the last days of fine weather.

To economic factors in his own times he attributed as much importance as to those of antiquity. Again and again he indicates precisely
the material and financial resources available to the principal belligerents, and he points out that, in the last resort, it would be Persian gold
that would tip the balance in favour of the Peloponnese, since it
would enable the Spartans to increase and maintain their fleet. Now,
in any large-scale war, victory will ultimately belong to the group of
powers who have, or achieve, mastery of the seas; a law that Thucydides understood and which seems to have been borne out in our
own times by the history of the last two World Wars.

Nevertheless, for him, it is human intelligence which, more than
any economic consideration, is the decisive factor, especially when
allied with courage and energy. It is this interest in psychological
analysis (which, as we have already noted, was characteristic of
Euripides) that distinguishes the historian as being very much a man
of his times. Where Herodotus had been content to present historical
figures simply in terms of their public attitudes and external behaviour,
Thucydides portrays their intellectual capacity, their will power,
their character. Before entering upon his subject proper, while he is
still discussing the Persian Wars, he praises Themistocles in these
terms:

By his native intelligence, which study neither prepared for nor added to,
thanks to his powers of swift reflection he excelled both in his judgment
of immediate problems and in his ability to form a correct view of the
future in its widest perspectives. . . . To sum up, by the resources of his own
intelligence and the ease with which he could draw upon them, he was a
man unmatched in his power to take quick decisions (I, *cxxxviii*, 3).

With this genius for improvization he compares the genius of Pericles,
the fruit of reflection and experience, and of an acquired lucidity.

It is unfortunate, perhaps, that Thucydides so completely neglects
the physical appearance of the great men he writes about, omitting
any personal details or anecdotes. Yet this does not prevent him from
bringing home to us, both by his analysis and by the opinions he
puts into their mouths, the profound and noble wisdom of Pericles,
the timidly scrupulous honesty of Nicias, the bold ambition of
Alcibiades and the careless impetuosity of Cleon.

With regard to the latter, it is possible that Thucydides failed to
maintain his usual impartiality. True, his account of him is fully

supported by what Aristophanes tells us about him, but both the comic poet and the historian were conservative in outlook and, on principle, would have felt hostile towards this 'Jacobin', this democrat who behaved like a revolutionary. And it is a little disquieting to find Thucydides agreeing with a poet whose portraits tend to be caricatures rather than genuine likenesses, and who, in the *Acharnians*, presents even Pericles in such an unflattering light. For though Cleon may have been lacking in manners and in personal distinction, he seems to have been both a brave soldier and a skilful leader.

It was not, however, only with individual psychology that Thucydides was concerned. He also carefully observed the distinctive, and very different, characteristics of the Athenian and Lacedaemonian peoples. In an elaborate speech, abounding with antitheses and the subtle distinctions between words affected by Prodicos, a spokesman of the Corinthians says to the Spartans:

The Athenians are innovators, quick to conceive and carry out their plans, whereas you tend to stick to your ideas, inventing nothing new, and when you do act on them, you fail to achieve even what is indispensable. Similarly, they act boldly without weighing their strength, take risks without pausing to reflect; whereas, when you find yourselves in a difficult situation, you are apt to despair of finding a way out. They are resolute, where you are dilatory. . . . To sum up, it would be true to say that they neither know what it is to be at peace themselves, nor are prepared to leave others in peace (I, *lxx*, 2–9).

As a general, Thucydides had had experience of public affairs; his knowledge of history was not acquired simply from books. When his activities were brought to an end by exile, he transferred his energies to reflection and meditation, though he was already naturally predisposed to the contemplative attitude of the philosopher. Knowledge was his religion, and such was his love of truth that impartiality came naturally to him. After all, it is by no means certain that he misjudged even Cleon. What is particularly striking is the way he refused to allow his judgment to be swayed either by success or by failure. He was not dazzled by Cleon's brilliant achievement at Pylos; and when the people of Chios defected from the Athenian cause and thereby brought about their own undoing, Thucydides was able to understand the political reasons for their decision, and to justify it. Again, the ultimate defeat of Athens in the Peloponnesian War, he

maintains, in no way proved that the plan conceived by Pericles had
been mistaken:

He survived the outbreak of hostilities by two years and six months, and
it was only after his death that men realized how correctly he had foreseen
events. For he had told the Athenians they would win, but only on condition
that they remained on the defensive on land and directed their energies
to operations at sea, without attempting to make new conquests and without
incurring risks during the course of the war. But, once Pericles was dead,
in every respect they did the contrary (II, *lxv*, 6 ff.).

Thucydides never allowed himself to be misled by appearances.
We have seen what he said of the real importance of Mycenae and of
Sparta. When he studies the causes of the Peloponnesian War he
does not accept the grievances put forward by the belligerents at their
face value, but points out the underlying cause of the struggle: the fact
that the expansion of the Athenian empire had reached a point that was
intolerable to Sparta and her allies. Good Athenian as he was, his
lucid judgment nevertheless enabled him to grasp that the imperialism
of his native city was the starting point of all the misfortunes suffered
by the Greeks in a war that lasted thirty years and destroyed the
living strength of Hellas.

Whenever possible, he consulted official documents. In Book v
he reproduces word for word the text of the treaty drawn up in 421
at the time of the Peace of Nicias; and recently discovered inscriptions,
notably the accounts for tribute paid to Athens by the subject cities,
have confirmed his veracity as a historian.

Herodotus was not only a believer, he was also credulous. The
outlook of Thucydides was always rational and positivist. Obviously,
it is no more possible in his case than in that of Euripides to understand exactly what he felt about religion. He quotes a number of
oracles that were current during the war because they excited the mob
and therefore exerted a significant influence on events, but it is clear
that he himself did not believe in them. When Athens was struck
by the plague, he says:

As happens in such circumstances, people recalled a prophecy that the old
men said had once been spoken: 'When there is war with the Dorians,
there will be plague as well.' There was some discussion as to whether the
word was really 'plague' (*loimos*) or 'famine' (*limos*) which differs by one
letter only, but it was generally accepted that the original word was 'plague',

since it was natural for men's recollections to accord with their sufferings (II, *liv*).

Thucydides never attempted to explain the course of history in terms of divine retribution or Nemesis. For him, events are determined in the main by men's will (*gnomê*) and, for the rest, by chance (*tychê*). At the same time, he includes amongst the signs of social corruption the diminished respect for the gods and, in his famous account of the plague, he considers the general lack of piety to be disquieting. 'His attitude of respectful seriousness in these matters,' Alfred Croiset wrote, 'has more in common with the school of Anaxagoras than with sophisticated atheism.'

What is indisputable is his sustained objectivity and unfailing realism. Thucydides never adopts a moral attitude towards human behaviour. In the well-known discussion between the Athenians and the people of Melos he refuses to take sides, even when the former justify themselves by an appeal to force. The small island of Melos was of little importance, except perhaps as a strategic base: it certainly threatened no one. Its only crime was that it obstinately desired to remain neutral between two rival blocs, the two 'Great Powers' of the period, Athens and Sparta. The dialogue between the Athenian and Melian envoys is as tragic as the scene between Creon and Antigone:

Mel: So you do not accept that we should remain at peace, as your friends, and without entering into any alliance?

Ath: No, for your hostility would be less injurious to us than your friendship, since in the eyes of our subjects that would be regarded as a mark of our weakness, whereas your enmity is a proof of our power. . . .

Mel: But, surely, if you yourselves are prepared to face such dangers in order to increase your empire . . . it would be base and cowardly on our part not to risk everything rather than submit to servitude?

Ath: Not if you are wise, for the contest would not be on equal terms. . . . We believe that both gods and men, by a necessity of their nature, have the same will to dominate. This is not a law that has been made by us; but we intend to profit by it and we shall hand it on for all time (v, *xciv–xcv, passim*).

One might be listening to Callicles in Plato's *Gorgias* (see p. 269). Never has the will to power been asserted with such utter lack of scruple, with such cynicism, and yet with such an easy conscience. But the capture of Melos and the frightful treatment inflicted on its inhabitants do not appear to have aroused any emotion in the historian, for he adds coldly:

The Athenians massacred all the Melians old enough to bear arms, and sold the women and children as slaves (v, *cxvi*).

In his descriptions he is above all concerned with clarity and precision. Yet if an event seems to him to be of special importance, he will interrupt his narrative to paint a picture, drawing upon all the resources of rhetoric in a display of bravura. For example, his account of the departure of the Sicilian expedition is a magnificent affirmation of the power of Athens:

At dawn the Athenians and their allies went down to Piraeus and boarded their ships. And they were accompanied by everyone that was in the city, both citizens and strangers. . . . Hopes for the conquests to come were mixed with tears for the men whom they might not see again. . . . Yet they only had to look around them to revive their confidence in their might. . . . These first military forces, equipped by a single city, were greater than any that had been seen before, both by reason of the expense involved and the luxury of their appointments. . . . When the embarkation was completed, the trumpet proclaimed silence, and prayers were said before putting out to sea, not separately on each ship, but by all together, led by a herald. Throughout the whole army wine was poured into the mixing bowls; and officers and men made libations with gold and silver cups. And on land, also, the whole throng of people and all who had come out of friendship joined in the prayers. Then, when the paean had been sung and the libations were concluded, the ships put out to sea, at first in single file, then racing one another towards Aegina (VI, *xxx–xxxii, passim*).

In contrast to this, consider the scene when the Athenians are abandoning camp after the loss of their ships at Syracuse, a retreat that marked the beginning of the army's collapse:

As the corpses were not buried, when anyone saw the body of a friend lying on the ground he was seized with grief mixed with fear; and more even than the dead, those that were left behind alive, the sick and the wounded, were a cause of grief to the living, for they were more to be pitied than those who had perished. Begging to be taken along, beseeching their comrades as they passed and clinging to them, they spread dismay . . . so that the whole army was plunged in grief, finding it difficult to leave, despite its being enemy country and though the sufferings they had already suffered and those they feared for the future were too great for tears (VII, *lxxv, passim*).

The speeches, as I have said, express the ideas appropriate to the speaker, but in addition they succeed in conveying his feelings as an orator: anger, irony, the desire to convince his hearers. During the deliberations that precede the Sicilian expedition, Nicias had intervened with counsels of prudence in opposition to the temerity of the younger men. Alcibiades replies:

Do not allow the policy of inaction advocated by Nicias or these quarrels between young and old to divert you from your purpose. We have a sound tradition: it was by taking counsel, young and old together, that our fathers raised our power to its present height. . . . Neither youth nor age alone can achieve anything: the true secret of strength is to associate and mix together what is less good or mediocre, with what is perfect (VI, *xviii*, 6).

The last phrase is obviously a sarcastic gibe at the pretensions of the old men to have achieved supreme wisdom.

When Pericles is made to speak, he does so with a loftiness of spirit and nobility of language worthy of 'the Olympian', particularly in his funeral oration for the first men killed in the war. Praise of Athens was a traditional part of such official speeches:

We love beauty, but shun luxury; we devote ourselves to wisdom, but without allowing ourselves to grow soft. Wealth we regard as something to be used, not as a subject for boasting. . . . We judge matters soundly, and conceive them in the same spirit; for, in our eyes, speech is no hindrance to action. . . . In a word, then, I make bold to say that our city is the school of Greece (II, *xl*).

The language used by Thucydides is an archaic form of Attic, close to the Ionic; powerful, rather than supple. His style, especially in the speeches and set pieces, tends to be abstract, concise, difficult sometimes even to the point of obscurity; it is full of asymetrical antitheses, sudden discontinuities, litotes and all the other figures of speech distinguished by the orators. It is a style that strives for effect, and it is occasionally meretricious; yet one is continually aware of the effort to express the finest and most subtle shades of meaning, to follow every turn of thought and to give ideas their full weight. Undoubtedly he owed much to the Sophists but, where they had almost nothing to say, with him the richness and density of the content is more important than the form, even at its most brilliant. Indeed, no writer is more original than this disciple of the sophists, and his style bears the imprint of his own powerful personality. His work dominates the whole of ancient historiography, for his qualities as a historian are such that he surpasses even those who came after him.

ARISTOPHANES

Like Thucydides, Aristophanes also speaks to us about Pericles, Cleon, Nicias, Alcibiades. He shows us the other side of the Peloponnesian War, what it meant to the ordinary people of Athens and the peasants of Attica, packed into the city. His comedies are an invaluable complement to the work of the historian.

His life, of which we know practically nothing, is for us inseparable from the history of his work. He was born about 445 and, despite assertions to the contrary by his enemies, both his parents were pure-born Athenians. He was extremely precocious. His first play, not preserved, the *Banqueters*, must have been performed before he reached the legal age of eighteen, for, in the parabasis to the *Clouds*, he says: 'Being still a virgin and forbidden to procreate, I exposed my child, and another young woman looked after it for me' (530–1); in other words, in 427, his play was put on in the name of one of his friends. It was the same with the *Babylonians* in 426 and with the *Acharnians* in 425, the earliest of his comedies that has come down to us. In the former, he made a violent attack on Cleon, who summonsed him for claiming to be an Athenian citizen when he was not. Aristophanes won his case and was in no way intimidated: he attacked Cleon again in the *Acharnians* and, even more savagely, in the *Knights*, both belonging to the year 424. The latter was the first of his plays that was performed under his own name (see above p. 173).

All these early comedies were successful, but in 423, with the *Clouds*, where he attacked the sophists and Socrates, he was beaten by Cratinos (see p. 174), and was only awarded the third prize. He did not resign himself to this setback and re-wrote the parabasis with a view to a second performance, though this did not take place.

The *Wasps* came in 422, and the *Peace* in the following year, when the negotiations that were to lead to the Peace of Nicias were already in train. Thus, from the *Acharnians* to the *Peace*, the first five of his plays that have been preserved date from the period of the War of Archidamos (see pp. 176–7), and appeared regularly year after year.

The following comedy however, the *Birds*, was not produced until 414, shortly after the Athenian fleet had set sail for Sicily. It would be a mistake to conclude from this that during this interval from 421 to 414 Aristophanes wrote nothing for the theatre, but the plays have been lost. In 411 came *Lysistrata* and the *Thesmophoriazusae*; then, in 405, shortly after the deaths of Sophocles and Euripides, the *Frogs*.

So far, all his plays belong to the time of the Peloponnesian War, but the last two that have been preserved, the *Ecclesiazusae*, 392, and *Ploutos*, 388, clearly belong to a later time. They deal with themes that were then in vogue, feminism and pauperism, and differ considerably from the previous plays. In all, he wrote forty-four comedies, eleven of which we still possess. And he seems to have died about 385.

In the Old Comedy, of Aristophanes and Cratinos, the form was rather rigid. The Chorus was larger than in tragedy, consisting of twenty-four members. In the first part of the play, after the exposition, which often led to a kind of parade, it played a most active part; violent struggles or arguments with the protagonist. In the *Acharnians*, the bellicose old men belonging to the deme of Acharnai who form the Chorus, fight the 'pacifist' Dicaeopolis. This first part ends with the triumph of one of the adversaries (in the *Acharnians* it was Dicaeopolis who won) and at this point the action proper is concluded. Then the members of the Chorus, left alone on the stage, took off their costumes to indicate that the action was temporarily suspended and, coming forward to face the public in a movement called the parabasis, spoke directly to the audience in the name of the author, voicing his grievances, criticisms and confidences (see p. 173). At the end of the parabasis the actors returned to the stage, and the play continued in a series of scenes that unfold in a humorous way the consequences arising from the situation reached at the end of the first part. These scenes were not so much integrated as simply juxtaposed, the total effect being not unlike a modern revue. In the latter part of the comedy the Chorus no longer played an active role, except to sing satirical couplets between the scenes.

Such was the basic structure of the Old Comedy, though writers sometimes took liberties with it: in the *Clouds*, for example, there are two parabases, though the plot is continuous throughout the play. Possibly this explains its comparative failure: the audience may have been put off by its unfamiliar construction.

The last two plays that have been preserved, the *Ecclesiazusae* and *Ploutos*, belong to the so-called Middle Comedy, a transitional stage on the way towards the New Comedy that was later introduced by Menander. In it we note a tendency that was also making itself felt in tragedy: the continually decreasing importance of the Chorus in relation to that of the actors. In the Middle Comedy, the coryphaeus takes part in the dialogue with the actors and the lyrical passages are progressively diminished. The Chorus tends to become a collective figure, still preserved on traditional grounds, but with its role more and more confined to occasionally giving advice to the actors or calling upon them to speak. True, the intermissions between the various episodes, or scenes, are still retained, and during them the Chorus dances, but it no longer sings. In the manuscripts, where we should expect to find the text of their songs, there is simply the stage direction: 'Dance of the Chorus'.

In the first parabasis of the *Clouds*, where Aristophanes compares himself with his rivals, he proudly insists:

So great a poet am I that I don't need to put on airs by wearing my hair long [he was, in fact, bald], nor do I cheat you by continually repeating the same subject, but of my skill invent new stories for you, all different and all ingenious (*Clouds*, 545 ff.).

This was quite true: the plots of his comedies, always new, brilliant and full of surprises, display an amazing power of invention. In the *Acharnians*, written when the war was at its height, an Athenian, Dicaeopolis, concludes a private peace treaty with the Peloponnesians, valid only for himself and his family, and as a result the second part of the play is able to emphasize all the advantages of peace. In the *Knights*, Cleon, the servant of Demos (the people), a stupid old rascal, finds himself supplanted in his master's favour by a pork-butcher, an even more impudent thief than himself. In the *Clouds*, the peasant Strepsiades wants to learn all the tricks of the trade of the sophists, represented by Socrates, so that he can swindle his creditors and avoid paying his debts, but as he is too old and thick-witted to do so he decides to send his son to the 'thinking shop' instead; the latter soon becomes so adept that he is able to prove to his father that he is justified in beating him, whereupon the old man, beside himself with rage, burns down Socrates' house. The *Wasps*, which provided Racine with the inspiration for *Les Plaideurs*, shows us an old man, Philocleon (Friend of Cleon), who has a mania for delivering judgments: his son, Bdelycleon (Enemy of Cleon), shuts him up in his house and, as a harmless outlet for his mania, makes him pass sentence on a dog that has stolen a piece of cheese. In the *Peace*, a wine-grower, Trygaeos, heart-broken by all the misfortunes Greece has suffered as a result of the war, flies up to heaven on a beetle's back to lay his complaint before Zeus, and releases the goddess of Peace from the cave where she has been imprisoned.

The second group of plays is less immediately concerned with social and political affairs, and in them the poet gives even freer rein to his fantasy. Like Trygaeos, the two Athenians in the *Birds*, Euelpides and Pisthetairos, go up to heaven, but in order to found there the city of Cloud-Cuckoo-Land; and in the end Pisthetairos seduces the goddess Royalty from Zeus and marries her. In *Lysistrata* it is the women of Athens who decide to take heroic steps to put an end to the war: they refuse their husbands' embraces until the latter agree to negotiate peace. In the *Thesmophoriazusae* Euripides, concerned by the hatred he arouses in women, sends his brother-in-law Mnesilochos, disguised as a woman, to the Thesmophoria, the festival of Demeter, at which no men were allowed, to spy on them and find out what plots they are hatching against the tragic poet: the identity of Mnesilochos is discovered, and Euripides has to employ all his cunning and subtlety to excuse him. In the *Frogs*, Dionysus, the god of the theatre, descends into the underworld to discover which is the greatest of the tragedians, because, since the death of Aeschylus, Sophocles and Eurpides there is a shortage of good poets.

The third group, consisting of the *Ecclesiazusae* and *Ploutos*, is of a different character as I have said, but the poet's imagination is still almost as lively. In the first, the women of Athens, led by Praxagora, take possession of the Assembly and proclaim a completely communist state: abolition of property and marriage, and communal ownership of goods and women. In the second, a brave Athenian, Chremylos, has discovered Ploutos (Wealth) disguised as a blind old man; he takes him to the sanctuary of Asclepius at Epidaurus to recover his sight and then keeps him in his own house: thus Ploutos, now gifted with second sight, will in future stop favouring rascals and bestow fortune on those who deserve it, firstly on Chremylos, who gives a banquet to his friends.

In most cases, the name of the play is taken from the Chorus, since it is they who have the most spectacular role: the old Acharnians, with their sacks of charcoal; the Knights mounted on their hobby-horses; the Clouds, worshipped by the sophists, with their 'cloudy' talk; the dicasts (lawyers) armed with their great styles as emblems of their profession, which make them look like Wasps; the members of the Chorus, dressed up to look like every kind of Bird; the Frogs from the infernal swamps; the Chorus of women admitted to the Eleusinian mysteries; and the women dressed in men's clothes and wearing false beards. The idea of Trygaeos' beetle, borrowed from one of Aesop's fables, the *Eagle and the Beetle,* also suggests an amusing setting; for instance, when Trygaeos is being hoisted up into the air by some sort of crane, he pretends to be worried and calls to the man working the crane to take care.

Aristophanes' sense of the comic is wide-ranging, but uneven. In the parabasis to the *Clouds*, which he claims to be a 'play for connoisseurs', he boasts that he has foresworn the crude and vulgar means employed by his rivals to make their audiences laugh:

Like Electra of old, my comedy hopes to find an enlightened audience; she will recognize at once the locks of her brother's hair! And notice how restrained she is by nature: to begin with she doesn't attempt to make the urchins snigger by wearing a piece of leather sown to her dress, painted red at one end; she doesn't mock the bald-pates, or dance the *Cordax*;[1] you won't find an old man poking his neighbour with his stick and mumbling his lines in the hope of getting away with stale jokes; nor does she fling herself about the stage with a lighted torch, crying 'ow, ow', but appears before you confident in her own merit (*Clouds*, 534 ff.).

At times, it will be seen, the parabasis fulfilled the same function as those 'Prefaces to the Reader' in which Molière and Racine defend themselves against their critics.

But as a rule Aristophanes was far from being as restrained and pure-minded as he here claims to be. He probably did away with some of the most obscene comic accessories, like the imitation phalluses and other stage business grown stale from constant repetition, but the dialogue of the actors and some of the songs sung by the Chorus

---

[1] An obscene dance.

are full of the coarsest smut. As one of the traditions of the Old Comedy, he could scarcely have dispensed with smut altogether even if he had wanted to; but there is little evidence that it was repugnant to him—he even seems to have enjoyed it. By comparison with Aristophanes, Rabelais appears almost decent. Moralists, such as Plutarch, were to prefer the comedies of Menander to plays like *Lysistrata*.

This amazing buffoon, with his staggering zest for life, could also arouse laughter of a very different kind. His dialogue and choruses are strewn with the most brilliant drolleries—an almost continual stream of puns, nonsense, parodies of tragedy, neologisms, ridiculous catalogues of words, in which the expected one is suddenly replaced by another with the most entertaining effect. Such a bewildering wealth of verbal invention presents the translator with a disheartening problem, especially as he is continually alluding to personalities and incidents we know nothing about. And yet the genius of Aristophanes is not difficult to appreciate; nor is there any other ancient writer whose works, even today, are so attractive and delightful to read.

In the *Clouds*, the peasant Strepsiades, who has taken a wife socially superior to himself, attributes all his troubles to his marriage. Parodying the tragic style, he exclaims:

O that she had died a miserable death, that match-maker who bestirred me to marry your mother! I used to lead a pleasant country life, not bothering to sweep up, lolling at my ease, and well supplied with honey, olives and sheep. Whatever possessed me, a simple countryman, to marry the niece of Megacles, a city dame, a simpering miss, completely Coesyrified![1] As I stood beside her at our wedding, I stank of new wine, cheese-racks and wool, the smell of plenty; while she breathed perfumes, saffran and lewd kisses, the odour of gluttony, extravagance and venery (*Clouds*, 41 ff.).

And here is how Strepsiades' son, as a result of a conjugal compromise, came to have the name Pheidippides (horse-lover):

Well, I and my good wife started quarrelling about what we should call him. She wanted some fancy name with 'hippos', Xanthippos, or Charippos, or Callipides; I preferred Pheidonides (son of thrift), his grandsire's name. And so the argument dragged on, until at last we agreed on Pheidippides.

---

[1] Coesyra was the typical fine lady, stuck up and affected. Molière, in an analagous way, created the verb *tartuffier* from the name Tartuffe.

So she took the boy and started spoiling him. 'When you are grown up,' she would say, 'you will drive your own chariot to the citadel, like Megacles, all dressed in purple.' But I used to tell him: 'You'll be lucky if you're bringing your goats back from the mountain as your father did, with a sheepskin jacket on your back.' But instead of listening to what I said to him, he proceeded to ruin me by starting a racing stable (*Clouds*, 60 ff.).

Dicaeopolis' explanation of the origins of the Peloponnesian War has very little in common with that given by Thucydides. He describes the Athenian ban on trade with Megara as follows:

Some good-for-nothings began denouncing the short woollen cloaks from Megara. Whenever they saw a cucumber, a hare, a sucking pig, a bit of garlic or a lump of salt, 'That comes from Megara,' they'd say, and straight away put it up for auction. Then some drunken young cottabus-players went to Megara and carried off the courtesan Simaetha. Smarting under the affront, the Megarians, as randy as cocks, stole a couple of Aspasia's hussies for revenge. And that's how war broke out, setting all the Greeks at odds on account of three whores! For, of course, this infuriated Pericles, so that the Olympian began thundering and hurling his thunderbolts, upsetting the whole of Hellas and issuing decrees that sounded like drinking-songs: 'Let all Megarians at once depart, And quit the sea, the mainland and the mart' (*Acharnians*, 517 ff.).

But this unscrupulous entertainer was also a great lyric poet, and V. H. Debidour is fully justified in applying to him some of the terms of La Bruyère's comment on Rabelais: thanks to his 'bewildering power of assimilation', his work reveals, side by side with the 'charm of the dregs of society', 'the most delicate dishes, at once excellent and exquisite'. In the *Birds*, one of the Hoopoe's serenades begins:

Epopopopoi, popoi, popopopoi, popoi, popoi, io, io! Come hither all my fluttering brothers, countless swarm that feed upon the peasant's well-sown fields, swift-winged barley thieves and twittering grain-peckers, all you who gather in the fields, crowding the furrows, and warble with your sweet, shrill throats, *tio, tio, tio, tio*. . . . (*Birds*, 517 ff.).

Or, again, this song sung by the Chorus of Eleusinian initiates in the *Frogs*:

O blessed Iacchos, you who dwell in these temples, join the members of our mystic throng, your brow encircled with its wreath of sweetly flowering myrtle, and boldly strike up the measure for our wild and joyous dance, the pure and holy dance of our sacred mystery (*Frogs*, 321 ff.).

Nor is it only in such lyrical passages that Aristophanes shows himself to be a genuine poet. In the *Clouds*, True Logic says to Pheidippides:

If you take my advice, you will go to the Academy gymnasium and there beneath the sacred olives, wearing a chaplet of rushes, walk with a friend of your own age, carefree, breathing the scent of the bindweed, watching the catkins falling from the silver poplars; enjoying the springtime of the year, when the plane trees whisper to the elms (*Clouds*, 1005 ff.).

Whenever he speaks of the Eleusinian mysteries, Aristophanes becomes serious. In the *Frogs*, with its Chorus of initiates, he puts into the mouth of Aeschylus the solemn prayer to which I have already referred (p. 155). But for the most part he treats religion with an utter lack of reverence, representing the gods as so many ridiculous puppets. In the *Birds*, Demeter, the corn goddess, is challenged to make a blade of wheat grow. In the *Frogs*, Dionysus, god of the theatre in whose sanctuary all tragedies and comedies were performed, is made to appear a contemptible braggart, morally inferior to his slave, Xanthias. In his last play, *Ploutos* maintains that Zeus is jealous of well-to-do mortals and Chremylos asks him: 'Do you really believe all your power and all your thunderbolts are worth tuppence?' (*Ploutos*, 124–5).

Yet Aristophanes was not, like the sophists he so much disliked, an atheist utterly lacking in piety. His disrespectful attitude to the gods was part of the comic tradition and, in this respect, the Athenians allowed their comic poets a surprising degree of freedom, considering the number and seriousness of the charges they brought for impiety; we have seen how careful even a tragic poet like Euripides had to be. The fact is, it was only comedy that enjoyed this licence, probably because it was not taken seriously.

Does this mean that Aristophanes regarded himself simply as a clown, whose only aim was to 'get a laugh from the gallery'? In the *Acharnians*, Dicaeopolis, whose name means something like 'justice of the city', parodying Euripides' *Telephos*, begins his great speech to the Chorus with the proud claim:

Think not ill of me, spectators, if I, a beggar, speak of our city in a comedy before you Athenians. For comedy herself can speak the truth (*Acharnians*, 496 ff.).

Aristophanes certainly regarded it as his right to criticize society, politics and literature in the name of good sense, morality and taste. He felt himself capable of giving his fellow citizens sound advice. By denouncing the demagogues and sycophants, the sophists and eccentric judges, he felt himself to be acting in the interests of a healthy public life, and thereby rendering an important service to his city; again and again he insists upon this. In the *Frogs*, he makes Aeschylus say that it is the duty of tragedy to teach the people, but he was convinced that comedy had an equal responsibility. The noble and haughty knights declare:

If one of our old comic poets had tried to force us to come and speak in the parabasis, he would scarcely have succeeded. But, on this occasion, the poet is worthy of the honour, for he hates those whom we hate, dares to speak the truth, and attacks Typhon, the destroying hurricane (*Knights*, 507 ff.).

Typhon the hurricane is Cleon.

Aristophanes dared to speak the truth, but he also hated the same people as the young aristocrats who formed the Chorus. From this it has been supposed that he belonged to the conservative faction, and was therefore opposed to the reigning democracy. This conclusion seems to me no more likely, however, than that, because he treated the gods with such freedom, he was therefore an atheist. True, he was continually praising the past, as conservatives do. He was full of admiration for the Marathonomachoi and for the old-fashioned kind of upbringing that had produced these 'mighty warriors, six foot high'. He enjoyed the works of Phrynichos, Aeschylus and Sophocles, hated the sophists, and was continually taunting Euripides. He also attributed to the Lacedaemonians more political wisdom than to the Athenians; and the 'Spartan dream' was one of the constant pre-occupations of the aristocratic party and its supporters.

All this is true, but with Aristophanes it is important to distinguish between the man and the writer. As a man, it seems probable that his political ideals were similar to those of Thucydides, a moderate democracy, with a peaceful foreign policy: for, as we have seen, at least with regard to Cleon, they were of the same opinion. But, as a comic poet, he had no hesitation about poking fun at such an authentic Marathonomachos as Aeschylus, or at the peasant Strepsiades, or at old Philocleon and the Acharnians themselves, all of whom, in contrast to the depraved behaviour of the poet's contemporaries, stood for 'the good old days'. Living in a democracy, he felt bound to criticize its vices and abuses: had he lived in a city ruled by the aristocracy, his target would have been, not Cleon the tanner, but the high-born Knights.

It must always be remembered that comedy originated in the *komos* (see pp. 170–1), and that unrestrained merry-making, stimulated by drinking and dancing, was the only rule to which it conformed. Aristophanes certainly 'chastised men with laughter', but it would be even truer to modify this slightly and say that he laughed as he chastised them: his primary aim was to win the prize by making the spectators laugh; only in the second place did he seek to improve the political, social and literary behaviour of his fellow citizens.

In his last two plays he seems to have had greater philosophical— one could almost say, sociological—pretensions than in his earlier ones: the *Parliament of Women* (the title *Ecclesiazusae* was itself a joke, for the participle of the verb *ekklesazo* was never used in the feminine) with its proposal for the community of women, looks forward to Plato's *Republic*; while *Ploutos* is in large measure a protest against inequalities of wealth and class. At the same time, it must be realized that Aristophanes was only concerned with such serious subjects because they were already being discussed in Athens. For a comic poet, the best subject is always the one that is in the news.

I have already noted the first signs of a kind of feminist movement in Athens when speaking of Euripides and Socrates. By keeping the men away from home and forcing the women to take greater initiative, the Peloponnesian War inevitably strengthened this tendency, and in the 'Funeral Oration' Thucydides made Pericles himself allude to new ideas about the emancipation of women, if only to express his opposition to them. Thus the theme of the *Parliament of Women* was already in the air; and, in any case, the play is a more or less incoherent farce, so that one would be hard put to it to discover in it any serious discussion of communist ideas.

Aristophanes excelled in reproducing the speech and ideas of common people, and showing them as they went about their everyday business. For anyone wishing to understand the atmosphere of Athens and the way of life of its people, he is far and away the most informative of all writers. In the *Parliament of Women*, Praxagora undertakes to prove that women are more sensible than men:

In the first place, they still soak their wool in hot water as they always did, and you won't see them trying to change that. The trouble with the men of Athens is that, however well things may be going, they refuse to believe they are safe unless they're dreaming up some new-fangled idea.[1] Now the women, they sit down when they cook as they always have done; they carry their bundles on their heads as they always have done; they bake their cakes in the way they always have done; they irritate their husbands as they always have done; they take lovers as they always have done; they eat sweets all day as they always have done; they drink their wine without watering it as they always have done; and they enjoy making love as they always have done (*Ecclesiazusae*, 245 ff.).

In the *Birds*, Pisthetairos sings the praises of the cock:

He has only to start crowing at crack of dawn and everyone leaps out of bed and sets to work: smiths, potters, tanners, shoemakers, bath attendants, lyre-makers and shield-makers. Why, some of them even begin putting on their sandals while it is still dark.

To which Euelpides replies:

You don't have to tell me! It was all through a cock that I was unlucky enough to lose my woollen Phrygian cloak. I had been invited to a child's Tenth Day feast, and on the way stopped in town to have a few drinks. I must have dozed off, because though it wasn't even time for supper, when a cock started crowing I thought it must be morning, and set out for Halimous. I had scarcely got outside the city walls, when a thief fetches me a terrible blow with his cudgel. Down I went, but before I could shout for help, he had whipped off my cloak and disappeared (*Birds*, 488 ff.).

No one else has described daily life in the city and the countryside as well as Aristophanes. If the purpose of history is to re-create the past in its entirety, and not merely to recall political and military events, his comedies are of invaluable assistance to the historian. The

---

[1] In speaking thus of the Athenian character Aristophanes is at one with Thucydides, see p. 226.

account of the session of the Assembly at the beginning of the *Acharnians* may be a caricature, yet it conveys the everyday atmosphere of the Pnyx better than Aristotle's *Constitution of Athens*. Aristophanes was interested in all the problems of his age. He defended his political and literary beliefs energetically, and often courageously. But above all he was one of the greatest comic geniuses of all time.

6

LAST STRUGGLES FOR FREEDOM
Fourth Century

Even if the future had been known to everyone beforehand, even
if you had proclaimed it, Aeschines, even so our city ought not
to have acted otherwise than she did, if she had the least concern
for her fame, for our ancestors and for posterity,

DEMOSTHENES: *On the Crown* (199)

HISTORICAL BACKGROUND

By the defeat of 404 Athens, whose man-power and resources had been
seriously depleted by the long war, lost both her fleet and her empire.
At the mercy of her conqueror Lysander, the city was governed from
404 to 403 by a commission, the Thirty, chosen from the aristocratic
party, which, after its ephemeral revolt in 411, now proceeded, in
collaboration with the enemy, to take its revenge on the democrats.
Protected by the Spartan garrison, the Thirty instituted a regime of
terror; and there were very few who, like Socrates (see p. 203), had
the courage to resist. Theramenes, a member of the Thirty and leader
of the moderate fraction within the party, was so concerned by the
excesses committed that he dared to criticize them: he was hailed
before the Senate by Critias and illegally condemned to death.

The reign of the Thirty lasted less than a year, however. The
democrats who had been banished to Boeotia recrossed the frontier
under Thrasyboulos and, having captured the fortress of Phyle,
advanced to Piraeus. Faced by the likelihood of a prolonged civil war,
Pausanias, the king of Sparta, magnanimously intervened between the
'men of the city' and the 'men of Piraeus' and under his aegis the two
parties concluded a peace, based on the understanding that no one
should be punished for his attitude in the past. Though this undoubtedly prevented the further excesses that would have resulted from a
general purge, the trial of Socrates in 399 may well have been a sequel
to these grave events, since a number of young aristocrats had been
his pupils (see above, p. 205).

In 401, Cyrus the Younger, with the help of Greek mercenaries and Spartan troops, attempted to overthrow his brother Artaxerxes, king of Persia. He was defeated and killed at Cunaxa; and the 'ten thousand' Greek mercenaries succeeded in crossing Asia Minor and regaining their own country—amongst them the Athenian Xenophon whose *Anabasis* is an account of their journey. This extraordinary achievement of the Ten Thousand exposed the military weakness of the Persian Empire, a colossus with feet of clay, since a few thousand Greeks succeeded in crossing it from end to end without being cut off by the armies the king sent in pursuit. Sparta thereupon undertook to liberate the Greek cities in Asia Minor; and in 396 her king, Agesilaos, succeeding a number of other generals, disembarked at Ephesus and won considerable success.

Meanwhile, Athens had once again begun to raise her head. Conon, a general who had escaped from the disaster of Aegospotami and had never submitted to Sparta, took service under the Persians and severely harassed the Lacedaemonian fleet. Athens, Corinth and Thebes, subsidized by the Great King, formed a coalition against Sparta who thus found herself obliged to recall Agesilaos and his army from Asia. At Nemea and Coroneia the Spartans were victorious, but in the long drawn-out campaign around Corinth the Athenian general Iphicrates distinguished himself; and, in order to maintain her hegemony, Sparta abandoned the cause of the Greeks in Asia. In 387 the Spartan Antalcides negotiated a treaty with the Persians, sometimes known as the King's Peace, but as a result of the quarrels amongst the Greeks Persia had become the arbiter of their fate.

Despite the peace, in 383 the Spartans aroused widespread hatred by seizing the Theban citadel, the Cadmaea, in a surprise attack. Soon, however, the exiled Thebans, led by Pelopidas, succeeded in overthrowing the oligarchical party and recaptured their city from its Spartan garrison. Thebes then formed an alliance with Athens who in 377 set up a second Maritime League, on a more liberal, less authoritarian, basis than that of the preceding century. At Leuctra in 371, and again at Mantineia in 362, the hitherto invincible Spartan army was defeated by the Thebans. Epaminondas, who had aroused the Peloponnesus against Sparta and founded the cities of Megalopolis and Messene, was killed at Mantineia. In 367 the Theban hegemony was acknowledged by the Great King in the Decree of Susa.

After its initial successes, the new Maritime League soon ran into serious difficulties. In 357 the War of the Allies broke out, that is to say, the principal cities in the League, Rhodes, Chios and Byzantium revolted. This revolt was encouraged, if not actually instigated, by Mausolous, king of Caria, whose capital, Halicarnassos, had been the birthplace of Herodotus more than a century earlier. In 355, in order to restore the King's Peace, Athens had to resign herself to the loss of a great part of the confederated cities: all that remained to her was the Euboea, the Cyclades, a few ports in Thrace and the Chersonese, and the colonies (*clerouchies*) of Lemnos, Imbrios and Samos.

Such was the sorry position of Athens when she suddenly found herself faced by the threat of Macedonia. Since the days of Pericles, her civic spirit had curiously declined: the teaching of the sophists for whom nothing was sacred, defeat, the demoralization resulting from recurrent civil war, the social tension caused by the excessive wealth of a small section of the people and the impoverishment of the mass of her citizens, all conspired to weaken and undermine the sense of patriotism. The Athenian army, which in the fifth century had consisted entirely of citizens, was now largely made up of foreign mercenaries. By 355 the most influential political figure was Euboulos, a skilful financier, but, as a supporter of peace at any price, in favour of coming to terms with Macedonia.

Since 359 Macedonia had been governed by the young and ambitious Philip II, at first as regent, later as king. He knew Greece well. From the age of fourteen to seventeen, he had been a hostage in Thebes, in the time of Pelopidas and Epaminondas. Now, he had completely reorganized his kingdom. By 356, when a third Sacred War over the question of the sanctuary of Delphi had split the whole of Greece into two camps, he had a well-stocked treasury and a solid army of thirty thousand men. It was at this point that the long struggle, destined to last almost twenty years, broke out between him and the Athenian orator Demosthenes.

Philip began by seizing the Thracian towns that still belonged to Athens: Maroneia, Methone and Abdera where Democritus and Protagoras had been born. In Chalcidice he attacked the city of Olynthos, an ally of Athens, capturing it in 348; while in central Greece, he intervened against the 'sacriligeous' Phocians who had seized the treasures of the Pythian sanctuary and whom the Athenians were supporting against Thebes and Thessaly. In 346 Demosthenes, thoroughly disheartened, had to resign himself to the Peace of Philocrates, by which Athens had renounced her claim to Amphipolis, Potideia and Cardia.

An Athenian mission, which included Aeschines and Demosthenes, was then sent to Philip to receive his oath and that of his allies. Philip dragged out negotiations as long as he could, profiting from the delay to pursue his own ends. It appears that some of the ten ambassadors were even prepared to assist him in this. As a result, on its return to Athens, the embassy was brought to trial, though it was not until 343 that sentence was passed.

In the west, in 344, Timoleon of Corinth liberated Syracuse from the oppressive government of the Tyrant Dionysus the Younger who had succeeded his father Dionysus the Elder in 367.

In 340 Philip renewed hostilities in Greece, seizing some Athenian merchant ships and laying siege to Byzantium, whose position on the Straits made it of great importance. But Athens dispatched a fleet under the command of Phocion and Philip was forced to raise the siege. Once again, however, Delphi was to become the centre of events and these were to prove favourable to Philip's aims. In the spring of 339 Aeschines, as *poliarchos*, persuaded the Amphictyonic League to condemn the Locri of Amphissa for ploughing up land dedicated to Apollo. The result was yet another Sacred War, and Philip who had been a member of the League since 346 seized the opportunity of bringing his army into central Greece on the pretext that he was the 'secular arm' of the Delphic Apollo. By capturing the Phocian city of Elateia, he was now only three days' march across Boeotia from the Attic frontier. In Athens feeling was intense. Demosthenes declared a state of emergency and at last succeeded in achieving an alliance with Thebes to protect their freedom. But in 338 the Athenian and Theban armies were overwhelmed by the Macedonian infantry at Chaironeia. The freedom of Greece was at an end.

In 337, Philip became the head (*hegemon*) of the Panhellenic League that was formed in Corinth and began to make preparations for a great expedition against Persia which was to be the historic parallel to the attempts of Darius and Xerxes to conquer Hellas. The Macedonian army had already crossed the Hellespont and encamped in Troas when in 336 Philip was assassinated by one of his nobles.

He was succeeded by his twenty year old son Alexander who was prepared to push forward with his father's plans, but had first of all to face a revolt of the Greeks. He quickly suppressed it. Then, having destroyed the city of Thebes as an example, he embarked for Asia, leaving behind Antipater as regent of Macedonia and responsible for

15. Head of the Hermes of Praxiteles, c. 350–330 (p. 250). *Olympia Museum*

16. The frieze of the altar of Zeus and Athena at Pergamon, 197–159 B.C., representing the battle of the Gods and the Giants (pp. 330–1). *Berlin Museum*

Greece. Thus began the epic of the 'new Achilles'. His defeat of Darius III at the Granicos opened up the whole of Asia Minor to him. He crossed the frontier into Syria and at Issus again defeated the Persian army, capturing Darius' family and treasure. Having conquered Phoenicia, he advanced into Egypt where in 332 he founded Alexandria. A third great victory at Gaugamela completed the ruin of the Persian Empire: Alexander entered the capitals of Babylon and Susa in triumph while Darius, fleeing for his life, was assassinated by one of his own satraps. He continued his triumphal march to the furthest eastern limits of the Empire, but having reached the frontiers of India was forced to retreat. In Babylon, he fell sick; and there he died at the age of thirty-three. In a reign of only thirteen years he had won for Hellenism the vast Asian empire of the Achaemenids.

As soon as they heard the news of Alexander's death, the Greeks, not yet prepared to accept servitude, rose against the Macedonians as they had done at the time of Philip's death. This resulted in the Lamian War, in the course of which the regent, Antipater, was besieged in the town of Lamia, a little to the north of Thermopylae, near the Maliac Gulf. But it was not long before Antipater regained the upper hand and captured Athens; and the patriots who had instigated the uprising, Demosthenes and Hesperides, were sentenced to death.

There now ensured the struggles between Alexander's many successors, the Diadochoi, in the course of which his vast heritage was broken up: Perdiccas who had received the royal ring from the dying conqueror, Eumenes, Seleucos, Lysimachos, Antigonos the Lame, aided by his son Demetrius Poliorcetes (the Taker of Towns), Ptolemy and Antipater himself who was succeeded by his son Cassander. Strife was unending, scarcely had one conflict died down than another broke out. Only Ptolemy had the wisdom to restrict his ambitions to securing control of Egypt. The others persisted in fruitless efforts to reconstitute the immense empire, but no sooner had they succeeded in carving out kingdoms for themselves, large or small, than they collapsed like card castles.

From 317 to 307, Athens was governed, on behalf of Cassander, king of Macedonia and with the support of a Macedonian garrison, by the philosopher Demetrius of Phaleron, a disciple of Aristotle and friend of Theophrastos. In this period, Athens was still a town of considerable size: it was estimated to have twenty thousand citizens and ten thousand aliens, not to mention the multitude of slaves.

In 309 Athens was 'liberated' by Demetrius Poliorcetes who nominally restored democracy while at the same time defiling the Acropolis with his debauches. Of all the Diadochoi, his father, Antigonos, had come nearest to reviving the Empire under his own rule, but his tenacious ambition led to the other Diadochoi forming a coalition against him; and in 301 he was defeated and killed at Ipsos in Phrygia. The fragments of Alexander's empire were never to be put together again.

ART

In the fifth century, Greek art was essentially Athenian art. In the fourth, Athens having lost her political supremacy, a certain decentralization of art took place, though Attic influence still remained considerable. Perhaps the most characteristic building of this period was the Mausoleum at Halicarnassos, built in honour of Mausolous, king of Caria (see p. 245), by his wife Artemisia about 350.

The development of individualism, one of the most striking features of the period, was especially marked in works of art: the first portrait busts now began to appear, for example, those of the great writers: Thucydides, Sophocles, Plato. There was, too, a general modification of sensibility: the serenity of Pheidias' art was beginning to give way to a freer display of feeling and pathos. Both sculpture and painting more frequently depicted the nude female figure, an unmistakable sign that homosexuality was giving way to heterosexual love, a change that is noticeable also in literature. And there was, too, a growing taste for abstract and allegorical themes such as Peace, Abundance, Love, Desire.

At Epidaurus, where the cult of Asclepius flourished, the principal monuments of his sanctuary were now erected: the temples of the god and of Artemis, the entrance gates, the mysterious *tholos* or *thymele*, and finally the theatre, the most magnificent of all those that still remain from Greek antiquity. Indeed, most of the theatres built of stone date from this period: Syracuse, Corinth, Argos, Tegea, Megalopolis and Athens itself where after the battle of Chaironeia architecture experienced a new burst of activity under the wise financial administration of the orator, Lycurgus. The graceful choragic monument to Lysicrates at the foot of the Acropolis dates from 334; and other important buildings were the Panathenaean Stadium and, at Eleusis, the portico of Philo running the length of the initiation chamber which remains unfinished to this day.

At Delphi, the sixth-century temple of Apollo, destroyed in the catastrophe of 373, was rebuilt in limestone, thanks to the gifts that poured in from all parts of the Greek world. The new limestone temple of Athena Pronaia also dates from this period, as well as a number of Treasuries, of which the one at Cyrene is perhaps the most remarkable: the proportions of this building seem to indicate a curious architectural application of the mathematical discoveries of the time. At Olympia there was the Metroon, the temple of Cybele, mother of the gods; at Nemea, the temple of Zeus; at Tegea, that of Athena Alea, where the master mason was Scopas and where the interior decoration, derived from the Corinthian order, reveals a number of architectural innovations.

But it was in Asia Minor that the most sumptuous monuments appeared: the new Didymeion at Miletus, to which I shall return later as its construction was to continue into the Hellenistic period; the Artemesion at Ephesus, rebuilt on the ruins of the old one destroyed by Erostratos in 356, to be reckoned among the Seven Wonders of the World; and, lastly, the temple-tomb of Mausolous at Halicarnassos.

This Mausoleum, which in general conception recalls the monument to the Nereids at Xanthus (see p. 181), is an enormous quadrangular building, with a funeral temple of the Ionic order surmounted by a pyramid upon which, high up in the air, was set a four-horsed chariot. Four sculptors worked on the statues and bas-reliefs with which it was decorated: Scopas, Bryaxis, Leochares and Timotheos.

The earliest sculptures of the period are anonymous, like the funerary ceramic bas-relief that represents the young Athenian horseman, Dexileus, in the act of killing an opponent at the battle of Nemea in 394. At Delphi the group of three exquisite dancers against a tall acanthus pillar is of uncertain date, still in dispute. Their light tunics clinging to their bodies, they are executing a stately dance, probably of a religious nature, since the baskets they carry on their heads are the sacred *kalathoi* used by priestesses. They are probably Caryatids, or Graces, or Thyiades, dedicated to the cult of Dionysus who was held in almost as much honour at Delphi as Apollo, though their calm and serene bearing would be more befitting the priestesses of Apollo himself.

Recently in Piraeus, at the same time as the great archaic *Kouros*, referred to earlier (p. 94), two bronze statues from the second half of the fourth century have been found: a colossal helmeted Athena in the same pose as the chryselephantine figure by Pheidias in the

Parthenon; and a smaller Artemis, the pure and delicate modelling of whose face is outstandingly lovely.

The three names that dominate the history of sculpture in the fourth century are: Scopas, Praxiteles and Lysippos. Scopas who was born at Paros worked on the temple of Athena Alea and on the Mausoleum. The head of a soldier, found during the excavations at Tegea, is remarkable for the intense pathos of the expression. Among the bas-reliefs on the Mausoleum, a number of the scenes from the *Amazonomachia* have been attributed to him; the nervous, muscular bodies display all the energy of battle; the swift movements make the folds of their clothing float round their shoulders as lightly as scarves; an Amazon, fallen to her knees, her right arm extended in a moving gesture, pleads with the Greek who is about to stab her. The famous Maenad by Scopas, of which we only have copies, with her arched back and dishevelled hair, is throwing back her head with a gesture whose violence admirably suggests Dionysian ecstasy. She is as different from the stately dancers at Delphi as the delirious Bacchanalian orgies were from the elegant movements of an Apollonian dance. Scopas is also known to have carved a melancholy statue of Pothos, the embodiment of Desire and Regret.

Praxiteles was an Athenian, one of a family of traditional sculptors: his grandfather Praxiteles the Elder and his father Cephisodotos, as well as his sons, were all well-known artists. The vigour and boldness of Scopas portrayed the human figure in moments of intense strain and effort: by contrast, Praxiteles preferred to show it in repose, and took a voluptuous pleasure in the supple modelling of flesh. Such works as the Satyr torso (in the Louvre), Apollo Sauroktonos (Killer of Serpents) and the Hermes from Olympia are distinguished by their grace and elegance, rather than their strength. Above all, Praxiteles was famous for his naked figures of Aphrodite, the model for which was his mistress, the courtesan Phryne. The best known of these is the Aphrodite of Cnidos, a supreme tribute to female beauty. His marble statues were painted to give the illusion of living flesh and Lucian was later to write a scabrous story about a young man who fell in love with the perfect goddess. Both the Cynic philosopher Crates and, later, Plutarch, the priest of the Pythian Apollo, condemned Praxiteles for erecting a gilded bronze statue of Phryne on a huge marble column.

Lysippos, born at Sicyon, worked mainly in bronze. The bodies of his athletes are taller, more slender and elegant than those based on the so-called 'canon' of Polycleitus (see p. 180). Somewhere about 336 Daochos, the tetrarch of Thessaly, dedicated a series of nine statues of himself and his ancestors to the temple at Delphi; these marble effigies are probably copies of original bronzes by Lysippos, executed in the master's own studio. The best preserved of them is that of Agias, the wrestler. Erect, most of the weight taken by the right leg, the pose skilfully balances the main muscular masses. With its broad shoulders and deep chest, the elegant strength of the limbs, and the rather small head supported on an almost exaggeratedly powerful neck, the statue presents a striking specimen of the human animal. Lysippos was to become the favourite sculptor of Alexander the Great, who posed for many of his statues, which were in effect portraits.

The great painters of the fourth century are today no more than names since all their works have perished and we only know the subjects of the most famous of them. The three most celebrated artists came from Asia: Zeuxis of Heracleia, Parrhasios of Ephesus, and Apelles of Colophon. Notable amongst the works of the last named were an allegorical painting, Calumny, and the Aphrodite Anadyomene (Issuing from the Waves) for which Phryne herself had posed.

Of the lost works of these great painters, whose influence was to make itself felt much later in the classic elements of the frescoes at Pompeii, fourth-century vase painting offers us only a pale reflection. Pottery, which in the fifth century had been the work of craftsmen, was tending to be produced on an industrial basis, with a consequent weakening in design and draughtsmanship and a general tendency towards conventional banality. An Attic hydria, dating from about 340, which depicts the rape of Thetis by Peleus, has some fine studies of nude women (reminiscent of Praxiteles) and a small winged Eros flying above Peleus' head; and there is some attempt to create an effect of perspective. Such representations of the god of love recur almost to the point of satiety: mythological scenes, in which the story of Aphrodite, the goddess of pleasure, and of Dionysus, the effeminate god of drunken ecstasy, become increasingly important. There is an unending succession of Silenuses pursuing nymphs, of Ariadnes sleeping or wantonly sporting with Dionysus among a crowd of Satyrs and Maenads, of judgments of Paris, of Helens flirting with her Phrygian lover. . . . In *genre* paintings, the most popular subjects are women dancing, playing the flute, or sitting naked at their toilet.

THE SOCRATICS

Though Socrates himself wrote nothing, he inspired others to devote themselves to philosophy and literature. Of the work of several of his disciples, we possess only fragments. This is the case with Aristippos of Cyrene, and with the Athenians, Antisthenes and Aeschines. Aristippos taught a hedonistic philosophy, and was thus a forerunner of Epicurus. He was one of the lovers of the famous courtesan Lais. When someone maliciously informed him that she did not return his love, he replied: 'Why should that matter to me? I enjoy drinking wine and eating fish, but this does not mean that I suppose that either of them have any liking for me' (Plutarch *Amatorius*, 750 D).

In contrast to Aristippos, Antisthenes and Aeschines maintained and extended the Socratic doctrine of the equality of the sexes; and both of them wrote dialogues which they called *Aspasia*. Antisthenes was the author of the maxim: 'Virtue is the same both for men and for women.' He wrote some forty philosophical works, as well as speeches and a commentary on Homer. He founded a school of his own in the Cynosarges ('the Agile Dog') from which his followers were known as Cynics (Dogs), though the name also came to symbolize the snarling and barking of these austere moralists who were noted for their intolerance of vice. Despising worldly possessions, they lived as beggars and tramps. Antisthenes was succeeded by Diogenes of Sinope, the philosopher who lived in a tub and who, when Alexander the Great asked him if he could grant him a favour, replied: 'Yes. Remove your shadow.'

In his *Aspasia*, Aeschines of Sphettos, thus known to distinguish him from Aeschines the orator, the opponent of Demosthenes, makes Socrates describe the following exchange between Aspasia, Xenophon and the latter's wife.

Aspasia first asked Xenophon's wife: 'Tell me, pray, if your neighbour's gold was of a higher carat than your own, which would you prefer, hers or yours?'—'Hers,' she replied.—'And if she had richer clothes and ornaments than yours, which would you prefer?'—'Hers'—'And if she had a husband better than yours, which would you love best?' Here Xenophon's wife blushed and was silent. Aspasia then turned to Xenophon and put a similar series of questions to him, substituting horses for gold and land for clothes. Then she asked: 'And if your neighbour had a better wife than yours, which would you love best?' At this point Xenophon also remained silent. Whereupon Aspasia continued: 'Since both of you refuse to answer the one question that interests me, I myself will tell you what is in your thoughts. *You* would like to have the most perfect of husbands, and *you*, Xenophon, the most accomplished of wives. Thus so long as you fail to become, you the most perfect husband on earth, and you the most accomplished wife, you will always regret perfection, you as a husband and you as a wife.' (Cicero, *De Inventione*, I, 31).

Here it is clearly taken for granted that the principle of moral equality between the sexes was fully accepted and, by implication, the ideal of marriage is a high one. In the time of Alexander the Great, the Cynic, Crates of Thebes, the man who had been shocked by the statue of Phryne at Delphi (see p. 250), married the sister of Metrocles, a philosopher of the same school of thought as himself; the rich, beautiful and high-born Hipparchia. So deeply was she impressed by Crates' teaching that she refused to marry anyone else, although her parents regarded him as a quite unsuitable match since, like all the Cynics, he insisted upon living in complete poverty. Hipparchia shared both his poverty and his philosophy, and they begged their way from house to house. She is mentioned by Diogenes Laertius in his *Lives of the Philosophers*. This successful marriage of the two philosophers was a practical expression of Socrates' theory of the equality of the sexes

Three of Socrates' disciples, however, left behind them an important body of work: Xenophon, Plato and Isocrates. Of these, the last, though born ten years before the other two, was to live very much longer than either of them.

XENOPHON

The Athenian Xenophon was, like Sophocles, the typical *honnête homme* of the French seventeenth century: well born, carefully educated, intelligent, cultured, pious, and endowed with all the moral and physical qualities (*kalòs kagathós*) requisite for success. This apart, however, the two men were separated by an enormous gulf: three-quarters of a century of historical development, which in Greece, and especially in Athens, had been both rapid and profound.

Xenophon was born during the early years of the Peloponnesian War, about 426. His father, Gryllos, though not of noble origin, belonged to the class of well-to-do landowners; the 'Knights', portrayed by Aristophanes as the natural enemies of the demagogues. From his childhood and family background, he derived a passion for riding and hunting. He was a good-looking youth, at a time when the Greeks regarded physical beauty as the reflection of moral beauty. Thus Socrates, happening to meet him one day in the streets of Athens, barred his way with his stick and enquired where he could procure the necessities of life. Xenophon told him. Whereupon Socrates said: 'But if you wish to become a good man, where would you go?' And when Xenophon could not answer, he added: 'Then follow me and I will teach you.' This was how Xenophon became one of Socrates' disciples.

Whether he took part in the last battles of the Peloponnesian War, was captured and taken to Thebes is not certain. But in any case, it was while on a visit to a friend in Boeotia, Proxenus, that the latter suggested they should join Cyrus' expedition against his brother Artaxerxes, where there was a chance of earning both money and glory. This was in 401. Xenophon consulted Socrates who pointed out that, by so doing, he would risk compromising himself in the eyes of his fellow citizens, since by subsidizing Sparta Cyrus had helped her to defeat Athens. However, as the young man seemed extremely anxious to go, he advised him to seek advice from the Delphic oracle. Xenophon did so, but in a disingenuous way: instead of asking Apollo whether or not he should take part in the expedition, he enquired which god he ought to sacrifice to, to ensure that his journey should be successful. Though Socrates was annoyed by this deception, he realized that it was useless to oppose the young man's intentions, and let him go.

As one of the Ten Thousand, Xenophon was 'neither general, nor officer, nor ordinary soldier': he joined the expedition out of curiosity, probably with a view to writing an account of it, like a modern war correspondent. In the *Anabasis* there is a description of the tragic circumstances that eventually forced him to take command, and though he perhaps exaggerates its importance, he certainly played an important part in leading the army to safety and handing it over to Thibron, the Spartan leader then fighting against the Persians in Asia Minor.

Meanwhile, Socrates had drunk the hemlock. Whether Xenophon was exiled from Athens in 399 or after the battle of Coroneia in 394, is not certain, but in any case he accompanied Agesilaos into Asia in 396; and, when the latter was recalled to Greece, Xenophon fought with the Spartans against his compatriots at Coroneia (see p. 244). What had become of the uncomprising patriotism of the Marathonomachoi —for Alcibiades, too, had already deserted the cause of Athens?

The fact is, with the approach of the Hellenistic epoch, intellectuals were beginning to regard themselves as cosmopolitans; citizens, not of a particular State, but of the world.

As a result of being banished, Xenophon was deprived of his property in Athens. But, in return for his services, the Spartans granted him a large country estate at Scillous in Elis, not far from Olympia, with woodlands, meadows, plough-land and orchards. There he settled down for the next twenty years with his wife Philesia, who bore him two sons, Gryllos and Diodoros, leading the life of a wealthy and cultured landowner, looking after the running of his farm, hunting, entertaining his friends and writing his books. In 371, the year of the battle of Leuctra, Scillous was ravaged by war. Xenophon went first to Lepreon, south of Scillous but still in Elis, and later to Corinth. In 367, at a time when Athens and Sparta were uniting to resist the Theban hegemony, Xenophon's sentence of exile was withdrawn; shortly afterwards he was pardoned and returned to his own country. In 362 both his sons were on active service with the Athenian cavalry: in the course of an engagement on the eve of the battle of Mantineia, Gryllos, after fighting bravely, was killed; and his eulogy was written by Isocrates. Xenophon himself probably died about 355.

Xenophon was a man of action, who was also a man of letters. The word we should use today to describe his literary activity would be 'essayist', though in fact his writings are of the most varied kinds. Some are inspired by his enduring veneration for Socrates: the *Apology*, the *Memorabilia* and the *Symposium*. Others are historical: the *Anabasis*, the *Agesilaos*, the *Hellenica* (Greek History). But both the *Anabasis* and the *Memorabilia* are also in a sense personal memoirs, since they deal with events in which he himself participated and describe his part in them. Others are technical and educational treatises on the best methods of training a cavalry officer, a huntsman, the head of a family or a statesman: the *Hipparchicus*, the *Hippike*, the *Cynegeticus*, the *Oeconomicus* and the *Cyropaedia*, though the last is also a historical romance. Again, there are others that deal mainly with politics and economics: the *Constitution of Sparta, Hiero: or the Tyrant*, the *Revenues of Athens*.

The portrait Xenophon paints of Socrates, though very different from Plato's, is probably more accurate (see p. 202). He sees the philosopher not only as a stern moralist, the begetter of the Cynics, but also as a charming and entertaining companion, full of gaiety and wit. The tone of the *Memorabilia* is often humorous and provides plenty of scope for Socratic irony, as for example in the account of Socrates' pleasant but quite innocent visit to the courtesan Theodota. But it also contains much that is serious, particularly when Xenophon is concerned to defend his master's memory against the charges of impiety and corruption of youth which cost him his life; a theme to which he returned in the *Apology*. Himself a devout believer, Xenophon sets out to demonstrate that Socrates was the most religious of men.

There can be little doubt that his purpose in writing the *Symposium* was to correct the portrait of Socrates in Plato's *Symposium;* the portrait of a philosopher who, though certainly witty, was often didactic and pedantic. I think Xenophon would have readily applied to Socrates the words that Pascal was to write of Plato and Aristotle: 'One cannot imagine them always dressed in scholar's robes. They were agreeable and sociable men, as ready to laugh with their friends as anyone else.' In the opening lines of the *Symposium*, Xenophon makes his purpose clear:

In my opinion, it is not only the serious deeds of eminent men that deserve to be recorded, but also their amusements. This I know, having myself been present at them (*Symposium*, 1, 1).

Writing as a reliable witness, the Socrates he reveals is a man who enjoyed company, who liked joking with his friends about everything under the sun, arranging a beauty contest between himself, noted for his ugliness, and the handsome Critoboulos, describing the exercises by which he attempted to reduce his excessive girth and, as was the custom at banquets, striking up a song. In this attractive work, as well as a description of the entertainment provided by an impressario from Syracuse, we also find a fuller and historically more exact account than in Plato's *Symposium* of the carefree atmosphere in which, having finished their meal, the Greeks like to relax over their wine. The whole dialogue presents a picture of Socrates that is at once familiar and full of life, without the least trace of pedantry. Yet, though Socrates is here in his most convivial mood, he explicitly condemns pederasty, a subject on which Plato, at least until his last work the *Laws*, always remained extremely equivocal.

There are few war books as varied and attractive as the *Anabasis*, which Xenophon published under a pseudonym. According to Plutarch, and we can accept what he says, 'Xenophon was his own historian: he described what he had done as general and the success he achieved, though attributing his book to Themistogenes of Syracuse. He renounced the fame of being its author in order to ensure more credence by speaking of himself as a stranger' (*De Gloria Athen.*, I, 345 E).

The word *anabasis* means 'ascent'. After leaving Sardis, where Cyrus' troops were concentrated, the Greeks did, in fact, ascend the high plateaux of Asia Minor, but later, after the battle of Cunaxa, they turned northward, finally descending to the coast of the Pontus Euxinus, where the sight of the sea at last assured them of safety: 'Thalassa!' Thus, the title only properly applies to the beginning of the work.

By Book III, Xenophon has become the leader and the principal character in the story, which from then on is largely autobiography. The speeches he made to the troops are reported at length. The ruses of the barbarians, the ambushes they set, the difficulties experienced by the Greeks in crossing rivers, the terrible weather, particularly the snow and frost, the lack of food that threatened to wipe out the army —all these are described as dramatic episodes that hold the reader spellbound. The book abounds in exotic local colour, and in his descriptions of the strange customs of the peoples they encounter, Xenophon recaptures something of Herodotus' skill. For example, this account of the Mosynochoi.

They showed the Greeks the children of wealthy parents who had been fed on boiled nuts: these children were fat and quite white, almost as broad as they were tall, with flowers tattooed on their backs and all over the front of their bodies. These barbarians wanted to copulate in public with the women accompanying the Greeks, as was the custom of the country. All of them had white skins, men as well as women. Our soldiers said they were the most barbaric people they had met on the whole expedition, furthest from our Greek way of life. They used to do in full public view those things that other people do in private, and when they were alone they behaved as though they were in company: they would talk to themselves and laugh when no one else was there; they would begin dancing wherever they happened to be, just as though they were performing before spectators (*Anabasis*, v, 4, 32–4).

The *Oeconomicus* is once again concerned with Socrates, and at first sight might be taken for a chapter of the *Memorabilia*, since it begins abruptly: 'One day I heard him express the following views on domestic economy' (I, I). Socrates then talks to Critoboulos, to whom he later reports a conversation he has had with Isomachos. But Xenophon is less concerned to acquaint us with the ideas of Socrates than with his own opinions—on agriculture, on the running of a country estate, on the role of the landowner's wife, on the cultivation of the land. Since Socrates, an out-and-out city dweller, could have had no experience of life in the country, it is obvious that Xenophon was simply making use of him, as Plato was to do, to express his own views. And indeed, the book is simply an account of what he himself had learnt from his experience as a country landowner at Scillous. Clearly Xenophon had a high opinion of agriculture, and one feels that for him, as for most well-born Greeks, there were really only two occupations worthy of a man of action: the army and the running of a country estate. Whether he is writing about sowing, harvesting, weeding, threshing, winnowing or the care of fruit trees, Xenophon is as much at home as Hesiod in *Works and Days*. But where Hesiod was simply a small peasant, working his wretched plot of land with his own hands, Xenophon regards the most prosperous landowner as a man who knows how to give orders and make others work for him, starting with his wife. The portrait he gives of Ischomachos is charming. He has just got married, and is determined to give his young wife the best possible advice about how to order the household methodically and economically. His manner of speaking to her is coldly reasonable, with scarcely a trace of affection, and he treats marriage simply as a partnership for the successful exploitation of the estate:

Tell me, wife, do you understand the reason why I married you and why your parents gave you to me? We were not worried about finding someone to sleep with, you must realize. But having duly considered, I on my own behalf and your parents on yours, as to the best partner we could take for our household and children, I for my part chose you, and your parents, it seems, chose me, as being the best possible match (*Oeconomicus*, VII, 10 ff.).

Certainly the book lives up to its title, for unlike the *Symposium* there is not the slightest mention of love. Indeed, it reminds one of Montaigne: 'In this sensible bargain, which is what marriage amounts to, the appetites are not so wanton. . . . One does not get married for one's self, whatever people may say; one marries as much, more indeed, for the sake of one's posterity, for one's family.'

It is possible that, before he died, Thucydides had asked Xenophon to revise and complete his history. Whether this was so or not, the two first books of the *Hellenica* take up the story at the precise point where Thucydides had broken off, 411; and they carry it on up to the reconciliation between the two Athenian parties in 403. As an historian Xenophon is certainly very inferior to Thucydides: and here, as in the *Anabasis*, he reminds one more of Herodotus, enlivening his narrative with picturesque details and dramatic episodes. Two of the most remarkable are the trial of the Athenian generals after their victory at Arginusae, and the session of the Council at which Theramenes was condemned. As the latter is being dragged across the Agora towards the place of punishment by Satyros, one of Critias' henchmen, Xenophon describes him trying to attract the attention of the passers-by with his cries:

When Satyros told him he would make him pay for it if he didn't hold his tongue, he asked: 'And if I do hold my tongue, shan't I pay for it just the same?' And again, when he had to drink the hemlock, he is said to have thrown away the last drop as though he were playing a game of cottabus, and cried out: 'To the health of mighty Critias!' These, I know, are only jests that are hardly worth mentioning, yet all the same, one cannot help admiring a man who, when death was so near, could so coolly crack a joke (*Hellenica*, II, 3, 56).

Thucydides would have omitted such a scene: Xenophon's description of it, and especially his comment, reminds one of the Plutarch of the *Lives*; they show the same interest in psychology, the same flair for characteristic detail.

The five further books of the *Hellenica* continue the history of Greece up to the battle of Mantineia, in 362; that is to say, for a period of forty years. The composition becomes increasingly slovenly, still more remote from the manner of Thucydides. For what happened in the year 395, even if one compares his account with that of the anonymous author of *Oxyrrhynchus* (an historical fragment preserved in a papyrus), Xenophon does not appear to advantage, for he idealizes the portrait of his friend Agesilaos, whereas the anonymous author makes no attempt to conceal the mistakes, and even thefts, committed by this great general. Moreover, Xenophon does not even mention such important events as the foundation of the second Athenian League in 377.

Yet, while it is true that the *Hellenica* is no more to be compared with Thucydides than Xenophon's *Symposium* is with Plato's, considered in itself it has undeniable qualities. For Xenophon's gifts include a rare power of observation, a feeling for the picturesque, and an urbane and subtle mind; in short, many of the best elements of 'Atticism'. His narrative is clear and straightforward: and it contains scenes of real comedy, as when he describes the behaviour of Dercylidas towards Meidias; moving passages, like the description of Agesilaos' grief at the death of a friend; and a number of remarkable speeches, some of which are such admirable pastiche that they provide an ironic comment on the speaker. Callias, the Athenian ambassador to Sparta, is about to speak. He was the rich and aristocratic Athenian whose house was the scene of Xenophon's *Symposium* and of Plato's *Protagoras*, and he held the important religious post of *dadouchos* (Torch Bearer) to the Eleusinian goddesses. Xenophon says:

The first to speak was Callias, the Torch Bearer. He was a man who delighted as much in his praise of himself as in that bestowed upon him by others. He began thus: 'Citizens of Lacedaemonia, I speak to you as an ambassador, not as an individual: my father's father inherited the title from his father and handed it on to his descendants. I would wish you to understand the consideration in which my family has always been held by the city of Athens: when she is at war, it is us she chooses as her generals; and when she wishes to bring hostilities to a close, it is us she sends to negotiate peace (*Hellenica*, VI, 3, 3 ff.).

One can see at once the naive vanity of the man; and the rest of the speech continues in the brilliant, affected, turgid style to be expected from an admirer of the sophists.

Xenophon's interests were continually divided between the intellectual demands of the writer and his activities as a soldier and landowner. Both aspects of his personality were typified by friendships, for his two greatest friends were Socrates and Agesilaos, the philosopher and the soldier. Not content with his frequent references to Agesilaos in the *Hellenica*, Xenophon composed a eulogy of him after his death, which is the first independent biography we possess: I have already drawn attention to the similarity between Xenophon and the Plutarch of the *Lives*. Agesilaos was king of Sparta and it was on his advice that Xenophon had his two sons brought up in the city of Lycurgus, whose institutions he so profoundly admired. Of all the Athenians who were impressed by the 'Spartan dream', none was more enthusiastic than he. His *Constitution of the Lacedaemonians* provides us with precise technical details about the Spartan army, its organization and tactics, which he had observed at first-hand. The same technical approach is to be found again in the *Hipparchicus*, the *Hippike* and the *Cynegeticus*. Xenophon was a fine horseman and a great huntsman; being also of a didactic nature, he was determined to pass on his experience of horses and hunting in the same way as, in the *Oeconomicus*, he had written about agriculture.

The *Hiero* is a short dialogue between this tyrant of Syracuse and the poet, Simonides of Ceos, (see pp. 108–9) on the vices of tyranny and how to reform it. The *Cyropaedia*, that is to say, the *Education of Cyrus*, deals, not with Cyrus the Younger who appears in the *Anabasis* and the *Hellenica*, but with the great Cyrus, the founder of the Persian empire in the sixth century. Here again Xenophon's purpose was primarily didactic: to provide an ideal recipe for the education of a prince. In fact, however, Cyrus' education only occupies the opening chapters of Book i; and if the rest of the work may be said to reveal the effects of this education, it also deals with many other subjects. Evidently, the reason Xenophon chose someone belonging to such a remote and little known period was to allow him to give free play to his imagination and fantasy. The account of Cyrus' childhood at the court of Astyages is delightful: the little boy's naïvety lends charm to the stern lessons about sobriety, discipline and hatred of lying that Xenophon derives from Socrates and Agesilaos. Once Cyrus has grown up, Xenophon describes his empire in terms of a Utopia. Despite the fact that in the centre of the capital there is a square called Freedom, the kingdom is organized like Sparta on the lines of an army, of which Cyrus is the commander-in-chief. Passive obedience and discipline, the main strength of all armies, are strenuously enforced. But Cyrus, the absolute monarch, is morally superior to any of his subjects; under his enlightened despotism the state enjoys perfect happiness and harmony. As Alfred Croiset aptly says: 'it was like Louis xiv's Versailles, revised and corrected by Fénelon.'

Thus, like Plato, Xenophon too wrote his *Republic*. The difference between the ideal monarchy of the one and the aristocratic communism of the other is profound. But there are also genuine analogies, for both these disciples of Socrates were concerned to describe an ideal state, whose institutions would be conducive to moral improvement and to the practice of the primary virtues of temperance and justice.

The *Cyropaedia* is also the earliest novel, since in Books v and vi, it contains the edifying story of Abradatas, king of Susa, and his wife Panthea. The latter, who is a great beauty, falls into the hands of Cyrus, who treats her with respect and hands her over to the care of one of his friends, the Mede, Araspes. This appears to be an excellent choice, for in the course of a curious conversation with Cyrus, Araspes has boasted of being able to control his passions: 'Love,' he says, 'depends on the will: one can make up one's mind who one will love.' Cyrus is sceptical:

I have seen people in tears for the misery love has caused them, who yet remain the slaves of their passion, though before they were in love they would have regarded such slavery as the greatest misfortune. Their attachment was like a sickness they could not cure themselves of, it was as though they were bound by some power stronger than links of iron. A man in love, despite the torments he endures, does not seek to escape the power of the beloved, but is in continual fear lest he should lose her (*Cyropaedia*, vi, 1).

This might almost be a scene from one of the Provençal 'Courts of Love'.

In the event Cyrus' scepticism is justified, for despite his high principles, Araspes quickly falls in love with his beautiful prisoner, and when she resists him and remains faithful to her husband, he threatens to violate her. Fortunately Cyrus gets to hear of this in time and intervenes, and husband and wife are re-united: 'Immediately they flung themselves into each other's arms in transports of joy, all the greater for being unexpected.' It is a wonder they do not actually swoon with passion; the heroes of some later Greek romances would certainly do so under the circumstances. Impressed by Cyrus' magnanimity, Abradatas becomes his devoted supporter. He sets out for the wars and bids his wife a fond farewell in a scene that is obviously inspired by Hector's parting from Andromache in the *Iliad*. Panthea, with all the fortitude of a woman of Sparta, urges her husband to prove himself worthy of her by his heroism. When at last he is in his chariot and she can no longer embrace him, she kisses his chariot instead, and has to be dragged away by her maids and eunuchs:

Then all eyes turned towards Abradatas: so long as Panthea was there, no one thought of looking at him, though the warrior and his chariot were indeed a sight worthy to behold (*Ibid*, vi, 4).

Such a melodramatic display of emotion is a poor substitute for Homer's simplicity; and Panthea is certainly no Andromache. Yet, in fairness to Xenophon, he must here be recognized as one of the originators of the novel, for the *Cyropaedia* is distantly related to the *Ephesiacs* and the *Ethiopics*; and, more remotely still, to Mademoiselle de Scudéry's *Le Grand Cyrus*.

Xenophon's style, with its occasional gentlemanly lapses, is both natural and elegant. After the acrobatics of the rhetoricians and the long, involved sentences of Thucydides, reading him is a relief; it is like listening to a man who does not pride himself on his fine writing, but writes as he speaks, clearly, wittily and with distinction. An essayist of considerable talent, Xenophon attempted too many kinds of writing to excel in all of them. Clearly he is not to be compared with Plato as a philosopher or with Thucydides as a historian. But the *Anabasis*, the *Symposium* and the *Cyropaedia* have a genuine attraction and, in many ways, are remarkable. For the literary historian, a writer who who may be said to have initiated two new kinds of writing, biography and the novel, is of outstanding importance. The 'Attic Bee', as Xenophon was called in antiquity, plundered many kinds of flowers, often haphazardly and nonchalantly, but thanks to his natural gifts he produced fine honey.

PLATO

It may well be that Xenophon, a man of action rather than a philosopher, did not fully grasp the philosophy of Socrates. Plato, however, on the basis of certain Socratic ideas, was to construct an imposing conceptual system that has made a lasting impression on the thinkers of every age. The word 'Platonic' has passed into the vocabulary of every European country. In the words of Ortega y Gasset, 'no one can say how deeply Platonic concepts have penetrated every level of Western thought. It is quite normal for the simplest people to employ expressions and ideas that stem from Plato.' As we turn from Xenophon to Plato, we pass from talent to genius. Plato's unique position is not only due to his greatness as a philosopher. He was also the most skilful and subtle of Greek prose writers, only comparable as a stylist, and then in a very different key, with Demosthenes.

He was born almost at the same time as Xenophon, in 427, and to begin with was known as Aristocles; the nickname Plato, which means 'broad-shouldered', being given him by his schoolmaster. His father claimed descent from king Codros and his mother also belonged to the highest ranks of Athenian society. He received an excellent education and as a young man wrote dithyrambs and tragedies. When he was twenty, he met Socrates for the first time and the effect on him was immediate and profound. It is said that he immediately destroyed all his poetical writings.

His social position offered him every opportunity to make a career in politics: he was related to such influential leaders of the aristocratic party as Critias and Charmides, both of whom were prepared to help him. But he was deeply shocked by the excesses of the Thirty, and above all, by the death of Socrates, whom he had come to regard as the best and noblest of men. In *Letter* VII he says: 'I was so disgusted that I turned my back on the wretchedness of the times' (325a). Owing to illness, he was unable to be with his master at the time of his death, which is described in the *Phaedo*. For the disciples of Socrates it was no longer safe to remain in Athens and, like a number of others, Plato left the city for Megara. Later he visited southern Italy, where he associated with the Pythagoreans, Philolaos, Archytas and Timaeus; Egypt, where he studied astronomy; and Cyrene, where he met the mathematician Theodorus.

These journeys were undertaken for purposes of study. His three later visits to Sicily were for a different reason. The philosopher Dion whom he had probably met in Italy had persuaded his brother-in-law, Dionysius the Elder, Tyrant of Syracuse, to invite Plato to his court as a political adviser. Plato who was then approaching forty hoped to find in Sicily an opportunity of trying out his political principles in practice. It was not long, however, before the Tyrant, taking umbrage at his ideas, arrested him and handed him over to the captain of a Lacedaemonian ship, Sparta being then at war with Athens. At Aegina, Plato was sold as a slave to a citizen of Cyrene who soon afterwards granted him his freedom. He then returned to Athens.

In 387, in the more propitious conditions created by the King's Peace, Plato began to teach at the Academy which was situated at the gates of Athens not far from the village of Colonos, the birthplace of Sophocles. Soon, people from every part of the Greek world, including women, were hastening to listen to him. In 367 Dionysius the Elder died and was succeeded by his son Dionysius the Younger. The faithful Dion immediately sent for Plato, hoping that the young Tyrant would prove more accommodating than his father. Once again,

The Writing*s* of Plato

however, Plato fell out with his patron and had to flee precipitately. A third and last journey to Sicily in 361 was no more successful: it was only owing to the intervention of Archytas, a philosopher and leading statesman of Tarentum who was a friend of Plato's, that he was able to return safely to his native land. He died in 347 at the age of 80.

His works have been preserved in their entirety and we possess forty-two Dialogues and thirteen Letters attributed to him, though the authenticity of several Letters and a dozen of the Dialogues is doubtful. The chronology of the Dialogues, or at least the grouping of Dialogues that belong to the same period, has been established with a considerable degree of certainty by careful statistical examination of their stylistic peculiarities. By this method it has been found that an author's way of writing, his personal idiosyncrasies of style, differ from one period to another. For example, with regard to the particles, in which the Greek language is so rich, comparison has shown that the frequency with which they occur varied from one stage of Plato's life to another. On the basis of such tests, it now seems probable that the *Phaedrus*, previously considered to be one of the youthful Dialogues, actually belongs to Plato's maturity, like the even later *Republic*.

His two most important works, his two *Summa* so to speak, are the *Republic* (*Politeia*), which might be better translated *State*, and the *Laws*, which remained unfinished at the time of his death. The very titles of these two great works clearly indicate one of the main orientations of his philosophy, which was always pre-occupied with political organization. Having, as a young man, refused to enter political life, Plato was able to stand back and reflect upon the problems of government. He always retained this interest and would have dearly loved to have put his principles to the test of practice, as may be seen from his three visits to Syracuse. It has even been said that his whole philosophy is actually 'dammed-up action'.

A first group of Dialogues sticks closely to the historical memory of Socrates: the *Hippias*, *Protagoras* and *Gorgias* show him among the sophists; the *Apology*, facing his judges; and the *Crito*, talking to a friend when he was in prison. Other works of the same period are called after *Alcibiades*, the mystic *Euthyphro*, the rhapsode *Ion*, Plato's uncle *Charmides*, the soldier *Laches*, and the young and good-looking *Lysis*. In all of these, Socrates behaves like the portrait of himself in the *Apology*: carrying out his 'mission' to the people of Athens

Last Struggles for Freedom

whom he meets in the street or on the Agora, first enquiring about
their occupation, and from there passing on to some general question,
such as the nature of beauty (*Hippias*), or wisdom (*Charmides*), or
friendship (*Lysis*), or religion (*Euthyphro*), or poetry (*Ion*).

Socrates skilfully directs the discussion, drawing his companion on
till he either contradicts himself or has to modify an opinion; and
almost invariably the argument ends in deadlock (*aporia*). But this
point is only reached after an amazing display of irony on the part
of Socrates, which transforms the Dialogues into admirably witty
comedies, sometimes with two characters (*Hippias, Euthyphro, Ion*),
sometimes with four or five (*Charmides* or *Lysis*). Even when a
considerable number of people are present, as in the *Protagoras* or the
Gorgias, rarely do more than four or five of them actually take part
in the discussion. The argument may begin at once, as in the *Hippias*,
or it may be introduced by Socrates, addressing some unnamed friend;
as in the *Lysis*; or, again, there may be a brief opening conversation
in which Socrates refers to a previous discussion, as in the *Protagoras*.

In the *Lysis*, Socrates is on his way from the Academy (where
Plato was to teach) to the Lyceum (where Aristotle was to teach)
when he falls in with a group of young men, one of whom, Hippothales, asks him to accompany them to a newly-opened gymnasium.
As they walk along, Socrates asks: 'First of all, I should like to know
what I am going to do there and what is the attraction of the place?'
Hippothales is evasive: 'Everyone's likes and dislikes differ.' But
when Socrates presses him, he will say no more and starts to blush.
Whereupon, one of his companions, Ctesippos, breaks in:

It is all very fine, Hippothales, blushing and refusing to give his name,
but Socrates would only have to talk to you for a few minutes and you
would be boring him to death by continually repeating the name you won't
mention. He drives us all crazy, Socrates, by talking about Lysis, and when
he has had one or two drinks he repeats his name so often that, next morning
when we wake up, we can still hear it. It's bad enough when he's content
just to talk about him; when the fit takes him to start pouring out poems
about him, it is even worse; but worst of all is when he begins singing about
his love in that terrible voice of his that there's no escaping from. Fancy your
question making him blush! (*Lysis*, 203 ff.).

Earlier, referring to a conversation between Cyrus and Araspes in
Xenophon, I used the expression 'Courts of Love'; it could be applied
even more aptly to the *Lysis*, in which Socrates debates, first with

266

him and then with Menexenes, the question: Who should be called the friend, the one who loves or the one who is loved? In the course of the discussion they refer to the view of Empedocles and Heracleitus, according to whom friendship arises either from resemblance or unlikeness. After considering these alternatives with considerable subtlety, both are rejected as inadequate, and the dialogue ends inconclusively. At this point, the 'pedagogues' arrive, noisy slaves rather the worse for drink, who have come to take the boys home.

The *Ion* is more of a farce than a comedy. Like the sophist Hippias, the rhapsode Ion of Ephesus claims to know everything, flattering himself especially on having a better understanding of Homer than anyone in the world. Now Homer had a thorough grasp of all arts and sciences, therefore. . . . And Socrates amusingly deflates his naïvely silly vanity. In doing so, he puts forward his famous theory of poetic inspiration, which he compares to the phenomenon of magnetism, manifested by the stone that was found in the peninsula of Magnesia: 'It is the Muse herself that inspires men and, through them, others are able to share her inspiration, thus forming a continuous chain' (*Ion*, 533 e). In trying to answer a number of searching questions, Ion gets bogged down in his own contradictions. Whereupon Socrates says:

Far from convincing me of your talent, you are not even prepared to tell me which subjects you are skilled in discussing, despite my insistence. Every time, you manage to escape by assuming a different shape, like Proteus. . . . If you really have some special understanding of Homer's art, yet refuse to tell me what it is when you have promised to, you are simply making fun of me, which is wrong of you. On the other hand, if you have no such knowledge, and it is by virtue of some divine privilege you share with Homer that, without knowing anything, you are able to speak so highly of this poet, then you are not wrong. So you must choose: either you are wrong, or else you are divine. I would prefer to be regarded as divine, Ion replied. Well then, said Socrates, we will grant you what seems best to you, Ion: that you are divine—and that being so, you have no knowledge of Homer's art (*Ibid.*, 541 e ff.).

By maintaining that it is impossible to attain absolute truth, the sophists Protagoras and Gorgias (see pp. 199–200) had made a clean sweep of all religious beliefs and morality. In the Dialogues named after them, Plato shows Socrates opposing these two famous men, in order to establish, by means of his new dialectical method, the supreme reality of virtue and justice. Thus the philosopher, whom Aristophanes in the *Clouds* and, later, the accusers at his trial, were to liken to the sophists, in fact stood out against them and boldly asserted the moral values they claimed to have disproved.

At the home of the wealthy Callias, Protagoras is walking beneath the portico, surrounded by a chorus of respectful admirers that he has brought with him, 'holding them beneath the spell of his voice like another Orpheus'. Socrates comments:

The graceful evolutions of this chorus, as they tried to avoid getting in Protagoras' way, delighted me: every time he and those nearest to him turned, those behind, with quite admirable unanimity, parted their ranks to right and left, and by a circular movement closed in again behind him. It was really wonderful to behold (*Protagoras,* 315 b).

Is the political virtue that Protagoras claims to teach really susceptible of being taught? In an attempt to prove that it is, the sophist first recalls the myth of Prometheus and Epimetheus, then delivers a lecture and, finally, cites the poets. Socrates criticizes each of these methods as inadequate, and sets out to demonstrate that the quite relative virtue Protagoras is talking about is not the true object of knowledge. Thus the debate is raised from virtue based on opinion, to virtue as strictly and objectively defined by the dialectic.

The *Gorgias* has a quite different bearing. Here, at least to begin with, the question at issue is the rhetoric taught by the great sophist. First with Gorgias himself, and then with his disciple, Polos, Socrates seeks to show that rhetoric is an empirical activity, like making one's toilet or cooking, rather than an art. Polos is drawn into arguing that it is possible for an unjust man to be happy, like Archelaos, king of Macedonia, who behaved like a tyrant, yet succeeded in everything he undertook. But Socrates traps Polos in the web of his dialectic and proves that it is worse to commit an injustice than to be the victim of one, and that not to expiate a sin one has committed is worse than being punished for it. These apparent paradoxes arouse the indignation of one of the bystanders, Callicles,[1] and his intervention introduces a touch of drama:

[1] According to J. Humbert (*Polycrates, the Trial of Socrates and the Gorgias*, Klincksieck, 1930), in creating the character of Callicles, Plato had in mind the sophist Polycrates who had written a pamphlet against Socrates.

Tell me, Socrates, do you mean us to take what you are saying seriously, or are you joking? For if you are serious, and if what you are saying is true, the whole of human life is going to be turned upside down. . . . (*Gorgias* 481, b–c).

As a matter of fact, in Plato's view, what Socrates was proposing was nothing less than a complete revision, or rather *inversion*, of all values currently accepted in Greece; in a word, a philosophical *conversion*. Callicles then goes on to defend the doctrine that might is right (like the Athenians in their argument with the Melians, described by Thucydides), and describes the laws of the city as an invention of the weak for the protection of their own interests. If philosophy is going to set itself up in opposition to the power and might of the 'superman', he says, it deserves nothing but contempt:

For young men, I strongly approve of philosophy. . . . But when I come across an old man who still insists on philosophizing, I say to myself, Socrates, that he deserves whipping. For, however naturally gifted such a man may be, he is bound to become less than a man if he is always avoiding the centre of the city and those public gatherings, where, as the poet [Homer] says, men achieve distinction, hiding himself away to the end of his days, chattering in corners with three or four young men, and never speaking out freely and generously (*Ibid.*, 485 c).

The orator, Isocrates, expresses a very similar opinion about the *eristics*, those addicts of 'disputation', confusing them with philosophers, although he himself was one of Socrates' pupils.

Socrates' reply is magnificent. He begins on a mocking note: 'If my soul was made of gold, Callicles, I should certainly be delighted to find one of those stones that are used for testing gold. It seems to me that, in you, that is just what I have been fortunate enough to discover' (*Ibid.*, 486 d). And, indeed, Callicles shows none of Polos' timidity: he follows his ideas through and expresses them frankly. What luck for Socrates to have come across such an opponent, whom he can treat as a friend! The long argument that ensues is like a duel. Callicles realizes that he is getting the worst of it; disheartened, he is ready to give up, and merely answers out of politeness. At last, only Socrates is left talking, and he concludes with a myth, very different from the one used by Protagoras. (When the dialectic arrives at presentiments of truth that are not actually demonstrable, Plato sometimes has recourse to myth in order to give depth to his ideas).

And now let me tell you a story, which, though you perhaps may look upon it simply as a tale, I believe to be true (*Ibid.*, 523 a).

And he goes on to recount the story of Hades and of the ultimate retribution of good and bad alike, when the souls of men will appear in all their nakedness before the three judges:

Then, Callicles, you will be summoned before Aiacos, and there you will stand, your mouth agape and your head in a whirl, just as I should feel before a human judge, and you will have to submit to seeing yourself struck and exposed to every outrage. . . . So take my advice, and come with me where you will find happiness in your lifetime and after your death, according to the dictates of reason. Let yourself be scorned, treated as a madman, beaten: and if you are really an honest man, devoted to the practice of virtue, you will find it does you no harm (*Ibid.*, 526 e and 527 c).

In the second group of Dialogues, written in his maturity, the *Republic*, the *Symposium*, the *Phaedrus* and the *Phaedo*, Socrates is still the chief character, as he was to remain in the rest of Plato's works, with the exception of the *Laws*, where his place is taken by an anonymous Athenian. More and more, however, one feels that Plato is using him as a mouthpiece to express his own ideas. Though it was to Socrates that he owed the awakening of his mind and his fundamental ideas, he also took over many elements of his philosophy from the pre-Socratics: Heracleitus, Parmenides, Anaxagoras and the Pythagoreans. The result of this, however, was in no sense merely eclecticism, for the powerful originality of his mind transposed and transmuted all his borrowings.

The perpetual flux of Heracleitus he regards as no more than an appearance. Behind the phenomena perceived by the senses, there is an invisible reality of the spirit and the intellect, comparable with the *being* of Parmenides or the *spirit* of Anaxagoras, but seen by Plato rather as a plurality: Forms or Ideas, those eternal realities of which all that man is capable of perceiving here on earth is but a poor imitation, a pale and imperfect reflection. The soul, too, is eternal: having contemplated these pure essences in a previous existence, here on earth it still has fleeting recollections of them. In the case of a philosopher, the soul's one aspiration is to recover these Ideas, in order to achieve once again the perfect vision of beauty and goodness in themselves. But, if it is to do so, it must first purify itself by ridding itself of material influences and of evil. For the body is the soul's tomb (*Soma = sema*, a Pythagorean idea); when the body dies, the soul is set free to experience real life, that is to say, 'assimilation with the divine'. But if, in the cycle of existences, the soul is weighed down with matter and with sin, it may also suffer a decline, and come to inhabit the body of some inferior human being, or even of an animal.

Such is the imposing conception expressed in the works of Plato's maturity and old age, not in the form of a dogmatic, fully worked out system, but rather as a succession of approximations, a picture that the artist was continually modifying and retouching, and many parts of which were only tentatively sketched in. Fundamentally, it matters little whether his philosophy underwent a crisis or a development: what is important to grasp is that his thought always remained open, never became static. Though he himself wrote so much, Plato distrusted books: they are incapable of answering objections, and once they have been written, they are 'finished', dead, in the sense in which we speak of 'finishing off' a wounded animal. Jean Guitton has said: 'The essence of Platonism, it seems to me, is not to choose. It is a circle; and from whichever point on it one sets out, ultimately one arrives at all the others. His dialectic, if we follow it to the end, infallibly leads to mysticism. If we regard mysticism as the true source of his doctrine, we shall be led on to politics, which is the art of adapting contemplation to the multitude.'

In the *Republic*, which is a whole world in itself, we can only hope to point out some of the peaks and note one or two of its peculiarities.

On a visit to Polemarchos at Piraeus, Socrates is chatting with the latter, his father Cephalos, Thrasymachos of Chalcedonia and Plato's two brothers, Glaucon and Adeimantos. Socrates finds that Cephalos has aged, and this leads to a witty discussion of old age, its drawbacks and advantages. But before long the conversation turns to the virtue of justice. If the ring of Gyges, which made its owner invisible, were given to a just man, it would turn him into a criminal; thus one cannot rely on current ideas, which remain on the surface of things. What is important is to define justice, both individual and social, since there is only one justice: in the *Republic*, the features of the individual microcosm are merely reproduced on a larger scale, and can therefore be better understood. In both cases, justice is harmony: in man, harmony between the three active principles of the soul, reason or intelligence (*nous*), passion or sensibility (*epithymia*), and courage or will (*thymos*). In the state, harmony consists in agree-ment between the three classes: the rulers, the warriors, and the workers and peasants. In our own times, Georges Dumézil has found evidence of this tripartite social division in the history and mythology of many Indo-European peoples; Plato had already either observed it or had a presentiment of it.

The rulers and warriors together comprise the 'Guardians'. They must be given an elaborate and advanced education, for no state can be happy unless its rulers have genuine scientific knowledge and are in some measure philosophers. Now, in Greece, children's intelligence and sensibility are developed in the first place by studying the works of Homer and other classical poets. Yet the *Iliad* and the *Odyssey* are full of legends and fictions, that is, of falsehoods—a fine way of teaching children to respect the truth! And when the poets talk about the gods, they portray them as tricksters, criminals, parri-cides and adulterers. On this point, Plato shares the views of Xenophanes of Colophon (see p. 115), but goes further.

Indeed, though Plato is a great exponent of the art of writing, and a genuine literary critic, [1] he maintains that, however admirable the intentions of the poets may have been, epic poetry, and even more tragedy and comedy, are harmful in themselves, because they are based on the principles of *mimesis*, of imitation of the passions.

Thus, if a man skilled in assuming any character and imitating any shape were to arrive in our city, and wished to perform and exhibit his poems in public, we would pay reverence to him as a holy, wonderful and charming person, but we should inform him that there was no place for him amongst us and we should send him elsewhere, having first anointed him with perfumes and crowned him with fillets (*Republic*, 398 a).

Perfumes and fillets were honours reserved for the gods and the rhapsode Ion has already been ironically acclaimed by Socrates as 'a god-like man'. But here it is Homer himself, not to mention Hesiod, Aeschylus and Sophocles, who is politely but firmly expelled from the Platonic republic. Later, however, in Book x, Socrates is to recall that 'throughout my life I have always felt a certain affectionate respect for Homer', though he adds 'Yet it would be wrong to honour a man at the expense of truth' (*Ibid.*, 595 b-c).

[1] See the recent and remarkable work by Paul Vicaire; *Platon, critique littéraire* (Klincksieck, 1960).

According to Plato, both truth and the common good demand that poets and artists shall be subject to strict control: it will be for the state to propose the subjects they shall deal with, and to supervise the manner in which they treat them. Today, his views have been implemented by the censorship and strict conformism that are found in certain totalitarian states.

The class structure described by Plato is more akin to the Indian caste system. The classes constitute a hierarchy, like the metals: day labourers are men of bronze; artisans, of iron; warriors, of silver; and rulers, of gold. Plato uses the ancient myth of Hesiod to express a very different idea. The Guardians must own no personal property and be free of all ties, including those of the family, so that they may be at liberty to devote themselves to the good of society as a whole. This is why, in their class, wives and children will be held in common. True, the women are to receive the same education as the men; they can even be soldiers. On this issue, Plato accepts the principle of equality of the sexes enunciated by Socrates, but far from drawing the same conclusions from it as Antisthenes and Aeschines, he is led on to the conception of complete sexual promiscuity, which he was certainly not the first to think of since it was the subject of Aristophanes' comedy, the *Ecclesiazusae*, first performed in 392 (see pp. 240–1). The passages in the *Republic* where Plato attempts to provide a recipe for the 'production' of leaders, remind one of Aldous Huxley's *Brave New World*.

Plato's genius, at once logical and fantastic, was not afraid of arriving at absurd conclusions. Moreover, his communism was very different from the universal, popular communism of today: it was an aristocratic communism, restricted to a class of leaders. It did not include the workers, but was more like the orders of Chivalry, the Teutonic Knights; and, still more, the Parties of a modern totalitarian state. But the *Republic* is also very different from the political Utopia described in Xenophon's *Cyropaedia*. In Book VII, it provides the best illustration of his doctrine of Ideas: the allegory of the Cave. The moral conversion demanded of Callicles in the *Gorgias* is only one aspect of the total conversion that philosophy must undergo, from the world of appearances and opinion to the world of knowledge and reality.

Now, consider our natural condition, so far as education and ignorance are concerned, according to this picture. Imagine men living in an underground cavern, the entrance to which, open to the light, stretches the whole length of the cave, in which they have been kept since childhood, their legs and necks fettered with chains so that they cannot move from their place and can only see straight ahead of them, because the chains will not allow them to turn their heads. Behind them, a long way off, a bright fire is burning. Between the fire and the prisoners is a raised roadway. And, along this road, imagine a little wall, like those screens that marionette players put up between themselves and the public, and behind which they perform their wonders (*Ibid.*, 514 ff.).

All that these curious prisoners could see, either of themselves, or of their neighbours, or of what was passing along the road, would be the shadows cast by the fire on the part of the cave facing them. For them, these shadows would be reality itself since they could know no other. If one of them happened to be set free, and he was turned towards the fire at the entrance to the cave, every movement would cause him pain and suffering; at first he would be dazzled and unable to see anything; and he would need a long course of re-education before he was able to perceive real objects. Like the Parables in the Gospels this allegory of Plato's requires a key, which he provides:

The visible world must be likened to the prison-house, and the light of the fire by which it was lit to the power of the sun. As for the return to the outside world and the sight of all its wonders, in this must be seen the soul's ascent into the sphere of the intellect (*Ibid.*, 517).

that is to say, the philosopher's approach to the supreme reality, God.

The *Republic* ends with an eschatological myth, on the same lines as that in the *Gorgias*, but more fully orchestrated. Er, son of Armenius the Pamphylian, is killed on the field of battle, and twelve days later is restored to life. He describes what he has seen in the other world. The story is set against a cosmography in which Plato's poetic imagination makes skilful play with the most recent scientific results of his time. He is at present at the scene of judgment, when souls are being punished or rewarded, and when they also choose their new forms of existence, which are assigned by Lachesis, one of the Fates. Plato, who despite his refusal to admit Homer to his *Republic* cannot do without him, tells us that Achilles chose to become a lion, Agamemnon an eagle, Thersites a monkey, and Odysseus an ordinary private citizen. The conclusion of the myth is quite clear: the soul is immortal, capable of everything that is good and everything that is evil; in order to find the road that, in the cycle of existence, leads upwards and not downwards, it must practise justice and wisdom. To make even more sure, it must call upon the upward strength inherent in the love of Goodness and Beauty, the wings that enable the soul to rise to heaven. Of Plato's doctrine of Love, which is an essential part of his philosophy, only the first outline is to be found in the *Lysis*, those elements, perhaps, that he owed to Socrates; the *Symposium* and the *Phaedrus* have a wider range, developing a metaphysic of Love that is at once dialectical and mystical.

Agathon's guests are a great deal more serious than those of Callias in Xenophon's *Symposium*: they dismiss the flute player and, with her, the entertainments customary on such an occasion. Each of them in turn has to speak in praise of Love—Phaedrus, Pausanias the doctor, Eryximachos, Aristophanes (who should have spoken earlier, but was prevented by an attack of hiccoughs), the tragic poet Agathon, and finally Socrates. Thus Plato admits the author of the *Clouds* to the Socratic circle, and his approach to the question of Love is by way of an anthropological fantasy. Originally, humanity comprised not only two sexes, but three. These creatures of the past were monsters,

with completely round backs, and each having four hands, four legs, two faces, four ears, and their privy parts also in duplicate: the sex organs of the first kind were both male, of the second, both female, while the third kind, having both male and female organs, was androgynous (*Symposium*, 189 d ff.)

Worried about the power of these first men, Zeus and the other gods cut them in two, 'as one cuts an egg with a hair' and Apollo then performed various operations on them, what we should call 'plastic surgery'. From that time on, each half has sought out its other half: those that were originally androgynous have heterosexual tastes, which we are accustomed to call 'normal'; the others, both men and women, were homosexual. As opposed to this myth, so indulgent to every form of love, Socrates then puts forward another, which he claims to have heard from a priestess, Diotima of Mantineia, who had attained to the highest degree of knowledge accessible to an 'initiate'.

According to Diotima, Love, or Eros, was not a god, but a daimon or spirit, that is to say a creature halfway between man and god, like the angels of Christianity, who were originally messengers. During a feast at which the gods were celebrating the birth of Aphrodite, who is usually regarded as the mother of Eros, Poros (Expediency) befuddled with nectar, begot a child on Penia (Poverty); and this child was in fact Eros. That is why Eros is poor and naked like his mother, 'unkempt, dirty, barefooted, homeless, sleeping on the bare ground'. And that is also why, like his father, he is virile, 'always on the look out for whatever is beautiful or good, an outstanding huntsman, keen on all inventions and fertile in resources, an incomparable sorcerer, magician, sophist and philosopher' (*Ibid.*, 201 e ff.). Because of his intermediate nature, he stands midway between ignorance and knowledge, like the philosophers who, in love with wisdom, eternally pursue it without ever attaining it. He is, too, continually in search of Beauty and Goodness for which he has a passionate longing.

Love tends to 'the begetting of beauty, both of body and soul', but this longing for an eternal projection of the self can be satisfied, at a higher level, by spiritual fecundation. This is what happens with great poets, inventors and law-givers: their love of Beauty drives them to seek immortality through their works. Indeed, though love begins with the love of bodily beauty, complete initiation consists in realizing that the beauty of a given person is the sister of the beauty inherent in another; more than this, it consists in valuing the beauty of the soul above that of the body, and in thus raising oneself by successive stages to the ultimate awareness, the highest degree of which is the revelation of immaterial and eternal Beauty, God. Love, supposed to be blind, becomes in Plato the condition of the highest knowledge and the supreme illumination.

After the noisy arrival of Alcibiades, reeling with drink, the *Symposium* contains yet another passage of splendid eloquence: the portrait of Socrates drawn frankly and with no attempt at concealment by the man who had sought to make him his lover, in the hope that this peerless philosopher, with the face of a Silenus and words as magical as the sounds of Marsyas' flute, would transmit to him his divine wisdom.

In the *Phaedrus*, Socrates, who was interested only in men and whom 'the trees had nothing to teach', as Paul Valéry said, finds himself for once in the country, on the banks of the Illissus:

See how this plane tree casts a shadow as broad as its own height, and how tall and splendidly shady this Agnus Castus is, filling the air with its lovely scent! How delightful this spring, flowing beneath the plane tree, and how refreshing it is to dip one's feet in it. . . . If we were to lie here on this bank, its slope is just right to support our heads in comfort (*Phaedrus*, 229 a).

Plato, who used to teach beneath the trees of the Academy, was very susceptible to the beauty of nature.

The dialogue begins by considering the principles of rhetoric and the writings of Lysis and Isocrates, but soon Socrates turns the discussion to the subject of Love. The rural setting reminds him of the story of the grasshoppers. Once upon a time, certain men were so possessed by the Muses that they could think of nothing else but the pleasure of music and, forgetting to eat and drink, they died of starvation. Whereupon they were turned into grasshoppers, upon whom 'the Muses had bestowed the privilege of being able to live without food, so that they were able to spend their entire lives singing' (*Phaedrus*, 259 b-c). Socrates then proceeds to distinguish between the four kinds of madness (*manía*) or divine possession (*enthousiasmós*) with which men are endowed by heaven: the prophetic madness of the Pythia, the religious madness of the Corybantes and the Dionysian mysteries, the poetic madness inspired by the Muses (that of the grasshopper men), and lastly, and most important of all, the madness of Love, which leads to ultimate knowledge. The human spirit is like a winged chariot, driven by Reason, and drawn by two horses, Thymos, the steady one, and Epithymia, the restless one. Here, once again we have the tripartite division of the spirit suggested in the *Republic*, but this time illustrated by a myth. For the chariot to be able to ascend so that it can join the heavenly procession of souls reaching out towards the gods, it is necessary to develop and strengthen its wings; and it is through its perception of beauty here on earth that the soul, recollecting the divine Beauty that it has contemplated in a previous existence, is able to acquire powerful wings like Eros, who is himself winged, and thus attain the highest state of all, the sphere of Ideas, where once again it will be able to contemplate the divine essence.

In both the *Phaedo* and the *Crito*, Socrates is in prison. It is the eve of his death, and he is talking to his disciples for the last time. At this solemn moment, the subject of their conversation is the immortality of the soul. The profound belief that Socrates expresses was certainly held by him, though many of the arguments that he uses to prove it are in fact Plato's. The Pythagoreans, Simmias and Cebes, raise an objection: if the soul is to be compared with the harmony of a lyre, what becomes of the harmony when the lyre is broken? Socrates ponders this a moment, then begins to compare himself with the swans, the melodious birds of Apollo who have the gift of prophecy:

As they feel the hour of death draw near, they sing more often and more loudly than ever, expressing their joy at rejoining the god who is their master. But men are so afraid of death that they slander the swans, saying that it is grief that makes them utter this last song: whereas, in fact, what inspires them on that day to sing more sweetly than ever before is their foreknowledge of the happiness awaiting them in the realm of Hades (*Phaedo*, 84 c).

What a contrast between this paradoxical joy at the approach of death and the melancholy displayed by the heroes in Homer.

The eschatological myth at the end of the *Phaedo* unfolds an even more amazing cosmology than those in the *Gorgias*, the *Republic* or the *Phaedrus*. Once again Plato makes use of the scientific knowledge of the times, but with a freedom of imagination that is bewildering. He first describes the various parts of the world, and then the fate of souls on their journeys. He reveals the unity of the cosmos and its influence on destiny, arranging the structure of heaven and earth according to a moral finality, decreed by the Idea of the Good. The account of Socrates' death at the end of the *Phaedo* completes the portrait of him already outlined in the *Symposium*, the *Apology* and the *Crito*. Written in a style of utter simplicity, in which the restrained emotion can be felt behind every word, these pages at once disregard and transcend the bounds of literature.

The *Parmenides* is a metaphysical dialogue in which Plato perfects and deepens his doctrine of Ideas, while at the same time paying homage, even in the title, to the great Eleatic philosopher and to his disciple Zeno.

In his great fresco, the *School of Athens*, Raphael imagined Plato holding the text of the *Timaeus* in his hand. And indeed from the earliest times, this Dialogue, with its account of the genesis of the cosmos, was looked upon, at least by professional philosophers, as Plato's masterpiece. Aristotle often quoted it; Plutarch devoted a favourable commentary to it; and the Christian, Arab and Jewish scholars of the Middle Ages and the Renaissance scrutinized it more closely than any other work of Plato's in order to discover his ultimate ideas about the creation of the universe, even comparing it with the Book of Genesis. Certainly, the spectacle it provides, of the demiurge copying the eternal model as he creates the world, is an impressive one. Like the *spirit* of Anaxagoras, this demiurge did not create the universe *ex nihilo;* such an idea was foreign to Plato, since for him matter, like the soul, was eternal. The demiurge is only the artificer of this mighty work.

If Plato's style has here become somewhat set, and occasionally lapses into didacticism, the *Timaeus* is far from being simply an edited version of a course of lectures given at the Academy. As elsewhere, the exposition is shared between various characters: Socrates, Timaeus the mathematician and astronomer from Locri, Hermocrates the Syracusan general who played so large a part in the defeat of the Athenian expedition to Sicily, and Critias, a cousin of Plato's and one of the Thirty.

All these characters recur in what was to have been a continuation of the *Timaeus*, the unfinished *Critias*, which, drawing upon an ancient and obscure tradition, describes the war between the Athenians and the people of Atlantis, that mythical continent, larger than Africa and Asia combined, that was supposed to have sunk beneath the sea. It was a kind of Eldorado, where, in the Age of Gold, a state of justice and happiness had obtained, ruled over by the god Poseidon—a legend that has haunted men's imagination and given rise to innumerable hypotheses. In his minute description of Atlantis, Plato displays all his usual imaginative gifts, even to the point of giving detailed figures in his account of the country and the divisions of its inhabitant into provinces and districts.

The twelve Books of the *Laws* constitute the second Platonic *Summa*; the first being the *Republic*. Here Socrates, who in the *Timaeus* and the *Critias*, was already tending to become a silent listener, disappears altogether. Three old men, an anonymous Athenian, the Cretan Clinias, and the Lacedaemonian Megillos, chat to one another as they make their way from Cnossos to the cave and sanctuary of Zeus. Since the laws of Minos and of Lycurgus were regarded in antiquity as having been the best, it is understandable that the Athenian should have come to Crete to learn from his two companions.

The first three Books form a long introduction, mainly concerned with the principles of education and the ancient history of Greece. As an 'archaeologist' Plato is inferior to Thucydides; he treats history as an agreeable pastime and devotes more attention to the ideas of the past than to the facts. There follows a detailed, even meticulous codification of the laws by which the perfect City should be governed. Plato returns to earlier conceptions, often to correct them or to bring them more in line with reality, even in the examination of certain concrete cases. All this is of great interest for the history of his ideas, but it is clear that death prevented him from revising this work, with the result that several more or less serious faults of style and composition remain, though without damaging the overall impression of grandeur and nobility.

In the works of his youth and maturity, Plato's language has a unique richness and flexibility. His style shows a tremendous range, from humour to seriousness, from seriousness to gravity, without the least vulgarity or over-emphasis, and all the characters who take part in his Dialogues are drawn from the life. With the skill of a dramatist he was able to catch the very quality of their speech: the artless enthusiams and spontaneity of young men like Lysis and Phaedrus; the pedantry of the sophists which he parodies brilliantly; the violence of men as ambitious as Alcibiades or as enigmatic as Callicles.

The wealth and brilliance of his imagery and metaphors never become tedious. His myths display an extraordinary power of imagination. The writings of this 'anti-poet' are strewn with admirably chosen poetical quotations which denote an immense culture, extending far beyond the literature of philosophy. Except in those passages—and it is true, there are plenty of them—where his use of the dialectic is purely technical and sometimes seems to be almost playing with words, reading Plato is fascinating. 'His art,' Alfred Croiset wrote, 'is the flower of Atticism. The very essence of long centuries of culture is there distilled into light and perfume by the supreme charm of his artistic genius.'

Plato's significance for Greek literature is only comparable with Homer's. Regretfully the philosopher banished the poet from his Utopia, but he was not so puritanical as to fail to appreciate Homer's greatness, and he often displays his admiration for the *Iliad*. Of the philosopher, Jean Guitton has said: 'After his death, Plato remained lord and master of the Western world. Every thinker in Europe since his time has been a Platonist: Aristotle, Plotinus, St Augustine, then all the Augustinians as far as Malebranche, Kant, Auguste Comte, Nietzsche (full of Plato, though opposed to him), Bergson, Husserl, Heidegger (who, through Plato, rediscovered Parmenides). All have been under the spell of Plato; none has been able to break it.'

There are some poets who are really only versifiers. Plato, who destroyed his early poetic efforts and left nothing but prose, was nevertheless a very great poet. By a curious contradiction, the man who condemned the inventions of Homer and the tragic poets, was himself a creator of myths. Most of these, it is true, have a moral purpose and it is only their form that is poetic, but there are some that were written simply for pleasure. Examples of this are the story of the grasshoppers in the *Phaedrus* or the myth invented by Aristophanes in the *Symposium*.

Who else has shown such a combination of genius, both as a writer and a philosopher?

<h3 style="text-align:center">ISOCRATES</h3>

At the end of the *Phaedrus*, Isocrates is mentioned by name: Socrates prophesies that the young man will go further than the other orators, because 'nature has implanted in his mind a certain philosophy'. At the time the *Phaedrus* was written, Isocrates would have been in his seventies. Was this praise of him merely sarcastic and intended as a snub? Or did Plato really consider him to be a thinker of at least a relatively high order? Plato's habit of irony makes it difficult to decide.

Isocrates was almost as long-lived as his master, Gorgias, who lived to be a hundred and five. He was born ten years before Plato and he died ten years after him, at the age of ninety-eight. At the time of his birth, in 436, under the government of Pericles and before the beginning of the Peloponnesian War, Athens was at the height of her power. The news of the defeat at Chaironeia, in 338, is said to have so upset Isocrates that he allowed himself to die of hunger.

His father was a middle-class Athenian who owned a workshop where slaves made musical instruments, flutes; and he was well enough off to be a *choragos* and to give his son a good education. As a child, Isocrates was as gifted at games as he was at his studies; he won several prizes for playing *keretizontes*, a game something like hockey. But after he grew up he frequently complained of poor health which, combined with a weak voice and incurable shyness, prevented him from playing an active part in politics or participating in the oratorical struggle in the Assembly. He studied under Gorgias and Prodicos; and, like Plato and Xenophon, was one of Socrates' followers, though less assiduous. By the time the Peloponnesian War came to an end, in 404, the fortune he had inherited from his father had been reduced to practically nothing, and in order to earn a living he had to become a *logographos*, that is to say, a man who composed speeches for litigants unable to write their own.

This did not satisfy his ambition, however, and about 393 he opened a school of oratory in Athens. Unable to become an orator himself, he nevertheless undertook to instruct gifted young men in the art of public speaking. He earned a great deal of money and was so well known that pupils flocked to him from all over Greece: orators like Isaeus, Hypereides and Lycurgus, generals, like Conon's son, Timotheos, who always remained deeply attached to him, as well as statesmen, poets and historians, like Ephoros of Kyme and Theopompos of Chios. By the end of his life, Isocrates had become a figure of considerable importance, thanks to his connections and influence. He corresponded with Archidamos, king of Sparta, Jason, the tyrant of Pheres, Euvagoras, king of Cyprus, and Philip of Macedon.

Of Isocrates' writings, we have six speeches that he wrote when he was a logographer, eight letters and fourteen epideictic orations. In order to attract the public and to keep his pupils, every teacher of rhetoric had to be able to produce such samples of his skill, in which the subject was of less importance than the rhetorical style. Isocrates' forensic speeches all date from the period before he started teaching in 393. From that moment, he not only completely dropped all judicial business, but even took to deriding the law and the profession of speech-writing which he had practised for some ten years.

His speech, the *On the Chariot Team*, which is incomplete, deals with a curious case. At the Olympic Games in 416, Alcibiades had aroused universal admiration by his luxurious display, his prodigality and his victories: seven chariot teams had been entered in his name at the races, and he had carried off the first three prizes. But a private citizen, who accused him of having unfairly laid claim to one of the winning teams, brought an action against him. Alcibiades' banishments and various military appointments prevented the case from coming to court before his death, in 404. However, as soon as his son, also called Alcibiades, attained his majority, he became legally responsible for the charges against his father; and it was for him that Isocrates prepared this speech for the defence, about 396. In the main it consists of a panegyric of the great Alcibiades, which, though extremely brilliant, is dishonest and full of artifice. Dates are either disregarded, or so arranged as to suit the needs of the case. Any attempt to excuse Alcibiades for the acts he had committed against his country while in exile was bound to be disingenuous, but here, casuistry is pushed to the extreme. Nevertheless, the speech is remarkable for its lively style, as well as for the skill with which it ties up the cause of the two Alcibiades with democracy and that of his accuser with the oligarchy of the Thirty, then held in horror and detestation.

The speech *Against Callimachus* has to do with an affair that occurred after the reconciliation between the Athenian parties, under the aegis of Pausanias, in 403. It is largely concerned with praising the peace agreements, and it was doubtless this political aspect of what was actually a forensic speech, that decided Isocrates to publish it. Towards the end, he returns to this point which he obviously regarded as decisive for his case. Throughout his life Isocrates was an ardent supporter of internal peace and national unity, and he must certainly have regarded the reconciliation of 403 as one of the great moments in Athenian history.

Then in 393 Isocrates opened his school. This was the occasion for a pamphlet, that was also a veritable manifesto: *Against the Sophists*. Of this we only have the opening, though he later revised several paragraphs of it and used them in the *Antidosis*. It is an ironical and mordant attack both upon the eristic philosophers and the rhetoricians. The first, philosophers like Plato, though he is not actually named, hold out to their pupils the promise of virtue and happiness, almost of immortality; they thus claim to be prophets. Yet, in return for these priceless gifts, all the payment they ask is a few miserable pence. Moreover, though claiming to teach justice, they distrust their disciples! Plato did not found the Academy until a few years later, in 387; but for a long time there was persistent rivalry and frequent polemics between the two schools.

It is the second kind of 'Sophists', however, that Isocrates criticizes most severely: the bad teachers of rhetoric, from whom he is careful to distinguish himself. The philosophers, he says, are at least concerned with justice and temperance, however little they succeed in teaching these virtues to their pupils, whereas the bad rhetoricians are only interested in intriguing and making money. It is passages like this, and there are several of them in Isocrates' writings, that remind us that he, too, was a follower of Socrates, even if not a very assiduous one; and they also show him to have been a loyal and upright man, with a genuine concern for morality. In my view they are sufficient to account for Plato's measured and somewhat ironical praise of him in the *Phaedrus*, despite the many disagreements between them and the fact that they taught in rival schools.

But it is in the epideictic discourses that his talent is seen at its best. One of the literary forms most in vogue among the sophists was the *enkomion*, in which Isocrates prided himself on excelling both his predecessors and his contempories. It was not unusual for rhetoricians to choose for these exercises such paradoxical themes as a fly, or salt, or the lives of exiles or beggars, or misfortunes in general; Alcidamos had even written *In Praise of Death*, and, very much later, Erasmus was to write *In Praise of Folly*. Isocrates, however, restricted himself to the classical themes provided by mythology and epic poetry. His master, Gorgias, had written an *Enkomion of Helen*, which still exists (see p. 199); Isocrates, without mentioning him by name, set out to surpass him. Helen's more than dubious virtue could be 'saved' in one of two ways: either by maintaining, like Stesichoros and Euripides, that it was only her ghost that went to Troy; or else by proving, what is suggested by Homer, that in following Paris she was simply the tool of Aphrodite and later bitterly regretted her involuntary sin. Gorgias had chosen the second method. Isocrates' aim is quite different, and essentially paradoxical: he tries to show that, though she did indeed go to Troy and was a free agent, she had always behaved in a correct and praiseworthy way; and he even extends his complete approval of her, to her two seducers, Theseus and Paris. In preferring Helen to all that the two other goddesses, Hera and Athena, could offer him, Paris had been inspired not by lust, but by the fact that, as the daughter of Zeus, she could confer on his descendants the noblest possible 'armorial bearings'.

The whole of this eulogy is full of rhetorical exaggeration, paralogism and sheer sophistry. Theseus is portrayed as a greater hero than Heracles, the originator of a kind of democratic monarchy, and thus a distant precursor of Pericles—a theme already used by Euripides in *The Suppliant Women*. What justifies Helen and her two seducers is that beauty is a gift from the gods, surpassing all others and monopolizing the mind: 'We would rather be the slaves of beautiful people than have mastery over others' (*Enkomion of Helen*, 57). When he is describing the wondrous power of beauty over men and gods alike, Isocrates' style rises to lyrical heights. This feeling for beauty is one of the fundamental characteristics of the Greek spirit[1]; in the *Symposium* and the *Phaedrus*, Plato insists upon it as the source of the highest wisdom. On this plane, and in the way they both share the deepest

[1] On this point I may perhaps be allowed to refer the reader to my book *Love in Ancient Greece* (Frederick Muller, 1960).

tendencies of their race, the orator and the philosopher for once find themselves in agreement.

Polycrates, an obscure sophist with an exaggerated taste for paradox, from whom Plato perhaps drew some of the characteristics of Callicles in the *Gorgias*, was the author of an *Accusation of Socrates*, in which he slandered 'the best, the wisest and the most just of men who ever lived'[1] and also of an *Enkomion of Busiris*, an attempt to rehabilitate a legendary king of Egypt who was usually regarded as typifying the cruellest and most bloodthirsty tyranny. In writing his own *Busiris*, Isocrates claimed to be showing Polycrates how it should be done, in the same way that he had prided himself on surpassing Gorgias in his *Enkomion of Helen*. Here he paints an enchanting picture of Egypt, a traditional theme in Greece, at least since the days of Hecataeus of Miletus; and attributes the origin of Egyptian institutions to Busiris on the dubious grounds that no other mythical king of Egypt appears to have a better claim. Busiris, he argues, cannot have committed the crimes he was accused of, because the dates make this impossible: just as, in *On the Chariot Team*, Isocrates had been prepared to distort the chronology of the Peloponnesian War, so, here, he bases his argument on a chronology derived from mythology! Moreover, he condemns the poets for committing blasphemy by accusing heroes and even gods of scandalous behaviour: it might almost be Xenophanes or Plato speaking, though, by the fourth century, this criticism of mythology on grounds of morality had become a platitude. Indeed, 'platitudinous' is a word no reader of Isocrates can avoid: even his great show pieces, the *Panegyricus*, *On Exchange*, the *Panathenaicus*, are all full of long, harmonious commonplaces.

In their *Olympian Discourses*, both Gorgias and Lysis had been concerned with important political ideas. Isocrates hoped both to imitate and to excel them. In his *Panegyricus*, so called because it is supposed to have been spoken at the solemn gathering of the Greeks (*panegyrie*) for the Olympic Games in 380, he expresses his views about the destiny of the Greek cities and of the whole of Hellas. In his opinion, Athens was, from every point of view, entitled to the hegemony: her antiquity, her services to Greece ever since mythical times and particularly during the Persian War, her brilliant achievements in literature and the arts. His praise of Athens as the true capital of the Hellenic world echoes Pericles' speech in Thucydides

---

[1] Plato at the end of the *Phaedo*.

(p. 230), but it is drawn out through an interminable succession of melodious oratorical periods. From the *Panegyricus* onwards, Isocrates supported the idea of Greek unity against the hereditary enemy, Persia. He considered that the shameful King's Peace should be rescinded and that, taking advantage of the military weakness of Asia, the empire of Darius and Xerxes should be attacked and destroyed.

With the *Antidosis*, which dates from about 354, he returned to the problems of education. At much greater length than in his manifesto, *Against the Sophists*, he expounded his theories with regard to the training of an orator, in the form of an imaginary speech for the defence: an Athenian citizen, summoned to the position of trierarch, is supposed to have claimed that Isocrates, being wealthier than himself, ought either to accept the burden of office, or agree to exchange fortunes; this process of exchanging property, strange as it appears to us, being provided for in Athenian law.

It is in this speech that Isocrates defines his 'philosophy', as he grandiloquently calls his teaching, putting forward his ideas for a kind of higher education, suitable for men in public positions and orientated towards practical action. The sterile arguments of dialecticians like Socrates and Plato 'only provide a form of mental gymnastics and an introduction to real philosophy', his own:

I would gladly recommend young men to devote some time to such studies, but without allowing their minds to become desiccated or themselves to be bogged down in the theories of the sophists, which are so much hocus pocus, of no use but to draw fools into a circle (*Antidosis*, 268).

This is like Callicles in the *Gorgias* (see p. 269), who regarded the philosophy of Socrates as simply an introductory course, suitable for providing young people with general notions and commonplaces, before they settled down to the only worthwhile subject, rhetoric. In contrast, Plato looked upon the rhetoric of Isocrates as nothing more than a technique; a completely opposite conception.

Despite his complaints about his health, Isocrates remained full of energy to a ripe old age. At the age of ninety-seven, a year before his death, he wrote the *Panathenaicus*, one of his longest and most famous speeches, in which, not without vanity, he congratulates himself on still experiencing the intellectual excitement of youth. It was, so to speak, his political testament, though he no longer believed, as he had at the time of the *Panegyricus*, that Athens was destined to

lead a great Panhellenic crusade against Persia. Taking recent developments into account, he now urged that the invasion of Asia should
be undertaken by a number of rulers, especially Philip of Macedon—
in the event, it was the latter's son who realized the old man's project.
Isocrates was concerned that the freedom of the Greek cities should
be preserved, and envisaged their unification being achieved by
peaceful means; not, certainly, as a result of the battle of Chaioneia.
In this respect, his dream of the future proved to be chimerical.

Yet one has only to remember how few Greeks at that time, even
the most intelligent of them, were able to rise above the narrow
concept of the City State and envisage the welfare of Hellas as a whole,
in order to appreciate how advanced Isocrates' political ideas were.
Moreover, though he was convinced that any hope of achieving
knowledge by means of the dialectic was doomed to failure, he never
wavered in his devotion to the moral teachings of Socrates. His
Panhellenic dream has often been taxed with ingenuousness and
naïvety; and Demosthenes' implacable hostility to Philip has, at
first sight, seemed more realistic. Yet the policy of the latter proved
to be a failure, whereas Isocrates' insistence upon the necessity of
agreement and friendship (*eunoia*) between the Greek cities was, in
the long run, to serve a good and useful purpose. Georges Mathieu
has expressed the opinion that, all things considered, he was 'perhaps
the most influential political thinker of the fourth century'. Yet the
word 'thinker' applied to Isocrates somehow seems not quite right.
For my part, I look upon him rather as a sonorous echo; a man who
gathered together ideas that were already in the air and, by virtue of
his eloquence, gave them the widest currency.

As a writer of Greek prose, Isocrates was a great artist. Following
the attempts of Gorgias and many of the other rhetors to write prose
discourses that would achieve the harmony and beauty of poems, he
achieved formal perfection, though at the cost of a certain monotony.
As he proudly asserts in the *Antidosis*, his most accomplished speeches
'are more like works of art in their music and rhythm than the language
to be heard in the courts'. And, indeed, with its fine, often protracted,
periods and rhythmical cadences, and with the same assonances or
internal rhymes that one finds in Gorgias, his prose has a genuinely
musical and poetic quality. In this respect, he was certainly the
precursor of Cicero. Not everyone will enjoy this type of eloquence,
where the choice and subtle arrangement of the words is of greater
importance than the ideas, noble and generous as these may often be;

and it must in any case be admitted that the formal perfection of this accomplished rhetorician often borders on a somewhat mannered preciosity.

Theodor Gomperz has described Isocrates as 'a great man within limits'. Madame de Romilly considers him not to have been very intelligent, but she at once adds that 'in one way or another, we are all indebted to him'. And Marrou justly points out that, as Plato was the precursor of our training in philosophy, so Isocrates was in the case of rhetoric, for in the history of classical education their antagonism continued to prove fruitful. At the same time, the opinion of Isocrates that the philosophy class was only to be regarded as an introduction to the study of rhetoric has not been widely accepted, and posterity has finally settled the argument in favour of Plato.

THE ORATORS

The next three writers were all distinguished for their forensic speeches, a kind of writing that Isocrates had given up as soon as he could and which he later decried.

Cephalos, the wealthy, agreeable and wise old man whom we have already encountered in the *Republic*, chatting with Socrates, was a native of Syracuse. On the advice of his friend Pericles, he had established himself at Athens as an alien, bringing with him the prosperous arms factory in which he employed as many as a hundred and twenty slaves. Of his three sons, the eldest was Polemarchos, who also appears in the *Republic* and was devoted to the study of philosophy; and another was Lysias, who was born in Athens about 440, that is to say, shortly before Isocrates. Despite being an alien, Lysias was brought up with the sons of the leading families and later travelled in Italy and in Sicily, where his family had originated and which was also the cradle of rhetoric (see p. 198). After studying under several masters, he returned to Athens in 411, where he and Polemarchos ran their father's factory until, in 404, their wealth attracted the rapacity of the Thirty. Polemarchos was forced to drink the hemlock and Lysias, though he managed to escape, was ruined. The whole affair is described by the latter in his speech *Against Eratosthenes*.

A year later he returned to Athens with the leading democrats, who thought of conferring citizenship upon him, though the project came to nothing. To earn a living, Lysias became a speech-writer, dying in his eighties about 360. It would thus seem probable that as an old man he may have read the *Phaedrus*, in which Plato refers to him, quoting from his *Discourse on Love*; though this may simply have been a pastiche written by Plato.

Lysias wrote an immense number of such speeches, of which some thirty have come down to us, many of them fragmentary. Some of these were epideictic, like the *Olympicus* of 388, in which, eight years earlier than the *Panegyricus* of Isocrates, he already advocated unity and political agreement for the Greeks; not against the Persians, however, but against tyrannical rulers like Dionysius of Syracuse. Only two pages of this speech have been preserved.

Of all his forensic speeches, the only one he himself delivered was *Against Eratosthenes* in which he demanded that his brother's murderer should be punished. It opens simply and directly enough, though his pretence that he was unused to speaking in public is simply one of the commonplaces of the *captatio benevolentiae*: the narrative that follows is as remarkable for its clarity of exposition as for the deep feeling of its content. In the refutation he disposes in advance of the arguments Eratosthenes was to urge in self-defence. The peroration, where he compares the justice obtainable under the Thirty with that of the democracy, is powerful, but completely lacks the thunder and lightning that Demosthenes would have displayed in arguing such a case. As a whole, it is a masterpiece of grave and measured eloquence, often tinged with irony.

As a logographer, Lysias excelled Antiphon (see pp. 201–2), and even Isocrates. His clients were for the most part ordinary people, peasants, merchants or artisans, completely inexperienced in public speaking, and the speeches he wrote for them display all the naturalness and simplicity that are the two great qualities of his art. His gift for entering into the minds and characters of his clients enabled him to provide them with typical arguments expressed in their own words, and so most likely to persuade and move the judges. What is particularly interesting about these speeches is the insight they give us, like the comedies of Aristophanes, into the daily lives of ordinary people.

On the Murder of Eratosthenes is an attempt to justify Euphiletos, an Athenian who had killed his wife's lover, Eratosthenes; a kind of Don Juan, having no connection with the politician of the same name. Despite being called the 'Well-Beloved', Euphiletos was unfortunately far from being loved by his wife. As he explains:

To start with, my wife was in every way a model: a clever and economical housekeeper and an accomplished woman. But I lost my mother and her death was the beginning of all my troubles. For it was during the funeral that Eratosthenes first set eyes on my wife and it was not long before he succeeding in seducing her; he used to wait till the slave had gone to market and then sought her out and ruined her. But first I ought to tell you, for these details are important, that my house has two storeys, with the women's apartment upstairs and the men's downstairs. Then came the birth of our child whom my wife used to look after herself. Every time she wanted to give him a bath she had to go downstairs, which meant that there was always a risk of her falling. Accordingly, I decided to live on the first floor, and let the women sleep downstairs. I used to hear my wife get up during the night and lie down beside the baby to suckle it and stop it crying. And for a long time things went on like this without arousing my suspicions, because I was fool enough to imagine that my wife was the most honest woman in the whole city (7 ff.).

Unfortunately, she soon began to take advantage of this new arrangement, to entertain her lover Eratosthenes on the ground floor while her husband was blissfully asleep upstairs.

The whole speech is a typical domestic drama, with a succession of varied scenes, sometimes indoors sometimes in the street, and lively dialogue, full of picturesque detail, never exaggerated yet sometimes deeply moving. The characters—trusting husband, artful wife, cowardly womanizer, jealous mistress, accommodating slave and shady go-between—are all lightly but deftly drawn, with that extraordinary naturalness that distinguishes Lysias' art.

The background to the speech *Against Simon* is very different. The plaintiff begins like this:

My chief grudge against Simon, citizens of the Council, is that he has forced me to speak about such delicate matters in public. The only reasons I have put up with his behaviour for so long is that I was ashamed of exposing my weakness. . . . If you do not find it unreasonable that, at my age, I should feel like this about a young lad, I would ask you not to think ill of me: for, as you are aware, this is a passion all men are subject to. . . . Simon and I were both in love with Theodotos of Plataea. But whereas I tried to win his affection by treating him considerately, Simon thought he could force him to accept his advances by violence. . . . Simon further claims that he had made a contract with Theodotos, by which he was to pay him three hundred drachmas; and that it was I who intrigued to seduce the youth away from him (3 ff.).

The rest of the speech is an entertaining and picturesque account of the squabbles and brawls that took place between the two elderly lovers, sometimes indoors, sometimes even in the street.

The speech *For the Invalid* is a little masterpiece. In Athens, the poor who were too ill to earn a living were given a small allowance. But the list of those entitled to it was revised every year by the Council; and Lysias' client had been accused of being neither sick nor poor. The weakness of his case seems to have been that, despite his infirmity, he managed to obtain a modest livelihood, in some unspecified manner that obliged him to visit various people, either hobbling along on sticks or riding a borrowed horse. However, he defends himself energetically and wittily:

As to my skill as a horseman, which my accuser did not blush to refer to, I will be brief. Those whom luck has forsaken have only one idea in their heads: how best to adapt themselves to their unfortunate situation. In the miserable circumstances to which I have been reduced, I looked for the easiest possible way of making the long journeys I have to undertake. . . . If I could afford it, I should travel on a properly saddled mule, instead of riding other people's horses. . . . He did not mention the fact that I have to have two sticks to walk with, while other people only need one; but he did not use *that* to prove that I am a fit man. It was because I sometimes go on horseback that he chose to kick up a fuss, arguing that, on that account, I cannot be completely impotent. Now, the fact is, whether I use two sticks or a horse, it is for one and the same reason (10 ff.).

The weakness of his argument is, of course, obvious: his plaintiff's reference to the horse was not an attempt to prove that he was in fact able-bodied, but to show that he must have some resources. The plaintiff had also asserted that his shop was a meeting place for a band of rascals. On which he comments:

These accusations are no truer of me than of any other shopkeeper, nor of my customers than of theirs. You are all in the habit of visiting the scent shop, the barber's, the cobbler's, whenever you fancy, though you usually patronize the shops near the Agora and only occasionally visit those in more remote districts. To accuse all my customers of being rascals amounts to accusing the customers of all my fellow shopkeepers; in other words, what he is saying is simply that *all* Athenians are rascals (19 ff.).

On two occasions Lysias had to compose speeches against Alcibiades the Younger who had been defended by Isocrates in the chariot-racing case (see p. 282). In both cases, he vigorously and pertinently rebutted the disingenuous arguments with which Isocrates had attempted to justify the behaviour of the famous Alcibiades while in exile:

He had the audacity to claim that Alcibiades did nothing particularly reprehensible in fighting against his country. Doubtless there are those amongst you who, when in exile, took part in the capture of Phylae, felling trees and scaling walls. . . . But there is all the difference in the world between a man who fights on the side of the enemy against his fatherland, and patriots striving to regain their city when it was occupied by the Lacedaemonians! (*Against Alcibiades*, XIV, 32–3).

From this it is clear that, when occasion demanded, Lysias was quite capable of expressing indignation, and was not afraid to expose an opponent's dishonesty.

Andocides, an Athenian of noble birth, was born, like Lysias, about 440. His life was a tempestuous one. In 415, at the time when the Sicilian expedition was preparing to sail, as a member of the fashionable and wealthy set who hero-worshipped Alcibiades he was involved with the latter in the scandal arising from the mutilation of the Hermae. Thrown into prison, but later released for denouncing some of those who had taken part in the affair, he was deprived of his right to speak in the Assembly or take part in religious ceremonies. Preferring exile to such a humiliating position, he wandered from place to place, leading the life of a clever and unscrupulous adventurer. At the time of the general amnesty in 403, he returned to Athens where he hoped to take up politics, but he could not live down his past. In 399, the year of Socrates' trial and death, he was accused of having profaned the mysteries of Eleusis, but his speech in his own defence, *On the Mysteries*, which is still extant, secured his acquittal.

In 392 he was sent as one of the ambassadors to Sparta, with the aim of ending the war against Corinth, and on his return to Athens he delivered his speech *On the Peace* before the Assembly. But Athens denounced the negotiators and they were banished. Now approaching his fifties, Andocides once more became an exile and from then on nothing more is known of him.

Though he is traditionally listed among the ten Attic orators, the speeches of Andocides are on the whole dull and mediocre. True, there are moving passages in *On the Mysteries*, as when he describes the night in prison, in 415, when, under pressure from his friends, he turned informer; or, again, when he overwhelms with invective his worthless accuser, Epichares, who had been one of the Thirty. But Andocides cannot sustain this vigour, and all too soon relapses into a diffuse and repetitive style.

Since we possess not a single speech by Alcibiades, Theramenes or Critias, nor one by Callistratos, whom both Demosthenes and Aeschines regarded as the most eloquent orator of the preceding generation, nor by Phocion, whom Demosthenes used to call his 'axe', nor by Demades whose brutally powerful eloquence created so deep an impression, one can only feel that chance unduly favoured Andocides, by deciding that a speech by him should survive.

Isaeus' chief claim to fame was that he taught Demosthenes. We know practically nothing of his life, and the twelve forensic speeches that we have, all of which deal with questions of inheritance, though of great interest for the historian of Attic law, are boring for the ordinary reader. At most, there are occasional entertaining passages, as when in the *Philoctemon* he tells of how the aged Euctemon abandoned wife, children and home, in order to instal a one-time prostitute, Alke, 'as tenant of the pottery works that belonged to him, near the postern in the wine market'.

Hypereides belonged to the well-to-do bourgeoisie. He was said to have been the pupil of both Isocrates and Plato, but the latter did not succeed in converting him to the austerity of a philosopher's life, for he was well-known for his immoderate taste for high living, wine and women. He was one of the lovers of the famous courtesan Phryne, the mistress of the sculptor Praxiteles. When she was accused by one of her old lovers of having committed fornication in a sanctuary, a serious crime punishable with death, Hypereides defended her in court. Only fragments of his speech are extant, but the gesture with which he accompanied it has since served many an actor: tearing open her tunic, he exposed her breast to her judges as the climax of his peroration. This anecdote, though often questioned, may perhaps be true, for the Greeks attributed a deep religious significance to physical beauty. In their eyes, 'the charming gifts of golden Aphrodite, which come from the gods and that no man can acquire for himself', as Homer makes Paris say, were the outward manifestation of divine approval. Because of her beauty, Phryne was not to be judged like an ordinary woman.

Hypereides was also the lover of several other lesser known

courtesans: Myrrhina, one of the most expensive hetairai in Athens, Aristagora and Phila. He set up the first in his town house, the second in Piraeus and the third on his estate at Eleusis. He must have made a great deal of money as a logographer to indulge such extravagant tastes. Always active in politics, he was for a long time a staunch supporter of Demosthenes, and it was he who proposed the honours that were heaped on him shortly before the battle of Chaironeia. After the defeat, he set about organizing the defence of the city without much concern for the rights of property, and when, later, Demados accused him of acting illegally in this respect, he replied: 'For me, the armed might of Macedonia concealed the law: it was not I who was responsible for passing the decree you reproach me with, but the battle of Chaironeia.'

Towards the middle of Alexander's reign, the long alliance between Demosthenes and Hypereides broke up. Demosthenes was compromised in the affair of Harpalos, Alexander's treacherous treasurer, who came to Athens and bribed some of the city functionaries with money he had embezzled. Hypereides was one of the first to accuse his old friend and Demosthenes was banished. Eventually, however, at the time of the Lamian war, the two men were drawn together again by their patriotism and love of liberty. Hypereides was chosen to deliver the funeral oration for the men who had been killed at Lamia. Forced to flee by Antipater's victory, he was caught and executed in 322, having first been tortured, and Demosthenes committed suicide to avoid a similar fate.

No manuscript of Hypereides' works has come down to us, but, in the middle of the nineteenth century, important fragments of his speeches were found in Egyptian papyri. Only one of them, *For Euxenippos*, is tolerably complete; *Against Demosthenes* and the *Funeral Oration* are mere fragments.

In two of his speeches, *For Euxenippos* and *For Lycophron*, Hperereides was opposed by the orator Lycurgus, a dour defender of law and morals, and was hard put to it to save his clients from severe punishment. The trial of Euxenippos was an impeachment (*eisangelia*), a procedure usually reserved for those accused of serious crimes against the state or attempting to overthrow the democratic government. In fact, he was suspected of having misrepresented a revelation, vouchsafed to him at the sanctuary of the hero Amphiaraos with regard to some land belonging to Oropos, in the neighbourhood of the temple. He therefore opened the defence on a sarcastic note:

I am surprised that the judges are not disgusted by an impeachment on such grounds. In the past, such trials have been reserved for politicians accused of crimes against the state. . . . What is happening in our city today is quite laughable: Diognidos and the alien, Antidoros, have been impeached for paying more for their flute players than the rate laid down by law; Agasicles of the Piraeus for registering himself as a member of the deme of Halimous, and now Euxenippos is impeached for what he imagines he saw in a dream! (*For Euxenippos*, 1–3).

Lycophron had been accused of adultery. Hypereides' defence consists of a lengthy recapitulation of his irreproachable career as an officer and official. How could a man with such an honourable record be guilty of such a crime?—an argument that would appear not entirely to have convinced his editor, Gaston Colin; 'surely it is not impossible,' he comments, 'that an excellent officer and administrator may have solicited, or accepted, the love of a married woman?'

In the speech *Against Athenogenes*, Hypereides is more convincing, as well as being more amusing. His client, Epicrates, had fallen in love with a slave girl who worked in a scent shop on the Agora belonging to Athenogenes. The simplest way for the wealthy Epicrates to obtain the girl was to buy up the whole business, which he succeeded in doing thanks to the scarcely disinterested intervention of Antigona, a woman of easy virtue who was Athenogenes' mistress. Between them, the two latter had so arranged the deal that the naïve Epicrates soon discovered he had been swindled. In describing this sorry affair, Hypereides shows himself to have been as witty as Lysias, with the light Attic sense of comedy that we shall later find in Menander. Writing this speech thoroughly amused him and he enables us to share his amusement without in any way weakening his client's case.

There is nothing like this to be found in the grave and austere eloquence of Lycurgus, the avowed spokesman of morality and a severe critic of men like Euxenippos, Lycophron, and also Leocrates. Yet, according to tradition, he, like Hypereides, had studied under Isocrates and Plato: one can only suppose, therefore, that the two men were of very different temperament.

A member of the old Athenian nobility, Lycurgus was, with Hypereides, despite the very different tone of their speeches, a staunch supporter of Demosthenes in the latter's struggle for the safety and greatness of their country. It was after Chaironeia, when he was already past fifty, that his qualities began to make themselves felt. In those disastrous times, his sternness and energy, as well as his absolute honesty—a rare virtue at this period among politicians—won for him the lasting trust of the Athenians; and for twelve years, as the man responsible for finance and public works, he was the leading official in the State. Thanks to his strict and economical methods, he was able to find the money for a huge programme of construction (see p. 248). He died on his sick bed in 324 and seventeen years later a bronze statue to him was erected in the Agora.

The only speech of his that has come down to us is *Against Leocrates*. Terrified by the defeat at Chaironeia, Leocrates secretly fled from Athens to Rhodes, taking with him his mistress and money. After living at Megara for some five years, he returned to Athens, hoping that he would have been forgotten. But he was impeached by Lycurgus who demanded the death sentence. He was acquitted, but only by a majority of one vote.

Lycurgus' speech on this occasion is typical of the man's intransigeant and implacable harshness, but it is also filled with a high sense of duty. After the solemn exordium, it establishes the facts of the case and passes on to a defence of patriotism, illustrated by endless quotations designed to impress upon the judges his own ideal of civic virtue; the oath of the Athenian youths, the oath taken by the Greeks at Plataea, a long patriotic tirade from Euripides' *Erecthea*, Hector's exhortation of the Trojans from the *Iliad*, a poem by Tyrtaeus (see p. 98), and the epitaphs written by Simonides for the glorious dead at Thermopylae and Marathon. It is a regular anthology. He concludes:

Thus I denounce, before you the dispensers of justice, a man who has violated every custom of our country. It is for you to punish Leocrates in the name of the law and of the gods. . . . He has shown himself guilty of every crime: treason, attacks upon democracy, impiety, outrages against his family, desertion of his country and insubordination. In view of this, who is there among you who would wish to spare him? Who, by saving such a man, would be so short-sighted as to entrust our safety to one who was ready to abandon us? Who, out of pity, would be prepared to let our country be laid waste by an enemy as pitiless as he? Who, out of weakness for a man who has betrayed his country, would expose himself to the vengeance of the gods? (*Against Leocrates*, 146 ff.).

With its antitheses, its repetitions, its thrusting questions and emphatic phrasing, the style is suited to the thought: it is strained and sententious, utterly lacking in grace or irony, but its noble vehemence goes straight to the heart of the matter.

Aeschines, on the other hand, was not lacking in humour and he was also a wit. Born at Athens in 390, his childhood and youth were impecunious: his father, Atrometos (who lived to the age of 95) had been ruined under the rule of the Thirty and, in order to provide a livelihood for himself and his family, had to adopt the ill-paid profession of school-mastering. Aeschines himself, until he was appointed secretary to the Council, had been a scribe, and later an actor. His whole family, poor though always respected, despite Demosthenes' slanderous statements about them, slowly retrieved its position; and Aeschines' two brothers became respectively a general and an ambassador.

In 348, in his first speech before the Assembly, Aeschines denounced the threatening advance of Philip, but before long he was to change his mind and join the party of Euboulos. The latter, famous for his financial administration in the period before Lycurgus, was primarily concerned with maintaining peace, the only hope of ensuring a balanced budget: like Isocrates, he therefore supported a friendly policy towards Philip. This may, perhaps, have shown political wisdom, but, in view of Philip's persistent encroachments upon the rights of the Athenians and the territory of their allies, it involved continual concessions. It was against this policy that Demosthenes, backed by Hypereides and Lycurgus, revolted, with the result that he and Aeschines became the leading spokesmen for two utterly opposed policies.

The three speeches by Aeschines that we possess are all connected with his struggle against Demosthenes: *Against Timarchos* (345), the *On the Dishonest Embassy* (343), *Against Ctesiphon* (330). Aeschines won the first two rounds in this struggle, but Demosthenes won the last and the most important.

In 346 Demosthenes and Aeschines had been two of the ambassadors sent to negotiate the peace of Philocrates (see p. 245) with Philip. On their return, Demosthenes was convinced that Aeschines had behaved treacherously. A rich and influential politician, Timarchos, made himself responsible for Demosthenes' public accusation of Aeschines. But the latter retorted by accusing Timarchos of having, in his youth, accepted bribes; a crime which, if proved, would deprive him of his political rights. The case presented in his *Against Timarchos* resulted in conviction: Timarchos was sentenced and disappeared from political life.

Demosthenes, however, continued to press his charge with regard to the embassy and in 343 the case came before the court. As the plaintiff, Demosthenes spoke first and was followed by Aeschines. Both speeches have been preserved and have the same title: *On the Dishonest Embassy*. Aeschines was acquitted by a majority of thirty. Eventually, after Chaironeia, a certain Ctesiphon proposed to reward Demosthenes, despite the defeat, by presenting him with a gold crown in recognition of his great services to his country. Aeschines immediately accused Ctesiphon of having made an illegal suggestion. This was the origin of the case, *On the Crown*, which, under pressure of political events, did not come to trial until 330. It was then that Aeschines delivered his *Against Ctesiphon*, to which Demosthenes' *On the Crown* was the reply. On this occasion, Aeschines having, as plaintiff, failed to obtain one-fifth of the votes, he was obliged to pay a fine of 1,000 drachmas. Rather than pay, however, he preferred to quit Athens for Asia, carrying on his profession in exile at Ephesus and Rhodes. When and where he died is unknown.

In his last trial of strength with his rival, Aeschines was overwhelmed by the oratorical genius of Demosthenes, and many Hellenists have accepted the verdict. Whether he was in fact a traitor and had been bribed by Philip, I do not know, but it was never proved. Alfred Croiset said of him that he had 'all the vanity of an upstart literateur and actor . . . with a very mediocre intelligence.' But this judgment needs to be reconsidered. In *Against Timarchos*, which throws a curious light on certain aspects of Athenian life and contemporary legislation, Aeschines displays extreme cleverness. At no point does he allude to the personal circumstances that had brought him into the case. Like Lycurgus in *Against Leocrates*, he quotes several passages from Homer and Euripides, treating them as so many arguments against his opponent, and poses as the vigilant defender of public morality. Whether or not his indignation was sincere, he nevertheless succeeded in impressing the judges and Timarchos was condemned. The *Embassy* opens with the traditional appeal to the judges to show mercy to the accused, but then Aeschines suddenly goes over to the attack:

Athenians, I beg you to hear me with mercy, having due regard to the great danger of my position and the many accusations against which I have to defend myself. Nor should you forget the artifice, the manoeuvres or the cruelty of my accuser, who has not shrunk from urging you—you who have sworn to listen impartially to both sides—to disregard the case for the defence. He did not speak thus out of anger, but out of hatred for the truth. . . . Listening to his speech, I found myself as ever moved by feelings of terror, indignation and joy. I was overwhelmed with fear and I still tremble lest some among you, misled by his insidious and malignant antitheses, should have formed a false impression of me. How could I remain calm when I had to listen to him accusing me of having violated, under the influence of drink, a free woman of Olynthos? But when, at the very moment he was perpetrating this slander, you saw fit to interrupt him, I experienced a sense of joy (*On the Dishonest Embassy*, 1–4).

Aeschines then goes on to give a clear and circumstantial account of the various missions, paying strict attention to the dates. In the course of one of them he says Demosthenes suffered a curious misadventure, which he proceeds to describe with relish:

Following this speech and a number of others, it was Demosthenes' turn to speak in the presence of the king. Everybody listened with the greatest attention, expecting a miracle of eloquence: Philip and his advisers, as we afterwards learnt, had been informed that the orator was to make an outstanding speech, so that the audience was all ears. But presently the 'lion' began mumbling an obscure exordium in a voice trembling with fright and, before he had begun to develop his theme, suddenly broke off, lost countenance and was apparently robbed of the power of speech. Seeing the state he was in, Philip urged him to recover his composure: it was not a catastrophe, like an actor forgetting his part; let him take his time and continue his speech as he had intended. But Demosthenes, having once lost the thread of what he was saying, was unable to recover his self-control. He tried again, but it was useless. The same thing happened again; and the silence becoming unendurable, presently a herald invited us to retire (*Ibid.*, 34–5).

True, many of the arguments used by Aeschines in this speech are not very convincing. At times he gives the impression of pleading his own credulity, blindness and incapacity. Yet, more often, he displays the qualities of a genuine artist in words and, as we know, he succeeded for a second time in convincing the majority of his judges.

In his speech *Against Ctesiphon* where he was again the plaintiff, his task was a more delicate one. The man he was seeking to discredit was no longer Timarchos, of unhappy memory, but Demosthenes himself. To maintain that the great patriot had never acted except from egotism, greed or cowardice, to attribute to him every setback to his policy, and every success to the gods or to fortune, was a gamble. As a great advocate, able to argue even a bad case with skill, Aeschines took the risk, but when we come to consider Demosthenes' speech *On the Crown*, we shall see why Aeschines' remarkable talent was powerless against his opponent's patriotism, and, especially, against the torrential force of his eloquence.

Even admitting, however, that the language of Aeschines sometimes rings as hollow as that of the Sophists, it nevertheless has considerable purity, brilliance and beauty. The orator shows a consummate art in his use of vehemence and irony, of indignation and sarcasm. He is able to arouse passion in his listeners at one moment, and to soothe them at the next. He has more grace and wit than Demosthenes. A 'very mediocre intelligence' could not have stood up to the greatest orator of Greece and twice emerged victorious. Belittling Aeschines adds nothing to the stature of his opponent, who from every point of view was a man without equal.

DEMOSTHENES

Demosthenes, son of Demosthenes, of the deme of Paiania, was born at Athens in 384. His father, like Lysias', was a wealthy arms manufacturer who died when the boy was seven years old, after having appointed three guardians. They, however, only squandered his fortune. According to Plutarch, Demosthenes was a delicate child and his mother would not allow him to take part in athletics and wrestling. At the age of eighteen, having attained his majority, he began proceedings against his dishonest trustees. The preliminary discussions and interviews lasted three years, during which Demosthenes studied under Isaeus who specialized in probate cases (see p. 293). In 363, when he was twenty-one, he pleaded his own cause before the court and won, but he had to undertake three further legal actions and in the end only recovered a small part of his patrimony. His speeches against his trustees, which have been preserved, already display remarkable oratorical gifts; and though these tedious proceedings did little to improve his financial position, they helped to stiffen his determination, as well as giving him legal experience.

At an early age he was drawn to the Assembly, at first simply to listen to the famous speakers, and it seems to have been a speech by Callistratos that inspired him to become a tribune of the people. Plutarch says: 'Demosthenes envied Callistratos' fame, but even more he admired the power of his eloquence which, as he saw, enabled him to dominate his fellows. Henceforward, putting aside all other occupations, he spent his time training himself as a political speaker' (*Life of Demosthenes* ch. v). Plutarch also tells the well-known, but probably legendary, anecdotes about Demosthenes putting pebbles in his mouth to improve his elocution, proclaiming his speeches against the roar of the sea, and retiring to a cave in order to study.

His first attempts at public speaking proved to be a dismal failure, and in order to earn his living, he became a logographer, as Isocrates and others had done before him. We have a number of the speeches that he wrote for clients, most of them for civil cases, but also such political ones as *Against Androtion, Against Timocrates* and *Against Aristocrates*. *Against Leptines*, a political speech, was delivered in 355 by Demosthenes himself, representing two citizens who were appealing against Leptines' decree on immunity. In 354, at the age of thirty, he delivered the first of his speeches that has survived, *On the Naval Estimates*. Three years later came the thunderbolt of the *First Philippic*, followed by a rapid succession of speeches over the next ten years. Of these, the most important were, in chronological order, *For the Rhodians*, the three *Olynthiacs, On The Peace* (of Philocrates, in 346), the *Second Philippic*, the *Chersonese,* and the *Third* and *Fourth Philippics* (in 341).

In 347, having been publicly struck in the face at the theatre by a rich citizen, a member of the Euboulos faction, Demosthenes, who was at the time the choragist, composed his speech *Against Meidias*. As a settlement was arrived at, the speech may never have been delivered, but it is possible that Meidias had already been declared guilty before the terms were agreed upon. Four years later came the affair of the embassy already referred to (see pp. 297–8). From 340 to 338, having been elected to power by the popular vote, Demosthenes was responsible for the political affairs of the city and no longer had time or inclination to revise his speeches for publication. It was during this period that he negotiated the alliance with Thebes, which, if the fortunes of war had not proved favourable to Philip, would have saved both cities.

With the defeat of Chaironeia, Athens ceased to be independent and for a time Demosthenes remained silent. Nevertheless the affair of the 'golden crown', which came before the courts in 330, provided an opportunity for him to defend his political career, then being violently

criticized by Aeschines. This tremendous duel not only profoundly
stirred the Athenians, it also attracted many Greeks from other cities
who flocked to the trial.

In 324 there was the Harpalos case, in which Hypereides was one
of the prosecutors. Demosthenes was convicted on suspicion of
bribery and escaped into exile (see p. 294). As soon as the news of
Alexander's death reached Athens, however, Hypereides and Demosthenes became reconciled and the latter returned to the city in triumph.
Almost immediately the Lamian war broke out; and Demosthenes,
once again banished by the Macedonian party, sought refuge in the
sanctuary of Poseidon on Calaureia, a small island off the coast of
Argolis. His whereabouts was soon discovered by his enemies who
were determined to arrest him, despite the rights of asylum. Thereupon
Demosthenes poisoned himself.

Almost all the speeches of Demosthenes that were known to the
Ancients have been preserved, the most regrettable loss being his
defence in the Harpalos case. But, of the sixty speeches bearing his
name that have come down to us, several, especially those dealing
with civil issues, are either dubious or definitely not attributable to him.

From the start, Demosthenes was a man of action, pledged to a
positive policy. Lulled by the material prosperity under Euboulos,
the Athenians had gradually allowed their political position to be
eroded. Suddenly the *First Philippic* confronted them with the
realities of the situation.

Do you not see, people of Athens, how impudent this Philip has become,
not even leaving you the choice whether you will take action or remain
at peace? While we temporize instead of acting, he is continually entangling
us in his net. When are you going to make up your minds to undertake
what has to be done? Do you want to delay until necessity forces your hand?
And if that were to happen, what name should we deserve? For my part,
the most urgent question for a free man is to maintain his honour. Answer
me: are you prepared to spend the rest of your lives running about the
streets, asking each other for the latest news? What news do you need but
this: that a Macedonian, a barbarian, is continually defeating the Athenians
and taking the control of Greek affairs into his own hands? Is Philip dead?
asks one. No, he is only sick, replies another. Dead or sick, what matters
it to you? Why, if he were to disappear from the face of the earth, you
yourselves, by your neglect of your own interests, would create a new
Philip. It is not only his strength that makes him so powerful: even more,
it is our own stupidity. . . . You, people of Athens, though you possess a

mightier force than anyone else, in triremes, in hoplites, in cavalry, in revenue, you have had no advantage of it up to now because, when Philip threatens you, you behave like barbarians who fight with their bare fists. As soon as one of them gets hit, he puts his hand to the spot: he gets another blow and again he covers up. He has no idea of parrying the blows and watching his enemy in order to forestall him. So it is with you. When you hear Philip is in the Chersonese, you rush reinforcements there; then he is at Thermopylae, so you hurry off again. You allow yourselves to be end-lessly manoeuvred, foreseeing nothing until after it has happened. Truly, it must be a god, blushing for the way you allow yourselves to be treated, who inspires Philip to act, simply in order to shake you out of your in-difference—unless, of course, you have already decided to give up. How can you expect to win, when the triremes you dispatch are armed with nothing but your hopes? Is it not time we ourselves began to man the ships? Should *we* not be fighting our own battles? Will it never be *our* ships that attack? (*First Philippic*, 9 ff.).

The short, breathless sentences, the insistent questions, the ironical picture of the Athenians worrying about Philip's state of health instead of acting, the sudden assertion that he is only a creation of their own fears, the metaphors of the inexperienced boxer and of the ships filled with hope instead of men—here was a kind of eloquence never before heard, utterly unlike the stately periods of Isocrates or the subtleties of Lysias. The eloquence of Demosthenes' great speeches is itself action; a thing of nerve and muscle, striking, lashing, dis-concerting, inspiring. One feels even in the printed word, the violence of his gestures. Aeschines says that, when he was speaking, he prowled about the platform 'like a tiger'. Even reading him, one can hear the vibration of his voice; as Montaigne says, 'his words leap from the paper as once they did from his lips'.

With Demosthenes, the springs of action were his burning patriot-ism, and his high conception of the politician's role in a democracy. Again and again, when describing a 'spokesman of the people' (*symboulos*), he portrays the kind of man he himself strove to be: 'a man who, despite you, seeks your good, a man whose words aim, not to win favour and popularity, but to attain the good of all.' The very reverse of a demagogue, he was fully justified in saying to the Athenians: 'I have given myself to your cause without reservation.'

Everything goes to show that, in addition to his utter devotion, his sense of responsibility and complete frankness, Demosthenes had a clear grasp of politics and unusual competence. Thus, in his speech

On the Crown, he was able to explain, without false modesty, why he was the one man whose advice the people were prepared to accept after the fall of Elateia (see p. 246):

It was in the evening; the occupation of Elateia had just been announced by the Magistrates. Immediately, some got up in the middle of their dinner and began driving the people from the booths on the Agora, and setting fire to them, while others summoned a council of war and ordered the trumpets to be sounded. The whole city had gone mad. Next morning, at daybreak, the Assembly met at the Pnyx to hear the report of the Magistrates and of the man who had brought the news. Then the herald demanded: 'Who wishes to speak?' Not a man moved. Several times the herald repeated his question, but still no one stood forth. Yet all the generals were there, and all the politicians, and our country was crying out for a man who would speak in her name, for the herald's voice was the legal voice of the people. . . . But what the times demanded was not just a man who was devoted, but a man who was in touch with everything that had happened from the beginning, who had considered seriously Philip's motives and his aims. And, that day such a man appeared, and it was I. . . . But where were you, Aeschines? What did you do in this crisis? You, who seek to malign me by nicknaming me *Battalos,*[1] you who brag that you used to play the hero on the stage, a Cresphontes or a Creon, even an Oenomaos, a part you once completely ruined? That day I proved that I, Battalos of Paiania, was worthier to serve our country than you, Oenomaos of Cothokeides (*On the Crown,* 169 ff.).

Beginning with the brief, but gripping account of the effect of the loss of Elateia on the Athenians, the passage ends with a wounding attack on his main political opponent. The reference to Aeschines, the one-time actor of 'bit parts' who had been hissed for forgetting his lines in the role of Oenomaos, shows a sense of humour rarely to be found in Demosthenes.

Politically, Demosthenes may well have been an idealist. Certainly, the prudent and realistic policy of Euboulos seemed to him unworthy of Athens; and, in opposing it he often invokes the Beautiful (*to kalon*) and the Just (*to dicaion*). At such moments, his style reminds one of Thucydides, whose works he had repeatedly studied, not only for their style but for the political lessons to be learnt from them. Beauty and Justice are ideals that governments as well as individuals must always strive for. Usually, moreover, they are conducive to expedience:

---

[1] Battalos means either *stammerer* or *backside.*

it was in the interests of Athens to behave honourably, to remain faithful to her historic role (*ethos*), while at the same time defending the weak and opposing every threat to her freedom. Fully aware that the time for the brutal imperialism of the fifth century had gone by, Demosthenes was nevertheless determined to save what he could of the moral and material heritage bequeathed by Themistocles, Cimon and Pericles. For him, the Athens of Pericles remained the supreme exemplar to which he constantly refers.

The effectiveness of this idealism is powerfully revealed in *On the Crown*, the great speech in which he justifies his policy against Aeschines who in *Against Ctesiphon* had repeatedly insisted that it had led to the disaster of Chaironeia. Shortly after the passage just quoted Demosthenes goes on:

Do not attribute Philip's success to my mistakes, for the result of the battle was in the hands of the gods, not mine. But if you can prove that I failed to take the best decisions available to human reason, that I omitted to act justly and zealously, exerting myself beyond my strength, or that the course upon which I resolved was in any way unnecessary, ignoble or unworthy of our country, only then can you accuse me. If the hurricane that was let loose proved to be too strong not only for us, but for all the other Greeks, what were we to do? It is as though a captain who had taken every precaution for the safety of his ship, who had provided it with every means of protection, should be held responsible when he ran into a storm that swept away the rigging. Surely he would say: 'But I was not the helmsman (as I might say, I was not the general). I am not the master of fate, who controls all things. . . .' Since Aeschines has chosen to dwell so much on the past, I will add this. It may appear paradoxical, but, by Zeus and all the gods, let no one be astounded by my insistence. Let him consider what I have to say with goodwill. Even if the future had been foreseen by everyone, if everyone had known it in advance, if you, Aeschines, had proclaimed it and borne witness to it, even then, our country should not have acted otherwise than she did, unless she had ceased utterly to care for her fame, her ancestors and her posterity (*On the Crown*, 193 ff.).

Since it was Aeschines who was convicted, it would appear that this paradoxical, or at any rate extremely bold, argument convinced the Athenians.

Demosthenes' idealism, moreover, never impaired his positive and realistic appreciation of political and military realities. Like a good general he foresaw everything that was humanly predictable. In his speech *On the Naval Estimates*, he outlines a whole plan for financial reorganization. In the *Philippics* and the *Olynthiacs* he lays down precisely what was to be done, the number of ships to be equipped and of infantry and cavalry to be despatched, as well as the stores and expenditure that would be required. More than this, with regard to Philip's intentions, he never shared the illusions complacently indulged by Euboulos, Aeschines and Isocrates.

Was Demosthenes solely influenced by patriotic motives? Aeschines and he continually accuse one another of taking bribes, but this is not proof; in any case, to accuse one's opponents of venality was a commonplace of political controversy. At the same time, there seems to be little doubt that, in the Harpalos affair, Demosthenes was embarrassed by the suspicion of complicity. According to Plutarch, 'he arrived in the Assembly with his neck carefully wrapped up in a woollen scarf, and when they shouted at him to mount the tribune he made a gesture of refusal, indicating that he had lost his voice, though ill-natured wits maintained that what the orator was suffering from was not a sore throat but a "silver" throat.' Later, his sore throat having disappeared, he defended himself, but was nevertheless sentenced to the enormous fine of 50 talents. Unable to pay it, he was committed to prison; but he managed to escape and fled into exile.

It is also possible that, at an earlier period, he may have accepted money from the Persians who, fearing an attack by Philip, were ready to support everyone who opposed him. But, even if he did, it is by no means certain that he kept the money for himself; it may well have formed part of one of the many voluntary donations he made to the Athenian treasury. Some scholars, particularly Germans, have tried to prove that Persian bribes largely accounted for his implacable hostility to Philip. But when the charge is examined against the whole background of his life and achievements, it seems impossible to sustain and may be dismissed.

No one was better aware of Demosthenes' redoubtable power than Philip himself. Plutarch has described how, after the battle of Chaironeia, where he was afraid that everything might be lost, 'he could not restrain his joy, but danced amidst the bodies of the slain, drunkenly singing the preamble to Demosthenes' decrees and beating time with his feet: I, Demosthenes, son of Demosthenes, of the deme of Paiania, hereby declare . . .' (*Life of Demosthenes*, ch. xxv.).

Unlike most of the orators who succeeded Gorgias, Demosthenes used the spoken Attic language of his day, without neologisms, archaisms or poetic borrowings. His speeches were not show pieces, designed to display his artistic skill and dazzle his listeners; he spoke with the sole purpose of convincing. But if his vocabulary was derived from everyday speech, his syntax was peculiarly his own; and the result was a natural, lively style, not afraid of the inconsistencies and vivid constructions that throw ideas into relief, and utterly unlike the monotonous uniformity of Isocrates. The key word always stands out, and every sentence is designed to express, not the cold logic of the orator, but the passionate ebb and flow of the speaker's feelings. And yet this vigorous, intensely original style is always perfectly clear. Metaphor and imagery are infrequent, never elaborated, but always appropriate and striking. They are the perfect embodiment of the thought behind them; one never feels they were added for the sake of ornament.

Argument is the soul of Demosthenes' eloquence. His purpose was to convince the Athenians; intelligent people for the most part, not easily misled. His dialectic, full of good sense and authority is tenacious, supple and compulsive. Often, to hold the attention of his audience, he suddenly introduces a paradox: 'What you have lost up to now, Athenians, is precisely what may yet save you.' Sometimes he insists: 'What I am about to say may sound like a paradox, yet, as you will see, it is the truth.' To give life and animation to his speeches, he makes use of dialogue, first stating the views of an imaginary opponent, then slashing his argument to pieces in an oratorical duel that reminds one of the *stichomythia* used by the tragic poets. But he seldom smiles; his rare flashes of wit are usually sarcastic insults.

From the point of view of their general structure, his speeches defy all the rules of oratory, except for a brief exordium and a weighty and powerful peroration. He sets out the essential ideas he intends to develop without any preconceived plan, but never loses sight of the conclusion he has in mind, to which everything is conducive, even his apparent digressions. His sole aim is to carry conviction. Many of the ancient teachers of rhetoric were shocked by his speeches; they considered them to be lacking in eloquence because they neglected the precepts of the schools and they preferred orators whom it was easier for their pupils to imitate. But behind his spontaneous passion lies an art that is at once consummate and inimitable.

In his *Letter to the Academy*, Fénelon said: 'Cicero's artistry is marvellous, but one sees through it to the orator himself: when he is speaking of the safety of the republic, he never forgets himself, nor does he allow us to forget him. Demosthenes seems to have left himself behind, so that all he sees is the fatherland. He does not strive for beauty: he creates it without thinking about it. He is beyond admiration. He uses language as a modest man uses clothes, to cover himself. He thunders and lightens, and the torrent sweeps everything before it. We cannot criticize him, because we are possessed by him; we think of what he is saying, not of the words he is using. We forget about him: Philip alone concerns us and absorbs our attention. Both these orators delight me: but I confess that I am less moved by the infinite artistry and magnificent eloquence of Cicero than by the swift directness of Demosthenes.'

ARISTOTLE

The life of Aristotle covers exactly the same period as that of Demosthenes; both men lived from 384 to 322. The philosopher was born at Stagira, a Greek colony in Macedonia, north of Athos. His father Nicomachos, was the personal physician and friend of king Amyntas II, so that Aristotle and Philip II knew each other from childhood. Possibly, before he died, Nicomachos may have had time to initiate his son in the science of Hippocrates.

In 367 Aristotle went to Athens to complete his studies. He was then seventeen and it is believed that he spent some time studying rhetoric under Isocrates: but, if so, it was not long before he left him to enter Plato's Academy, where he was to remain until the latter's death some twenty years later. Plato soon noticed his disciple's outstanding gifts, and used to call him 'the intelligence' or 'the reader' (he read practically everything and was a kind of walking encyclopaedia), and to start with he put him in charge of the rhetoric class. Aristotle is said to have begun his first lecture by parodying a line from Euripides, 'Should I, then, remain silent and allow the barbarians to speak?' substituting "Isocrates" for barbarians'.

With the exception of Socrates, every ancient philosopher spent some time in travel, both to see the world and to gather information. After Plato's death, Aristotle left Athens with his friend, Xenocrates (after Seusippus, he was to become Plato's second successor as head of the Academy), and went to live at Atarneos, a town in Asia Minor, opposite Lesbos. Aristotle's guardian, Proxenos, was a citizen of Atarneos, and the chief magistrate of the town, Hermias, had invited the philosopher to visit him. This Bithynian eunuch, who had risen to become the tyrant of the district, later became devoted to philosophy and transformed his tyranny into a liberal government. Aristotle was much more readily welcomed by Hermias than Plato had been by Dionysius of Syracuse, and he was able to achieve for the small state of Atarneos what Dion and Plato had vainly dreamt of for Sicily. Hermias installed Aristotle and Xenocrates at Assos, a town in Troas that belonged to him, where they were joined by Calisthenes, Aristotle's nephew, and Theophrastos, a native of Eresos in Lesbos. Here, Aristotle formed his first group of disciples, whom he later took with him to Mytilene, on the neighbouring island of Lesbos.

In 342 Philip appointed Aristotle as tutor to Alexander, then aged fourteen. Until 335, therefore, he lived in Macedonia with his pupil, usually at the royal palace at Mieza, near Pella, sometimes visiting his native town of Stagira, which had been destroyed and rebuilt. His influence on Alexander was undoubtedly profound. Above all, he strove to inculcate in him the spirit of 'magnanimity', the heroic virtue that lies at the heart of Aristotelian morality; and Alexander came to regard himself as another Achilles. It was from Aristotle, too, that he derived his interest in science and scientific investigations, and later used to send him from Asia specimens of rare plants and animals. Like Napoleon in Egypt, he surrounded himself with scientists: he despatched a scientific mission to the Sudan to study the flooding of the Nile, a problem that had interested Herodotus; and it was on his orders that Nearchos navigated the coast of Asia and explored the Euphrates and the Indus.

When, in 341, Hermias was captured by the Persians and crucified, his young sister, Pythia, fled to the Macedonian court, where she became the wife of Aristotle, then aged forty-five: but shortly after the birth of a daughter, also called Pythia, she died. Later, Aristotle took a second wife, Herpyllis, a native of Stagira, by whom he had a son, Nicomachos.

In 335, his pupil having set out to conquer Asia, Aristotle left Macedonia and returned to Athens, the Mecca of philosophers, where he remained for thirteen years. There, near the shrine of Apollo Lykeios, he set up his own school at the Lyceum, whose pleasant 'walks' (*peripatoi*) were to bequeath their name to his disciples: the Peripatetics. In the nature of things, the Lyceum became the rival of the Academy, at that time under the direction of his friend Xenocrates. The creation of a second school was fully justified, for though Aristotle never lost his veneration for Plato, there were several important issues on which his own philosophy differed from that of the master: *Plato amicus, sed magis amica veritas*.

In 325 Callisthenes, Aristotle's nephew, who had accompanied Alexander as official historiographer, was condemned to death for refusing to prostrate himself before the emperor in the oriental manner. From that moment, all correspondence between the conqueror and the philosopher ceased. After Alexander's death, when Hypereides and Demosthenes were once again summoning the Greeks to fight for freedom, it was dangerous for Aristotle, a known friend of the Macedonians, to remain in Athens. He was charged with impiety. Whereupon, wishing, as he said, to spare the Athenians 'another opportunity to commit a crime against philosophy'—they had already put Socrates to death—he fled to Chalcis on the island of Euboea. There, in 322, after a long period of suffering, he died of a disease of the stomach. His will, preserved for us by Diogenes Laertius, proves him to have been an affectionate and devoted husband and father; nor did he forget his slaves and their children to whom he granted freedom.

The volume of Aristotle's writings was prodigious: some four hundred works, dealing with every aspect of knowledge and philosophy, *de omni re scibili*, of which forty-seven have come down to us almost complete, as well as fragments of about a hundred others. Unfortunately for the history of literature, what we have today are the *esoteric* or *acromatic* writings, those addressed to his intimate circle and not intended for the general public. His *exoteric* works, in which he described the progressive development of his austere and rigorous science for the general reader, have been lost; those, precisely, that would have most interested and delighted us today. It is known that, like Plato, he did write dialogues for publication and we are assured by the Ancients who had the opportunity of reading them that, though they lacked the magical beauty of Plato's style, they were admirably written, in a language that seems to have been closer to oratory than to poetry. Thus, as a writer, Aristotle's position is exactly the opposite of Plato's: in the case of the latter, we have only his literary works, of the former, only his teaching. In fact, the extant works of Aristotle, being of a largely technical nature, are lacking in charm and have little literary merit. The language they are written in is simply a means of intellectual communication and not, as is so often the case with Plato, a medium for poetic and musical incantation. Moreover, Aristotle's insistence upon absolute precision in the expression of his ideas frequently involves the use of a special vocabulary, abstract and difficult, with such expressions as 'things in themselves' and 'quiddities'. Presumably this kind of jargon is inevitable for the expression of subtle and precise ideas, since so many philosophers, theologians and scientists (in other languages as well as Greek) have found it necessary to imitate Aristotle in this respect.

Yet Aristotle was a very great philosopher and a very great scientist. As a philosopher and metaphysician he was much more practical and realistic than Plato. He was the originator of induction, that is to say, before arriving at a synthesis, he inisted upon the scientific accumulation of documentary evidence and observed facts. He did not completely dismiss the dialectic, but he no longer relied upon it as Socrates and his immediate disciples had done, as the sole means of attaining ultimate truth. According to him, it is impossible to grasp the essence of things (*ousia*) by pure logic. His conception of Ideas differed from Plato's; he regarded them as existing, not outside and above the universe, but within it and by means of it. The philosopher, he considered, ought not to withdraw from the visible world and lose himself among more or less personified abstractions such as the Good or the Beautiful, but should study every kind of reality patiently and at first-hand before claiming to have arrived at its essence.

It was this conviction that led Aristotle to undertake his immense investigations into art and history, as well as nature. For him, concrete study must precede and condition philosophy, which was to be the final synthesis of all human knowledge. That is why, with the help of his pupils and even of Alexander, he set about providing a prodigious encyclopedia of the learning of his period. Unfortunately, in a number of fields, this knowledge was dubious and tentative; today, it sometimes even appears laughable, as when we find him accepting Herodotus' description of the anatomy and behaviour of certain animals that he himself had been unable to examine.

As regards their fundamental ideas, there is a close connection between the ideas of Aristotle and Democritus, (see pp. 295–6), in the sense that both were aware of the importance of scientific observation (not, I should say, of experiment). In the Hellenistic period, this was to achieve remarkable results, but in the course of centuries it was above all to lead to the prodigious growth of human knowledge and technical attainment of the present day.

Here, I only propose to speak, and then briefly, of those of Aristotle's works concerned with aesthetics, morality and history.

Both the *Poetics* which consist of unfinished lecture notes and the three books of his *Rhetoric* are of the greatest value, and quite indispensable to the student of Greek literature. They are full of new and profoundly intelligent insights, for Aristotle had devoted as close and serious attention to the works of poets and orators as to natural history, the physical world and metaphysics. We have already quoted some of the opinions expressed in the *Poetics*, particularly with reference to Homer and Euripides (see pp. 16, 25 and 210). Here, too, the well-known theory of the 'three unities' was formulated for the first time, although only the unity of action is explicitly mentioned. Again, Aristotle notes:

The difference between the historian and the poet does not consist in the fact that the one writes in prose and the other in verse (one could put the works of Herodotus into verse and it would still be history); what distinguishes them is that the historian describes events that have already happened, the poet describes those that might happen. Moreover, poetry is more philosophical and of a higher order than history, for it describes the general aspect of things; history, the particular (*Poetics*, IX, 1451 b).

Like Plato, he considers imitation to be the basis of epic poetry and tragedy, as indeed of all the arts, but he does not on that account condemn them, since he believes that true poetry is more philosophical in its nature than history.

The *Nicomachean Ethics* accepts the principle that happiness is the aim of all men, though each individual will understand it in his own way. More liberal-minded than Plato, he does not reject either pleasure or ambition, but a careful study of human existence leads him to the conclusion that of all goods the most reliable and enduring are those of the spirit, through which men attain virtue by the habitual exercise of free will. Moral good consists in applying the doctrine of the mean; in generosity, which is the mean between greed and prodigality, in courage, which avoids the extremes of cowardice on the one hand and of temerity on the other, and so on. *In medio stat virtus*. Of all the virtues which, like the vices, he carefully analyzes, the one he most admires is spiritual greatness, magnanimity. The full meaning of this conception can only be understood by reading his splendid description of the magnanimous man, the sage, in Book IV, Chapter 3 of the *Ethics*.

With regard to this portrait, it is interesting to note the increasing attention that the Peripatetics were to devote to the study of character.

Theophrastos of Erosos, whose real name was Tyrtamos, had first joined Aristotle's circle at Assos and was to become his most devoted disciple and friend. When the master had to flee Athens in 323, it was to Theophrastos that he entrusted the direction of the Lyceum. He lived to a great age and, like most of the Peripatetics, he wrote prolifically. One of his works that has survived, written about 319, is a short book that was to be translated and imitated by La Bruyère, his *Characters*, in which he describes, not the magnanimous man, but the vices and peculiarities of the flatterer, the chatterbox, the niggard, the superstitious man, the vain man, the coward and so on.

The conception of love advanced in the *Nicomachean Ethics*, is also very different to that held by Plato. Love is seen as a form of friendship (*philía*). Even the magnanimous man, though in a sense self-sufficient, needs friends, since man is above all a 'social being'. In fact,

friendship is necessary if we are to practise virtue. A virtuous friend is indispensable to the virtuous man. He will provide him with the opportunity of doing good, and nothing is better than doing good to a friend, for the sake of friendship, because one loves him. Through friendship, too, the magnanimous man will experience the pleasure of accepting. And again, it teaches him the value of giving, of sacrificing himself, which we see as the highest manifestation of life; as it were, the peak of greatness and of beauty.

Married love is only a particular case of friendship. Plato, a celibate, had little to say about marriage. Aristotle, who had two wives and was devoted to both of them, writes in the warmest terms of this abiding, mutual affection. Though he does not fully accept the equality of men and women, he condemns infidelity on either side as 'a shame and infamy'. Like Socrates, he is strongly opposed to pederasty, which, whether it is a vice or an illness, he regards as a barbarian practice, unworthy of the Greeks.

Like Plato, Aristotle was passionately interested in politics, though in a rather different way. He describes man as 'a creature intended to live in cities'. But instead of propounding a series of somewhat contradictory conclusions, like the *Republic* or the *Laws*, he makes a close study of all known constitutions. The Alexandrians possessed a hundred and fifty-eight treatises, by him or his immediate disciples, describing the political institutions of various countries of which we should have had nothing but a few fragments, had it not been for the chance discovery in 1891 of a papyrus containing the major part of the *Constitution of Athens*.

This work comprises two parts: the first historical, the second descriptive. It starts with an account of Athenian institutions from the time of Solon onwards (an earlier section is missing), then proceeds to give a detailed account of government and the administration of justice in contemporary Athens: the registration of citizens, the appointment of magistrates, either by lot or by election, the courts of law. The account of the Heliaion and its different sections may be somewhat meticulous, but it throws a brilliant light on an amazingly complex organization. The discovery by American archaeologists, on the Agora, of some of the machines used for drawing lots for the judges (*kleroteria*) has recently served to clarify and confirm this exhaustive description.

Aristotle did not underrate the history of events, but he also fully understood the importance of institutions, of political and social structure, and also, like Thucydides, of economic factors. This may be clearly seen from his *Politics*, the synthesis of a lifetime's reflection, and a work of fundamental importance, though unfortunately incomplete and containing a number of interpolations and regrettable transpositions.

In it, he first studies the elementary forms of society, based on the economy of the family, but in a spirit very different from Xenophon's. Here he expresses some curious views about slavery, the necessary basis of the city in antiquity. He then goes on to consider what are the best forms of government, taking into account not only the actual constitutions that he has already described, but also the Utopian proposals of Plato and several other writers. From this he derives a general theory that monarchy degenerates into tyranny, aristocracy into oligarchy, democracy into demagogy. This is not unlike Plato, but Aristotle stresses the point that the decline of the best form of government, monarchy, leads to the worst, tyranny: *corruptio optimi pessima*. Oligarchy does less harm than tyranny; and, taking everything into account, demagogy is better than oligarchy. He then tackles—something Plato never attempted, even in the *Laws*—the problem of practical politics: like the naturalist and biologist that he was, he attempts to provide what we should call the morphology and pathology of government. And, finally, he too puts forward his proposals for the ideal city and the best kind of education.

Apart from physics and metaphysics, of which I have said nothing, one sees what it is that distinguishes Aristotle from Plato. He does not reject all syntheses, but he insists that they must be based on tremendous practical research, which explains why his work is one immense encyclopaedia. For him, documentation, information and observation are the first duty of a philosopher, who must therefore be, in the first place, a scientist; and a universal scientist at that. For Plato, the *Idea* is the first and ultimate reality: for Aristotle, *Facts* are primary, and philosophy will only lose itself in cloudy abstraction if it loses sight of or fails to appreciate their significance. As one might expect, Plato, whose work, according to Pascal 'is a fitting introduction to Christianity', was admired and used by many of the Fathers of the Church, but—what is at first sight surprising, and what I shall not attempt to explain—of the two, it was Aristotle who became for the Middle Ages and for Aquinas the most reliable guide, the 'philosopher' par excellence.

POETRY: MENANDER

Aristotle wrote two poems: an elegy to his disciple, Eudemos of Rhodes; and a *skolion*, written in memory of his friend Hermias of Atarneus. The latter is of considerable interest:

Virtue, object of men's labours, noble aim of human life, for your beauty, O virgin, Greeks tirelessly strive and even give their lives. Mighty is the desire for fame you instil in our hearts, that immortal fruit, more precious than gold or noble birth, more precious than sweetest sleep! What sufferings did Heracles, son of Zeus, undergo in pursuit of you, or the twin sons of Leda! For love of you, Achilles and Ajax descended into Hell; and for the sake of your beloved beauty, the son of Atarneus, too, forsook the light of day. Thus his deeds deserve to be sung, that the Muses shall grant him immortality, the daughters of Memory, who shall make the glory of welcoming Zeus shine in his honour and the gifts of faithful friendship (*Athenaea*, xv, 696 a).

Plato, too, wrote tragedies in his youth. As Alfred Croiset has said: 'In the fourth century, educated Greeks could compose an ode or an elegy without being poets, in the same way that an eighteenth-century Frenchman would produce a rhymed epigram or a letter in verse.' But whereas even in the fifth century, philosophers like Parmenides or Empedocles were still using verse to express their ideas, by the fourth century poetry had for many writers become simply a *parergon*, as the Greeks used to say, a graceful and rather frivolous accomplishment. Socrates himself had set the fashion when, in obedience to the god's command to 'make music', that is to devote himself to the service of the Muses before he died, he set about turning Aesop's fables into verse. The fourth century marked the end of a long period of literary development, admirably defined by Plutarch (see pp. 112 ff.); though it still produced some genuine poets, it was essentially the century of prose.

The choral lyric was not yet dead, especially in Athens. One proof, amongst many, is the inscription to be found on the monument of Lysicrates, dating from the year 334.

Lysicrates, son of Lysitheides, of the deme of Cicynna, being master of the ceremonies, the tribe of Acamantis won the children's prize. Theon played the flute; Lysiades taught the choir; Euainetos was archon (*Sylloge Insc. Gr.* III, 1087).

There were dithyrambic as well as children's choirs, who were accompanied sometimes by the flute, sometimes by the lyre; and the men who trained the choirs were poets. Each of the ten tribes provided a choir which was recruited and maintained by a choragist. Performances took the form of contests, as with the plays that developed out of the dithyramb. At ordinary festivals, the prize, which was offered by the government, consisted of a tripod; at the Panathenaia, it was a gold crown. The choragist Lysicrates had been the winner of a tripod which may still be seen surmounting his charming monument. Much information about these choirs is to be found in the works of orators such as Antiphon, Demosthenes and Lysias.

Amongst the inscriptions at Delphi are two hymns by the poet Aristonoös of Corinth, to Hestia and to the Pythian Apollo. The latter, consisting of six strophes, begins like this:

If in sacred Python, on the rock of Delphi, it is always you who sit in the seat of the divine oracle—all hail, O Apollo—you, the lordly son in whom Leto, born of Coeos, and almighty Zeus take pride, it is by the will of the Blessed—hail, all hail! (*Fouilles de Delphe*, III, 2, 190).

The hymn to Hestia, 'mistress of Olympus and the earth', though much shorter, lacks neither variety nor eloquence. The author, who wrote these poems for the Delphic festival, and who, on his return about 335, was overwhelmed with honours by the people, was a skilful versifier.

The best known lyric poets of this period were Timotheos of Miletus, and Philoxenos. The former lived to the age of ninety, from 447 to 357, and during his long artistic career was as famous as Pindar. He competed in almost all the important cities of Greece and Asia Minor, performing his dithyrambs, *nomes*, hymns and odes. In his *Birthpangs of Semele*, he attempted to express realistically, in words and music, the heartrending cries of the mother as she gave birth to Dionysus. In Athens he sang the title role in his own *Artemis*. His *Persae*, of which a considerable part has been recovered, was especially famous: Plutarch records that two centuries later, in the time of Philopoemen, this kind of lyric tragedy was still being performed. In the *Poetics*, Aristotle maintains that the kind of imitation practised by Timotheos was the best, because it embellishes the subject.

Philoxenos was born in the island of Cythera in the south of the Peloponnese in 435 and died at Ephesus in 380. He was invited to Sicily by Dionysius the Elder, but before long he was thrown into prison in Syracuse. He managed to escape, and took his revenge by making savage allusions to the tyrant in his *Cyclops*, the most famous of his dithyrambs, a scene from which is parodied in Aristophanes' *Ploutos*. He took his subject from Book ix of the *Odyssey* and a satyr play by Euripides, but gave it a fresh twist by introducing the theme of Polyphemus' love for the water nymph, Galateia. Spurned by her, as he drives his sheep to pasture, he sings: 'O lovely face, O Galateia's golden curls and ravishing voice. O flower of love. . . .' Then he sends dolphins to find the nymph in the depths of the sea and tell her that he is cured of his love. Seeing this man-eating brute transformed into a love-sick troubadour one thinks of Euripides: 'Love can make a poet of the veriest boor.' The dithyrambs of Philoxenos were amongst the masterpieces that Alexander instructed Harpalos to send to him in Asia; and two centuries later, in the time of Polybius, the Arcadians were still reciting his lyrics and those of Timotheos at the Dionysian festivals.

If the latter's *Persae* in some ways resembled a tragedy, so the former's *Cyclops* had much in common with a satyr play: and, indeed, genuine tragedy survived in Athens after the great period, even if Aristophanes' *Frogs* seems almost to have proclaimed its death as early as 405. When celebrating one of his tragic victories, Agathon, the host of Plato's *Symposium*, substituted simple musical interludes for the chanted Choruses and this innovation was soon adopted in comedy as well. Iophon and Sophocles the Younger, the son and grandson of the poet, as well as Euripides the Younger, all continued to write tragedies, though these proved to be so inferior to the masterpieces of the fifth century that there was an increasing tendency to revive the latter, especially the plays of Euripides. In the last two comedies by Aristophanes to have survived, the emphasis on political satire is much slighter and the Chorus places a much smaller part (see p. 233): they mark the transition from the Old to the Middle Comedy, and already point forward to the New Comedy, of which Menander was to be the typical representative.

Middle Comedy (about 400 to 336) is best illustrated by the work of Antiphanes, who was not an Athenian and lived from 404 to 330, and of Alexis of Thurii, who lived to be a hundred years old. Only fragments of their writings have survived, however. Alexis was especially interested in the world of procuresses and courtesans, 'Fillies of Cypris' as he called them. Of the former, he says:

They get hold of inexperienced young girls and utterly transform them, not only their faces and figures, but even their feelings. If one of them is too short, they sew thick corks soles in her sandals. Too small in the hips, they pad her out till everyone exclaims 'What a charming rump!' Too fat in the tummy, and they fix her up with stays. And if she happens to have ginger eyebrows, they blacken them with soot. But any special beauty she may have, she must expose to public view (Kock: *Com. Att. Fragment* 98).

New Comedy lasted from about 336 to 250; and it is much better known to us than the Middle because considerable passages of Menander's work, and recently a complete comedy, have been discovered in papyri. It is distinguished from the classical comedy of Aristophanes by certain technical innovations, the most obvious of which are the introduction of a prologue, in the manner of Euripides, and the diminished role of the Chorus, which, as in Agathon's tragedies, tends to be restricted to singing and dancing between the acts, a kind of intermission unrelated to the subject of the play. But a more important difference is apparent in the subject matter and the way it is treated, which reflect the tremendous change that had taken place in the social and political life of Greece between the Peloponnesian and Lamian Wars

Social behaviour had become much more urbane and refined. As Aristotle says in the *Nicomachean Ethics*:

One of the signs of good breeding is to speak and hear only what befits a free and distinguished person. . . . This may be seen by comparing the comedy of the old days with that of today. One used coarse words to make people laugh; the other expresses itself by implication; from the point of view of seemliness, the difference between these two methods is considerable (IV, 13).

In addition, heterosexual love and marriage play a much greater part in the New Comedy than in all Greek literature of earlier times. Indeed, the imaginative freedom of the ancient comedy ceased to appeal to the literary taste of the fourth century, which was already beginning to show traces of Hellenism. It was a time of prose writers, of moral and philosophical reflection; poetry was still acceptable, provided it conformed to common sense. There was a growing interest in studies of character and behaviour, as may be seen from the work of Theophrastos, which appeared about 319 (see p. 313). Menander was then twenty-three, and he and Philemon were the two outstanding representatives of the New Comedy.

Like Antiphanes and Alexis, Philemon was not a native of Athens though it was there that he made his name. Born in 361, he was only a year short of a hundred when he died. As the rival of Menander he was often successful, but though we have the names of sixty of his comedies, only fragments have survived. In one of them a countryman praises the advantages of peace, like Aristophanes' Trygaeos, though for very different reasons:

They tell me philosophers are always trying to find out what they mean by the Good. But though they seem to spend an awful lot of time at it, they don't yet know—some say virtue, some intelligence, or anything you care to mention. But it is none of these things. I, who have spent my whole life digging from morning to night, have just discovered what it is: Peace is what is Good. O dear Zeus, what a wonderful and beneficent goddess she is! Weddings, festivals, relations, children, friends, wealth, health, corn, wine, pleasure—all these things are her gift. Without her, everything that makes life worth living disappears (Kock: *Com. Att., Fragment* 71).

But the star of the New Comedy was the Athenian Menander, who was born in 342 and died fifty years later, in 292. He was a pupil of Theophrastos, but the teaching of the Epicureans seems to have influenced him more strongly than that of the Peripatetics. Good looking and elegant, he appears to have shown very little interest in politics. He led a peaceful and studious life with the courtesan Glykera at his villa at Piraeus, writing prolifically; and he also appears to have been one of the lovers of Thais. Ptolemy Soter invited him to Alexandria, but Athens suited him so well that he refused. The ten years spent under the peaceful government of Demetrius of Phaleron, the Peripatetic philosopher, were probably the happiest of his life.

Like Euripides, Menander was more appreciated by posterity than by his contemporaries, and he often had the disappointment of losing the prize to Philemon, who was certainly less talented. But, in the third century, the criticism of Aristophanes of Byzantium raised him to the front rank of Greek poets, alongside Homer. He even became so famous that one of his lines is quoted by St Paul in the New Testament[1] and Athens ordered a bronze statue of him by the two sons of Praxiteles to be erected in the theatre of Dionysus. There are several busts of him in existence, most of them probably inspired by this statue, which was executed at a time when both sculptors and painters were much concerned to provide a likeness. Georges Méautis has said: 'It would be hard to find a nobler and more aristocratic head. What is most striking is the expression of supreme intelligence, the luminous gaze, and the almost disabused expression in the disdainful curve of the lips. Looking at this handsome face, one is inevitably reminded of another comic writer, Molière, who, because he too had a profound experience of human nature, also understood the meaning of bitterness and sadness.'

Menander wrote quickly, and with unusual facility. Plutarch records that, one day, a friend, meeting him in the street said to him: 'The feast of Dionysus will soon be here, Menander. Haven't you written your comedy?' To which the poet replied: 'My comedy is finished: I've got the whole plan of it in my head—all that remains is to write the words.' In thirty years of creative activity, he wrote a hundred and eight comedies, an average of three or four plays a year.

Until 1898 Menander was only known to us from passages quoted by other writers, from what the ancients had said of him, and from Latin comedy, for both Plautus and Terence took a lot from his work: it is possible to obtain a fairly complete idea of the *Man who Punished Himself* (*Heaūton Timorouménos*) from Terence's plagiarized version. Then a series of papyrological discoveries in 1898, 1905 and 1957, revealed one whole play, the *Misanthrope* (*Dyskolos*), and considerable

---

[1] St Paul in I Cor. xv, 33 quotes the line; 'Evil communications corrupt good manners.' See the edition of *Menander* by A. Coerte No. 187, *p.* 74.

parts of several others: the *Arbitration* (Epitrepontes), the *Woman of Samia*, the *Hero*, the *Beauty whose Hair was Cut* (Perikeiroméne) and the *Flatterer*.

The first edition of the *Misanthrope*, prepared by Victor Martin, was published at the beginning of 1959. This play is chronologically the earliest of those known to us otherwise than by name, for the *didaskalia* tells us that it was performed at the Lenaean festival in January 316. Menander was then twenty-five, but had already been writing for the theatre for five years.

The god, Pan, emerges from a grotto sacred to him and to the Nymphs, to speak the prologue, which sets the action at Phyle, in Attica, and describes the themes: Cnemon, an old curmudgeon, who lives with his daughter and an old servant near the grotto and is separated from his wife and from Gorgias, her son by a previous marriage:

So assiduously does the girl venerate my companions, the Nymphs, that we have decided to look after her. There is a young man, the son of a wealthy citizen, who has come to hunt in the neighbourhood with a friend. I have inspired in him a violent passion for the girl. That, broadly speaking, is the situation: as for the details, those you may learn, if you have a mind to.

The lover, Sostratos, sends his slave to Cnemon who is digging, but before the slave can give him the message he is chased away by a hail of pears and clods of earth. Sostratos' reception is not much better, though he does succeed in making the acquaintance of Gorgias, who decides that his intentions are honest, since the wealthy Sostratos asks nothing better than to be allowed to marry the poor girl. Gorgias agrees to help him, though it proves to be difficult. Because of a dream she has had, Sostratos' mother decides to offer a sacrifice to Pan and the Nymphs at their grotto, and sends her slave and a cook ahead with the sheep that is to be slaughtered (every sacrifice was followed by a meal). As they have nothing to cook it in, they try to borrow a pot from Cnemon, but he refuses and angrily drives them away.

The *peripeteia* is rather far-fetched: Cnemon's old servant drops a bucket down the well and in trying to rescue it drops a spade too. To retrieve his precious tools Cnemon lowers himself down the well, but the rope breaks and he thinks his end has come. Then Gorgias manages to pull him out, with the help of Sostratos, and the old man realizes that it is Gorgias, to whom he never speaks, who has saved his life.

He therefore agrees to let his stepson decide who his half-sister shall marry; to the delight of Sostratos, who in turn persuades his father to let his sister marry Gorgias. The sacrifice then becomes the occasion for a double betrothal. Cnemon, who is lying on his bed covered with bruises, has to put up with the sarcasm and brutal jokes of the slave and cook he had beaten.

The plot is lively and well contrived. The scenes follow one another in rapid succession, with only four breaks, during which there is singing and dancing by the Chorus, 'a band of merry-makers, rather the worse for drink'. But the important thing is the drawing of the characters, especially Cnemon's, the only one of the leading parts that is not sympathetic. Even when he is rescued from the well he remains as surly as ever, and only wants to be left alone, though in Act IV he relents slightly: 'My great mistake was to believe that I could do without other people, and didn't need anybody's help. Now I see that death can catch you unawares, and I realize I was mistaken' (*Dyskolos*, 713 ff.).

The *Arbitration*, of which we only have rather more than half, belongs to the poet's maturity and was one of the plays most enjoyed by the Ancients. Charisios is married to Pamphile and loves his wife. But, after only five months of marriage, she secretly has a child, which she exposes, leaving with him a gold ring and some jewels. Charisios, however, getting to hear of it, abandons his wife and goes to live with a courtesan, Habrotonon. Meanwhile, the child has been found by a slave, Daos, who hands him over to a poor charcoal burner called Syriscos, whose wife wants to have a child to bring up. Daos, however, has kept the jewels for himself and when Syriscos demands them Daos refuses to hand them over. They take the matter to an arbitrator, who turns out to be Pamphile's old father, Smicrines. Daos insists that he owes nothing:

It is Syriscos who owes thanks to me for granting his request. . . . I freely gave you part of what belonged to me. If you want to, keep it. If you don't, and are regretting that you ever accepted it, give it me back. What is certainly not fair is that you should have the lot, both the part I freely gave you, and the part I want for myself. [Syriscos agrees that what Daos says is correct, but he says to the arbitrator:] Against Daos, sir, the child itself has a case. Wife, fetch me the baby (*he takes it in his arms*). It is he, Daos, who demands the necklace and other things by which you can be recognized. He says the jewels were given to him, not to provide a living for you. and I have a claim to them as well, because I'm your guardian: he appointed me such by handing you over to me. The point that has to be decided is this: are these jewels and gold to be kept for the child, as his mother intended, until he is grown up; or is this thief to keep them because he happened to be the first to find them? And here is another point to be considered, sir. It may be that the child is better born than we are, and that though we bring him up he will refuse to do our kind of work. He may be forced by his nature to do deeds worthy of a free man: to hunt the lion, to carry arms, to run in the races. You've been to the theatre, so you must know what happens. What about heroes like Neleus and Pelias? Weren't they found by an old goatherd who wore a sheepskin like me? And when he found out they were high born, didn't he tell them, and give them a little wallet with things in it they could be recognized by? And instead of being goat-herds they became kings (*The Arbitration*, 125 ff. and 157 ff.).

The old man's naïvety is charming, imagining that life in the great world is like some tragedy he happens to have seen. Daos is obliged to give up the jewels, and finally, thanks to the good-hearted Habroto-non the child is identified by them as the son of Pamphile and, even more surprising, of Charisios as well. For the gold ring turns out to be his: one night, during the feast of the Tauropolia, he had begotten the child on his future wife when it was too dark for them to recognize one another; and the unknown man, from whom Pamphile had snatched his ring as she tried to defend herself, had, indeed, been Charisios. As happy an ending to a romantic intrigue as anyone could wish, which Menander took from a lost tragedy by Euripides, the *Alope*.

Almost invariably, the subject of Menander's plays is thwarted love, either before or after marriage, though he plays a hundred variations on it. Yet it is not only to the skill and variety of his plots that Menander owes his reputation; it rests above all on that subtle insight into every shade of feeling, every aspect of personality, thanks to which his characters have the vitality of men and women drawn from life. The language they speak is simple, relaxed and natural, yet full of zest, like the easy conversation of witty, well-educated people. He has a marvellous gift for portraying human beings in all their diversity. His work is the exquisite expression of that genuinely human wisdom that had slowly matured in the privileged conditions of Attic civilization. True, he lacks the purely comic quality of Aristophanes, very rarely does he make one want to laugh out loud; but the human situation which he presents with such truth and delicacy, and with such admirable good humour, is always entertaining and delightful.

7

THE HELLENISTIC AND ROMAN PERIOD
Third Century B.C. to Third Century A.D.

Therefore [Paul] disputed. . . . in the market daily with them that
met with him. Then certain philosophers of the Epicureans, and of
the Stoics, encouraged him. . . . And they took him, and brought
him unto Areopagus. . . .

(*Acts of the Apostles*, XVII, 17–19)

HISTORICAL BACKGROUND

After the battle of Corupedion in 281, at which Lysimachos lost his
life (as Antigonos Cyclops, the One-Eyed, had done twenty years
earlier at Ipsos) the empire of Alexander was eventually divided into
three parts: Macedonia, ruled by the Antigonid dynasty, descendants
of Antigonos Cyclops; Egypt, under the Ptolemies (Ptolemy I Soter
was the son of Lagos); and finally Syria, where the Seleucid kings
reigned, alternatively taking the name of Seleucos or Antiochos.

In Thrace, Lysimachos had to fight the Celts, or Galatians, whose
warlike tribes were advancing towards the shores of the Mediterranean
from the lands of the Danube. In 279, in an attempt to halt the invasion,
the king of Macedonia was killed and the Celts, after invading Thessaly,
penetrated as far as Thermopylae. Hurriedly, the people of central
Greece set about organizing resistance. The largest contingent came
from Aetolia, a country that had hitherto played a minimal part in
the history of Hellas. Hoping to loot the sanctuary, the Celts made
a rapid thrust in the direction of Delphi, but they were overtaken by
bad weather in the steep defiles of Parnassus, decimated by the Greeks,
and put to flight.

The new king of Macedonia, Antigonos Gonatas (the Slothful),
and the Aetolians won considerable prestige by the defeat of the Celts.
At Delphi, where it was said that the sanctuary had been miraculously
saved by Apollo himself, a new festival was instituted, the *Soteria*, or
Salvation, under the patronage of the Aetolians.

Throughout the third century, the Aetolian League dominated

324

the Delphic Amphictyony and considerably increased its power in central Greece. But it soon came into conflict with the rival League of the Achaeans, which had been formed in the coastal region of the Peloponnesus known as Achaea, a name going back to Homeric times which, in the Roman epoch, was applied to the whole province of Greece.

The history of Greece in the third century is essentially the history of the incessant quarrels between the Macedonians, Aetolians and Achaeans, in which victory was determined by the various forms of alliance. Thus, in 250, the leader of the Achaean League, Aratos of Sicyon, attempted to liberate Greece from Macedonian influence, but eventually, to defend himself against the Aetolians and Sparta, he was obliged to turn to the king of Macedonia for help. Moreover, the Ptolemaic and Seleucid rulers, remote as they were, were not above intervening in Greece; especially the powerful Egyptian fleet which for a long time dominated the Aegean.

In 280 the king of Epirus—a country which, like Aetolia, would hardly have been regarded as Greek in the time of Pericles—the ambitious and warlike Pyrrhus (319–272), having taken part in the struggles for the succession and vainly attempted to seize Macedonia for himself, crossed over to Italy, in response to an appeal from the Greek town of Tarentum, at that time threatened by the Romans. He may have hoped to conquer the West, as Alexander had conquered the East; but, after winning the battle of Heracles and carrying the war into Sicily, he was defeated in Italy and in 275 was obliged to return to Greece. Three years later, Rome, by then mistress of practically the whole of Italy, captured Tarentum. Whether she intended to attack Greece, as a reply to Pyrrhus' threat, is not known, but in any case her expansion to the east was to be retarded by her great struggle against Carthage in the two Punic Wars (264–201).

It was during the second of these wars that the Macedonian War broke out (211–205). Philip v revived Pyrrhus' designs on Rome under more favourable circumstances, having formed an alliance with Hannibal. Roman diplomacy retorted by concluding an alliance with Philip's bitterest enemies, the Aetolians, thus preventing the Macedonian army from joining up with the Carthaginians. But the peace that was concluded in 205 was, on the whole, favourable to Philip.

By the time of the second Macedonian War (200–196), Rome, having overcome the danger from Carthage, had her hands free: she sent her legions into Illyria, and Flaminius, having overwhelmed the

Macedonian army with the help of his Greek allies, seized on the occasion of the Isthmian Games to proclaim the freedom of Greece, liberated from Macedonian domination by Roman arms. In fact, the legions withdrew from Hellas, leaving her to her freedom and her recurrent squabbles. The Aetolians, hitherto friendly to Rome, now turned against her and concluded an alliance with Antiochos III, king of Syria, the new champion of Hellenism against Rome. But the Seleucid empire was by this time considerably shaken by defections both in the east and in the west. Chief among these dissident powers was Pergamon, in Mysia, where, towards the middle of the third century, Eumenes, the adopted son of Philetairos, succeeded in increasing the extent of his domains. Eumenes had no royal title, but was a 'dynast', a vassal of the Seleucids. In 279, his successor, Attalus I (241–197), defeated the Celtic Galatians, who were then spreading terror throughout Asia Minor as they had previously done in Greece; and as a result of this victory, he became king. He proved to be a great ruler, who united most of Asia Minor under his sway. Wisely, he agreed to an alliance with the Romans.

His son, Eumenes II, stood by Rome when Antiochos III declared war against her. Antiochos was defeated at Thermopylae, and again at Magnesia in Asia Minor (192–189). The power of his Aetolian allies was decisively reduced, and they lost control of Delphi, where, in 191, the Roman general granted independence both to the sanctuary and the city. Antiochos himself, like Philip V, had to accept Roman suzerainty; while Eumenes II gathered up the spoils. For the kingdom of Pergamon it was a golden age, though under Attalus II Philadelphus, (159–138) her splendour began to decline.

However, the love of liberty was not yet dead in Greece. For a time, the Achaean League succeeded in unifying the whole of the Peloponnesus, thanks to the efforts of Philopoemon of Megalopolis, the successor of Aratos. Then, in 183, the 'last free Greek' was taken prisoner by his enemies in Messenia and, like Socrates, was forced to drink the hemlock.

Perses, Philip V's son, dreamt of revenge against the Romans. In 172 the Senate declared war on him; at Pydna in 168 he was defeated by Paulus Aemilius and taken prisoner. It was not long before Macedonia was reduced to a Roman province; and in 146, when a last attempt at revolt had given Mummius the excuse to conquer Corinth, the same fate overtook Greece herself. From then on, the history of Greece was bound up with that of Rome.

Did the Romans behave like 'savage conquerors' which, in the long run, would have been the only way in which they could have overthrown a civilization so superior to their own? Especially after the taking of Tarentum, the whole ruling class of Rome came to know and admire Greece, whose freedom had been proclaimed by Flaminius in 196. Despite their exactions, coupled with a considerable amount of looting, Roman rule was probably milder than that of the Macedonians had been, and it permitted a certain degree of autonomy in many cities, at least as regards municipal and local affairs. In 67 A.D., Nero attended the Isthmian Games and renewed the pledge made by Flaminius, publicly assuring the Greeks of their freedom, and even granting them immunity—doubtless an ostentatious and meaningless gesture, but at least an indication of benevolent intentions.

Be that as it may, the benefits of the *Pax Romana* were many and substantial. Towards the end of his life, about 125 A.D., during the reign of Hadrian, the most philhellenic of the emperors, Plutarch wrote: 'I am grateful for the tranquillity we enjoy, for on every side there is calm and peace; all fighting has ceased; there are no more emigrations and no more revolts, nor those other scourges and sicknesses native to Greece' (*On the Pythian Oracles*). We of the twentieth century can only envy such a happy state of affairs!

The Roman epoch in Greece appears to have been a continuation of the Hellenistic period, without any sudden break or violent changes. True, political power had passed from the hands of the Antigonids, Ptolemies and Seleucids to the Romans, but society continued to develop along the same lines as previously. Apart from a few Roman innovations, like the cruel gladiatorial shows that now spread throughout the whole of Greece and the east, it could be said that Greek influence on Rome was more profound than Roman influence on Greece. In his third Satire, Juvenal complained that 'the Orontes now flows into the Tiber', but one would hardly find a Greek of the period complaining that the waters of the Cephissos or the Ilissos had been contaminated by the Tiber.

There is, indeed, considerable truth in the apparently paradoxical view expressed by Pierre Grimal:[1] 'People gradually came to realize that Rome was not a barbarian city, the haunt of savage conquerors bent on the destruction of a priceless and defenceless Hellenism, but, indeed, an outpost of Hellenism, a landmark preceding and encouraging its expansion into the western Mediterranean. Later, men came to

[1] *A la recherche de l'Italie antique* (Hachette, 1961), p. 25.

realize that it was Rome that had enabled Hellenism to survive, at the very moment when it was in danger of being overwhelmed by the flood of oriental mysticism. At no time was the struggle between Rome and Greece a conflict between the spirit of destruction and the spirit of creation: architectural forms, decorative and historical friezes, monumental sculpture, painting, all originated in the east, but it was the Roman public that gave them a new impetus. Without Rome, the creative genius of Hellas would have died away as swiftly as it had arisen; it would have remained a miracle without a future.'

HELLENISTIC ART

While the art of the Hellenistic period was mainly a continuation of that of the fourth century, there were also important modifications and new developments. Once Alexander had thrown open the huge Persian empire, a genuine fusion took place between the east and Greece itself; and similarly, after the Roman conquest between the east and the west. But what Hellenism gained through this extension and irradiation she often lost in purity. Hellenistic art is more sumptuous, more varied and ambitious, more grandiose than classical art, but it is much less balanced: by the second century it had become almost baroque.

Large numbers of temples continued to be built as in the past, either in newly founded cities, or in ancient towns on the site of earlier buildings that had been destroyed. The Didymaion, rebuilt by the Milesians in the time of Alexander, was an example of the latter. The foundations of this vast and curious edifice measured some 350 feet by 160, compared with the Parthenon's 210 by 90 feet, and the whole temple was surrounded by a double range of columns, reinforced at the entrance by a dozen more, disposed in three rows. Moreover, in place of the usual *naos*, was a courtyard, at a lower level and open to the sky, containing a *naiscos*, a small Ionic temple of Apollo. Several similar plans, unusual in Greece, bear witness to eastern influences.

However, it was not in religious architecture that Hellenistic art showed its greatest originality, but in town planning. Like Athens, most Greek towns had developed haphazardly, without preconceived plan, and consisted of a tangle of twisting, evil-smelling streets, which apart from wholesale demolition offered little scope for the town planner, except to improve the Agora by adding monumental porticos to the buildings.

As propaganda for the benefits derived from their 'philhellenism', the kings of Pergamon devoted part of their immense wealth to buildings of this kind at Delphi, Delos and Athens. In the Agora at Athens, Attalus II built the great portico of white Pentelic marble, that has recently been restored by archaeologists from the American school. Visitors may find its whiteness rather dazzling, but in the heat of summer they will appreciate the cool shade of its galleries as much as the Athenians used to. This type of portico, of which there are many examples, is evidence of a new preoccupation with comfort that is typical of the Hellenistic period: the word *tryphe*, denoting an easy and luxurious existence, and hitherto used as a pejorative, now acquired a favourable meaning. It was even accepted as an ideal, that was to be realized in 'the inimitable life' of Antony and Cleopatra.

In the towns that were actually founded in this period, the past was no obstacle to town planning; and innumerable cities were, indeed, founded by Alexander and his successors. The one that was to give its name to the whole period—Alexandrian is almost equivalent to Hellenistic—was founded in 331 B.C. 'Alexander had the plans for his new city, between the sea and lake Moeris, prepared by Deinocrates, an architect of bold originality. These were first studied by the king, who carefully considered the advantage of the site. . . . He himself took a special interest in his project, and chose the lay-out for the principal buildings, particularly the agora. Strabo makes it clear that the whole original site was divided up by avenues, broad enough for horses and chariots, and all intersecting one another at right-angles. The main avenue, almost in the centre of the town and running east and west, was a hundred feet in breadth.'[1]

The plan of the original Greek town of Alexandria has not yet been completely traced: those of Priene and Pergamon, however, provide a much clearer picture. Though both these towns existed long before the Hellenistic era, they were then so drastically enlarged and re-planned that to all intents and purposes they became new cities. Priene is laid out geometrically, like Alexandria, with the streets crossing each other at right angles and running north-south and east-west. The temple of Athena Polias, which was not completed till the middle of the second century, was famous. The altar, situated at the entrance to the temple, stood on a high plinth, carved with sculptures representing the Gigantomachy, and it was flanked by porticos of carved pillars. The area of the market place, in the centre of the town,

[1] R. Martin, *L'Urbanisme dans la Grèce antique*, p. 116.

corresponded exactly to two *insulae*, with two vast covered porticos facing one another. Nearby were the meeting place for the Assembly and the Prytaneum; and the magnificent plan was completed by a theatre, two gymnasia and a stadium.

The houses in Priene, like those on the island of Delos, bear witness to the same feeling for comfort and luxury that we have already referred to. The dwellings of the rich and comfortably-off are much more spacious and ornate than in classical times. To ensure privacy, they have no windows on the outside, but the rooms give on to a central courtyard, usually square, with a fountain surrounded by a cloister. The floors are decorated with ornamental mosaics, sometimes representing mythical subjects: at Delos there is one of Dionysus, the great god of the Alexandrian period, riding a panther. The walls were covered with painted stucco, or even sheets of marble, and there were often statues. The houses at Pompeii clearly derive from this type of dwelling, which originated in the Greek orient.

Priene was a democratic city, Pergamon a centre of royal power. Before proceeding to improve other Greek cities, the kings of Pergamon were at pains to make their own capital, which had previously been little more than a glorified village, a truly princely city. In contrast to Alexandria, built on flat ground at the edge of the sea, Pergamon is a citadel, perched on a steep hill and sloping down to the plain of the Caicos. On a long, strongly underpinned terrace, stands the theatre, which takes advantage of the natural slope; high above it stands the temple of Athena Polias, while on a vast open space below is the altar of Zeus and Athena Nikephoros, and lower still, the agora. Because of the slope, the latter is laid out as two oblongs, facing one another at right angles on either side of the road leading up to the acropolis, and surrounded on three sides by sumptuous porticos, forty feet in depth, whose Doric columns are almost fifteen feet high.

The great altar of Zeus and Athena is ornamented with sculptures that are amongst the best preserved and most characteristic Alexandrian carvings we have. A small frieze, carved in 'pictorial' low relief tells the story of Telephos, the mythical founder of the city. A much larger one, seven or eight feet high and about a hundred and forty yards long, represents the old story of the battle between the giants, like the one at Priene; and is an extremely original work, full of strength and grandeur. Scholars have discovered the names of the rarest of the giants that are engraved on the lower edge of the frieze, amongst

them Eurytos and Brontes who has wings sprouting from his
shoulders and legs that end as serpents' bodies. The powerful torso
of Zeus indicates a detailed knowledge of anatomy. Athena, crowned
by Nikê, is in the act of felling the giant Alkyoneus, whose mother,
Ge (the Earth), half buried in the ground, reaches upwards in a gesture
of supplication. The whole frieze is carried out in a brilliant but
rather theatrical style, with minute realism and astonishing virtuosity.

At the beginning of the third century, a pupil of Lysippos (see
p. 250), Chares of Lindos, erected a bronze statue of the Sun God,
the tutelary divinity of the island, at the entrance to the port of
Rhodes. The hundred foot high Colossus was regarded as one of the
Seven Wonders of the world and is typical of the contemporary taste
for the gigantic.

Both the realism and the tense feeling revealed in the great frieze
at Pergamon are also to be found in other works: for example, the
torture of Marsyas, Menelaus with the corpse of Patroclus, or the
famous Laocoön. The convulsive pose of the Trojan priest and his
tortured expression, with his two sons anxiously straining towards
him, are undoubtedly moving, despite their theatricality.

The art of portraiture, unknown in classical times, had been
introduced in the fourth century and continued to develop throughout
the Hellenistic epoch, reaching its highest point under the Romans.
On the splendid sarcophagos discovered at Sidon are two portrait
figures of Alexander; and busts like those of the Seleucid monarchs
or the eunuch Philetairos, the first dynast of Pergamon, are amazingly
realistic. A marble head found at Delphi and a bronze head from
Delos, though both subjects are unknown, are highly individualized;
while the fine portraits of Aristotle, Demosthenes and Menander
all date from this period. Some sculptors of the time were particularly
concerned to stress distinctive racial characteristics, especially in the
case of foreigners. To commemorate his defeat of the Gauls, Attalus I
commissioned a number of bronze statues of Galatians for his city
of Pergamon, copies of which we still have. The 'Wounded Gaul'
is certainly a portrait of a particular gladiator, and his features, as
well as the torcs he wears round his neck, his oval shield and trumpet,
all clearly indicate his Celtic origin. Even more moving is the group,
in which a Gaul, supporting with his left arm the wife he has just
stabbed, is about to kill himself.

Now, also, practically for the first time, sculptors began to show an
interest in children, unlike the classical masters: the infant Dionysus

on the shoulder of Praxiteles' Hermes, for example, is a very mediocre piece of work. But the child struggling with a goose, by Boethos, or the little Eros teasing a Centaur, are both examples of a kind of statuary much appreciated by the Alexandrians.

The pastoral aspects of Hellenistic civilization, typified in the *Idylls* of Theocritus, were also a feature of the plastic arts, notably in the frieze of Telephos at Pergamon. Hitherto, bas-reliefs had been completely dominated by the human figure; at most, they might include the trunk of a tree or a rock in the background. Now interest began to shift to the landscape itself, possibly with some human figure, a peasant leading his cow to market, also depicted. At the same time we find a growing taste for symbolism and allegory. A pupil of Lysippos, Eutychides of Sicyon, executed a large bronze-gilt statue for the town of Antioch, representing Tyche, the goddess of luck and chance, who, like Dionysus, was one of the favourite divinities of the period. She is shown as a woman, seated on a throne and wearing an embattled crown, while the river Orontes, represented as a swimming nymph, issues from the ground at her feet.

At the same time that these new developments were taking place, sculptors also continued to work in the classical tradition, and sometimes, as may be seen from two famous works in the Louvre, produced masterpieces. The *Victory of Samothrace* bears comparison with the *Nikai* of the Attic age. She is standing on the prow of a trireme, and some recently discovered fragments of the right hand suggest that originally her arm was raised in a solemn gesture of triumph. It is hard to determine the precise date of this splendid work, but it may belong to the end of the third, or the beginning of the second, century B.C. Even more difficult to establish is the date of the marvellous *Venus of Milo*. Certainly it is later than the Victory, but Praxiteles would not have been ashamed to acknowledge it. As the work of a great, though unknown, artist, it proves that the classical idea was still alive in the Alexandrian, possibly even in the Roman, epoch.

Vase painting, which already in the fourth century was very inferior to that of the fifth, had now become completely decadent. In the main, it relied on floral or geometric decorative motifs, though one still finds plenty of representations of Eros flying about: the little winged god, like his mother Aphrodite, as well as Dionysus and Tyche, obsessed the Alexandrians. A hydria, on which two goats confront one another, about to charge, is a good example of the kind of carefully observed *genre* picture, stemming from the same inspiration as the *Idylls* of Theocritus or the pastoral epigrams of the *Anthology*.

The main demand in this period was for vessels decorated in relief, and for the intricately sculpted vases that compete with the art of the goldsmith or the modellers of figurines. The so-called 'Megarian' bowls are sometimes ornamented with scenes from epic poetry. There is a sculpted vase in the Louvre in the shape of an owl; while another, in the Berlin Museum, represents Adonis holding Aphrodite on his knees, a typical Alexandrian theme. Many of the figurines from Tanagra and Myrina are third century: elegant women or young men, sometimes naked, sometimes clothed, are shown sleeping, playing games or dancing. Both intaglios and cameos were produced in great numbers at this time, and the fashion lasted until the end of the Roman period. The cameos with twin portraits of Ptolemy Philadelphus and his sister-wife, Arsinoe, are extraordinarily beautiful.

Frescoes of the period, which certainly inspired the pictorial bas-reliefs and mosaics, have all perished, but there can be little doubt that they were greatly superior to those at Pompeii. The closest approximation to them, perhaps, is the fine mosaic of the battle of Issos, which though discovered at Pompeii, was actually produced in Alexandria.

Roman art was a continuation of Hellenistic art, with certain distinctive features that need not concern us here. A fresco in the basilica of Herculaneum, painted in the first century A.D. and representing Theseus killing the Minotaur, was certainly inspired by a Greek painting of the third, perhaps of the fourth, century B.C. What better symbol of the continuity of Greek and Roman art could be found, than this classical picture of an Attic hero at Herculaneum?

PHILOSOPHY AND SCIENCE

In the Hellenistic period the Greek city, even when it retained more or less theoretical autonomy, was enclosed in a constricting network of external influences and was no longer really free; it was part of a vast kingdom and, later, of the Roman empire. In classical times, men had always seen themselves in relation to the City; this is what Aristotle meant when he said: 'Man is a creature who lives in a City.' When this framework collapsed, the individual found himself disorientated and alone, confronted by quite new problems. At the same time, religious beliefs, partly related to official religion, had either worn thin or broken down altogether: what confidence could men feel in all-powerful gods who had failed to prevent the defeat of the government they were supposed to protect? This helps to explain why the philosophies that arose in the third century, Stoicism and Epicureanism, were concerned, much more explicitly than the systems of Plato or Aristotle, with the idea of personal happiness, often presented under the religious aspect of salvation. The attainment of wisdom remained the purpose of philosophy, but the wise man was one who relied upon himself for strength and encouragement, since he could no longer count on help from the gods.

The teaching of the Cynics, more directly descended from that of Socrates than was either the Academy or the Lyceum, was also better suited to the needs of the new age. Menippos of Gadara, a native of Phoenicia, born in slavery, lived at the beginning of the third century. His numerous writings achieved an immense success, but none of them has survived; a most unfortunate loss. He gave his name to that burlesque mixture of prose and verse which he was the first to practise and which is still known as 'Menippean satire'. Some idea of his originality and audacious wit is to be obtained from the work of Lucian who imitated him closely.

The founder of Stoicism, Zeno, was a pupil of the Cynic Crates (see p. 253), and the two philosophies have certain features in common: both proclaim a high ethical ideal; and they also share a taste for allegory and moral interpretations of myth. Zeno who was born at Keition was a Greek from Cyprus, but about 301 he came to teach in Athens, establishing his school in the *Stoa Poikile* (the Painted Portico) from which his philosophy derived its name. Many of his ideas were taken from those of Heracleitus of Ephesus (see p. 116). He died in 264 at the age of seventy-two; it is said, by his own hand. His successor was Cleanthes of Assos, in Mysia, who arrived in Athens with only four drachmas in his purse and used to earn his living by drawing water during the night so that in the daytime he could attend Zeno's lectures. Of his many works, we still have his *Hymn to Zeus* in which, reviving the ancient tradition of philosophical poetry, he expounds the Stoic doctrine. He died in 332, aged ninety-nine, also by his own hand; and was, in turn, succeeded by Chrysippos of Soles, in Cilicia. A redoubtable dialectician and a writer of prodigious fecundity (seven hundred and fifty works were attributed to him), he was regarded as being, second only to Zeno, one of the founders of Stoicism. When he died, about 206, he was over seventy years old.

Apart from Cleanthes' *Hymn to Zeus*, the only extant writings of these 'ancient Stoics' are a few fragments.

Though their interpretations of mythology were naturalistic and their ideas about the physical world fundamentally materialist, nevertheless the Stoics were not hostile to religion. They believed in divination and sought to justify it rationally by their principle of 'cosmic sympathy' between all living creatures in the universe: there is no single fact which cannot ultimately be related to the totality of facts, present, past and future. The effect of a man raising his finger is felt throughout the entire world. The role of Providence, in which the Stoics deeply believed, is precisely to reveal these subsidiary connections, these slender threads that are imperceptible to ordinary logic: to interpret them is the task of augurs and prophets, inspired by the gods.

The meaning of the word 'stoical', today, is attributable to the high moral outlook of the Stoics, which was closely related to their logical and scientific teachings. Man's first duty is to free his soul from the influence of the passions which produce madness. Virtue, of itself, is sufficient to secure happiness. There are no degrees either of virtue or of vice: all moral weakness, even the most anodyne, is a crime against reason. Only the wise man can be happy and free; even were he to be deprived of all his possessions and to become a slave, he would still be a king amongst men.

In the second and third centuries B.C., the chief representatives of Stoicism were Panaetios of Rhodes, who for a long time lived in Rome where he associated with the Scipios and knew Polybius; and Posidonios of Apamaea, in Syria, an eclectic philosopher whose lectures were attended by Cicero and Pompey and to whom certain scholars have recently attributed more influence than he in fact had. Under the empire, when, doubtless because of an affinity between its rigorous moral teaching and the Roman temperament, Stoicism exerted a wide and profound influence in Rome, two names stand out, those of a slave and of an emperor.

Epictetus, born in Phrygia shortly before 50 A.D., was a slave, who lived at Rome in the reign of Nero and attended the lectures of the Stoic, Musonius Rufus. Having been granted his freedom, he himself became an exponent of the doctrine. Expelled from Rome in 94 A.D. by the Senatus Consultus which in the reign of Domitian banished all philosophers from Italy, he retired to Nicopolis in Epirus, where one of his disciples was Arrian. Like Socrates, Epictetus wrote nothing, but, thanks to Arrian, we are familiar with his teaching. Indeed, in his admirable *Conversations* and *Manual*, Arrian of Nicomedia provides a more reliable account of Epictetus' ideas than Xenophon and Plato did of Socrates. We shall return to him later.

Marcus Aurelius was almost a personification of Plato's dream; the philosopher-king, absolute ruler over a vast empire and passionately devoted to philosophy. Being a Roman, he normally carried on his correspondence in Latin, and Greek must have been a foreign language to him. Yet when he wrote his *Meditations*, the fruit of long hours of solitary thought and self-examination, he did so in Greek, the language he had been taught in, the language of the philosophers he admired, above all of Epictetus. The Stoicism of Marcus Aurelius is in no way original, but his deeply sincere book reveals in an extremely personal and intimate way an unusually engaging moral character.

The earliest Stoics had been natives of Cyprus or Asia. Epicurus was of pure Athenian stock, of the deme of Gargettos. That he happened to be born at Samos, in 341, was due to the fact that his father Neocles was living there at the time as Athenian ambassador. In 323, the year of Alexander's death, the eighteen-year-old Epicurus went to Athens to perform his military service. One of his fellow conscripts was the poet Menander (see p. 319 ff.), who was later to become an Epicurean. After a period of teaching at Mytilene and at Lampsacos, Epicurus returned to Athens in 306 to set up a school, buying an estate known as the Garden for the purpose. His health was always poor and in 207, after a period of intense suffering, he died at the age of seventy-one. Shortly before his death he wrote to a friend:

The best day of my life draws near, the last. The pains in my bladder and stomach, always severe, continue to plague me. But against this, I set the joy I feel in my heart when I recall our discussions in the past. You, who from your youth have been doubly faithful, to me and to philosophy, I beg you to take good care of Metrodoros' children (*Vita Epicuri*, 22).

Unmarried and childless, Epicurus was deeply attached to the children of his beloved disciple and friend, Metrodoros, who had died seven years earlier. The friendship between the two men, which was to be perpetuated in sculpture by several double portraits, deserves to rank with that of Achilles and Patroclus or of Montaigne and La

Boétie. Epicurus seems to have had an exquisite spiritual delicacy. He taught his slave Mys, to whom he was devoted, to appreciate philosophy. It is not surprising that *philia*, friendship, was regarded as an essential part of the Epicurean way of life, the unifying principle of the Garden. Just as Zeno of Keition drew upon Heracleitus for inspiration, so Epicurus turned to Democritus and his atomic philosophy (see p. 194 ff.). On every issue, his teaching was opposed to that of the Stoics, and often to Platonism and the various more or less idealist schools deriving from Socrates. As against the divine providence of the Stoics, Epicurus sets Tyche, Chance, the great goddess of the Hellenistic period. It is Chance alone that determines the infinite variety of encounters and combinations of atoms, from which all matter and all life arise. But, for Epicurus, natural science is of comparatively little account; in his eyes its primary importance was that it could deliver mankind from the superstitious fear of the gods that poisoned their existence.

Epicurus was not, however, an atheist. Father Festugière has written an admirable little book called *Épicure et ses dieux*. The gods are remote and utterly unconcerned with mankind: to intervene in human affairs, like the gods of the *Iliad*, would be contrary to the perfect serenity (*ataraxia*) that constitutes their beatitude. In his own way, Epicurus was a pious man, and in performing his public religious duties he seems to have been sincere, though he insisted upon his radical disbelief in divination. Whereas, for the Stoics, a manifestly false prophecy was not an adequate logical reason for rejecting the oracles, for Epicurus, a correct prediction, was not, equally logically, sufficient reason for accepting the truth of divination. Basically, by his rejection of any kind of Providence, Epicurus abolished theology: for mankind, the gods, since they neither know of nor care for humanity, were effectively non-existent.

Epicureanism was a religion based on friendship and happiness, though Epicurus was at pains to distinguish between true pleasures and the false ones that entail suffering. Vice and debauchery were to be condemned because they are a bad bargain. Happiness is essentially negative, in the sense that it consists in the absence of passion and anxiety, that inner state of ataraxy that raises the sage to the level of the gods.

At times, this serenity strikes one as scarcely distinguished from an old bachelor's egoism, for the wise man is recommended not to marry, unless he finds himself 'on fire', nor to participate in public affairs, since marriage and politics are both a source of anxiety. The kind of love advocated by Plato, he must avoid like the plague, even if he could control the desires of the flesh by indulging them. As his disciple Lucretius says: 'To avoid love does not mean depriving oneself of the pleasures of Venus; on the contrary, it means enjoying their benefits, without leaving behind a hostage' (*De Rerum Natura*, IV, 103–4),—a wonderful motto for libertines of any period.

The members of the Garden included seven women, only one of whom was married. The others were courtesans, though doubtless they abandoned their profession when they devoted themselves to philosophy. 'One cannot help feeling somewhat surprised,' Father Festugière gravely comments, 'at the large number of hetairai, and undoubtedly their presence at the school gave rise to unpleasant rumours.' Athenaeus, for instance, maintains that: 'In the shady groves of the Garden, Leontion used to give herself to the Epicureans and did not conceal the fact that she bestowed her favours even on Epicurus himself' (XIII, 588 b); but Athenaeus was a malicious scandalmonger. In fact, Epicurus seems to have been extremely ascetic, though many of the later frequenters of the Garden were certainly self-indulgent. This increased the number of his adherents, even if all they accepted of his teaching was one or two maxims unrelated to their context; for example, 'I spit upon morality (*tò kalón*) and on men's empty admiration of it, unless it be a source of pleasure' or 'The principle and root of the Good are the pleasures of the belly' (*Epicurus*, fragments 79 and 59). Certainly *Tryphe*, as well as *Tyche*, was better adapted to Epicureanism than to Stoicism.

Epicurus wrote a great deal, though all we have are a few fragments. This is all the more regrettable in view of the outstanding importance of his own contribution to the body of ideas associated with him; much greater than that of Zeno or Chrysippos with regard to Stoicism. While the latter has never been known as 'Zenoism' or 'Chrysippism', the fact that we speak of Epicureanism emphasizes the tremendous role he played as its founder and guiding spirit, as well as through his writings. Indeed, so much was this the case that his successors appear as little more than shadows; it is here scarcely necessary to mention Hermarchos of Mytilene and Colotes of Lampsacos, though Plutarch was to write a refutation of one of the latter's works. To obtain a clear grasp of Epicurus' philosophy as a whole, we must turn to the *De Rerum Natura*, the long and serious poem by his devoted follower Lucretius (94–55 B.C.).

The contradictions inherent in Epicureanism and Stoicism encouraged scepticism and led to a revival of interest in the ideas of
Pyrrho of Elis. Born in 360, and living to be some ninety years old,
he accompanied Alexander into Asia, then returned to Elis where he
taught for forty years. He also studied the philosophy of Democritus,
but the conclusions he drew from it differed from those of Epicurus.
Like all the philosophers of this period, he was concerned to discover
the nature of happiness; boldly attributing it to a complete disregard
for learning and knowledge, thus rejecting the whole Greek tradition.
Here are one or two of his sayings: 'This is as good as that', 'There
is no argument that cannot be refuted', 'Truth is unknowable'.
Pyrrho's position was similar to that of Gorgias and Protagoras,
though he arrived at it in a very personal way. According to him,
the wise man should suspend judgment (*epoche*) and seek to attain
serenity (*ataraxia*) through indifference, ignorance and silence. When
Montaigne says that doubt and lack of curiosity constitute 'a soft
pillow for a well-made head', he is obeying these precepts.

Pyrrho himself wrote nothing: what was the point? His disciple,
Timon of Philious, who died at the age of ninety, in the second half of
the third century, left a number of works in prose and verse. The best
known of these was the *Silloi*, of which some 250 lines are extant. It
was a kind of humorous review of all previous Greek philosophers,
whom he treated with savage sarcasm and considerable wit. His own
ideas were to be expounded, ponderously and at length, in a number
of writings by Sextus Empiricus, towards the end of the third century
A.D., but, already in the Hellenistic period, the influence of Pyrrhonism
made itself felt on the 'middle' Academy. The philosophical schools
established prior to the origin of Epicureanism and Stoicism, notably
the Academy and the Lyceum, had never ceased to function, though
their original teaching was to some extent modified by these later
developments.

In 260 Arcesilaos of Pitane, in Aeolis, had been appointed to the
chair of the Academy. By affirming that absolute truth is beyond the
reach of the human mind and that the wise man should be prepared to
suspend judgment, he had certainly abandoned the philosophy of
Plato. At the same time his scepticism was only relative and provisory:
in accordance with the Delphic maxim, 'Nothing in excess', he
refused to commit himself to any categorical statement; without
going so far as to reject all knowledge, he confines his ambitions to
probabilities.

Carneades of Cyrene (215–129), who was also a professor of the Academy, maintained that objective truth was beyond man's grasp, but he distinguished three degrees of probability, the highest of which, though practically irrefutable, was only logically superior to the other two. This was an extension of the theory of probability outlined by Arcesilaos. Carneades, in addition to being a remarkable dialectician, was a gifted orator. In the course of a dispute with Sicyon in 156, the Athenians sent him to defend their cause before the Roman Senate, together with the Peripatetic philosopher Critolaos and the Stoic Diogenes. The three philosophers all took advantage of their mission to deliver lectures while in Rome. Carneades took as his subject Justice; one day proving that it existed, and the next day that it did not. His audience was shocked; and had Plato been present, he would certainly have disowned this faithless disciple who, despite being the head of the Academy, was behaving like the sophists in Socrates' day. It was this philosophy of the Middle, or New, Academy that Cicero adopted.

As for the Lyceum, it exerted a decisive influence on the intellectual institution most characteristic of the whole period, the Museum of Alexandria. Demetrius of Phaleron, having been expelled from Athens in 307 after governing the city for eleven years (see p. 320), was made responsible, by Ptolemy Soter, for organizing what we should today call the University of Alexandria. He was a pupil of Theophrastos who had studied under Aristotle. Ptolemy Philadelphus began by acquiring all the books that had once belonged to Aristotle; and the Library, which formed part of the Museum, eventually comprised almost five hundred thousand volumes. The Museum was a kind of religious foundation, administered by a priest or president appointed by the king, and it was responsible for the maintenance of scientists and scholars, dedicated, as they had always been in Greece, to the worship of the Muses. The kings of Pergamon, who rivalled the court of Alexandria in their patronage of the arts, also founded a richly endowed library. Parchment, which was here made for the first time, became known as 'Pergamon paper'. Rhodes and Syracuse were other important centres of learning, but for a long time the primacy of Alexandria remained unchallenged.

The scientists and scholars adopted the method laid down by Aristotle. It was based on observation and the scrupulous compilation of facts, but, thanks especially to their magnificent library, the means at their disposal were far greater than those available to the Athenian

Lyceum. As a result, notable advances were soon achieved in the exact sciences, as well as in philology, geography and history. This prodigious extension of literary and scientific knowledge can only be compared with that of the Renaissance in the fifteenth and sixteenth centuries. Yet this period of great discoveries was long regarded as one of decline and decadence, for the simple reason that its art and poetry were inferior to those of the classical period.

It was in the third century B.C. that the 'cycle' of ancient education (*encyclopaedia*), as envisaged by Plato and Isocrates, was really established; and it was Rome that gathered its fruits, for the German historians are fully justified in speaking of 'a Hellenistico-Roman culture' and refusing to separate Rome and Greece. It was only with the generation after Aristotle and Alexander the Great that education in the ancient world really found itself, really assumed its classical and, indeed, definitive form. From then on it remained unchanged.

The great scientists of this period were: Euclid, who systematized the elementary geometry of the classical epoch; Eratosthenes of Cyrene, head of the Library of Alexandria, founder of historical chronology and scientific geography, who measured the circumference of the earth by a quite new and much sounder method; Archimedes of Syracuse, geometer, engineer and the actual originator of modern physics, whose amazing inventions delayed the capture of Syracuse by Marcellus in 212; Aristarchos of Samos whose inspired guesses and knowledge of astronomy anticipated Copernicus' discovery that the sun moves round the world;[1] Hipparchos of Nicea (in Bithynia) who in the second century discovered the Precession of the Equinoxes and was, according to Bigourdan, the 'greatest astronomer of antiquity and perhaps of all time'; Herophilos of Chalcedon and Erasistratos of Ioulis (Ceos) who, by the vivisection of animals and condemned criminals, discovered the circulation of the blood twenty centuries before Harvey.

At the same time there was tremendous progress in the history of literature, originating at the Lyceum. The poet, Callimachus, prepared a catalogue of all the Greek writers whose works were in the Library of Alexandria. In the previous generation, Aristoxenes of Tarentum, a pupil of Aristotle and a great musical theoretician, had written the first lives of the poets and philosophers. Grammar and philology

[1] The Stoic Cleanthes, author of the *Hymn to Zeus* (see *p.* 334), claimed that Aristarchos had been charged with atheism for insisting that the sun and not the earth was the centre of the universe. One is reminded of the trial of Galileo.

were highly esteemed. Zenodotos of Ephesus prepared a famous edition of the Homeric poems. Aristophanes of Byzantium edited the principal Greek poets, as well as the works of Plato; he was also the originator of the grammatical theory of analogy. Aristarchos of Samothrace, his successor in charge of the Library of Alexandria, continued his philological and exegetical work, and, as the editor of Homer, his name became synonymous with careful and impeccable criticism.

POETRY

I have already mentioned Callimachus as a scholar and the author of a catalogue of the Library at Alexandria. Erudition, which today strikes us as being remote from creative literature, was an almost continuous feature of Alexandrian poetry. Callimachus, the son of Battos, was born at Cyrene in Africa about 315 B.C. He studied philosophy in Athens, then went to Alexandria where, to begin with, he earned a modest livelihood as a schoolmaster. It is likely that he had already written a considerable number of poems during his youth. Ptolemy Philadelphus patronized him and gave him a post in the Royal Library, where he wrote his famous catalogue, the *Tablets* (*pinakes*). But it is as a poet that he especially interests us.

In the second half of his life Callimachus was the official court poet and, at the same time, known as the leader of the Alexandrian school of poetry. His most important work was the *Aetia*, or *Origins*, learned verse chronicles describing the foundations of certain towns and the myths connected with them. Some fragments of this still exist, the most interesting being the story of the love of *Acontios and Kydippe*. The Alexandrian poets delighted in poems of love and passion. We also have some hymns by him: *To Zeus, To Apollo, To Artemis, To Delos, For the Bath of Pallas* and *To Demeter*. Many of these hymns were commissioned by the king of Egypt or by the priests of a temple for some religious ceremony. They are full of mythological, geographical and theological erudition, but they also contain vigorous and brilliant passages as, for example, in the hymn *To Delos*, a later version of the Homeric hymn (see pp. 78–9), with its description of the birth of Apollo and the miracle of gold that follows it. Lastly, there are a few epigrams by him, as well as fragments of elegies, iambics and lyrics of various kinds, as well as of an epic, the *Hecale*. As an aristocratic poet (he claimed to be a descendant of the kings of Cyrene), he only wrote for connoisseurs, disdaining the general public whom he regarded as ignorant and incapable of appreciating this refined and delicate art. In one of his epigrams he declares:

I detest cyclic poems, disliking a path that has been trodden by a crowd as much as a lover who has given himself to everyone. I do not drink at the communal fountain. Everything which is public is repugnant to me (*Epigram*, xxviii).

In his *Reply to Telchines*, the name he used to denote his enemies who had criticized his lack of inspiration and the slightness of his poems, Callimachus says:

I sing to those who delight in the shrill song of the cicada, not in the noise of donkeys. Let others bray if they will; I am content if I resemble the winged and graceful creature!

Again, in the *Hymn to Apollo*, Envy whispers in the god's ear: 'I do not like the poet whose song is not as mighty as the sea.' But Apollo spurns him and retorts:

The current of the Assyrian stream is also mighty, but see how much slime and foul mud it brings with it. The priestesses of Deo do not serve their goddess with any kind of water that comes to hand, but only with that which flows clear and limpid from the sacred spring, a few drops only, crystal bright.

Indeed, the works of this poet, though many in number, are always short and carefully written. In the *Anthology* it is his epigrams that stand out. Here is how he praises a friend who had died, who was also a poet:

When I heard of your death, Heracleitus, I wept as I remembered how often you and I communed beyond the setting of the sun. Now, my guest from Halicarnassos, you are only ashes. . . . But your nightingale songs still live and Hades who destroys everything shall not lay his hand upon them (*Epigram* ii).

Callimachus was the leader of the modernist school, to which Theocritus and Aratos also belonged. Their ideal was an exquisite, learned kind of poetry, expressed in short, highly contrived poems, written in modern but erudite language. In their eyes, the epic, as understood by Homer, had served its turn. It was an exhausted form and it was useless to try to bring it back into fashion. The only time that Callimachus assumes the epic manner is in the *Hecale*, a charming account of a little known episode from the cycle of Theseus, in which a gentle old peasant woman, Hecale, offers hospitality to the hero whom she treats with the tenderness of a mother. Theocritus writes in the same spirit of the childhood of Heracles.

'Detesting cyclic poems', as he did, what must Callimachus have felt when his friend and disciple, Apollonius of Rhodes, glibly proposed to recount the whole story of Jason and Medea in the four books of his *Argonauts?* Tradition has it that the two poets quarrelled, though this is not certain.

Apollonius was some ten years younger than Callimachus who, on the death of Zenodotos of Ephesus, about 270 (see p. 342), had secured his appointment as chief Librarian in Alexandria and had suggested him as the tutor for the future Ptolemy III Euergetes. Moreover, as Vian has said, 'In many respects Apollonius upheld the new aesthetic: he was fond of unusual traditions and erudite mythology and geography: he devoted considerable space to themes dear to the Alexandrians, especially to love; and he treated the traditional epic theme in a contemporary manner. . . . More than this, his *Argonauts* include a large number of references to the work of Callimachus, and in these imitations there is no trace of malicious intention.'

Book III is much the most attractive of the four books of the *Argonauts*; in it Apollonius describes Medea's love with considerable power and not without some echoes of Euripides. When she sees the Greek hero for the first time she is overwhelmed:

Every anxiety that Eros arouses stirred in her heart. Once again everything that had happened passed before her eyes: the form of Jason, the clothes he was wearing, the words he had spoken, how he had sat, the way in which he had left her. In the ferment of her heart, it seemed to her that no other man like him could exist in the whole world. Her ears could hear nothing but his voice, and the words he had spoken were sweeter than honey. She was afraid for him, fearing lest the bulls of Aietes himself should harm him. She wept as though he were already dead; tears of pity and of anguish streamed down her cheeks. . . .

And when Jason returns to her:

Her heart leapt in her breast, her eyes were dimmed with tears, the blood

344

flushed her cheeks, she was so overwhelmed with weakness she could neither advance nor retreat. It was as though her feet were glued to the ground (*Argonauts*, III, 451–61).

Obviously, Apollonius was familiar with the odes of Sappho.

Callimachus had set the fashion for verbal virtuosity and 'artistic writing'. Lycophron, known as the 'Obscure', was to go much further in this direction than any other poet of the time. He was, really, the 'connoisseur's poet', unintelligible to the public, though appreciated by a few initiates. Born at Chalcis in Euboea towards the end of the fourth century, Lycophron came to Alexandria where he acquired a great reputation both as a scholar and as a tragic poet. His most famous work, the *Alexandria*, is a strange poem of almost fifteen hundred lines, each of which requires laborious exegesis if it is to be understood. In this long burlesque monologue a slave reports the prophecies of Alexandria, that is to say, of Cassandra the daughter of Priam—prophecies which embrace the lifetime of the author. Lycrophron may have been attempting to revert to the poetry of the fourth century and to revive the abrupt and splendid style, the bold and disconcerting metaphors, of Aeschylus and Pindar. But the imitation is so persistent and systematic that the reader soon loses the thread. He was not without talent, however, and some of his lines have an astonishing power and virtuosity. Anybody in our time who derives pleasure from hermetic or sibylline poetry would enjoy the *Alexandria*.

Of all the Hellenistic poets, more even than Callimachus, it is Theocritus who is most worth reading today. And it was he, moreover, who exercised the greatest influence on Latin literature, especially on Virgil. He was a Greek from Sicily, born in Syracuse about 300 B.C. or a little earlier; so that he was slightly younger than Callimachus. About 275 B.C. he dedicated his sixteenth *Idyll*, the *Graces* or *Hieron*, to Hieron II, the tyrant of Syracuse who had proclaimed himself king, hoping to obtain his help and protection. But Hieron turned a deaf ear. The poet then approached Ptolemy Philadelphus who replied favourably. After spending some time in the island of Cos, Theocritus settled in Alexandria where he wrote his *Idyll* XVII, in praise of Ptolemy. He was, like Callimachus, a court poet and also a lovable man, indolent and sensual, opposed to any kind of constraint, always ready to tease and mock, an indulgent companion, a refined and courteous host, and a faithful friend.

As a literary form, the Idyll seems to have been invented by

Theocritus. The word *eidyllion* is a diminutive, meaning a small picture or poem. Its use implies that Theocritus belonged to the same literary circle as Callimachus and was a master of *oligostichia*, that is to say, of short poems. Moreover the word *idyll*, like the word *elegy*, only refers to the form, not to the content, which could be extremely varied: an epic fragment, a scene from everyday life, rustic or urban, pastoral or bourgeois. If, today, the idyll is usually associated with love poetry, it is because, in the main, Theocritus, like most Hellenistic poets, was obsessed with the subject.

The Cyclops in *Idyll* XI owes much less to Homer than to the famous dithyramb by Philoxenos of Cythera (see p. 317). He is both ridiculous and touching. He is in love with the Nereid, Galateia, and asks her:

O white Galateia, why do you repulse my love, you whose skin is whiter than curded cream, you who are gentler than the lamb and friskier than the heifer, and whose sheen is like that of green grapes? I know why you flee from me. It's because I have a shaggy eyebrow stretching across my face from one ear to the other, with only one eye and a crooked nose. . . . O that I had been born with gills, so that I could dive into the water after you, and if you would not grant me your lips I would be content to kiss your hand. . . . (*Id.* XI, 19 ff.).

It must be admitted that this gallant Cyclops, who is ready to become a fish in order to be with his love, is mawkish, precious and arch, weaknesses to which Alexandrian poetry has all too great a tendency. But, in *Hylas*, Heracles' love for the child stolen from him by water nymphs is powerfully described:

Wretched are those who love! What sufferings Heracles endured! A prey to madness, he approached the cruel god, who tore out his liver (*Id.* XIII, 66–7).

In the *Sorceress*, Theocritus expresses the wild passion of a young woman, Simaetha, for the lover who has left her. To bring him back she has recourse to magic: she spins the 'bird wheel' (*iynx*), and the piercing refrain occurs like a litany: '*Iynx*, bring back this man to me, bring back my lover,' while another refrain repeats an incantation to the moon: 'Thus know my love and whence it came, august Selene' (*Id.* II, 17 and 87).

As Callimachus had done in the *Hecale*, Theocritus transposes epic into a more contemporary key. The *Cyclops* is one example of this, but the Idyll on the *Childhood of Heracles* is even more typical. It relates the story of the hero's first exploit when, still in his cradle, he succeeded in strangling the serpents that Hera had sent to kill him. This is how it goes:

Alcmena heard his cries and was the first to wake, 'Get up, Amphitryon, I am too frightened to move. Hurry up, don't waste time putting on your sandals. Can't you hear, it's the baby crying. Something unusual is going on. (*Id.* XXIV, 34 ff.).

And, in obedience to his wife's orders, he got out of bed. The epic heroes, Amphitryon and Alcmena, have become ordinary parents, peaceful citizens who have been woken up in the middle of the night. The myth is interpreted in terms of everyday life, as one finds so frequently in the plastic arts of the period.

The somewhat conventional pastoral vein that had so much influence on Virgil's *Eclogues* is found in many of the Idylls: *Thyrsis,* the *Shepherds,* the *Goatherd and the Shepherd,* the *Country Choir,* the *Thalysies.* In his last poem there is a description of a warm day at the end of summer, where colours, sounds and scents conspire to create an effect of stifling heat. In the *Syracusan Women,* two young women from Syracuse have come to Alexandria for the feast of Adonis. First, one calls for the other, who welcomes her in a friendly and vivacious way: they discuss the question of husbands with all the light-hearted bawdiness of popular speech, to which snatches of Syracusan dialect give added point. Then the two friends set out for the temple, admiring the crowd of passers-by in the street and the horsemen who almost knock them down:

What a lot of people. However are we going to get through this crowd? Its as busy as an ant-heap. Truly, Ptolemy, you've done a lot of fine things since your father joined the gods: no more rascals, trying to get off with a girl, like the Egyptians. . . . O Gorgo, my dear, whatever's going to become of us? Look, here come the king's cavalry. All right, my man, there's no need to ride me down. Look at that chestnut, how wildly it is rearing. Thank goodness I left the child at home! (*Id.* xv, 44 ff.).

Its interesting to note the way she praises Ptolemy's police. When at last they reach the royal palace, the two women are overwhelmed with admiration at the splendour of everything they see and hear.

347

This Idyll is a veritable mime, imitated perhaps from Sophron; its vivacity and lively realism make it a small masterpiece.

Theocritus avoided the shoals of erudition more successfully than the other poets of his time. He can still move us with his deep vibrant sensibility, his love of nature and his sense of drama. The varied nature of his talent, the beauty of his descriptions of countryside and town, his wit, the virtuosity with which he manipulates language and dialect, combine to make him a great poet.

In the fifth century, Sophron of Syracuse, almost a contemporary of Euripides, had made a name for himself in the kind of mime imitated in the *Syracusan Women*. He had been influenced by Epicharmos (see pp. 171 ff.). His homely farces, which he wrote in popular Doric, were full of animation and brilliant observation; Plato admired them and, it is said, was influenced by them when writing his Dialogues. Such short fragments of Sophron's works have been preserved, however, that the best examples we have of the Greek mime are those by the Hellenistic poet Herondas or Herodas. A dozen mimes by him, several of them considerably mutilated, were discovered in papyrus in 1889. They are written in the Ionic dialect, though with a considerable number of Doric and Attic expressions, in *choriambic* verse, that is to say, iambic trimetres, in which the final iamb is replaced by a spondee.

Where Herondas came from is unknown, but he seems to have been more or less contemporary with Theocritus. The titles of the mimes that have been discovered sufficiently indicate his general approach: the *Go-Between*, the *Whoremonger*, the *Schoolmaster*, the *Women of Asclepius' Temple*, the *Jealous Woman*, the *Cronies*, the *Shoemaker*, the *Dream*, *Women at Breakfast*, the *Spinning Girls*, etc. An old procuress visits a woman whose husband is travelling abroad and makes immodest proposals to her. The landlord of a public brothel brings an action because of the damage done to his premises by a rowdy client. A mother begs a schoolmaster to punish her good-for-nothing son for the wicked tricks he plays. A young wife visits another because, at a friend's house, she has seen a leather dildo, and is dying to find out the address of the maker.

The way the two friends talk about their slaves is like Theocritus' women of Syracuse:

Corytto: Sit down Metro. (*Turning to the servant*) Bring a chair for Madam. Come on, be quick.—I have to tell her everything.—Can't you do any-

thing without having to be told, idiot? Really, I might just as well have
a block of stone in the house, for all the use you are. . . . Wonderful!
So this is the moment you decide to start polishing the chair. You can thank
your stars I've got a visitor, or you'd soon feel the weight of my hand,
my girl. . . .
Metro: My poor Corytto, I have to put up with just the same sort of thing.
From morning to night I gnash my teeth, chasing these wretched girls
like a dog. But the reason I came to see you. . . . (*Mime*, VI, 1–15).

These brilliant little sketches of social behaviour were written
either to be read, or performed in public: short scenes, with two or
three entertaining characters. These are caught in their most typical
everyday pursuits, with all their trivial worries, their passions and
amusements, and the vivid tang of colloquial speech. Here, we are a
long way from the formal erudition of Callimachus. Herondas'
realism knows no limits and is quite unscrupulous: he is not afraid of
obscenity when occasion arises, though he can hardly be accused of
introducing it for its own sake. He is content to reproduce the most
outrageous conversation, without complacency or insistence. The
whole unpretentious charm of these miniature comedies lies in the
vitality and naturalness of the often crude dialogue. Herondas'
extreme freedom may sometimes be shocking, but apart from the
fact that we learn a great deal about the manners of ancient society
from these snapshots, he is never boring and often highly entertaining.

Aratos of Solis, in Cilicia, was a poet, or versifier, of a very different
kind. With him we are back once more with that type of erudite
Alexandrian literature that logically tends towards didacticism, which
ever since Hesiod's time had always enjoyed respect in Greece. Aratos,
probably born about 315, was a friend of Theocritus, who mentioned
him several times in his *Idylls*. He spent some time at the court of
Antigonos Gonatas, king of Macedonia (see p. 324) and also lived in
Alexandria where he knew Callimachus. Philosopher, mathematician
and scholar, as well as poet, Aratos wrote a great deal. But he was
known to his contemporaries, as to posterity, above all as the author
of the *Phenomena*, a verse popularization of the astronomy and
meteorology of his time. It has none of the brilliance and conviction
of a Lucretius, yet it is a work of talent, distinguished for its elegance
and clarity.

With Nicander of Colophon, born towards the end of the third
century, we reach a much lower level of didacticism and popularization.

Nevertheless the two poems of his that have survived, the *Theriaka* dealing with the bites of various animals and their remedies and the *Alexipharmaka*, are not without interest to the specialist.

Amongst the Delphic inscriptions, not only are there two poems by Aristonoos of Corinth (see p. 316), but also two hymns to Phoebos Apollo, written by Dionysiac artists from Athens in the second half of the second century, after 146. What is unusual about them is that they are accompanied by their musical notation, so clearly carved that it has been possible to restore the melody (with what degree of certainty I do not know) so that they can be performed. These two hymns allude to the 'miraculous' preservation of the Pythian sanctuary in 278 at the time of the Celtic invasion which led to the foundation of the festival of the *Soteria* (see p. 324). The second hymn contains these words:

Thus, Lord Apollo, you stood guard near the holy navel of the earth when the barbarian horde, seeking to profane the home of your oracle to steal its treasure, perished in the damp whirlwind of snow. . . . With the aid of Apollo, of Artemis and of Leto, may the empire of the Romans, crowned with spears and always flourishing in its imperishable youth, increase, as it marches forward from victory to victory! (*Fouilles de Delphes;* III, 2, 138, l. 31 ff.).

GEOGRAPHY AND HISTORY

At the beginning of the Hellenistic epoch, as in our own fifteenth century, the world suddenly expanded; at least man's knowledge of what had hitherto been *terrae ignotae* was enormously enlarged and deepened. It was a period of great voyages of discovery and exploration. Moreover, thanks to the methods bequeathed by Aristotle's Lyceum to the scientists of Alexandria and elsewhere, the history of Greece's past now became the subject of much more precise and methodical research than previously, particularly as regards chronology and the synchronization of historical events in different parts of the known world. While Thucydides had confined himself to what happened in Greece during a period of twenty-two years, men now began to conceive of Universal History, extending from the origin of society up to the present.

The prince of scientific geography and historical chronology, Eratosthenes (see p. 341), was a universally gifted man, like Leonardo da Vinci and other great artists of the Renaissance. He was a poet, philosopher, literary critic, geographer, historian, mathematician, geometrician, astronomer and physicist. Born at Cyrene like Callimachus, in 273, Eratosthenes completed his studies at Athens under the most famous members of the Academy and the Stoics. When Callimachus persuaded Ptolemy Euergetes to invite him to Alexandria and put him in charge of the Library, he was thirty years old. He lived to be over eighty, and according to tradition, allowed himself to die of hunger because his eyesight failed.

Not only did Eratosthenes measure the circumference of the earth with remarkable accuracy (250,000 *stades*, i.e., 39,375 km.—an error of only about 4%), but in his descriptive geography, taking into account the views of Pytheas on the latitude of Marseilles, and also the theories of Dicaearchos, a Peripatetic of the fourth century, on the configuration of the Peloponnese, he produced a much more correct map of the world than those of his predecessors and the majority of his successors. Strabo often criticized the positions attributed to places by Eratosthenes, but almost always modern science supports Eratosthenes rather than Strabo.

His dating of historical events is equally remarkable for the extent of his information, and especially for his bold and vigorous criticism. He was the first to equate the beginning of historical times in Greece with the origin of the Olympic Games (776 B.C.) and regarded everything prior to this date as belonging to the mythical period. At the same time, he also studied the traditions relating to the origin of the country and his *Chronological Tables* start with the Trojan war. The chronology he established deserved the authority it achieved, and even today, despite certain criticisms with regard to the Mycenaean period, it still seems, to those best qualified to judge, the safest and most credible.

Not a single work of Eratosthenes has come down to us. As regards his poems and philosophical treatises the loss is probably not very serious. But his scientific works, known to us only from quotation and discussion of them by later writers, were certainly of the first rank. There can be no doubt that he was one of the greatest scientists of the Alexandrian epoch, on a level with Archimedes and Hipparchos.

In the time of Polybius, that is to say in the second century B.C., the historian who enjoyed the greatest reputation was Timaeus of Tauromanion in Sicily, who died at the age of a hundred, about 250. Only a few passages of his *History of Sicily* and *History of Pyrrhus* are known to us. Polybius continually attacked him, accusing him of partiality, ignorance and untruthfulness; he also reproached him for writing in the bookish, tortured style of the rhetoricians. This kind of criticism was customary amongst historians: Herodotus' handling of Hecataeus was not exactly gentle. Nevertheless, it is clear from Polybius' criticism that Timaeus had considerable qualities: an immense output of scholarly work based on original documents, and a judicial mind.

But Polybius was to throw Timaeus in the shade. An Achaean of noble birth, the son of Lycrotas, who was a friend of Philopoemen (see p. 326) and a general, Polybius was born at Megalopolis about 208. He soon began to take part in the political and military life of his father. In 183, it was to Polybius that the honour of bringing back Philopoemen's ashes to the fatherland was entrusted. Later, he accompanied his father on an embassy to Egypt, and there he found himself closely involved in the affairs of the Achaean League until 168, the year of the battle of Pydna (see p. 326). After the Roman victory, the Senate insisted that a thousand Achaeans should be handed over as hostages and Polybius was one of them. Thus, at the age of forty, he set out for Italy, spending eighteen years there at a time which, in the opinion of Cicero, was the Golden Age of the Republic. The discipline and civic virtues of the Romans amazed him. As has been said: 'There was, so to speak, a pre-ordained harmony between his vigorous intelligence and this new world; no one was better fitted than he to understand and appreciate it.' Like Thucydides' exile, Polybius' forced stay in Italy and at Rome had a beneficial effect on his work as an historian. Roman society was certainly better suited to his temperament than the troubled and quarrelsome Achaea of the time. His admiration for Rome was enthusiastic but also clear-sighted.

Fabius and Publius, the sons of Paulus Aemilius, the victor of Pydna, became his friends; the latter, known as Scipio Aemilianus, was the future conqueror of Carthage and Numantia. In a charming passage, Polybius tells how this friendship began with the loan of some books, and how the younger of the two brothers, then eighteen years old, modestly asked for Polybius' attention and advice, as up till then he had been mainly concerned with his elder brother. In this household, where he was treated not as a hostage but as a respected friend, Polybius met Laelius and the flower of Roman aristocracy. Out of friendship for Polybius, Scipio pleaded for the Achaean hostages with Cato, and in 150 the latter decided to liberate them. Polybius returned home, but Rome had become his second country. He revisited it several times and accompanied Scipio on his campaigns: he was with him in 146 at the capture of Carthage.

Rejecting the wise advice of Polybius, however, the Achaeans revolted against Rome, and as a result, Corinth was taken and Greece was reduced to a Roman province. Polybius used his influence with the conquerors to save a number of his fellow countrymen who had been compromised, and he earned the gratitude of certain Greek cities, especially Elis, which erected a statue to him at Olympia. He continued to lead an active life until he was well on in years, and died about 126 at the age of eighty-two, as a result of a fall from his horse.

His *Life of Philopoemen*, his treatise on *Tactics*, and his *Account of the Taking of Numantia*, have all been lost, but we still have several complete books, and some fragments of his principal work, the *Histories*, which originally consisted of forty books. The first two form an introduction, covering the period 264–221, but the real subject of this great work is the account of the Roman conquest, from 221–146. He claimed to have written a history that was pragmatic, universal and apodeictic. By *pragmatic*, he meant, quite simply, that it was a history of political and military events (*pragmata*), in contrast to those ancient works which were largely concerned with mythical accounts of genealogies and the founding of cities. It was *universal* because it included the whole known territory (*oikoumene*), at that time under the domination or protection of Rome. And lastly, it was *apodeictic*, in the sense that it was demonstrably true: Polybius had a positive, realistic mind; he studied the causation of events, particularly the origin of wars, in a rigorously methodical and precise way, based on the logical categories established by the school of Aristotle. He was fully conscious of the novelty of his purpose and the originality of his principles, though these owed much to Thucydides.

Polybius was also a geographer. He travelled extensively, and made a careful study, particularly from the point of view of ethnography and economics, of all the countries he passed through, above all, of Spain, still little known in his time, and parts of Africa. He sought to rectify the false ideas that were current before his day; he took a stand on the geographical problems of his time, on the geography of Homer, on the existence of a southern continent, and on the question as to whether the equatorial zone was inhabited. Following the general tendency of the period, though he began as a man of action, he later became a serious scholar. This is why, like the Peripatetics, he was so interested in the constitutions of countries. His studies of the constitutions of Sparta, Carthage and especially of Rome, as well as the military organization of the Romans, have justly remained classics. His one weakness as an historian was his prejudice with regard to certain enemies of the Achaeans, such as the Aetolians, whom he goes out of his way to condemn for their greed and brutality.

As a writer, though he is extremely clear, his style is dull and lacking in artistry, and he has not unjustly been criticized as one of the originators of political and journalistic jargon: had he been writing today, he would certainly have used such expressions as 'activize', 'factors' and 'organisms'.

Compared with Livy, who drew heavily upon his work, it is Polybius, the *Graeculus*, who gives the impression of being a strict and methodical historian, while the Roman is much more concerned with style and rhetoric. His account of the Roman conquest is lucid and profound. All the essential qualities of Thucydides, except his style, are to be found in Polybius, which is saying a great deal.

In the first century B.C., the historians and geographers who wrote in Greek were mainly compilers of facts, without much originality, though such of their works as have been preserved are valuable for the information they give about the ancient world: Diodorus of Sicily, author of a vast *Historical Library*; Dionysius of Halicarnassos, a literary critic as well as an historian whose *Roman Archaeology* is still very useful; and lastly Strabo, an historian, but especially a geographer, who sought to follow in the footsteps of Polybius in the same way that Xenophon continued the work of Thucydides. His *Geographica* provides a complete picture of the ancient world at the beginning of the Roman empire.

In the second century A.D., Arrian of Nicomedia who in his youth had heard Epictetus (see p. 335), became a high official of the empire, thanks to the favour of Hadrian who held him in high esteem. Amongst several historical and geographical writings, the work devoted to *India* contains many curious passages, notably the account of the navigations of Nearchos, one of Alexander's officers, who explored the northern coast of the Sea of Erythrea and the Persian Gulf, from the mouth of the Indus to Susa. Though this book is completely secondhand, it displays qualities of style and taste which show Arrian to have been something more and something better than a merely elegant popularizer.

PLUTARCH

In the Foreword to his *La Vie quotidienne à Rome à l'apogée de l'empire* Jérome Carcopino writes: 'Since a choice had to be made, I have deliberately chosen the generation which, born at the end of the reign of Claudius or the beginning of the reign of Nero, towards the middle of the first century A.D., lived on into the time of Trajan (98–117 A.D.) and Hadrian (117–138 A.D.). This was the generation that witnessed Roman power and prosperity at its height.'

It was above all, the generation of Epictetus (see p. 335), Dio of Prusa and Plutarch. Dio, later known as Chrysostomos (the golden-mouthed), was born about 40 A.D. at Prusa in Bithynia where his family was one of the richest and most influential in the town. With a natural gift for eloquence, and educated by the best teachers of rhetoric of the time, Dio soon became a well-known orator who, in the manner of the ancient sophists, travelled from country to country, giving his lectures and everywhere receiving enthusiastic applause. He lived in Rhodes, in Egypt and, above all, in Rome, where he aroused the suspicions of Domitian by his friendly relations with L. Flavius Sabinus, the emperor's first cousin who was put to death in 82 A.D. Dio was banished and not allowed to live either in Italy or in Bithynia.

His exile, which lasted fourteen years until the death of Domitian, changed not only his life, but also his character and outlook. He became a homeless wanderer, travelling throughout the east with nothing but his cloak, wallet and staff, like one of the Cynics. The experience was to transform him from a rhetorician into a sincere and profound philosopher, despite the fact that he had earlier written a violent discourse, *Against Philosophers*. It was, indeed, a veritable conversion. The only two books he took with him were Demosthenes' *The Embassy* (he had not lost his taste for eloquence), and Plato's *Phaedo*.

Under Nerva (96–8 A.D.) and Trajan (98–117 A.D.) Dio was restored to favour, but he remained a philosopher and continued to preach the need for moral conversion. His many journeys were not unlike those of a missionary. His success was tremendous. Summoned to Rome, he delivered two speeches *On the Monarchy*, addressed to Trajan. He died in 112 A.D. Among his extant works, those belonging to the first half of his life, before his exile, are mainly virtuoso performances. The second *Trojan Discourse* set out to prove that the

Achaeans had never captured Troy; and he also wrote eulogies *On a Fly* and *On a Parrot*.

The political and moral speeches written during and after his exile are of much greater interest. The thought is scarcely original: Dio's eclectic philosophy owes much to the Stoics, as his theology does to Platonism. He is continually chiding his listeners for the slackness of their behaviour, their love of money and well-being, their blindness to true spiritual values, that is to say, virtue and the search for God. His preaching displays considerable talent, as well as grace and wit. The *Huntsman: a Story of Euboea* is one of his most attractive works. Paul Mazon, who has translated it into French, says that at first it seems to be 'a kind of sermon on the dignity of peasant life, but later becomes propaganda in support of the policy of "back to the land" which was constantly advocated by the Roman emperors, particularly by Nerva and Trajan, with whom Dio was personally friendly.'[1]

Plutarch was a much more genuine philosopher than Dio. Because of his most famous work, the *Parallel Lives* of Greeks and Romans, he might be included amongst the historians, though he himself never laid claim to this title. What interested him in the lives of great men was not their outstanding military or political deeds, but their character, their moral physiognomy or, as we should say today, their 'psychology'. Plutarch regarded himself not as an historian, but as a philosopher, which, in fact, he was. True, he was not the creator of a system, but he was an accomplished psychologist, moralist, metaphysician, and theologian. The second part of his extant work, not so well-known as the *Lives*, has been mistakenly given the title *Moralia*: it does contain some moral treatises, but it also deals with many other subjects. A more suitable title would be *Essays on Various Subjects*, and anyone who has read the *Lives* knows how full they are of philosophical asides.

Chaironeia, where Plutarch was born about 46 A.D., in the reign of Claudius, is a little town in Boeotia, quite near Parnassos and the frontier with Phocis, where Delphi is situated. Several battles had been fought there, notably in 338 B.C. Plutarch belonged to a prosperous and well-known family: his great-grandfather Nicharchos, his grandfather Lanprias, and his father Autoboulos were all witty, cultured men, many of whose sayings he recorded. Somewhere around his twentieth year, like all young men of good family in those days, he went to Athens to conclude his studies.

---

[1] Paul Mazon: *Lettres d'humanité* II (1943), p. 47–8.

At that time, Athens was above all a university town, a kind of Oxford. Distinguished teachers lived there and well-known personalities were always passing through. Fifteen years before Plutarch's arrival, in about 51 A.D., a certain Paul of Tarsus, then scarcely known, had preached the Gospel there. He was in the habit of engaging in conversation with anyone he met in the Agora, as Socrates used to do, and the author of the *Acts of the Apostles* noted a feature of the Athenian character that recalls a remark of Demosthenes: 'the favourite pastime of all Athenians and aliens was to exchange the latest news.' The news brought by Paul was important: 'The Unknown God whom ye ignorantly worship, him I declare unto you,' (XVII, 23). This solemn confrontation of Christianity and Hellenism had little immediate result beyond a handful of conversions. Paul was to have greater success with the workmen of Corinth than with the philosophers of Athens. Plutarch himself, who was familiar with the Jews and their teaching, never mentions Christianity or the Christians; he seems to have known nothing about them.

Ten years after Paul, a very different personality arrived in Athens, the Pythagorean miracle-worker, Apollonius of Tyana on his first journey to Greece. Philostratos, in his *Life of Apollonius* says, 'He arrived at the port of Piraeus during the time of the Eleusinian mysteries, a time of year when Athens is the most crowded city in Greece. He landed and made his way up to the town, meeting many philosophers who were going to Phaleron. Some of these were sunning themselves, for the autumn is very warm in Athens, others were reading, practising declamation, or arguing. All of them, as soon as they learnt that it was Apollonius, hailed him joyfully, and stood aside for him to pass. When a group of ten young men met him, one of them, raising his hands towards the Acropolis, cried: "By Athena, standing there on high, I swear that we were just on our way to take ship from Piraeus, in order to visit you in Ionia".'

At Athens, Plutarch began by studying rhetoric, and we still have some of his youthful exercises; for example, a treatise on the question, Which is the more useful, fire or water? But, whereas Dio followed the profession of orator until his forties, Plutarch soon gave up public speaking. His grave and serious nature led him to study things rather than words, that is to say, science and philosophy. He took a passionate interest in mathematics, and also studied physics, the natural sciences and medicine. But it was above all philosophy that held him. His outstanding teacher was the Platonist Ammonios, to whom he sometimes accords the same place in his Dialogues as Plato had done to Socrates. Though he studied all the Greek philosophical systems, it was the philosophy of the 'divine' Plato that became the basis for his own conception of the world and of mankind.

Later on, Plutarch often returned to Athens to meet his friends and enjoy 'the books and varied conversation' that he could not find at home. He was made an honorary citizen of Athens. As a young man, he had already visited Alexandria to listen to some of the well-known teachers. His fellow citizens entrusted him with a mission to the Roman pro-Consul living at Corinth, and later sent him to Rome. By the time he arrived in Italy, towards the end of the reign of Vespasian (69–79 A.D.), he had himself become a teacher, lecturing on philosophy to cultured Romans, one of whom was 'that famous J. Arulenus Rusticus, whom Domitian later executed because he was jealous of his fame.' In the latter part of his life, Plutarch, like Dio, 'preached' philosophy and morality and acted as a kind of spiritual adviser. He visited many towns in Italy and returned to Rome on at least one other occasion, under Domitian.

Plutarch, however, was not cut out for the life of an itinerant lecturer. He returned to live at Chaironeia, lest, as he says, 'this little city should be still smaller for my absence'; and there he married. His wife, Timoxena, also a native of Chaironeia, bore him five children, four of whom were sons. He was an hereditary Archon, and seems also to have held the position of 'Boeotarchos' which gave him jurisdiction over the whole of Boeotia.

If, during the first half of Plutarch's life, the influence of Athens was predominant, the sanctuary of Apollo at Delphi began to affect him deeply from the moment that he accepted office as one of its priests, a position which he continued to fill until his death. Already a citizen of Athens, he now became a citizen of Delphi and had a house there, though without ceasing to live at Chaironeia. It was only a days' journey from Chaironeia to Delphi over Mt Parnassos and Plutarch often went there by horse or mule to fulfil his duties. Even while still primarily a philosopher, Plutarch had maintained his religious beliefs; when he became a priest, he was more and more drawn to religious and theological problems. At Delphi, he also became *epimeletos* to the Amphictyony and a director of the Games. After his death, his statue was erected in the holy city with the following elegiac couplet: 'Delphi and Chaironeia here honour Plutarch in accordance with a decree of the Amphictyonie.'

Despite all these public offices and his intense literary activity, Plutarch still managed to pay short visits to his friends at Athens, Corinth, Elis, Patras, Aedepsos (in Euboea) and Thermopylae. At home in Chaironeia, he led the simple, unostentatious life becoming to a philospher. People came from far and near to seek his advice, and among his guests were important magistrates, and an Assyrian prince, Philopappos. In this way he lived serenely and austerely, surrounded by family affection and the duties of friendship, and devoting himself to his literary work, the service of the gods and his public responsibilities. After the accession of Hadrian (117–138 A.D.), he had the pleasure of seeing the emperor, an archaeologist and lover of Greece, take an active interest in restoring the Pythian shrine, thus encouraging a revival of the Delphic religion and 'ancestral faith' to which Plutarch remained wholeheartedly attached until his death in his eighties, about 126 A.D.

Though a great part of his work has been lost, the volume of his extant writings remains considerable. The *Parallel Lives*, which were so widely read in Europe and exerted so great an influence from the sixteenth to the eighteenth century, are one of the most valuable sources for our knowledge of Greek and Roman history. As he himself says:

It so happened that I began to write these *Lives* to give pleasure to friends, but I have persisted with the project for my own sake, and I delight in it. For me, history is like a faithful mirror in which I observe these great men in order that I may seek to model my own life on their virtues (*Paulus Aemilius*, 1, 1.).

It was their author's intention that each of these biographies should constitute a chapter in a study of the heroic virtues. Then, one day, it struck him that the spectacle of vice could be as useful as that of spiritual greatness, 'after the manner of the Spartans who, having forced the helots to get drunk, would bring them into the room where the communal meal was being eaten, in order to inspire the young people with a horror of drunkenness' (*Demetrius*, 1, 2). He, therefore decided to write the lives of such unedifying characters as Demetrius Poliorcetes and Antony. True, in the *Lives*, which prove him to be a first-rate storyteller with a high sense of drama and a gift for picturesque and revealing detail, one is always coming across Plutarch's own feelings and ideas. Yet it is in his other, much less famous, works

359

that he reveals himself most directly and completely in all the rich diversity of his gifts.

Doubtless, there is a certain amount of padding in the *Moralia*. As a writer, he was occasionally diffuse and long-winded, and he scarcely ever revised what he wrote. Yet throughout his work, one continually encounters passages that are either profound or curious, amusing or instructive, and most of his dialogues, particularly those *On Love, On the Reprieve of Divine Justice* and the three *Pythian Dialogues*, are works of art, which, though they do not attain the literary beauty of his model, Plato, are nevertheless remarkable achievements. So good a judge as Montaigne called Amyot's translation of Plutarch 'his breviary' and he added: 'Plutarch is everywhere to be admired. . . . His teaching is the cream of philosophy. . . . He is so universal and so full of matter that, for every occasion, he fulfils our needs, and with a liberal and inexhaustible hand offers us his riches and his beauties. . . . I can scarcely stir, without running into him. . . .' And, indeed, the *Essays* are full of quotations from Plutarch, more even than would appear at first sight, for Montaigne sometimes forgot to use quotation marks.

In the history of philosophy, Plutarch represents what is called 'Middle' Platonism. He is much truer to Plato's thought than Arcesilaos or Carneades. Occasionally, on points of detail, he appeals to Aristotelian ideas or to the theories of the Stoics, though he frequently raises objections to the philosophy of the latter. The only philosophical school to which he is resolutely opposed is Epicureanism, despite the fact that his treatise *Of Superstition*, written when he was a young man, develops certain of Epicurus' ideas. The older he grew the more religious he became and, under the influence of the Delphic sanctuary, the mystical tendencies of Platonism increasingly appealed to him. Nevertheless, in this respect he remained a long way from the Neoplatonists.

The reader will perhaps have noticed how frequently, in the preceding chapters, I have quoted from Plutarch. In fact, Plutarch was both a literary and an art critic, and, in the best sense of the word, an antiquarian. He had a wide familiarity with all the poets and prose writers of Greece and was also interested in works of art, inscriptions and numismatics. His opinions and the information he provides us with are all the more valuable because so many of the works of his predecessors which he had read have since disappeared, and many of the monuments which he saw in their full beauty have either been completely destroyed or are now only ruins. Certain passages in Plutarch have an interest comparable to the *Description of Greece* that Pausanias wrote towards the end of the second century A.D., a kind of tourist's guide to Hellas, though Plutarch was a more cultivated man with much better taste. Plutarch's work is in a sense a resumé and recapitulation of the whole history and literature of Hellas. He has sometimes been regarded, in his attitude towards the past, as a mere compiler of facts, but nothing could be further from the truth or more unjust, for the power of his personality is persistently to be felt in all the writings authentically attributed to him.

THE NOVELS

Plutarch's conception of love and its significance is essentially the same as Plato's, though in the *Dialogue on Love* there are certain differences. For Plutarch, Eros is no longer the 'daimon' of the *Symposium*, a creature half god, half man, a kind of mediator, but a great god who was worshipped by the Greeks at Thespiae in Boeotia. Moreover, for him, it is no longer homosexual love that draws men to the Idea of the Beautiful and ultimate knowledge: the love between men and women, particularly in marriage, is equally valuable and efficacious. 'Conjugal intercourse,' says Plutarch, 'is a source of friendship like a common participation in the great mysteries' (*Amatorius*, 769 A).

On this last point, Plutarch is at one with the authors of the Greek novels, since in them homosexuality plays practically no part. This is not a question of literary influence: several of the novels appear to have been written before Plutarch's time. It is a result of the general evolution of ideas and social behaviour in ancient Greece. Already in the New Comedy of Menander (see p. 319 ff.) far more stress is placed upon affection and tenderness and the love between betrothed and married people; and this theme had become a commonplace of the Alexandrian poets.

In Greece Celtic women enjoyed a high reputation for loyalty and courage, which is one aspect of that idealization of the barbarians that we frequently find in the period we are now discussing. Some of the love stories told by Plutarch, for example, those of the Galatian, Canna, and the woman of Gaul, Empona, though they are partly based on fact, may already be regarded as short novels or, preferably, 'long short stories'. The Greeks had no word exactly corresponding to our 'novel', though they were familiar with the conception of fiction from the Homeric and Platonic myths and were never lacking in creative imagination. However, the Greek novel is not just any kind of myth but a particular kind of story that recounts the life and deeds of a number of characters, in relation to a hero and a heroine, who are in love with one another and are the central characters.

In a certain sense it may be said that the earliest Greek novels were the *Iliad* and the *Odyssey*. Adultery adds spice to the story of Helen; moreover the novelists were frequently to refer to her as the prototype, at least as regards beauty, of all their heroines. And the *Odyssey*, even more than the *Iliad*, is a 'romantic epic'; after twenty years of adventures, Odysseus returns to his beloved Penelope, whom he has never forgotten and who has remained patiently faithful to him.

In prose, Xenophon's *Cyropaedia* (see p. 262) contains at least the outline of a novel, as Mademoiselle de Scudéry realized when she came to write the *Grand Cyrus*, the purely fictional story of Abradatas and his wife Panthea. But in Xenophon one does not yet find the complexity of plot and the improbable accumulation of events characteristic of the novels that have come down to us. This type of work can be defined as follows: the Greek novel is, in essence, a decadent epic that employs facile methods of moving the reader: opposition of good and evil; confidants, and triangular situations; the affliction of the heroes with such misfortunes as tempests, shipwrecks, attacks by highwaymen and pirates; and yet another danger, no less redoubtable and quite unavoidable, the outstanding beauty of both hero and heroine. They have only to meet, and they immediately fall passionately in love with each other, with or without various degrees of moral scruple. . . . All these setbacks delay the final consummation of their happiness, sometimes threatening to prevent it altogether. The novel thus becomes a description of a pursuit, interspersed with mishaps, so that the anxiously awaited marriage is continually delayed by disheartening fatalities.

The titles of the Greek novels are always taken from the hero and heroine: e.g. *Chaereas and Callirhoe, Habrocomes and Anthea* (or *The Ephesians*), *Daphnis and Chloe, Theagenes and Charicleia* (or *The Ethopians*), and *Leukippe and Cleitophon*. The earliest of these appears to have been written about the first century B.C. by a Greek from Asia, Chariton of Aphrodisias in Caria. The historical background is detailed, although the chronology allows considerable scope for fantasy: it takes place in Greece at the end of the fifth century B.C.

The story opens in Syracuse where the leading citizen is General Hermocrates who defeated the Athenians at the time of the Sicilian expedition. From there it goes to Miletus, to Babylon during the reign of Artaxerxes, to Phoenicia, to Cyprus, and finally back to Syracuse. Hermocrates' daughter Callirhoe who is as lovely as 'the still virgin Aphrodite', and Chaereas are struck by 'Love's thunderbolt' the first time they set eyes on each other. From then on they are bound to one another for life. They get married and, to begin with, they are happy, but it cannot last: out of jealousy people slander Callirhoe and Chaereas foolishly believes them. I do not propose to describe the incredible misfortunes they both undergo during their long separation, each believing that the other is dead. Eventually, when Callirhoe is erecting a cenotaph for her husband, she remarks, and the author obviously does not intend us to miss the point: 'We are reciprocally burying each other.'

The novel is full of quotations from Homer and, like the *Iliad* and the *Odyssey*, includes numerous divine interventions, though it is always Aphrodite who appears, no longer Zeus, Athena or Apollo. At last, when after so many adventures Chaereas and Callirhoe once more find each other, they faint three times in succession, overwhelm each other with their tears and stories, then embrace and 'once more experience the bliss of sharing their marriage bed'. This sentence, imitated from the end of the *Odyssey*, confirms that the whole tale is based on the story of Odysseus and Penelope.

Xenophon of Ephesus, the author of the *Ephesians*, probably lived in the second century A.D. Once again we are concerned with the heroic constancy of a husband and wife, Habrocomes and Anthea. What gives this novel its special character, however, is its consistently religious, almost mystical, tone. The story is concerned less with the lovers' passion than with their virtue, which is destined to ensure their happiness, both now and in the hereafter, once it has triumphed over the tests to which it is subjected. The author frequently insists upon the happiness they will enjoy in the after life because they have always been ready to sacrifice material interests to the purity of their love.

The only one of these tales that is still well-known is also the shortest and most erotic, *Daphnis and Chloe*. It is a pastoral rather than a novel, written by Longus who, like Xenophon of Ephesus, seems to have lived in the second century A.D. Here one is reminded of Theocritus (see p. 345 ff.), for as Grimal has pointed out it is 'the development of a country idyll in prose'. On the isle of Lesbos, not far from Mytilene, some shepherds find two children who have been abandoned by their parents, a boy and a girl, accompanied with rare objects that will one day enable them to be identified. This is a frequent theme in the New Comedy and had earlier been used by Euripides.

Daphnis and Chloe watch the flocks belonging to their foster parents. Before long they are plighting their troth to each other and also talking a lot of nonsense; for Longus has no objection to using the stalest platitudes: 'Courage, Daphnis, the sun is warm. —O, my Chloe, if only it were as hot as the fire that burns in my heart!' How Chloe remains a virgin, after the obliging Lycenion has instructed Daphnis in the art of love is only to be explained on the grounds that the romantic convention insisted that physical intercourse, at least between the leading characters, should not take place until after marriage.

The *Ethiopians*, or, *Theagenes and Charicleia*, is by Heliodorus, who certainly lived in the second century A.D. and may perhaps have been successively a priest of the Sun at Emesos in Syria, and, having been converted to Christianity, Bishop of Tricca in Thessaly. It would not be surprising that a tale by a future bishop should turn out to be even more edifying that the *Ephesians*, full of priests and sanctuaries. Indeed, the masters at Port-Royal were being uncommonly strict when they forbade the fifteen year old Racine to read it; their prohibition would have been more understandably applied to *Daphnis and Chloe*.

Unlike the tales by Chariton and Xenophon, the hero and heroine are not married; though they are already betrothed. Indeed, it is only right at the end of the book that they succeed in getting married, after a hundred narrow escapes from death and having been again and again almost forced to marry someone else. The tone of the novel may be gathered from the account of their first and decisive meeting by Calasiris, a priest of Isis: 'Here was evidence that the soul is of divine origin and that its affinities are in heaven. For, immediately they set eyes upon one another, these two young folk loved each other as if their souls at this first encounter had recognized a kindred being and had leapt to meet the one spirit destined to belong to them.' Obviously, this account of falling in love is influenced by Platonism. Theagenes, a young man of exemplary virtue, swears: 'In the names of Pythian Apollo, of Artemis and Aphrodite, to act in all things in accordance with Charicleia's wishes'— the kind of vow one might expect to hear from the lips of a knight errant.

Whether Achilles Tatius of Alexandria, the author of *Leukippe and Cleitophon*, was earlier or later than Heliodorus is not known. Here the story is told by Cleitophon himself. He falls in love with Leukippe, but his feeling is not immediately reciprocated, and he only succeeds in winning his mistress after a prolonged courtship. Tatius continually compares love with initiation into the 'mysteries of Eros'. At the beginning of the book Cleitophon is described as 'an initiate of the god' and his instructor in the *ars amatoria* says to him: 'If you are accepted by the girl, you must observe silence, as though you were participating in the Mysteries.' It is true that this association of love with the Mysteries is of ancient origin and is already to be found in Xenophon's *Symposium*, as well as in Plato; but though it had become a platitude, it does contribute to the religious atmosphere found in most of the Greek novels.

Pierre Grimal has said: 'The countries the Greek storytellers use as the setting for the adventures of their heroes were certainly not imaginary. Indeed, the authors pride themselves on their veracity, and in this they differ from their modern imitators like Mademoiselle de Scudéry and her followers. The account of the king of Persia's court is realistic and the description of various Greek cities is exhilaratingly alive. . . . Their noisy, colourful world is taken from real life. If we sometimes find it disconcerting, it is because we have become accustomed to a Greece of marble ruins, whose public squares have long been deserted by the swarming oriental crowds.'

Indeed Heliodorus' descriptions of Egypt or the temple of Delphi, for example, were substantially correct. Readers of these novels—and from the sixteenth to the eighteenth century there were many of them —could have obtained a genuine understanding of the world of antiquity from them, though they were, of course, primarily attracted by the story. Admittedly, they rely too much upon convention and far too little on probability, and the modern reader tends to be bored by their length. Only in the case of Longus is his work redeemed by its brevity, its naivety, the charm of its pastoral setting and the bold realism of certain passages.

LUCIAN

The second century A.D. when several of these novels first appeared is also the age of Lucian. Though he produced no such long drawn out ove stories, many of his imaginative tales, for example, the *True*

Story, are related to the same type of romance. But Lucian's complete rejection of metaphysical and religious ideas, his underlying rationalism, were utterly opposed to the dominant intellectual current of his time, which, from the 'middle Platonism' of Plutarch to neo-Platonic mysticism, is felt as the background of most of the novels. He was born about 125 A.D., during the reign of Hadrian, at Samosata, the ancient capital of Commagene, on the upper reaches of the Euphrates. The mother tongue of this great Greek writer was, therefore, Syrian. His family, whose social status was modest, intended him to become a sculptor, but he proved to be an awkward apprentice and, having smashed a piece of marble that he had been given to polish, he fled from the workshop and persuaded his parents to let him continue his studies.

It was in Ionia, where there was no lack of teachers, that he perfected his knowledge of the Greek language and literature; and he devoured the poets, from Homer onwards, and all the great writers of the Attic period with enthusiasm. This was the start of his exclusive admiration for the kind of classical culture typified by Isocrates, for, though he may have read Plato, his particular cast of mind made him prefer the rhetorician to the philosopher: a preference that sets him poles apart from Plutarch.

At Antioch, he was for a time an advocate, but soon abandoned this profession to become a wandering Sophist, like Dio Chrysostomos in exile. He visited Rome, but was not happy there: born a barbarian and doubtless on this account having all the more admiration for the culture that had made him a Hellene, the Romans appeared to him to be pretentious louts. He gave displays of oratory in Italy, Gaul, Macedonia, Greece and Asia Minor, but, apart from his native country, which he perhaps despised, the only city where he felt really at home was Athens. In 165 A.D., at the age of forty, he settled there with his family and stayed for twenty years. It was during this time, it seems, that he wrote most of his masterpieces of which he used to give public readings before publishing them. But, despite his popularity, his gift for mockery attracted many enemies; and, though he became famous, he did not earn enough to satisfy him. Despite his poor opinion of the masters of the world, he therefore solicited a stable and well-paid post in the Roman administration. His request was granted and he was appointed legal adviser to the governor of Egypt, a position which he apparently continued to fill until his death, shortly before 192 A.D., towards the end of the reign of Commodus.

Ninety-two works are attributed to Lucian, none of them very long; but, of these, a dozen are either doubtful or definitely apocryphal. The literary form he preferred was the dialogue which in his hands was transformed into veritable comedy. Almost certainly he was influenced by Menippos of Gadara (see p. 334), for in the *Fisherman* he acknowledged his debt to him, and he also made him the principal character in several of his famous *Dialogues of the Dead*. The *Icaromenippos*, a story that makes curious reading in our epoch of astronauts and cosmonauts, *Charon*, the *Nekyomanteia*, remind one of the fantastic inventions of Aristophanes. His *Timon* was inspired by Menander's' *Misanthrope*. The *Courtesans' Dialogues* and some of the *Sailors' Dialogues* are closely related to the Mimes of Herondas and the Idylls of Theocritus.

All these literary influences, it has been suggested, had the effect of stifling, if not obliterating, Lucian's originality. It is true that, like many of his contemporaries during this second wave of Sophism, he accepted as the basis of his literary work the principle of *mimesis*, that is to say, the imitation of earlier writers. It is also true that he displays a somewhat bookish tendency. But this does not mean that we should accept the view that his relative originality is simply a superior kind of imitation. Any reader of Lucian who is familiar with the authors he imitates must immediately feel the novelty of tone, the individual touch and accent that distinguish him from all earlier writers. One has only to compare him with other representative writers of the period, like the declamatory Aelius Aristides, well-known in his day, or Maximus of Tyre, many of whose writings are still in existence, to appreciate the full extent of his originality.

Of those works not in dialogue form, the *Treatise on the Writing of History*, the fantastic *True History*, and the *Ass* (in my view this entertaining fable is correctly attributed to Lucian) are undoubtedly the most remarkable. They are all light-hearted, swift, ironical and full of a mocking and mordant wit which, though chiefly at the expense of the gods and the philosophers, is also directed at the poets: for Lucian did not spare the Greek writers he so much admired, not even Homer.

Here is a typical passage, from the beginning of the *Double Accusation*. It is Zeus himself who is speaking:

Plague take all these philosophers who insist that happiness is only for the gods! The truth is, if only they knew everything we have to put up with for the sake of mankind, they certainly wouldn't envy us our nectar and ambrosia. Why should they accept Homer's word, a blind man and an imposter, who insists upon our happiness and describes everything that goes on in heaven, while he couldn't even see what was happening on earth, at his very feet?

As an example, Zeus takes Helios, the Sun God, who, as he ceaselessly moves around the world, 'hasn't even got time, they say, to scratch his ear', and then Apollo who, 'thanks to the absorbing profession he chose, of being a prophet, is continually chasing from one sanctuary to another, to find answers for those who come to consult the oracle, and who has to sort out his prophecies if he doesn't want to ruin his prestige.' Then, Zeus turns to himself: 'However, what the other gods have to do amounts to very little compared with the disagreeable jobs that I, king and father of the entire creation, have to put up with. Why, with all the business I have to cope with, I'm almost over-whelmed with worry.'

In the *True History*, even the title is a joke, for the whole point is to make fun of all the writers of fantastic stories, in a tale that is itself pure invention:

Since I have nothing true to relate, never having had an adventure of the slightest interest, I have had to resort to lying, though the way I do so is much more honest than that of other men, for there is one point on which I am completely truthful: I admit that I am a liar. . . . The tale I am about to tell, therefore, is about things that I have neither seen, nor experienced, nor heard from anyone else; things that not only simply do not exist, but that are utterly incapable of ever existing. In consequence, my readers would be well advised not to believe anything I say.

No one has more aptly defined Lucian's intellectual outlook than Marcel Caster: 'Lucian understood culture as implying a state of harmony, of complete intellectual clarity. Everything that disturbs the mind reveals itself in ridiculous and mischievous actions. . . . He is distinguished by a certain Epicureanism, the influence of which may be continually felt. To sweep away the fog of metaphysics seems to him an essentially civilizing act: only the dry, somewhat artificial light of rationalism makes any appeal to him. For him, religion, even in the best of men, is simply an unpleasant exaltation, crazy hopes, stupid beliefs, and half truths (*pseudos*). He is not, in any special sense, hostile to paganism, so much as opposed to virtually all religion. . . . The irreligious outlook of Epicureanism is what he regarded as the true mark of Greek culture. Thus he rejected an important part of the classical heritage. His conception of culture is impoverished compared with that of Plato, Aristotle or even Isocrates, since his whole character prevented him from assimilating that spirit of religion that underlies the whole of Athenian culture. For him, the two essential features of culture were: firstly, that it was the privilege of a minority of educated Greeks; and, secondly, that it was based on scepticism. Philosophers (with the exception of Epicurus) and bigots he held in abhorrence. Living in the second century A.D., he had the outlook of a contemporary of Menander—a gap of five hundred years.'

It has become a commonplace to compare Lucian with Voltaire. As regards their ideas, however, the difference between these two great writers seems to me greater than their resemblance. The one thing they have in common is a style, a tone of voice: their short, incisive sentences, the savage thrusts that always reach their target, their icy clarity, and their sarcastic grin.

Alciphron seems to have lived about the same time as Lucian. He left a collection of one hundred and eighteen imaginary letters which are one of the most agreeable products of second century Sophism. The work consists of four parts: letters from fishermen, peasants, parasites and courtesans. Like Lucian, he borrows something from everyone: he was strongly influenced by Longus, the author of *Daphnis and Chloe*, and by the comic theatre, particularly that of Menander. The result is a series of valuable and delightful pictures of contemporary life. He describes the facile, brilliant and dissipated life of the hetairai, but he does not overlook the misery of the poor, nor the back-breaking toil of the peasantry. Here is a letter supposed to have been written by Menander's mistress, Glykera, to her friend Bacchis in Corinth:

My Menander has decided to go to Corinth for the Isthmian Games. This visit does not at all please me, for you know what it is to be deprived of such a lover, even for a short time. However, I could scarcely ask him not to go since he is so rarely away. Now that he is about to set out for the town where you live, how can I entrust him to you? But then, how can I help doing so, since he is hoping that you will look after him? I think that in writing this letter I am being quite sensible. Certainly I have not forgotten the close friendship between us; and knowing how superior your character is to your profession, I am much less afraid of you than of him. He is so easily swept off his feet and even the most austere of men would find it difficult to resist you, my dear. I cannot help feeling that the real purpose of his journey is not to attend the Games, but to meet you. You may perhaps resent this suspicion. You must forgive me, my dearest. We courtesans cannot help being jealous and to lose Menander's love would be a serious blow to me. Besides, you must remember that, if ever I upset him in the slightest, I am sure to have to listen to myself being bitterly abused on the stage by some Chremes or Pheidylos. If you send him back to me as he was when he left me, I shan't know how to thank you. Goodbye.

This letter is as delightful for its naïve sincerity as for the naturalness of the style, and one has only to open Alciphron's works where one will to find plenty of others as pleasant and entertaining.

The grammarian, Athenaeus, a native of Naucratis in Egypt, is typical of the scientific Sophists, erudite and even pedantic. His *Symposium of the Sophists*, probably appeared about 230 A.D., a lengthy compilation that was later abridged. The scene in which it is set follows an ancient tradition, of which Plutarch's *Table Talk* is a good example. The wealthy Roman pontiff, Larentius, is entertaining a number of friends, all of whom are scholars in various fields. In the form in which it has come down to us it is a massive and indigestible work, but it is an inexhaustible mine of information on almost every aspect of ancient life and society.

In the fourth century, the great rhetorician Libanius of Antioch was to be the friend of the emperor Julian, known to the Christians as the Apostate because he attempted to defend and restore Hellenism. Libanius represents the best tendencies of latter-day Sophism, and the considerable body of work he produced bears witness to his profound knowledge of Attic eloquence.

PLOTINUS

Accepting the Pythagorean view of the body as the tomb of the soul (*soma = sema*), Plato had called upon philosophers to accept a life of renunciation and asceticism as a necessary condition of that spiritual ascendancy and moral purity which alone enabled men to contemplate the Idea of the Good. He did this in several Dialogues, such as the *Symposium*, the *Phaedrus* and the *Phaedo*, but, even more explicitly, in the *Theaetetus*:

Evil inevitably exists in the region of the earth. That is why we should seek to escape hence as quickly as possible, in order to attain the other world. This journey consists in becoming like God as far as it is possible for us to become like him, that is to say, in being just and holy in the light of the spirit (176, a–b).

Plotinus accepted this mystical and ascetic way of life more fully than Plutarch or any other ancient philosopher. He was born in 205 A.D. at Lycopolis in middle Egypt. He was convinced of his vocation for philosophy when, at the age of eighteen, he was attending the lectures given in Alexandria by the Platonist, Ammonius, whose name was the same as that of Plutarch's teacher.

With regard to this vocation, Émile Bréhier has said: 'This was not Plotinus' first introduction to philosophical theory; philosophy was a fashionable subject, and the whole of rhetorical education was then imbued with it as may be seen from the dissertations of Maximus of Tyre, or the discourse of Aelius Aristides (see p. 367). But since the time of Epictetus, and even of Philo of Alexandria, genuine philosophers had always been opposed to this superficial approach to philosophy, simply as part of the educational curriculum. For them, the function of philosophy was to change men's souls and lead them to a new way of life. It was not a subject for students, but for mature men, capable of taking decisions that would provide them with a new orientation to life. Plotinus' enrolment in Ammonius' school did not merely mean acceptance of the Platonic doctrine: it was more nearly equivalent, despite the obvious differences, to the conversion of St Augustine.'

Plotinus remained with Ammonius for eleven years. Feeling drawn towards the Orient, however, in 242 he left Alexandria to accompany the army of the emperor Gordianus, then moving east against the Persians under king Sapor. He was probably hoping for an opportunity to obtain first-hand knowledge of the teachings of the Persian *Magi* and perhaps also of the *Gymnosophists* of India. But, after being defeated in Mesopotamia, Gordianus was forced to retreat. Plotinus fled to Antioch, and later to Rome, where he was henceforward to remain.

Here, his modest, but spiritually radiant, personality attracted many followers, a studious elite who attended his public lectures. Amongst them were professional philosophers like Porphyry and Amelius, important public figures, senators,[1] the emperor Gallienus and his wife,

---

[1] The example of the senator Rogatianus that Porphyry gives in his *Life of Plotinus* is both instructive and amusing; 'Rogatianus reached such a state of detachment from life that he gave up all his belongings, dismissed all his servants and renounced his offices. . . . He even refused to live in his own house, but stayed with friends or acquaintances. He only ate every other day. This renunciation and this heedlessness, at a time when he was so ill with gout that he had to be carried in a litter, restored his health: and whereas previously he had been incapable of opening his hand, he became more skilled in the use of it than any manual worker. Plotinus loved him.'

Salonia. Yet Plotinus made no claim to any kind of revelation or new religion. Neither rhetorician nor thaumaturge, he did not seek to win the crowd. His activities were confined to a small circle of distinguished men who felt an enthusiastic attachment to him. If he succeeded, it was because he possessed in so a high degree those qualities of mind and heart that all classes of Roman society looked for in a spiritual leader.

Plotinus dreamed of founding in the Campagna a city of philosophers, which would be governed by Plato's laws and was to be called *Platonopolis*. Had his dream been realized, the city would probably have become a kind of monastery; but the project collapsed.

In 268 Porphyry left Plotinus. The latter had always had bad health, aggravated by his disregard for hygiene, inadequate food and complete neglect of the 'rags of the flesh'. Now he became almost blind and appears to have contracted leprosy. More and more the world neglected him, and in 270 he died, alone, in a house in the Campagna belonging to one of his friends.

From 254 onwards, at the request of his followers, he had started to transcribe some of his lectures; and before long he had produced a treatise, which he later entrusted to his disciple Porphyry for revision. It was the latter who arranged the fifty-four chapters in six *Enneads* (or *Novenas*), so-called because of the mystical theory of numbers. Each chapter purports to be a commentary on a text from Plato or Aristotle, which is either quoted or assumed to be known. These texts serve as the starting point for Plotinus' own random reflections which he proceeds to develop in a very spontaneous sometimes disorderly, manner. Beneath the tense, nervous, hurried, style, it is possible to grasp the essential meaning, despite the frequent parentheses, repitions and abrupt transitions. It is as though the writer had as little respect for the rules of literary composition as for the material world. Nevertheless, certain chapters more carefully written than others, like the justly famous *On the Beautiful* (1, 6), are remarkable for their power of expression and wealth of accurate imagery, as well as for the profundity of his ideas.

Porphyry not only edited Plotinus' work, he also wrote his life. Here, after noting that the master 'seemed to be ashamed of inhabitating a body' (*Life of Plotinus*, 1), he proceeds to discuss a prophecy that Amelius had obtained from the Pythian oracle, whom he had asked where the soul of Plotinus now dwelt. 'These verses tell us that he was full of simple goodness and sweetness. They also say that his mind never slept, that his soul was pure and always striving towards what was god-like, which he loved with his whole being. He did everything to free himself, in order "to escape the bitter flood of this life, avid for blood". Thus, thanks to the inspired illumination, which often, through the intelligence, attains to God and the Beyond, following the path prescribed by Plato in his *Symposium*, he beheld the God who, because he exists beyond the intelligence and the intelligible, has neither form nor essence. . . . Plotinus was granted a clear vision of the end to be attained. For him the end and aim of life was the fullest unity with God, who is above all things. While I was with him, he achieved this aim on four occasions, thanks to an ineffable act which was not within his control' (*Ibid.*, 23).

From this it appears that Plotinus believed himself to have attained, though but rarely, a state of mystical ecstasy. According to him human beings have a spontaneous tendency towards perfection, which assumes the possibility of complete union with the First Principle, but this 'salvation', which is only attained by those who have achieved complete purity, is never 'given', for the immanence of the one remains imperfect by virtue of its very transcendance. Thus it is only at the conclusion of its laborious ascent that the human soul can hope to reach, by some mysterious means, the pure summit itself. In doing so, it embraces within itself, so to speak, the whole universe, which only exists through the presence within it of something greater than itself.

'Whence comes it then,' Plotinus asks, 'that souls have forgotten their father, God, and that, being but fragments of him and completely belonging to him, they are ignorant of themselves and of him?' (*Enneads*, I, I, I). The approach to God is a return to the soul's native country, to its spiritual home, but it is only possible, by means of complete purification and absolute renunciation; 'Having renounced everything here on earth, and having made itself as beautiful and as like God as possible, the soul suddenly becomes conscious of his presence within it: then nothing separates them, they are no longer two, but two in one' (*Enneads*, VI, 7, 34).

One sees how complete is Plotinus' mastery of the inner life of the spirit. He says: 'We must turn completely to the life within. . . . God is not outside any creature; he exists within all men, though they do not know it. They flee from him, or rather from themselves, but the wise man is he who turns in upon himself, and finds everything within himself' (*Enneads*, VI, 9, 7). The words *panta eiso* (everything within) might well serve as epigraph to Plotinus' teaching.

It is not surprising that, despite his hostility to their faith, so many Christians have been attracted to Plotinus' teachings; or that he had so much influence on St Augustine and many other Christian writers. It was St Bonaventure who, as late as the thirteenth century, accorded him the supreme title *Nobilissimus*.

What distinguishes the 'religion' of Plotinus from that of the Neo-Platonists who succeeded him is that it was based entirely on a kind of contemplative rationalism (if it is possible to use these two words together) and in no way depended upon prayer or sacrificial rites, even less upon 'theurgic magic'. According to Porphyry: 'Amelius liked to offer sacrifices; he never missed the ceremony of the new moon, but observed all the feast days throughout the year. One day he wanted Plotinus to accompany him, but Plotinus answered: "It is for the gods to come to me, not for me to go to the gods." What was he thinking as he spoke these proud words? We could not understand, but we dared not ask him' (*Life of Plotinus*, 10).

In a recent article, Professor E. R. Dodds wrote: 'The technique of union with God was, for Plotinus, neither physiological nor magical, but intellectual: mystical union was not a substitute for moral effort: 'Without true virtue,' he says, 'all talk about God, is only idle chatter.' Finally, in his philosophy, the experience of union was a *natural* occurrence, not, as in Christian mysticism, the result of supernatural grace... On all these points, Plotinus remained an authentic Hellene. Mystical union, though a completely personal experience as regards the way in which it was achieved, was nevertheless the achievement of a mind brought up in the tradition of classical Greece and determined to preserve the integrity of this tradition against the intrusion of any foreign mode of thought[1].'

This could not be said of the development of Neo-Platonism after Plotinus: the recourse to the magical rites of 'theurgy' was a departure from the normal practice of Greek philosophy, and was to lead to strange and aberrant doctrines. I prefer to end with the pure and 'most noble' Plotinus, who, though an ascetic and a mystic, was at the same time a true sage of Greece.

[1] *Journal of Roman Studies*, pp. 1-7.

8

CONCLUSION

Let us seek refuge in the beloved country. How, by fleeing, shall we return thither? We will do as Odysseus did, who, they say, fled from the sorceresses Circe and Calypso, refusing to remain with them, despite the pleasures of the eye and all the beauty that he found there. Our country is the place from whence we came, the dwelling of our Father (*Plotinus*, 1, 6, 8).

We have briefly surveyed the thousand years between Homer and Plotinus and in doing so have doubtless overlooked much of the wealth and splendour of ancient Hellenism. In most ancient literatures the earliest poems are concerned solely with the gods and the creation of the world. The *Iliad* and the *Odyssey* do not neglect Olympus, but in both of them it is men who hold the centre of the stage; and when they are called Achilles, Hector or Odysseus, they prove to be more exemplary than the gods. With their earliest crude attempts in the eighth century B.C., the Athenian vase painters introduced the human form into their geometrical designs; and later, the whole of classical and Hellenistic art was to exalt the physical beauty of men and women.

In Ionia, it was to the physical world that the first philosophers directed their attention, but the revolution effected by Socrates and the Sophists in the fifth century, turned their attention towards man. In a certain sense the maxim Socrates took from the wisdom of Delphi 'Know thyself' merges with Protagoras' 'Man is the measure of all things.' For, though Protagoras suggests that the gods and the universe itself have only a contingent and subjective existence in relation to man, he nevertheless implies that man, the unique subject, is the centre of everything and constitutes essential reality. Socrates does not share this relativism: he is concerned only that man should first have confidence in himself and be aware of his own powers before setting out to conquer the world. Yet both the Athenian and the man of Abdera are equally humanistic in their outlook.

For the poets, too, mankind became the centre of their world surprisingly early. In *Prometheus*, Aeschylus attributed the origin of human civilization to the Titan: yet only a generation later Sophocles makes the Chorus in *Antigone* say: 'In this world are many marvels, but none greater than man. .... Speech, thought swift as the wind, the aspirations from which cities are born, all these he taught himself.' And Menander was to echo Sophocles: 'How splendid a creature is man, when he is truly man!'

In the political sphere, it was the Greeks who invented civil liberty, that idea that Demosthenes was to defend so nobly. For them, the dignity of the individual, of the citizen, was the basis of society. True, the huge number of slaves and the inferior position of women were dark shadows on this brilliant picture. Marxist historians regard the slave society of ancient Greece as infamous: they overlook the fact that, at a time when technique was only embryonic, the terrible price of slavery was an essential condition of all human progress. And, at least, the honour of Greece was saved by the memorable protests of Socrates, Aristotle and Epitectus against both slavery and the social inferiority of women.

With the ending of the classical City State, the Stoics proclaimed man to be *cosmopolites*, that is to say, a citizen of the world. In place of Aristotle's definition of man as 'a being who lives in a City,' Chrysippos substituted: 'Man is a member of a universal society (*koinonikon*).' Thus the Greeks were ready to break out of the narrow framework of political particularism and strive towards universality.

If there were so many great writers and artists among the Greeks, it was primarily because of their cult of beauty. Admiration for every kind of beauty, but above all for the mutually dependent moral and physical beauty of man, is a persistent theme from Homer to Plotinus, and beyond. Beauty naturally inspires love, but, whereas others regard love as being blind, for Plato it became the primary condition for the highest form of knowledge, for the supreme illumination, for the approach towards intelligible Goodness and Beauty, that is to say, towards God. The fact that the religion of ancient Greece was anthropomorphic was already, surely, a sign that the Hellenes could find no more beautiful way of representing the Immortals than as human beings?

Traces of this ancestral belief are still to be found in the writings of the Greek Fathers of the Church, especially Clement of Alexandria, Gregory of Nyssos, and John Chrysostom. In the *Pedagogue*, for example, Clement says: 'The creative force of the world, regarding man as its highest achievement, submitted his soul to the direction of the intelligence and of temperance and adorned his body with beauty and harmony.' Who but a Greek would have thought of arguing, not only from the heavens 'that tell the glory of God,' but also from the moral and physical beauty of mankind?

At first, it was to the beauty of man that the Greeks award the palm, but from the fourth century B.C. onwards, to that of women. Yet, always, they regarded any human being endowed with physical beauty as being morally constrained to strive for equal spiritual beauty. In his *Journal*, Julien Green was expressing an essentially Greek attitude when he wrote: 'Is beauty the sign of a latent spiritual perfection, the mark, as it were, of a higher vocation? It has always seemed to me that a completely beautiful being who commits evil is betraying his real self, where an ugly person who commits evil is merely adapting his inner to his outer self' (20 November 1944). The hideous Thersites was also a bad man; Achilles, the typical Greek hero of the classical period, was both 'beautiful and good', *kalos kagathos*.

In addition to philosophy and history, the Greeks also discovered the positive sciences. They foresaw the technical achievements of the future in their dreams: aeroplanes, in the legend of Icarus; robots, in the iron slaves of Hephaestus in the *Iliad*; inter-planetary travel, in Lucian's *Icaromenippos*. But, above all, they created the supreme instrument of man's control of nature: mathematics. 'Let no one enter who is ignorant of geometry' was inscribed over the doors of the Academy; and the Alexandrians developed mathematics still further.

Yet, for a long time, some scruple prevented the Greeks from undertaking physical experiments. Was this simply because they involved a degree of manual work, which, being restricted to slaves, was considered undignified by comparison with the noble political activities of the citizen or the contemplative life of the philosopher? Or did the Greeks also have an obscure presentiment that by embarking on this powerful, but dangerous method of taming nature, mankind would run the risk of being overwhelmed by their own discoveries and the power thus conferred on them? 'Nothing in excess' was also a Delphic precept. Inevitably, this prudently limited humanism differed from the humanism of our own times, which have seen the smashing of the atom and the conquest of cosmic space. Time cannot be reversed.

Does this mean, then, that for us Greek philosophy and Greek

Conclusion

civilization only have an historical interest? Has Hellas nothing more to teach us? On the contrary. It is perhaps precisely today, when man finds himself more than at any time in the past threatened with 'dehumanization' by the machine and the marvellous and terrible developments of technique, that he needs to seek reassurance in the deepest roots of his being by reference to his own origins. And it was in Greece that our contemporary civilization was born. As André Bonnard has said: 'All the most important achievements which, taken as a whole, constitute Greek civilization, had the same end in view: to increase man's power over nature, thereby increasing his own humanity. This is what we mean when we speak of Greek civilization as humanistic. It was man, the life of humanity, that the Greek people strove to improve.'

The literature and aspirations of ancient Greece were not limited exclusively to the earth and to mankind. If reason was the Hellene's essential guide, it was not his only one. In 1951 Professor E. R. Dodds wrote a remarkable book on this theme, *The Greeks and the Irrational*. Few were the Greeks who, like Epicurus and Lucian, shut their eyes to divine mysteries, for they were conscious of the limitations of all human knowledge. The only thing Socrates knew was that he knew nothing. Dialectical reasoning could not of itself attain reality. One could only reach, and hold fast by, ultimate truth, said Plato, 'by participation, by divine grace'. Thus philosophy soared into that supra-celestial region where the soul, liberated by asceticism from the burden of matter and of evil and borne upon the wings of love, could contemplate the Eternal Ideas. For Plotinus, that was the road that led to certain mystical union.

It also explains why to many of the Fathers of the Church the pagan philosophy of Greece appeared to be a remote preparation for Christianity, a kind of Old Testament *in partibus infidelium*. Aristotle, though so far from being a mystic, was to become for the Middle Ages and for Thomas Aquinas the depository of all human knowledge, 'the philosopher' *par excellence*. Thus, at different stages in its development, Christian theology has appeared to be a synthesis of Revelation and Greek philosophy. In the eyes of a modern Christian philosopher, Jean Guitton, all that was lacking in the wisdom of Greece was 'a grasp of those key concepts, which were an essential part of the heritage of Jewish thought: transcendence, creation, the absolute value of the individual. Plato sometimes seems to have been intuitively aware of them, but they were not justified by his principles.'

378

In the fullness of time, the admirable Greek language which had expressed the poetry of Homer and the philosophy of Plato, was used to transmit the Revelations of St John, and later it was for a time the principal idiom of the Christian church. In our own time, the literature of modern Greece, though it has fewer readers, continues the great tradition of antiquity, with such notable writers as Kostis Palamas, Angelos Sikelianos and Nikos Kazantzakis.

In the history of humanity, the Greek people were the first to become fully conscious of man's powers and to confront the world in the light of reason, without forgetting the role of the mysterious and the ineffable. Contemporary civilization, which is the direct descendant of that of Greece, passed on by the Roman empire and Christianity, is beginning to realize that it is not immune from death. The atom, predicted and named by Democritus, has been smashed and the world itself is in danger of being destroyed in an apocalyptic conflagration. Such an *ekpyrosis*, which the Stoics considered to be a periodical event in the history of the universe, would be definitive, at least for the human race. Thanks to the astounding advances in the science and technology that originated in Greece, this possibility might at any moment be realized. Lacking the wisdom of the Greek philosophers (even the Epicureans were not atheists), there are today many who proclaim the death of God. What appears to be only too possible is the death of humanity. For myself, the one thing I know is, that as long as the earth lasts and is inhabited by man, Homer, Plato and many other Greek writers will find devoted readers.

CHRONOLOGICAL TABLE

DATES B.C.	POLITICAL HISTORY	ART	LITERATURE
2500–1500	Minoan civilization	Cnossos, palace	
1600–1100	Mycenaean civilization	Mycenae, acropolis and tombs	
c. 1400	Capture of Cnossos by the Achaeans		
c. 1180	Capture of Troy		Inscribed tablets of Mycenae and Pylos
1100–1000	Dorian invasions		
c. 800			Homer
776	First Olympiad; beginnings of Greek colonization	Geometric pottery	
c. 725			Hesiod
c. 680		Heraeum of Olympia	Terpander, Tyrtaeus, Archilochus
c. 640	Cypselus. tyrant of Corinth	Corinthian pottery	Mimnermos
627–585	Periander, tyrant of Corinth		Thales of Miletus
c. 621	Draco's Laws		
c. 600	Foundation of Marseilles		
594	Solon's archontate		
Beginning of sixth century	Pittacus of Mytilene	François vase; Argian statues at Delphi	Solon, Sappho, Alcaeus
566	First Panathenia		
560–530	Peisistratus, tyrant of Athens	The Artemesion of Ephesus; the Heraeum of Samos	Alcman, Arion, Anacreon, Theognis, Thespis, Aesop, Heracleitus
533–522	Polycrates of Samos		Pythagoras, Xenophon
c. 530		Treasury of the Siphnians; Vix crater; Kouros of Piraeus	First tragedy contest at Athens; Phrynichos, Hecataeus, Simonides
525			Birth of Aeschylus

Chronological Table

DATES B.C.	POLITICAL HISTORY	ART	LITERATURE
c. 518			Birth of Pindar, Bacchylides and Epicharmos
508	Cleisthenes' reforms in Athens	First red-figured pottery	
496	Birth of Pericles		Birth of Sophocles and Empedocles
494	Capture of Miletus	Korai of the Acropolis	
490	Marathon	Athenian treasury at Delphi	
485			Birth of Herodotus and Gorgias; First comedy contest at Athens
480	Salamis, Himera	Temple of Aphaea at Aegina	Birth of Euripides; Parmenides' poem *On Nature*
478	Foundation of the Delian League	Charioteer of Delphi	
476			Phrynichos' *Phoenicians*
472		Polygnotus of Thasos	Aeschylus' *Persae*
469			Birth of Socrates
468	Victory of Cimon at Eurymedon		Aeschylus' *Seven Against Thebes*
c. 460	Beginning of Pericles' rule	Temple of Zeus at Olympia; change from severe to free style in red-figured pottery	Birth of Democritus and Hippocrates
458			Aeschylus' *Oresteia*
456			Death of Aeschylus
c. 450	Peace of Callias		
446		Building starts on the Parthenon	Birth of Aristophanes
443	Foundation of Thurii		Herodotus at Thurii
441	Expedition of Samos		Sophocles' *Antigone*; Birth of Lysias and Andocides
438		Building starts on the Propylaea	Death of Pindar; Euripides' *Alcestis*

Chronological Table

DATES B.C.	POLITICAL HISTORY	ART	LITERATURE
436			Birth of Isocrates
431	Beginning of the Peloponnesian war; Siege of Plataea		Euripides' *Medea*
430	Plague at Athens	Trial of Pheidias	Trial of Anaxagoras
429	Death of Pericles		
428			Euripides' *Hippolytus*
427	Capture of Mytilene; Arrival of Gorgias in Athens		Birth of Plato and Xenophon
425	Battle of Sphacteria	Temple of Athena Nike	Aristophanes' *Archanians*
424	Battle of Amphipolis Battle of Delium		Thucydides exiled; Aristophanes' *Knights*
423			Aristophanes' *Clouds*
421	Peace of Nicias	Building of the Erechtheum	Aristophanes' *Peace*
420			Euripides' *Andromache*
415	Beginning of the Sicilian expedition		
414			Aristophanes' *Birds*
412			Euripides' *Electra*
411	Revolution in Athens; Thirty Tyrants		Death of Antiphon and Protagoras
c. 410		Tholos (Athena Pronaia) of Delphi	
406	Battle of Arginusae		Death of Sophocles and Euripides. Aristophanes' *Frogs*
404	Capture of Athens		
403	Democracy restored at Athens		Lysias' *Against Eratosthenes*
401	Expedition of Cyrus the Younger		Xenophon with the Ten Thousand; Production of Sophocles' *Oedipus at Colonus*
399			Trial and death of Socrates; Andocides' *On the Mysteries*

Chronological Table

DATES B.C.	POLITICAL HISTORY	ART	LITERATURE
396	Agesilaus in Asia		Xenophon accompanies Agesilaus
394	Battle of Nemea	Monument of Dexileus	Isocrates opens his school
392		Birth of Praxiteles; Scopas at Tegea	Aristophanes' *Ecclesiazusae*; Andocides' *On the Peace*
388			Aristophanes' *Plutos*
387	The King's Peace		Plato founds the Academy and works on the *Republic*
c. 385			Plato's *Symposium* Death of Aristophanes
384			Birth of Demosthenes and Aristotle
380			Isocrates' *Panegyric*
377	Second Athenian confederation		
after 373		Reconstruction of the Temple of Apollo at Delphi	
371	Battle of Leuctra		Xenophon leaves Scillus
c. 367	Reconciliation of Athens and Sparta		Xenophon returns to Athens Aristotle at the Academy
362	Battle of Mantineia		
357	War of the Allies	Destruction of the Artemesion at Ephesus	
356–346	Holy War		
c. 354			Isocrates' *Antidosis*
351		Mausoleum of Halicarnassus	Demosthenes' *First Philippic*
348	Fall of Olynthus		
347			Death of Plato, *Laws* unfinished; Demosthenes' *Against Meidias*
343			Demosthenes and Aeschines, *De Falsa Legatione*
342			Aristotle tutor to Alexander; birth of Menander

Chronological Table

DATES B.C.	POLITICAL HISTORY	ART	LITERATURE
341			Birth of Epicurus
339	Battle of Amphissa		Isocrates' *Panathenaiaics*
338	Chaironeia		Death of Isocrates
336	Accession of Alexander	Lysippus' Agias	Aristotle back in Athens
334		Monument of Lysicrates	
331	Foundation of Alexandria		Lycurgus' *Against Leocrates*
330			Aeschines' *Against Ctesiphon*; Demosthenes' *On the Crown*
323	Death of Alexander		
322	Lamian War		Death of Demosthenes and Hypereides; death of Aristotle
317–307	Athens governed by Demetrius of Phaleron		
316			Menander's *Dyscolus*; Birth of Callimachus and Aratos
306			Epicurus founds the Garden
301	Battle of Ipsos		Zeno of Keiton at Athens; Birth of Theocritus
292			Death of Menander
285–246	Ptolemy II Philadelphus		Library and museum of Alexandria
281	Battle of Corupedion	Colossus of Rhodes	
279	Invasion of the Gauls		
272	Death of Pyrrhus		Birth of Eratosthenes
c. 270			Death of Epicurus and Pyrrho; Apollonius of Rhodes becomes head of the library at Alexandria
c. 260			Arcesilaos becomes head of the Academy
241–197	Attalus I of Pergamon	Monuments of Pergamon	

Chronological Table

DATES B.C.	POLITICAL HISTORY	ART	LITERATURE
232			Death of Cleanthes
222–187	Antiochus III		
212	Capture of Syracuse		Death of Archimedes
211–205	First Macedonian War		
c. 207		Winged Victory of Samothrace	Death of Chrysippus; Birth of Polybius
200–196	Second Macedonian War		
183	Death of Philopoemen		
168	Pydna		Polybius deported to Italy
159–138	Attalus II of Pergamon	Stoa of Attalus II at Athens	
156			Carneades at Rome
146	Greece becomes a Roman province		
c. 126			Death of Polybius
First century		Laocoon	Chariton of Aphrodisias; Strabo; Diodorus of Sicily; Dionysus of Halicarnassus
A.D.			
c. 40	Caligula (37–41)		Birth of Dio Chrysostomos
c. 46	Claudius (41–54)		Birth of Plutarch
c. 50			Birth of Epictetus
c. 125	Hadrian (117–38)		Death of Plutarch; Birth of Lucian; Arrian official of the Empire
	Marcus Aurelius (161–80)		Marcus Aurelius' *Meditations*; Longus
End of second century			Pausanius; Alciphon
Third century			Heliodorus; Achilles Tatius; Athenaeus
205–70			Plotinus
229	Second consulship of Dio Cassius		
314–95			Libanius

AUTHOR'S BIBLIOGRAPHY

GENERAL WORKS

Alfred and Maurice Croiset, *Histoire de la littérature grecque*, 5 vols., Paris, 1928.

Von Christ, *Geschichte der Griechischen Literatur*, 6th ed., Munich, 1920.

Albin Lesky, *Geschichte der Griechischen Literatur*, Bern, 1958.

Fernand Robert, *La Littérature grecque*, Paris, 1946.

Jean Defradas, *La Littérature grecque*, Paris, 1960.

W. Nestle and W. Liebich, *Geschichte der Griechischen Literatur*, Berlin, 1961.

G. Glotz, Robert Cohen, Pierre Roussel, *Histoire grecque*, 4 vols, Paris, 1925–38.

Karl Julius Beloch, *Griechische Geschichte*, Strasbourg, 8 vols., 1912–27.

The Cambridge Ancient History, Vols. v–viii, Cambridge, 1923–39.

André Aymard and Jeanine Auboyer, *L'Orient et la Grèce*, Paris, 1953.

Hermann Bengston, *Griechische Geschichte*, Munich, 1950.

André Bonnard, *Civilisation grecque*, 3 vols., Lausanne, 1959.

H.–I. Marrou, *Histoire de l'éducation dans l'antiquité*, Paris, 1948.

C. Picard, *Manuel d'archéologie grecque: la sculpture*, Paris, 5 vols., 1935–54.

Jean Charbonneaux, *La Sculpture grecque classique*, Paris, Vol. i, 1943, Vol. ii, 1945.

*Martin Robertson, *Greek Painting*, Geneva, 1959.

Roland Martin, *L'Urbanisme dans la Grèce antique*, Paris, 1956.

Léon Robin, *La Pensée grecque*, Paris, 1923.

Werner Jaeger, *Paideia*, Berlin, 1934.

*E. R. Dodds, *The Greeks and the Irrational*, Berkeley, 1951; Oxford, 1956.

CHAPTER I

*Michael Ventris and John Chadwick, *Documents in Mycenaean Greek*, Cambridge, 1959.

Paul Mazon, Pierre Chantraine et al., *Introduction à l'Iliade*, Paris, 1942.

Friedrich Matz, *Le Monde égéen: Troie, Crète, Mycènes*, Paris, 1956.

Raymond Matton, *La Crète antique*, Athens, 1955.

Albert Severyns, *Homère*, 3 vols., Paris, 1945–8.

—— *Grèce et Proche-Orient avant Homère*, Brussels, 1960.

Fernand Robert, *Homère*, Paris, 1950.

Gabriel Germain, *La Genèse de l'Odyssée*, Paris, 1954.

Felix Buffière, *Les Mythes d'Homère et la pensée grecque*, Paris, 1956.

Yves Béquignon, *Paysages et images de l'Iliade*, Paris, 1945.

*C. M. Bowra, *Tradition and Design in the Iliad*, Oxford, 1930.

Author's Bibliography

Victor Bérard, *Les Phéniciens et l'Odyssée*, Paris, 1902.
——, *Les Navigations d'Ulysse*, Paris, 1927–9.
——, *La Résurrection d'Homère*, Paris, 1930.
——, *Le Drame épique*, Paris, 1930.
Édouard Delebecque, *Télémaque et la structure de l'Odyssée*, Aix-en-Provence, 1958.
——, *Le Cheval dans l'Iliade*, Paris, 1951.
Jules Labarbe, *L'Homère de Platon*, Liège, 1949.

CHAPTER 2

Jean Bérard, *L'Expansion et la colonisation grecques jusqu'aux guerres médiques*, Paris, 1960.
*C. M. Bowra, *Greek Lyric Poetry from Alcman to Simonides*, Oxford, 2nd ed., 1961.
*A. R. Burn, *The Lyric Age of Greece*, London, 1960.
Jacqueline Duchemin, *La Houlette et la lyre, I: Hermès et Apollon*, Paris, 1960.
François Lasserre, *Les Épodes d'Archiloque*, Paris, 1950.
E. Bethe, *Die griechische Dichtung*, Potsdam, 1929.

CHAPTER 3

Clémence Ramnoux, *Vocabulaire et structures de pensée archaïque chez Héraclite*, Paris, 1959.
Jean Carrière *Théognis de Mégare*, Paris, 1948.
Aurelio Peretti, *Teognide nella tradizione gnomologica*, Pisa, 1953.
Mario Untersteiner, *Senofane, testimonanzie e frammenti*, Florence, 1956.
H. Fraenkel, *Dichtung und Philosophie des frühens Griechentums*, New York, 1951.
D. L. Page, *Sappho and Alcaeus*, Oxford, 1955.

CHAPTER 4

*Sir Arthur Pickard-Cambridge, *The Dramatic Festivals of Athens*, Oxford, 1953.
Mario Untersteiner, *Le Origini della tragedia e del tragico dalla preistoria a Eschilo*, Milan, 1955.
Max Pohlenz, *Die griechische Tragödie*, 2nd ed., Göttingen, 1954.
Albin Lesky, *Die griechische Tragödie*, 2nd ed., Stuttgart, 1958.
——, *Die tragische Dichtung der Hellenen*, Göttingen, 1956.
Albert Willem, *Melpomène: Histoire de la tragédie grecque*, Liège, 1932, and Paris, 1932.
Jacqueline Duchemin, *Pindare poète et prophète*, Paris, 1955.

Author's Bibliography

Edmond Pottier, *Douris et les peintres de vases grecs*, Paris, 1905.
Jacqueline de Romilly, *La Crainte et l'angoisse dans le théâtre d'Éschyle*, Paris, 1958.
——, *L'Évolution du pathétique, d'Éschyle à Euripide*, Paris, 1961.

CHAPTER 5

*G. M. Kirkwood, *A Study of Sophoclean Drama*, Ithaca, 1958.
Jacqueline de Romilly, *Thucydide et l'impérialisme athénien*, Paris, 1947.
——, *Histoire et raison chez Thucydide*, Paris, 1956.
Charles Dugas, *Aison et la peinture céramique à Athènes à l'époque de Périclès*, Paris, 1930.
Pierre Devambez, *L'Art au siècle de Périclès*, Lausanne, 1955.
Maurice Solovine, *Démocrite*, Paris, 1928.
Fernand Chapouthier, *Euripide et l'accueil du divin*, Geneva, 1954.
Yves Battistini, *Trois contemporains: Héraclite, Parménide, Empédocle*, Paris, 1955.
Jean Beaufret, *Le Poème de Parménide*, Paris, 1955.

CHAPTER 6

Édouard Delebecque, *Essai sur la vie de Xénophon*, Paris, 1957.
Ulrich von Wilamowitz-Moellendorff, *Platon, sein Leben und seine Werke*, 5th ed., Berlin, 1959.
Pierre-Maxime Schuhl, *L'Œuvre de Platon*, Paris, 1954.
Jean Guitton, *Les Pages immortelles de Platon*, Paris, 1960.
Georges Mathieu, *Les Idées politiques d'Isocrate*, Paris, 1925.
——, *Démosthène: l'homme et l'œuvre*, Paris, 1948.
Georges Méautis, *Le Crépuscule d'Athènes et Ménandre*, Paris, 1954.
Ph.-E. Legrand, *Daos, tableau de la comédie grecque pendant la période dite nouvelle*, Paris, 1910.

CHAPTER 7

*W. W. Tarn and G. T. Griffith, *Hellenistic Civilization*, 3rd ed., London, 1959.
Ph.-E. Legrand, *La Poésie alexandrine*, Paris, 1924.
——, *Étude sur Théocrite*, Paris, 1898.
Pierre Grimal, *Romans grecs et latins*, Paris, 1958.
R. Helm, *Der antike Roman*, Berlin, 1948.
Marcel Caster, *Lucien et la pensée religieuse de son temps*, Paris, 1937.
Jacques Bompaire, *Lucien écrivain*, Paris, 1958.
Maurice de Gandillac, *La Sagesse de Plotin*, Paris, 1952.

SUPPLEMENTARY READING LIST OF
WORKS IN ENGLISH

In addition to works in the author's bibliography marked with an asterisk, the reader may also wish to consult the following works, all of which are available in English.

GENERAL WORKS

N. G. L. Hammond, *A History of Greece to 322* B.C., Oxford, 1959.

H.–I. Marrou, *A History of Education in Antiquity* (tr. G. Lamb), London, 1956.

G. Richter, *A Handbook of Greek Art*, London and New York, 1959, 3rd ed., 1963.

A. Bonnard, *Greek Civilization* (tr. A. Lytton Sells), 3 vols., London. Vol. I *From the Iliad to the Parthenon*, 1957; Vol. II *From the Antigone to Socrates*, 1959; Vol. III *From Euripides to Alexandria*, 1962.

A. W. Lawrence, *Greek Architecture*, London, 1957.

W. Jaeger, *Paideia* (tr. G. Highet), 3 vols., Oxford, 1944–54.

C. Hignett, *A History of the Athenian Constitution*, Oxford, 1952.

M. P. Nilsson, *A History of Greek Religion* (tr. F. J. Fielden), Oxford, 2nd ed., 1949.

A. J. Toynbee, *Hellenism: the History of a Civilization*, Oxford, 1959.

H. D. F. Kitto, *The Greeks*, Harmondsworth, 1951, reprinted with revisions, 1957.

H. C. Baldry, *Greek Literature for the Modern Reader*, London, 1951.

Morton Smith, *The Ancient Greeks*, Cornell, 1960.

CHAPTER I

J. Chadwick, *The Decipherment of Linear B*, Cambridge, 1958, 2nd ed., Harmondsworth, 1961.

L. R. Palmer, *Mycenaeans and Minoans, Aegean Prehistory in the Light of the Linear B Tablets*, London, 1961.

Alan J. B. Wace and Frank H. Stubbings (ed.), *A Companion to Homer*, London, 1962.

D. L. Page, *History and the Homeric Iliad* (Sather Lectures), Oxford, 1959.

——, *The Homeric Odyssey* (Mary Flexner Lectures), Oxford, 1955.

C. W. Blegen, *Troy and the Trojans*, London, 1963.

J. D. S. Pendlebury, *A Handbook to the Palace of Minos at Knossos*, London, 2nd ed., 1954.

T. B. L. Webster, *From Mycenae to Homer*, London, 1958.

M. Scherer, *Legends of Troy in Art and Literature*, London and New York, 1963.

F. Matz, *Crete and Early Greece: A Prelude to Greek Literature*, London, 1962.

Supplementary Reading List of Works in English

CHAPTER 2

A. R. Burn, *The Lyric Age of Greece*, London, 1960.

C. M. Bowra, *Early Greek Elegists*, Oxford, 1935, reprinted 1960.

CHAPTER 3

B. Snell, *The Discovery of the Mind* (tr. T. G. Rosenmeyer), Oxford, 1953.

T. B. L. Webster, *Greek Art and Literature 700–530 B.C.*, London, 1960.

K. Freeman, *Companion to the pre-Socratic Philosophers*, Oxford, 3rd ed., 1953.

CHAPTER 4

A. H. M. Jones, *Athenian Democracy*, Oxford, 1957.

A. W. Pickard-Cambridge, *Dithyramb, Tragedy and Comedy*, 2nd ed. revised by T. B. L. Webster, Oxford, 1962.

P. D. Arnott, *Introduction to the Greek Theatre*, London, 1959.

V. Ehrenberg, *The Greek State*, Oxford, 1960.

H. D. F. Kitto, *Greek Tragedy, a Literary Study*, London, 2nd ed., 1950.

George Thomson, *Aeschylus and Athens*, London, 1946.

CHAPTER 5

V. Ehrenberg, *Sophocles and Pericles*, Oxford, 1954.

J. de Romilly, *Thucydides and Athenian Imperialism* (tr. P. Thody), Oxford, 1963.

C. A. Robinson, *Athens and the Age of Pericles*, New York, 1959.

P. W. Harsh, *A Handbook of Classical Drama*, Stanford and Oxford, 1944.

F. M. Cornford, *Before and After Socrates*, Cambridge, 1932.

G. M. A. Grube, *The Drama of Euripides*, London 1941, reprinted 1960.

M. Bieber, *The History of the Greek and Roman Theater*, Princeton, 1961.

CHAPTER 6

T. B. L. Webster, *Art and Literature in Fourth Century Athens*, London, 1956.

E. A. Havelock, *A Preface to Plato*, Oxford, 1963.

G. C. Field, *The Philosophy of Plato*, Oxford, 1949, reprinted 1956.

A. E. Taylor, *Plato, the Man and his Work*, London, 6th ed., 1955.

CHAPTER 7

M. Rostovtzeff, *Social and Economic History of the Hellenistic World*, 3 vols., Oxford, 1941.

A. H. M. Jones, *The Greek City from Alexander to Justinian*, Oxford, 1940.

C. A. Robinson, *The History of Alexander the Great*, 2 vols., Providence, R. I., 1953–63.

W. W. Tarn, *Alexander the Great*, 2 vols., Cambridge, 1948.

INDEX

Names of Greek authors are distinguished thus: HOMER. Individual works are only entered where they have been discussed or quoted in some detail; and then in italic.

Index

Index

Index

Index